Final Basel III Modelling

Ioannis Akkizidis • Lampros Kalyvas

Final Basel III Modelling

Implementation, Impact and Implications

palgrave
macmillan

Ioannis Akkizidis
Employed by Wolters Kluwer
Zurich, Switzerland

Lampros Kalyvas
Employed by European Banking Authority
London, UK

ISBN 978-3-319-70424-1   ISBN 978-3-319-70425-8   (eBook)
https://doi.org/10.1007/978-3-319-70425-8

Library of Congress Control Number: 2018941825

Cover illustration: David Nixon / Alamy Stock Photo
Cover design by Henry Petrides

Printed on acid-free paper

This Palgrave Macmillan imprint is published by the registered company Springer International Publishing AG part of Springer Nature.
The registered company address is: Gewerbestrasse 11, 6330 Cham, Switzerland

Foreword

Ladies and Gentlemen

Given my current roles and duties, I have the great opportunity to explore the evolution of risk management and regulation in the financial sector from both an academic and a practical perspective.

Moreover, this dual perspective is often shared with Dr Ioannis Akkizidis, one of the authors of this book, an active colleague in the Board of the Swiss Risk Association. I am therefore pleased to provide a foreword to this book.

As the title indicates, the book focuses on the latest Basel modelling aspects, highlighting the challenges that banks may face by adopting the latest framework proposed by the Basel Committee on Banking Supervision (BCBS) and endorsed by the Group of Central Banks Governors and Heads of Supervision (GHoS) on Thursday, 7 December 2017.

After the financial crisis, the BCBS started to reform the existing, at that time, framework, in order to address its deficiencies. In many aspects, this regulatory development moves towards a more transparent and unified method in assessing financial risk, irrespective of whether banks follow the standardised or the advanced approaches.

Banks must implement the new rules not only to comply with the new framework but also to understand and manage the financial and operational risks, enhancing the financial stability of the banking system. Since 2010, when BCBS started introducing the reforms (known at that time as Basel III), banks have been claiming that the implementation of the reforms relates to significant implementation and compliance operational costs. Likewise, from 2018 onwards, banks will face new challenges when applying the latest reforms.

I would like to emphasise the significant work that the authors have done in order to examine the latest set of the revised standards of the BCBS frameworks. Focusing on vital elements of the BCBS papers, the authors question and/or recognise the impact of utilising the new framework. To this extent, I found the book novel and well aligned with today's market and regulatory requirements.

It is essential for all banks to understand why and how to progress with fulfilling the new requirements. Accordingly, the book assesses the impact of the transition to new BCBS frameworks with respect to the methodology for the estimation of capital requirements. The book addresses the question of what is the resulting capital impact by implementing the new approaches.

Given the changes in the calculation of risk-weighted assets (RWAs) and capital requirements, the book evaluates the revised framework vis-à-vis the current. The detailed analysis and examples facilitate the readers to identify the impact of RWA applied to the assets under study.

Regarding the credit risk framework, the book facilitates banks to measure the impact of the horizontal migration, that is, from the current to the revised standardised approach and from the current to the revised internal ratings-based approach, and eventually the capital needed under the new framework. Also, it separately examines the quantitative impact of applying the foundation internal ratings-based approach (FIRBA) and the advanced internal ratings-based approach (AIRBA) under the final frameworks. Using this book, practitioners should be able to compare the complexity and suitability of the different approaches and choose the one that matches the needs of the bank in question.

With regard to the developments in market risk, the book covers the fundamental review of the trading book (FRTB), particularly elaborating on the measurement of sensitivities under the standardised approach and the expected shortfall (ES) under internal models' approach for the estimation of the regulatory capital. The authors provide vital details that banks should cogitate when applying the FRTB. Furthermore, it addresses the impact of the transition from the value at risk (VaR) to ES measures.

Moving towards the pricing of over-the-counter (OTC) financial instruments, the book provides extensive coverage of credit valuation adjustments (CVAs) by exploring the elements needed for the estimation of the CVA capital charge.

Besides financial risks, the book also covers the amendments in the estimation of operational risk regulatory capital by providing evidence on the behaviour of the parameters and their interaction with the capital charges produced under the standardised measurement approach.

I find the examples included in this book very helpful to understand deeply the implementation of the final framework.

Having considerable experience in the arena of designing and implementing risk management systems and regulations, the two authors have combined their knowledge and quantitative skills to create a practical and informative book, which aligns with the latest BCBS framework.

I warmly recommend Ioannis' and Lampros' book as a "must-read" material. I can say—without reservation—that this book is a "clear translation" of the theoretical provisions of the new framework into a practical tool that would be highly beneficial to practitioners working for banks, regulators, and supervisors. It would also be a valuable tool for researchers and academics introducing the concepts of the new banking regulations into academia.

I, myself, very much enjoyed reading and reviewing this book.

UZH ETH, Zürich, Switzerland   Erich Walter Farkas
Swiss Risk Association, Zürich, Switzerland
Swiss Finance Institute, Zürich, Switzerland
AAAccell Ltd, Zürich, Switzerland

Acknowledgements

The authors would like to express their gratitude to Erich Walter Farkas for providing the preface of the book; Andrea Enria, Adam Farkas, Philippe Allard, and Cyril Demaria for supporting this publication; as well as Vivianne Bouchereau for her useful drafting comments.

Also, the authors appreciate the invaluable help of Palgrave's excellent team, particularly that of Tula Weis and Jazmine Robles, who turned our ideas into the book you are reading and provided their knowledge and energy towards its finalisation.

Disclaimer

The views expressed in this book are solely the responsibility of the authors and should not be interpreted as reflecting the views of any of the institutions the authors work for or are related to.

All remaining errors/inaccuracies are those of the authors only.

Contents

List of Abbreviations

General

AddT1	Additional Tier1 capital, i.e. 'Tier1 – CET1'
CD	Consultative document
CET1	Core equity Tier 1 capital
D-SIB	Domestic systemically important bank: used by the BIS (equivalent to O-SII)
EBA	European Banking Authority
ESCR	External credit rating assessment
GHoS	(The Group of Central Bank) Governors and Heads of Supervision
G-SIB	Global systemically important bank: used by the BIS (equivalent to G-SII)
G-SIIs	Global systemically important institution: used by the EU (equivalent to G-SIB)
LR	Leverage ratio
MRC	Minimum required capital
NSA	National supervisory authorities
O-SII	Other systemically important institution; used by the EU (equivalent to D-SIB)
SCRA	Standardised credit risk assessment
SFL	Shortfall of capital (from current capital ratio to minimum final Basel III capital ratio)
T1	Tier 1 capital
T2	Tier 2 capital
TRC	Target required capital

Mathematical Expressions

Abs	Absolute value of the expression that follows
h	Time horizon
H	The cumulative generalised extreme value distribution function
Max	Maximum value of the expression that follows
Min	Minimum value of the expression that follows
Δ	Difference between two values
ζ	"Shape parameter" for Fréchet and Weibull cumulative distribution functions
Λ	Gumbel cumulative distribution function
ξ	"Shape parameter" of the cumulative generalised extreme value distribution
ρ	Correlation between two variables
Φ	Fréchet cumulative distribution function
Ψ	Weibull cumulative distribution function
$W(t)$	Brownian motion
t	Time
δ	Recovery rate
λ	Intensity
μ	Drift
σ	Volatility factor
τ	Time of financial event
ϵ	Random value

Credit Risk

AIRBA	Advanced internal ratings-based approach
b	Maturity adjustment
BE	Bank exposures
CCF	Credit conversion factors
CE	Corporate exposures
CF	Commodities finance
EAD	Exposure at default
ECRA	External credit rating assessment
EL	Expected loss
EqE	Equity exposures

FI	Financial institutions
FIRBA	Foundation internal ratings-based approach
HVCRE	High-volatility commercial real estate
IPRE	Income-producing real estate
IRBA	Internal ratings-based approach, i.e. AIRBA and FIRBA
K	Capital requirement
Kd	Capital arising from dilution risk of purchased receivables
LTV	Loan-to-value
M	Maturity
MDB	Multilateral development banks
NIF	Note issuance facilities
ObF	Object finance
OffBS	Off-balance sheet exposures
OFR	Output floor rate
OnBS	On-balance sheet exposures
PF	Project finance
PIT	Point-in-time (estimation of PDs)
PRC	Corporate purchased receivables
PRR	Retail purchased receivables
RE	Retail exposures
RUF	Revolving underwriting facilities
RW	Risk weights
RWA	Risk-weighted assets
S	Sales (input to the formula for the calculation of SME capital requirements)
SA	Standardised approach
SCRA	Standardised credit rating assessment
SE	Sovereign exposures
SME	Small- and medium-sized entities
TTC	Through-the-cycle (estimation of PD)
UCC	Unconditionally cancellable commitments

Market Risk

ACC	Aggregate capital charge for the market risk
Advanced CVA	Advanced CVA risk capital charge (Basel III)

BA-CVA	Basic approach of CVA framework (FRTB/Minimum capital requirements for CVA risk under Basel III: Finalising post-crisis reforms)
CCP	Central counterparty
CCR	Counterparty credit risk
CDS	Credit default swap
CIR	Cox–Ingersoll–Ross model
CRD	Capital requirements directive
CSR	Credit spread risk
CTP	Correlation trading portfolio
CVA (VaR)	CVA value-at-risk
CVA	Credit valuation adjustment
CVR	Curvature risk charge
DJS	Direct jump-to-simulation date
DP	Default probability (equivalent to probability of default, PD)
DRC	Default risk charge
EE	Expected exposure
EEPE	Effective expected positive exposure
ELGD	Expected loss-given default
ENE	Expected negative exposure
EPE	Expected positive exposure
ES	Expected shortfall
FRTB	Fundamental review of the trading book
FX	Foreign exchange
GIRR	General interest rate risk
IM	Initial margin
IMA	Internal model approach of FRTB framework
IMM	Internal model method
IRS	Interest rate swap
JTD	Jump-to-default
LCR	Liquidity coverage ratio
LGD	Loss-given default
MPoR	Margin period of risk
MTA	Minimum transfer amount
MTM	Mark-to-market
MVA	Margin valuation adjustment
NICA	Net independent collateral amount
NMRFs	Non-modellable risk factors
Non-CTP	Non-correlation trading portfolio

NS	Netting set
NSFR	Net stable funding ratio
OTC	Over-the-counter
P&L	Profit & loss
PD	Probability of default
PDS	Path-dependent simulation
PFE	Potential future exposure
PLA	P&L attribution
RFET	Risk factor eligibility test
R-SbM	Reduced sensitivities-based method
RWR	Right-way risk
SA	Standardised approach of FRTB framework
SA-CVA	Standardised approach of CVA framework (FRTB/ Minimum capital requirements for CVA risk under Basel III: Finalising post-crisis reforms)
SbM	Sensitivities-based method
SCAO	Stressed Capital Add-on
SFT	Securities financing transactions
Standardised CVA	The standardised CVA risk capital charge (Basel III)
TB	Trading book
VaR	Value-at-risk
VM	Variation margin
WWR	Wrong-way risk

Operational Risk

AMA	Advanced measurement approach
BB	Banking book
BI	Business indicator
BIC	Business indicator component
DI	Dividend income
FC	Fee component
FE	Fee expense
FI	Financial income
GPD	Generalised Pareto distribution
IE	Interest expenses
IEA	Interest earning assets

II	Interest income
ILDC	Interest, lease, and dividend income component
ILM	Internal loss multiplier
LE	Lease expenses
LI	Lease income
NIM	Net interest margin
OOE	Other operating expenses
OOI	Other operating income
P&L	Profit & loss
SC	Services component
SMA	Standardised measurement approach
TB	Trading book
uBI	Unadjusted business indicator (does not include high fees adjustment)

List of Figures

List of Tables

List of Boxes

1

Introductory Remarks

Before they became standards on Thursday, 7 December 2017, the proposals (BCBS, 2015a, 2015b, 2016a, 2016b, 2016c) of the Basel Committee on Banking Supervision (BCBS) had spurred a heated debate amongst regulators, banks, and politicians on the merits that the new supervisory standards would bring to the resilience of banks as opposed to the potential burden that they would bring to the operational cost and the cost of capital. Since they became standards, the Basel reforms pose challenges as to the implementation of the new rules that the international banks have to cope with.

The new framework recommends supervisors to impose new capital requirements for going concern to mitigate the riskiness of non-defaulted exposures. The current chapter intends to provide the reader with the initiative of the publication, describe the target audience, and portray the applicability of the book's content by the stakeholders. In doing so, it briefly discusses the content of the book and describes why and how it is beneficial for each of the stakeholders.

1.1 Initiative of the Publication

The main argument of those who oppose the implementation of the new framework is that it would pose an additional operational burden to some banks, which already struggle to comply with the existing set of regulatory and reporting requirements on capital, leverage, and liquidity. It is undeniable that the compliance with the new framework will put an additional operational burden on banks. This burden translates into the additional effort and

© The Author(s) 2018
I. Akkizidis, L. Kalyvas, *Final Basel III Modelling*,
https://doi.org/10.1007/978-3-319-70425-8_1

human capital for the implementation of the new provisions. However, the most prominent concern of the criticism relates to the additional regulatory capital which the new framework may imply for most of the banks. The additional required capital could also lead to some second-order effects which relate to reputational risks, market confidence, and funding costs as well as competitiveness. The implementation of the new framework becomes even more challenging if we consider it in the context of the social pressure on international banks to boost economic recovery through the provision of credit to corporates and retailers.

Given that the various pieces of regulation seemed to have been designed in isolation, the actual integrated impact could be above the sum of the impacts of each individual component. Moreover, a set of changes to one type of risk may also require further amendments in the future to another type of risk, which could only be identified in practice (Deloitte, 2015).

Apart from the one-off operational burden arising from banks' internal reorganisation to implement the new framework, some associate the new rules with high ongoing compliance costs. Even before the publication of the final Basel III reforms, the banking industry was mindful of the increased costs of compliance with the existing version of Basel III regulation at that time (English & Hammond, 2015). The completed Basel III package will add to the regulatory cost of the existing Basel III part before even the full implementation of the latter.

Against this background, the book provides the reader with guidance on the methodology for the estimation of capital requirements under the final Basel III and with evidence on its impact with a view to inform banks, regulators, and supervisors. This would enhance their awareness and facilitate timely future reactions, ensuring a smooth transition to the new supervisory environment. The present book also unveils implications that the new framework may have when banks try to interpret the new regulatory framework or when they apply it.

Currently, large and internationally active banks continue arguing on the need to reduce the increased capital requirements but, due to the wide spectrum of the proposed revisions, it is likely that they will, anyway, have to invest in infrastructure and human expertise to address future compliance requirements, especially those relating to internal models. On the other hand, smaller banks, which do not have the capacity to build costly internal models, should reflect on the transformation of standardised approach (SA) methods which have now become more complicated than they used to be under Basel III (BCBS, 2016a, 2016b). In the absence of adequate human resources, banks of all sizes and banking models may also consider outsourcing the ongoing compliance to external providers of this service. The outsourcing of the implementation of the Basel reform package implies that the current book would be particularly useful for consultants who are the natural candidates for assisting banks in implementing the new framework.

Thus, the book intends to provide guidance on the implementation of the incremental elements of the final Basel III framework and its subsequent impact, as well as to shed light on the most common issues and dilemmas that banks are likely to face. Furthermore, it addresses the open question as to whether the social benefits of additional banking resilience, arising from the implementation and ongoing application of the reforms' package, offset the final cost in terms of additional capital requirements.

One of the aims of the reforms is to reduce the variability of risk-weighted assets (RWAs) by introducing a framework that would be less reliant on fluctuating risk parameters. To address this issue, the book compares the differences between SA and the internal ratings-based approach (IRBA) under the existing Basel III and the final Basel III, seeking evidence on whether the new framework achieves its scope. The wide variation of internal models' specifications, which is the result of a bespoke application of the rules, implies that two different models could result in different amounts of minimum capital requirements for the same institution.

The book investigates the impact of setting minimum values in the inputs and outputs of credit risk internal models as well as the impact that banks would have to face for the application of alternative specifications of the standardised measurement approach (SMA) for operational risk. Concretely, it assesses the capital impact of the BCBS's proposals in terms of additional future Pillar I (Chap. 2) capital requirements (final Basel III) on the current minimum Pillar I capital requirements (existing Basel III). To this end, it does not take into account any amount of Pillar II (Chap. 2) capital requirements mainly because the nature and applicability of Pillar II capital requirements differ amongst jurisdictions but also because there is no information on Pillar II capital that is readily available to researchers.

The assessment of the impact will focus on "analysis of delta", that is, the analysis of the incremental impact assuming full implementation of Basel III. To this end, the elements of Basel III, which remain unchanged in the new framework, are not considered in the analysis of the impact. These parts include the liquidity coverage ratio (LCR) and the net stable funding ratio (NSFR) as well as capital requirements which do not change under the new framework, that is, the treatment of sovereign exposures, settlement risk, qualifying central counterparties, and other Pillar I capital requirements. Although some of these parts of Basel III are in the pipeline for updates in the near future, the book does not include them in the final Basel III package, as there is no evidence on the direction that these updates will take. As Basel III adopted some parts of the Basel II framework, such as the treatment of specific types of exposures under credit risk, the "analysis of delta" of these parts will implicitly refer to comparisons with the Basel II framework too.

For the purposes of the analysis of this book, the set of Basel reforms includes the revised framework for minimum capital requirements for market risk (BCBS, 2016a), the revisions to the SA for credit risk (BCBS, 2015b), the revisions to the IRBA for reducing variation in credit RWAs arising from the use of internal model approaches (BCBS, 2016c), the revisions to the Basel III leverage ratio (LR) framework (BCBS, 2016d), the SMA for operational risk (BCBS, 2016b), the review of the credit valuation adjustment (CVA) framework (BCBS, 2015a, 2017b), and the reduced-form SA for market risk capital requirements—consultative document (BCBS, 2017a). The book does not consider any proposals or revisions to the above consultation documents announced, finalised, or made publicly available after 7 December 2017.

The methodology refers to the estimation of capital requirements for both current and proposed frameworks examining simultaneously the attributes of their application. In turn, it refers to the estimation of the impact of the final Basel III on the current RWAs and the minimum required capital (MRC). The presentation of the methodology for the estimation of the impact aims at assisting the bankers/researchers to apply it on the metric they would be most interested in their intended analysis.

It is worthwhile to underline that, unless stated otherwise, the analysis throughout the book refers to Pillar I regulatory capital (BCBS, 2006). The regulatory capital may be, and in most cases it is, much different from the accounting capital, that is, the capital shown in the accounting statements of a bank.

The quantitative impact studies presented so far by various agencies, institutions, or organisations (BCBS, 2017c; EBA, 2017) rely on data which includes a certain level of processing by the banks participating in these exercises. The involvement of the banks in processing the data set before its submission entails a certain level of model-error risk since it is natural that some of them have not yet adequately digested or understood the final Basel III proposals in the same way. The model-error risk and the inconsistency in the application of the reform proposals could lead to erroneous estimations of the total impact. Our approach does not use any results which imply banks' intervention.

To achieve this, we mainly analyse the differences per asset class and per risk category arising from model specifications and/or changes in risk weights which arise from different models specifications of the existing Basel III and the final Basel III based only on (realised) default rates (DRs) and realised loss-given default (LGD) observations. The independence of the analysis from bank-specific data will allow the analysis to remain unbiased. Along the same line, the inputs used in the internal models are retrieved or inferred from either publicly available sources (e.g. EU-wide transparency exercises, Pillar III disclosures) or observed variables (e.g. [realised] DRs instead of probabilities of default [PDs], realised LGD, instead of estimated LGD).

Regarding market risk and CVA, the final Basel III presents a new Fundamental Review of the Trading Book (FRTB) SA, which does not resemble the one currently applied by banks. Instead, it assumes the implementation of a unique model for the estimation of correlations and risk weights, which will be applicable to all banks. To this end, the book presents the implementation of this modelling together with illustrative examples in the boxes of the relevant chapters.

The BCBS proposal for a reduced-form SA, aka R-SbM (BCBS, 2017a), for the assessment of the market risk by small, non-systemic banks calls for a comparison with the SA of the FRTB (SA-FRTB) (BCBS, 2016a). Again, the book presents this comparison through illustrative examples, enabling the reader to apply the methodology for a portfolio of her/his preference to estimate the differences between the SA-FRTB and the reduced-form SA-FRTB.

1.2   Target Audience

The book aims to provide a concise but complete overview of the proposed changes, clarify pending implementation issues of the new framework, and provide evidence about the impact of the proposals.

There is a vast audience waiting for a comprehensive analysis of the new proposals and their recent amendments. This includes banking professionals (risk managers, compliance officers, other bank administrators, etc.) who will get involved in the implementation of the new framework; regulators and supervisors who will need to decide on the national implementation of the rules and the supervision of its application; consultancy firms that would offer their services in the implementation of the framework; IT companies, which are interested in programming the code and assisting banks to comply with the regulatory framework and its reporting requirements; and academics and students interested in research in this area.

The book targets all audiences, who have at least basic knowledge of banking (economists) or banking regulation (legal experts or compliance officers). To fulfil the needs of both audiences, the book presents the notions in mathematical terms, but it also describes them in plain text to make them digestible for audiences that are not acquainted with mathematical expressions. In principle, the book presents the notions in a way that is as comprehensive as possible to provide the readers with a clear idea about the implementation of the key sections of the final Basel III framework.

The book also provides many illustrative configurations that would facilitate senior professionals to get a good grasp of the regulation without having to go through the numerous cross-references. The book also aims at assisting younger professionals and university students and serves the purpose of a reference book. Like another book by the authors, the book is also aiming at being used as tutorial material by any of the global (risk or finance) associations.

To be of assistance to practitioners, the book will provide not only a set of concise illustrative examples but also a more analytical application to be used on a web-based platform. Finally, through simple examples shown in the boxes of each chapter, the book provides material to be used for teaching topics, such as risk management, banking and finance, and banking regulation.

1.3   Conclusions

The current chapter provides the readers with a brief description of the initiatives behind the publication of the book, and its target audience, to assist them figuring out why the book is useful for each of the involved stakeholders. In particular, it designates the high-level changes initiated by the new framework and elaborates how the content of the book is beneficial for bankers (risk managers, compliance officers, and other operational executives), economists, academics, and finance students alike.

References

Basel Committee on Banking Supervision. (2006, June). Basel II: International convergence of capital measurement and capital standards: A revised framework – Comprehensive version. Retrieved December 2016, from http://www.bis.org/publ/bcbs128.pdf

Basel Committee on Banking Supervision (BCBS). (2015a, July). Review of the Credit Valuation Adjustment (CVA) risk framework – consultative document. Retrieved July 2015, from http://www.bis.org/bcbs/publ/d325.pdf

Basel Committee on Banking Supervision (BCBS). (2015b, December). Revisions to the Standardised Approach for credit risk – second consultative document. Retrieved December 2015, from http://www.bis.org/bcbs/publ/d347.pdf

Basel Committee on Banking Supervision (BCBS). (2016a, January). Minimum capital requirements for market risk – Standards. Retrieved January 2016, from http://www.bis.org/bcbs/publ/d352.pdf

Basel Committee on Banking Supervision (BCBS). (2016b, March). Standardised Measurement Approach for operational risk – consultative document. Retrieved March 2016, from http://www.bis.org/bcbs/publ/d355.pdf

Basel Committee on Banking Supervision (BCBS). (2016c, March). Reducing variation in credit risk-weighted assets – constraints on the use of internal model approaches – consultative document. Retrieved March 2016, from http://www.bis.org/bcbs/publ/d362.pdf

Basel Committee on Banking Supervision (BCBS). (2016d, April). Revisions to the Basel III leverage ratio framework – consultative document. Retrieved March 2016, from http://www.bis.org/bcbs/publ/d365.pdf

Basel Committee on Banking Supervision (BCBS). (2017a, June). Simplified alternative to the standardised approach to market risk capital requirements – consultative document. Retrieved June 2017, from http://www.bis.org/bcbs/publ/d408.pdf

Basel Committee on Banking Supervision (BCBS). (2017b, December). Basel III: Finalising post-crisis reforms – Standards. Retrieved December 7, 2017, from https://www.bis.org/bcbs/publ/d424.pdf

Basel Committee on Banking Supervision (BCBS). (2017c, December). Basel III Monitoring Report – Results of the cumulative quantitative impact study. Retrieved December 7, 2017, from https://www.bis.org/bcbs/publ/d426.pdf

Deloitte. (2015). Basel III framework: The butterfly effect. Retrieved from https://www2.deloitte.com/content/dam/Deloitte/sg/Documents/financial-services/sea-fsi-basel-III-framework-noexp.pdf

European Banking Authority (EBA). (2017, December). Ad hoc cumulative impact assessment of the Basel reform package. Retrieved from https://www.eba.europa.eu/documents/10180/1720738/Ad+Hoc+Cumulative+Impact+Assessment+of+-the+Basel+reform+package.pdf/76c00d7d-3ae3-445e-9e8a-8c397e02e465

English, S., & Hammond, S. (2015). *Cost of compliance 2015*. London: Thomson Reuters.

2

The Roadmap to the Final Basel III

The current chapter describes the international bodies and the interaction amongst them that leads to the development of international banking supervision standards. It also depicts the market or regulatory failures that contributed to the creation of new supervisory standards and the significant changes that flagged each reform. In particular, it describes the evolution of banking standards from the Basel Capital Accord (aka Basel I) to Basel III.

Also, it elaborates on the final Basel III amendments on each of the risk categories (credit, market/credit valuation adjustments [CVAs], and operational risk) compared to Basel III, in an attempt to assess the direction of the impact of such changes. Finally, it briefly presents the changes in the leverage ratio (LR) framework.

2.1 The International Setting of Banking Regulation and Supervision

The G20 is an international forum of 20 countries[1] founded in 1999 to discuss international financial and monetary policies, reforms of financial institutions, and world economic developments. Although initially comprising finance ministers and central bank governors, after 2008, the G20 has become a forum of country leaders (*Heads of State and Government of the Group of Twenty*) to discuss international economic cooperation to facilitate progress in global economic governance. Occasionally, the G20 invites some international organisations[2] to discuss developments in the economy and support the decision-making process.

© The Author(s) 2018
I. Akkizidis, L. Kalyvas, *Final Basel III Modelling*,
https://doi.org/10.1007/978-3-319-70425-8_2

In 1999, the G7,[3] a Group of finance ministers and central bank governors, established the Financial Stability Forum (FSF) to recommend "new structures for enhancing cooperation among the various national and international supervisory bodies and international financial institutions to promote stability in the international financial system" (FSB, 2017). Following a call of the G20, the FSF expanded its membership to "strengthen its effectiveness as a mechanism for national authorities" (Draghi, 2009: 1).

In its 2009 forum in Pittsburgh, the G20 established the Financial Stability Board (FSB), the successor to the FSF, with the aim of taking the lead in proposing reforms in international financial regulation and, ultimately, of ensuring financial stability. In 2011, the G20 "agreed to strengthen the FSB's capacity, resources, and governance" (FSB, 2012: 1). Since then, the FSB sets international standards and promotes their implementation to comply with the G20 policy recommendations.

The FSB aims at enhancing cooperation amongst the national competent authorities, such as treasuries, central banks, and supervisors, and sustaining financial stability under adverse economic circumstances. As with other sectors of the economy, the FSB brings together banking regulators and supervisors to address vulnerabilities and develop international regulatory and supervisory standards of good practices with the objective of sustaining financial stability. More importantly, though, the FSB monitors the national implementation of such standards and makes high-level policy recommendations for the correction of the market or regulatory failures in the banking sector.

In 1974, the G10[4] countries established the "Committee on Banking Regulations and Supervisory Practices" (CBRSP) in response to the disruption in the financial market, in 1973, caused by the collapse of the foreign exchange system of managed rates of Bretton Woods (TIME, 2008) and the default of Herstatt Bank (Economist, 2001). CBRSP, which was made up of central bank governors of the participating countries, was eventually renamed "Basel Committee on Banking Supervision" (BCBS).[5] It expanded its membership in 2009 and 2014 and currently includes 28 country members,[6] 3 state observers,[7] and 5 international bodies.[8] It aims at sustaining and enhancing financial stability by exchanging knowledge on banking supervision amongst its members and, based on the strengths and weaknesses of national regulatory frameworks, to create new standards for improving the quality of banking supervision worldwide.

The BCBS reports to an oversight body, the Group of Central Bank Governors and Heads of Supervision (GHoS). This Group consists of central bank governors and (non-central bank) heads of supervision from BCBS member countries. The BCBS's decisions have no legal force but aim at putting forward the standards, guidelines, and sound practices, which its member countries are expected to implement. To ensure effective, efficient, and consistent implementation of banking supervision standards, the BCBS also monitors the application of supervisory practices in the national regulation.

Moreover, in 2012, the BCBS started overseeing the convergence of the jurisdictions with the minimum banking supervisory requirements by conducting regular assessments of the implementation of Basel III through two different channels. The GHoS endorsed a comprehensive process, known as the "Regulatory Consistency Assessment Programme (RCAP)", to monitor members' implementation of Basel III. This programme assesses the consistency and completeness of the Basel III framework. Separately, there are regular monitoring exercises to evaluate the convergence of the participating jurisdictions concerning the quantitative minimum requirements of Basel III. The BCBS communicates the results of the monitoring exercise to the public to promote confidence and to ensure a level playing field in banking regulation and supervision for internationally active banks.

As mentioned before, the FSB proposals, as specified by the BCBS and GHoS, have no legal force. The national jurisdictions, which would like to entirely (or partially) adopt these decisions, should transform these standards into binding regulation in their jurisdictions. In the case of the European Union (EU), a big part of the BCBS standards become mandatory through the adoption of the Capital Requirements Regulation (CRR) by the European Parliament and the Council (2013a). In areas where the EU decides that national discretions should be allowed, the Capital Requirements Directive (CRD) includes the majority of the BCBS standards (the European Parliament and the Council, 2013b). In turn, national authorities apply the CRR and transpose the CRD in their respective national regulations.

To prevent systemic crises which could affect the banking, securities, and insurance sectors, a Joint Forum was established and has been operating under the auspices of three different entities, that is, the "BCBS", the "International Organisation of Securities Commissions", and the International Association of Insurance Supervisors for insurers. The Joint Forum has been dealing with issues involving all three sectors. The equivalent body of the EU, the Committee of the European Supervisory Authorities (ESA), consists of the European Banking Authority (EBA), the European Securities and Markets Authority (ESMA), and the European Insurance and Occupational Pensions Authority (EIOPA).

2.2   Basel I: The Basel Capital Accord (1988)

At the beginning of 1980, the world economy entered a recession. The rise of nominal interest rates forced commercial banks to charge higher interest rates for loans and shorten repayment periods. As a result of the accumulated debt and interest, Latin American countries could not sustain their debts (Devlin & Ffrench-Davis, 1995). The sovereign defaults started eroding the capital buffers of international banks, which were net lenders to Latin American countries, thus increasing concerns about their resilience and the global financial stability. The international economic and financial developments encouraged the BCBS to intervene for setting up an objective framework for risk measurement. The G10 governors approved a "capital measurement system commonly referred to as the Basel Capital Accord (1988 Accord) and released it to banks in July 1988" (BCBS, 1988, 2016e). The main characteristic of the new framework was the risk weighting of on- and off-balance sheet asset classes according to the risk they bear and the setting of a minimum capital ratio of capital to risk-weighted assets (RWAs) of 8%.

The Basel I framework intended to measure the capital adequacy against exposures which bear credit risk. The BCBS published an amendment for providing clarifications on the definition of general provisions included in the calculation of the capital adequacy ratios (BCBS, 1991). It also allowed the recognition of bilateral netting of banks' credit exposures in derivative products (BCBS, 1995) and, finally, acknowledged the effect of multilateral netting (BCBS, 1996).

Moving beyond credit risk, the BCBS issued the so-called Market Risk Amendment (1996) to incorporate a capital requirement for market risks arising from banks' exposures to foreign exchange, traded debt securities, equities, commodities, and options (BCBS, 2016e). The main characteristic of the Market Risk Amendment was the permission to banks, subject to strict quantitative and qualitative standards, to use internal models for measuring their market risk capital requirements.

2.3   Basel II: A Radical Change of the Supervisory Framework (2004)

The increasing use of innovative financial products by the banking sector after the implementation of Basel I and the scandal of Enron led to the design of a new regulatory framework. As a response to the Enron scandal, the US published the "Sarbanes-Oxley Act of 2002" (SOA, 2002). The new Basel framework was finalised shortly afterwards (BCBS, 2006). The Basel II framework introduced more sensitive capital requirements to cater for the high complexity of on- and off-balance sheet items. It also provided measures for bespoke capital requirements (Pillar II), above the minimum, to address risks not captured by Pillar I. Basel II also included measures for increased transparency (Pillar III).

Overall, the new framework Basel, widely known as "Basel II", was released in 2004. Basel II comprised three pillars (BCBS, 2006):

- *Pillar I*: the minimum capital requirements which sought to develop and expand the standardised rules set out in the 1988 Accord;
- *Pillar II*: the supervisory review of an institution's capital adequacy and internal assessment process; and
- *Pillar III*: the efficient use of disclosure for strengthening market discipline and encourage sound banking practices.

As with Basel I, the amendment of the treatment of the market risk in the trading book[9] followed the release of the Basel II part referring to the credit risk in the banking book. Nonetheless, the integrated version of Basel II (BCBS, 2006) implies that both elements belong to the Basel II framework.

2.4 Basel III: Capital and Liquidity Reform Package (2010)

The outbreak of the financial crisis after the collapse of Lehman Brothers (2008) brought to light the excessive leverage of the banking sector and the lack of adequate liquidity buffers to absorb the consequences of the financial turbulence. The excessive leverage was the natural consequence of inadequate governance and risk management practices, which led to excess credit growth.

In light of the deficiencies revealed by the financial crisis, the BCBS strengthened the treatment of certain complex securitisation positions, off-balance sheet vehicles, and trading book exposures. Following the endorsement of the G20 Leaders' Summit in Seoul, the BCBS released, in 2010, two documents setting the standards of Basel III (BCBS, 2011, 2013).

The Basel III framework revised and strengthened the three pillars established by Basel II. Moreover, it added several new capital and liquidity requirements:

- **The capital conservation buffer (CCB)**, which adds to the minimum required capital. This capital requirement was designed as an additional buffer to protect the current minimum required capital. If this extra buffer requirement starts eroding, the payouts of earnings are restricted, enhancing the accumulation of the minimum required capital;
- **The countercyclical capital buffer**, which is complementary to the minimum required capital. This buffer limits the participation of banks in system-wide credit growth and aims at reducing their losses in credit downturns;
- **The capital surcharge for global systemically important banks (G-SIBs)**, which is accompanied by strengthened provisions for cross-border supervision and resolution;
- **The LR**, which is a metric of the minimum amount of loss-absorbing capital relative (T1 capital) to total on- and off-balance sheet bank's exposures. The definition of total bank's exposures to calculate LR is close, albeit not identical, to the measure of non-risk-weighted total assets shown in a bank' financial statements;
- **The liquidity coverage ratio (LCR)**, which sets the minimum standards for the adequacy of cash, or high liquid assets, to cover funding needs over a 30-day period of stress;
- **The net stable funding ratio (NSFR)**, which is a longer-term ratio designed to monitor maturity mismatches over the entire balance sheet.

Overall, the minimum capital requirements for the full implementation of Basel III would be the following:

As from 1 January 2015, the minimum Common Equity Tier 1 (CET1) was set at 4.5% while the T1 was at 6.0% implying that the additional T1 capital should be at the most 1.5% of the total RWAs. The minimum total capital (TC) requirement would remain unchanged, in comparison to Basel II, at 8.0%. The level of minimum TC requirement implies that T2 capital would be at the most 2.0% of the total RWA. As from 1 January 2016, a capital surcharge of up to 3.5% applies to G-SIBs.[10]

As from 1 January 2018, a minimum T1 capital requirement of 3% of the LR total exposure measure will become the new LR requirement under Pillar I. The appropriate calibration of this requirement is still under review.

As from 1 January 2018, the NSFR of 100% will become a minimum standard requirement, while as from 1 January 2019, the CCB will stand at 2.5% of RWA. The CCB will comprise CET1 and will be an add-on to the 4.5% CET1 minimum required capital.

Finally, as from 1 January 2019, the LCR will be set at 100%. The LCR, which is the buffer of high-quality liquid assets sufficient to deal with the cash

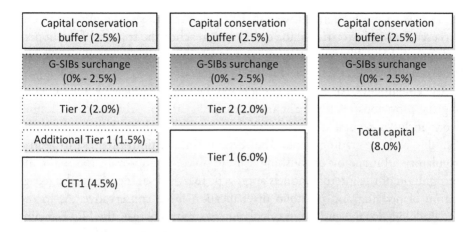

Fig. 2.1 Basel III minimum Pillar 1 risk-based capital requirements

outflows encountered in an acute short-term stress scenario, will be set at 100%. Figure 2.1 exhibits graphically the minimum capital requirements presented earlier.

2.5   Heading Towards the Final Basel III (2015–)

In January 2016, the GHoS endorsed the BCBS proposals for the revision of the market risk framework, which is otherwise known as the Fundamental Review of the Trading Book (FRTB). In the press release after the meeting (BIS, 2016a), the GHoS also called upon the BCBS to address the problem of excessive variability in internal models' RWAs by the end of 2016.

Regarding the revisions related to credit risk, the new framework addresses the issue of mechanistic reliance on external ratings by allowing two alternative approaches for the calculation of RWA (BCBS, 2015b): the External Credit Rating Assessment (ECRA) approach and the Standardised Credit Risk Assessment (SCRA) approach. The former revises the risk-weighting scheme, which currently applies according to ECRAs, while the latter introduces, for the first time, a proposal for the reduction of the reliance on ECRA. The SCRA applies to unrated exposures of banks incorporated in jurisdictions that allow the use of external ratings for regulatory purposes and for all exposures of banks incorporated in jurisdictions that do not allow the use of external ratings for regulatory purposes. The SCRA requires an assessment of credit risk exposures and their subsequent classification under Grade A, Grade B, or Grade C. As part of a due diligence process, a bank may classify an exposure to a grade with a higher risk weight (RW) even if it meets the minimum criteria set out in a lower-risk grade or has not breached the triggers of the upper-risk grade. Due diligence should never result in an RW lower than the one determined by the criteria set out for each grade.

In September 2016, the GHoS endorsed the FRTB framework after amending the provisions relating to market risk (BIS, 2016b). The proposed framework includes revised definitions on how to set the boundary between the banking and the trading book. The revisions in question intended to reduce regulatory arbitrage by establishing a more objective approval process for the recognition of the internal models approach (IMA). Also, they make the recognition of hedging and portfolio diversification more conservative. As to the methodology for the end-point calculation of capital charges, the FRTB retains the IMA and the standardised approach (SA). Nonetheless, the FRTB enhances the relationship between the two approaches by converting the latter into a credible "fallback" and simultaneously into a floor for the revised IMA. Nonetheless, the long-lasting negotiations amongst BCBS members led, on 7 December 2017, to further revisions of the FRTB framework and the postponement of its application to 2022. In January 2016, the GHoS delegated the BCBS to investigate ways to address the issue of excessive variability in RWAs (BIS, 2016a) by

- removing the advanced measurement approach (AMA) for operational risk; and,
- setting [input and output] floors on the capital requirements produced by the internal ratings-based models for credit risk.

On 7 December 2017, the GHoS also agreed that the LR should be based on a new definition of total exposures measure and endorsed the implementation of an additional surcharge for G-SIBs.

The GHoS delegated the BCBS to conduct a quantitative impact study (QIS) and to come up with specific proposals. Based on the evidence included in this QIS, the GHoS endorsed the risk-based framework in December 2017. Following the GHoS intention, the revisions do not result in significant increase of capital requirement. The significant revisions of the framework, endorsed by the GHoS, are the following:

- Changes in RWs applied to some asset classes and modifications in the credit conversion factors under the SA to credit risk;
- Changes in the internal ratings-based approach (IRBA), including the migration of some asset classes from the advanced internal ratings-based approach (AIRBA) to other more lenient methods (i.e. SA or Foundation Internal ratings-based approach (FIRBA));

- The implementation of input floors in the determinants (exposure-at-default [EAD], PD, and loss-given default [LGD]) of credit risk internal models' capital requirements;
- Inclusion of a LR add-on linked to a bank's G-SIB surcharge (if applicable);
- Removal of the AMA for operational risk;
- The replacement of all operational risk methods with the standardised measurement approach (SMA); and
- The inclusion of an output floor in the calculation of RWAs using internal ratings-based (IRB) approaches, set at 72.5% of the SA-equivalent RWA, assuming the complete absence of internal models.

For the sake of clarity, it is worth mentioning a difference between the naming convention used throughout the book and the one that the BCBS and GHoS use to refer to the Basel reforms. The book refers to the "final Basel III", being aligned with the terminology used by the GHoS, BCBS, and bank for international settlements (BIS), despite the fact that, for a long time, the industry has been referring to the reforms as "Basel IV" due to their extent and importance.

The book adopts the view that the reforms heralded a new era in banking regulation because of the severity of the changes in many components of the existing framework. Another reason is to avoid the confusion when referring to the Basel III set of revisions that took place between 2011 and 2015 (LCR, NSFR, LR, and some revisions to credit risk), and those adopted in December 2017 (the revisions examined in the present book). Irrespective of how one names the reforms, the book considers that they constitute a large-scale set of changes in banking regulation and supervision. That is why the analysis throughout the book believes that the FRTB, CVA, SA for credit risk, IRBA, operational risk, and LR reforms are all part of a new set of reforms which form the final Basel III framework.

The output floor is a newly implemented supervisory requirement that applies horizontally and produces an add-on amount of RWAs to that calculated for the individual risk categories. The output floor aims at addressing inefficiencies in the functionality of internal models or, in other words, at confronting with the model-error risk resulting from the use of internal models, which could lead to the underestimation of capital requirements. In addition to the risk-based capital requirements (individual risk category capital requirements plus additional capital requirements for output floor), the revisions in the LR may further affect the capital requirements produced by the risk-weighted framework.

The book deems it essential first to describe the current framework, and then the final Basel III revisions, with a view towards portraying a broad picture of how the completed regulatory setting would look like. In a few cases, the book assesses the impact arising from the potential adoption of alternative options, which deviate from the proposals, to examine the relative impact had these alternatives been adopted. Chapters 3 and 4 provide a detailed presentation of the changes between the final and current Basel III frameworks.

2.6   The Final Basel III: The Standardised Approach to Credit Risk

The revised SA for credit risk changes the treatment of exposures to banks, corporates, equities, specialised lending and commercial and residential real estate exposures (CRE and RRE). Unlike the IRBA framework, the SA does not imply any impact of the migration of exposures to other regulatory risk assessment approaches. However, certain asset classes are subject to different methods for the calculation of minimum capital requirements under the final Basel III (e.g. "buy-to-let" mortgages).

2.6.1   Bank Exposures

The revisions to the treatment of bank exposures refer to both ECRA and SCRA. The analysis of the book focuses on the impact of introducing capital requirements according to the ECRA, as it is the only approach which offers evidence for the comparison between the final and current Basel III frameworks. However, there is no evidence to estimate the incremental impact of the implementation of SCRA as the latter was not part of Basel III. Nonetheless, the book will also present the proposals relating to the SCRA and provide information about the direction of the impact compared to the proposals laid out in the second consultative paper on the revisions to the SA for credit risk (BCBS, 2015b).

The final Basel III framework allows for a preferential RW treatment of exposures to covered bonds, competed to the provisions of the initial Basel III framework which treated them as regular bank exposures.

The risk-weighting schedule of externally rated bank exposures under the ECRA remains somewhat the same (BCBS, 2015b) compared with the current framework. Under the SCRA, bank exposures rated as Grade A receive an

RW of 40% (BCBS, 2017a) while Grade B and Grade C bank exposures receive RWs of 75% and 150%, respectively (BCBS, 2017b). The reader could assess the impact of the changes in the risk-weighting scheme of the SA framework by applying the methodology described in the pertinent part of the book.

2.6.2   Corporate Exposures

The part of the final Basel III, which relates to corporate exposures, has not implemented material changes compared to the current framework. According to the Basel reforms (BCBS, 2017a), corporate exposures rated from BBB+ to BBB– under the ECRA will receive an RW of 75%. The jurisdictions, which do not allow the use of ECRA, that is, only SCRA is applicable, will apply an RW of 65% to corporate exposures considered as "investment grade". The "non-investment grade" exposures will receive an RW of 100%. In general, the final SA standards treat corporate exposures more favourably than the second consultative document (CD) (BCBS, 2015b). Amongst others, it is not surprising that the new framework suggests a preferential RW for small and medium-sized enterprises (SMEs) treated as corporates (85%), and an even more preferential RW for SMEs regarded as retail exposures (75%).

2.6.3   Equity Exposures

The first CD suggested the distinction between RWs falling under two discrete subclasses of equity exposures: the "publicly traded equity" and "all other equity holdings". The former subclass would receive a 300% RW while the latter 400%.

The second consultative paper introduces a general RW for equity exposures at 250%. Given that not all equity exposures (traded and non-traded) bear the same risk, the final revisions distinguish amongst four categories of equity, that is, "subordinated debt and capital other than equity" (RW of 150%), "equity exposures to certain legislative programmes" (RW of 100%), "speculative unlisted equity" (RW of 400%), and all other equity exposures (RW of 250%).

Given that the impact of the implementation of the two subclasses and the relevant RWs would point to opposite directions (positive impact for the first subclass, negative for the second subclass), the analysis cannot approximate either the direction or the magnitude of the impact of implementing these changes. Therefore, the decisive factor for the impact is the bank-specific allocation of equity exposures. Thus, the book refrains from providing any estimation regarding the general impact of the new framework on equity exposures. However, individual banks can assess the impact of the final Basel III on their capital requirements by applying the methodology after using the bank-specific allocation of equity exposures amongst the four equity subclasses.

2.6.4 Specialised Lending Exposures

Although the definition of the specialised lending exposures comprises several definitions stemming from the relevant subcategories, the current section examines only the RWs assigned to these subcategories. Regarding the project finance (PF) exposures, the issue-specific rated exposures receive the RW of the general corporates. The RW of PF exposures, where an external rating is not available, is 130% during the pre-operational phase, 100% during the operational phase, and 80% for high-quality exposures which are risk-weighted during the operational phase. The BCBS considers that the "operational phase is defined as the phase in which the entity that was specifically created to finance the project has (i) a positive net cash flow that is sufficient to cover any remaining contractual obligation, and (ii) declining long-term debt" (BCBS, 2015b: 32).

The RW for rated object finance (ObF) and commodity finance (CF) is the same as for general corporates, while the unrated exposures receive an RW of 100%.

2.6.5 Residential and Commercial Real Estate Exposures

The baseline Basel III SA applies a 35% RW to all exposures secured by mortgages on the residential property, provided there is a "substantial margin of additional security over the amount of the loan based on strict valuation rules" (BCBS, 2014: 15). As this approach does not specify the margin of additional security required to achieve the 35% RW, it allows for deviations in the treatment of mortgages on residential property across jurisdictions depending on the interpretation of "substantial margin of additional security". The new framework uses the loan-to-value (LTV) ratio as a proxy for the borrower's ability to service the RRE exposures (previously defined as mortgages) and assigns RWs accordingly. The proposed RWs range from 20% (LTV ≤ 50%) to 70% (LTV > 100%). A bank should measure the value of the property (denominator of the LTV ratio) at the origin and keep it constant throughout the life of the RRE exposure. The Basel revisions allow the splitting of the exposure across different LTV buckets by assigning a 20% RW to the part of the exposure that exhibits LTV of 55% or less, while the rest of the exposure receives the RW of the counterparty. The most recent proposals treat "buy-to-let" arrangements[11] less preferentially, compared to the RRE which do not significantly rely the repayment on cash flows on the property. The "buy-to-let" arrangements, i.e. income-producing RRE, receive RWs which range from 70% to 120%.

The new framework differentiates between the risk of commercial real estate exposures (CRE) and the risk of the RRE. Hence, the RW for commercial real estate exposures (RW = 60%), assigned to the least risky bucket of the CRE (LTV $\leq$ 60%), is much higher than the lowest assigned to the RRE exposures (RW = 20%–25%).

2.6.6   Retail Exposures

The pre-final Basel III provisions on retail exposures distinguish between "regulatory retail" and "other retail" exposures and assign 75% and 100% RWs, respectively. The definition of each category depends not only on the orientation criterion (to individuals or SMEs) but also on the product and granularity criteria as well as on a standard of low value of individual exposures.

2.7   The Final Basel III: Internal Ratings-Based Approach

2.7.1   Migration Dynamics

The BCBS (2016c) proposes the migration from the AIRBA to SA of exposures to banks, other financial entities, and large corporates (corporates with revenues above EUR 200 million). The final agreement provides that only the corporates with revenues above EUR 500 million, banks, and other financial entities will migrate to the FIRBA (instead of the SA), while equity is the only exposure that will migrate to the SA. It also proposes not to allow the use of the AIRBA for certain other corporates which do not exhibit reliable estimates of LGD.

This modification in the migration dynamics is expected to mitigate the impact of changing approaches, as the FIRBA generally produces lower RWs than the SA for the same asset classes. The analysis presents an estimation of the impact of corporate exposures' migration from AIRBA to FIRBA.

The specialised lending exposures will not add to the overall impact of the migration as they remain under the AIRBA. The migration of bank and corporate exposures from the AIRBA to FIRBA implies an increase in RWs compared to the currently applied AIRBA. The same applies to equity exposures which migrate from the AIRBA to SA. By providing a comparative analysis of the RWs, and implicitly of capital requirements, stemming from the final Basel III AIRBA, FIRBA, and SA, the authors enable the readers to apply the parameters relating to their exposures to estimate portfolio-specific impacts. Nevertheless, when comparing the final to current Basel III provisions, the impact of migrating AIRBA exposures (BCBS, 2016c: 3–4) to any of the other approaches implies an increase in the Basel III RWs for the same asset classes. The question is "how much?" Chapter 4 attempts to answer this question.

2.7.2 Changes Specific to AIRBA/FIRBA

The main innovation introduced in the IRBA estimates of capital requirements is the introduction of input and output floors in the calculation of the minimum required capital. The initial proposal on IRBA calibration includes a set of input floors for PDs, LGDs, and the level of EAD, complemented by an output floor that would further increase the capital requirements arising from the application of IRBA. Although it mainly impacts credit risk, given its majority in the formulation of RWA (see EBA, 2017: 26), the output floors apply to the entirety of RWAs calculated according to internal models, that is, IRBA for credit risk and IMA for market risk.

The analysis in Chap. 4 refers to changes in AIRBA and FIRBA, which may have an impact on the current level of RWA generated by the IRBA. The analysis also investigates different calibration scenarios as to the degree of input floors. We consider that the implementation of input and output floors intends to address the model-error risk arising from the development of IRBA models. We also deem that the "1.06 scaling factor", that is, the 6% add-on currently applicable to all RWAs calculated under IRBA, also addresses the same kind of risk. To this end, the authors believe this is correctly removed from the final provisions and, therefore, they conduct the estimations without considering it.

Although the removal of the 1.06 scaling factor writes down the additional buffer previously used to cover for potential erroneous model specifications, the input and output floors counterbalance, and potentially further increase, the safety net for the excessive model-error risk in the final calculation of RWA.

Chapter 4 also examines several alternatives for the calibration of FIRBA and AIRBA focusing on the potential reduction of the supervisory LGD (currently at 45%) assigned to corporate exposures under the FIRBA. Given that the revised framework sets the supervisory LGD at 40%, the analysis examines the impact of applying the reduced supervisory LGD for various collateralisation levels (from 0% to 200%).

The analysis of the book does not depend on the changes in the definition and potential subsequent reclassifications of exposures, which may occur amid the implementation of the final Basel III standards. Since any reclassification of exposures relates to bank-specific or contract-specific exposures, the analysis cannot make any generalisation relating to the impact of definitional changes on the output of IRBA modelling.

2.8   The Final Basel III: Market Risk

As mentioned earlier, the BIS (BCBS, 2013, 2016a, 2018) provides new standards to minimum capital requirements for market risk including some significant changes and improvements in both the SA and the IMA. In the SA, banks have to estimate the capital charges by employing the sensitivities-based method (SbM), the default risk charge (DRC), and the residual risk add-on. Indeed, these methods provide a sufficient level of standardisation to identify, measure, and manage market risk for those financial institutions that have no need to apply sophisticated approaches. Moreover, for those banks that have simpler and smaller trading portfolios, the BIS proposed an alternative and less demanding method to estimate market risk capital, aka the reduced sensitivities-based method (R-SbM). However, only banks that meet specific criteria would be able to use the alternative approach.

The SbM includes delta and vega sensitivities as well as curvature risk analysis applied to eight risk classes. Banks should use the DRC approach for estimating the capital charge against trading book exposures to counterparty credit risk (CCR), while an additional capital charge should apply against market-driven residual risks, which are not captured by the other approaches.

By applying the IMA, banks estimate a capital charge against market risk by employing the expected shortfall (ES), the DRC, and the stressed capital add-on for "non-modellable" risk factors (NMRF). The shift from the value at risk (VaR) to an ES metric ensures that the "tail risk" arising under stress market conditions is more accurately measured and captured.

2.8.1   Sensitivities-Based Method

According to the SbM, banks have to calculate delta and vega risk capital charges across all buckets by following a step-by-step process. First, it associates its portfolio to risk classes predefined by the regulators; second, it identifies the buckets which are associated to specific counterparties' and exposures' categories; third, it calculates the net sensitivities of each risk class; fourth, it estimates the weighted net sensitivities for each risk factor; and, fifth, it estimates the delta and vega risk positions for each bucket.

Also, a bank has to estimate the curvature risk charge across all buckets under the SbM. The sensitivity risk charge aggregation is based on stress scenarios on the formulation of correlation. On the other side of the fence, regulators provide the rules for the identification of the appropriate RWs, the formulae used for the estimation of sensitivities, as well as the step-by-step process for the calculation of capital charges. Chapter 6 provides examples for estimating capital charges. It also examines the impact of the parameters driving the SbM, to optimise the portfolio resulting in a minimum capital charge.

2.8.2   Standardised Default Risk Charge

Under the standardised DRC, banks apply the jump-to-default (JTD) methodology, which focuses on the tail of the loss distribution, where extreme events may arise, necessitating the need for a possible hedge. The new framework provides guidelines on the estimation of DRCs against JTD losses for correlated or uncorrelated securitised or non-securitised positions, covering the full spectrum of the trading book portfolio. The main elements of DRC consist of the measurements of gross and net JTD for long and short positions, the weighted-to-short ratio, as well as the RWs driven by the rating classifications. Chapter 6 explores these parameters using concrete examples for estimating the DRC of non-securitisations products.

2.8.3   Residual Risk

The new standardised approach includes additional capital charges against residual risk, including gap, correlation, and behaviour risk. The FRTB defines the exact types of risks which are subject to the residual capital charge add-on calculation.

2.8.4   Internal Models Approach

The IMA introduces three approaches for the estimation of capital charge against market risk. These approaches are the "ES", the "DRC", and the "stressed capital add-on" for "non-modellable" risks. Amongst the above-approved approaches, the liquidity and market stress conditions play a pivotal role in the estimation of ES and DRC. Chapter 6 explores the IMA approaches, highlighting the main elements and drivers for estimating the regulatory capital charge.

Moreover, banks should comply with the minimum back-testing and P&L attribution requirements to be eligible for calculating capital charges under the IMA. In addition to back-testing, which was already a requirement in Basel III, the new framework requires banks to pass the P&L attribution criteria, which are mainly based on *risk-theoretical* and *hypothetical* P&L measurements.

The number of outliers arising from the back-testing exercise results from the times that the ES underestimates the actual loss and has a direct impact on the capital charge through the multiplication factor applied. Finally, the bank should account for the regulatory valuation rules which could directly impact the level of liquidity especially for the trading positions associated with unexpected stress conditions.

2.9   The Final Basel III: Credit Valuation Adjustments (CVA)

In post-crisis regulation, there is intensive focus on CVAs. Both the BIS (BCBS, 2011, 2015a, 2017b) and the International Accounting Standards Board (IASB) responsible for the International Financial Reporting Standards (IFRS) regulation have extensively referred to the importance for banks to be able to consider the valuation adjustment due to CCR as well as to capture the corresponding losses. The new Basel documentation quotes that "under Basel II, the risk of counterparty default and credit migration risk were addressed, but mark-to-market losses due to credit valuation adjustments (CVA) were not" and that "during the financial crisis, however, roughly two-thirds of losses, attributed to counterparty credit risk, were due to CVA losses and only about one-third were due to actual defaults".[12] International Financial Reporting Standards (IFRS) requires banks to measure the fair value of over-the-counter (OTC) derivatives, which includes the adjustment of values according to credit quality. The IAS39 highlights that for non-defaulted derivatives the fair value needs to be considered to determine CVA. In Chap. 7 the regulatory approaches on CVA risk is explored in detail.

2.9.1   Exposure Analysis

The exposure analysis considers the netting rules as well as margin agreements in place in the new framework. The mechanism of margin agreements can be a rather complex process but must be well-defined and considered during the time steps of the evolution of exposure. The distribution of exposures' evolution based on different market scenarios is an essential factor in the estimation of CVA and is used in both banking and trading books. Based on the supervisory standards, banks may apply the accounting-based or the internal model method (IMM)-based approach for generating market scenarios. In addition to the valuation and accounting rules, which discount the distributed derivatives exposures, the bank has to identify the turning point where derivatives change from "in-the-money" to "out-of-the-money" positions for each scenario. The scenarios use certain probabilities for the evolution of P&L, indicating alternative paths for the evolution of potential future exposures and their effects in P&L over time. The models used in the exposure evolution must be calibrated considering real world and risk-neutral probabilities. Chapter 7 covers the exposure analysis and examines the challenges in estimating the distribution of the evolution of exposures to be used as inputs in CVA calculation.

2.9.2   Approaches in Estimating CVA VaR

An additional important factor in estimating the CVA VaR measurement is the consideration of CCR factors under the probability of default analysis. The evolution of the counterparty credit spreads is associated with the evolution of default probabilities defined through intensity and hazard rate functions. Chapter 7 uses the Cox–Ingersoll–Ross approach to estimate the intensity functions to stochastically simulate the credit spreads together with the derivation of survival and probabilities of default. Based on the stochastic exposures and credit spreads the CVA (VaR) approaches are applied in the estimation of the regulatory capital adequacy (BCBS, 2011, 2017b).

2.9.3   Regulatory Approaches in Estimating CVA Capital Charge

According to Basel III (BCBS, 2011), banks have the choice of applying between two approaches to compute the regulatory CVA capital charge for the banking book: the standardised method and the advanced method. Chapter 7 identifies the impact of the EAD and credit rating parameters on the calculation of CVA capital charge under the standardised approach. The advanced approach is based on internal models that have to be approved by regulators. The calculation of the capital charges accounts for counterparty credit spreads as the only decisive factor responsible for the changes in the CVA. Thus, the hedging CVA risk refers only to credit spreads.

However, the new framework (BCBS, 2015a, 2017b) estimates the minimum capital relying on variations of both market and credit spreads. The FRTB-CVA framework (BCBS, 2015a) is replaced by the new revised market risk framework on minimum capital requirements for CVA risk (BCBS, 2017b). Banks can choose in the new revised CVA framework between the *reduced* or the *full* version of basic approach (BA-CVA); or the standardised approach (SA-CVA) for calculating CVA capital charge. Banks do not have, however, the option to apply the IMA-CVA approach proposed by the FRTB-CVA framework. An alternative option to set the CVA capital equal to capital charge estimated for CCR may be exercised for those banks exposed to non-centrally cleared derivatives up to the materiality threshold defined by the BCBS.

Chapter 7 describes in detail the new revised BA-CVA approaches and explains how to optimise the components comprising the *full* version of the basic approach to minimise the capital charges.

In the standardised approach, the bank follows the SbMs for the trading book defined under the FRTB-SA. However, there is a reduction in the granularity of risk factors and sensitivity measures in the version of FRTB used under the CVA. CVA uses only delta and vega risk in the estimation of capital charge. Chapter 7 describes all the necessary steps for the application of the standardised approach alongside the impact on the current capital charges from their application.

2.10   The Final Basel III: Operational Risk

The BCBS proposed an alternative approach for the calculation of regulatory capital requirements (BCBS, 2016b), the SMA, which will replace the existing approaches for operational risk. The new approach proposes that the minimum capital requirement for operational risk relies on indicators of observed losses and indicators of business size, which is likely to generate operating losses of proportional magnitude in various banking activities.

Although flagged as a standardised approach, the SMA contains some elements of modelling and the use of past data, which would require banks to apply some expert judgement instead of blindly applying a standardised approach as known now (which does not rely on large data sets of internal data). The impact of the SMA implementation is subject to set the loss materiality thresholds.

The analysis in Chap. 8 examines alternative categorisations and subsequent assignments of RWs to business size, as well as different modelling specifications for the estimation of the loss component. It also introduces a dampening factor for the estimation of the loss component and alternative specifications for the loss multiplier. Finally, the analysis scrutinises the interactions between the business indicator component (BIC) and internal loss multiplier (ILM) on the one side and the SMA capital requirements on the other side. It also examines the potential effect of adopting a neutral ILM component (ILM = 1) in estimating SMA capital requirements.

The application of a neutral ILM (ILM = 1) for all banks would render the estimation of the SMA capital only dependent on the BIC component. The application of ILM equal to one would reduce the SMA capital for banks with actual ILM higher than unity, while it would increase it for those with actual ILM below unity. Thus, a potential application of ILM = 1 would depend on whether the cost of additional operational risk capital requirements offsets the benefits arising from the enhanced financial stability that the high capital would entail. If a national supervisor judges that the additional capital requirements accounting for the actual ILM overcome the incremental benefits from the enhanced financial stability, then they could favour the application of the actual ILM and vice versa.

The above expert judgement may differ across different jurisdictions. Based only on the mechanistic selection of the lowest SMA capital requirement, national banking systems which underwent high operational losses in the past would opt for the option of ILM = 1. On the contrary, jurisdictions which underwent very low or zero operational losses would promote the actual ILM as the component for determining SMA capital requirements.

Based on the above ad hoc analysis, the book assumes that the final SMA framework allows jurisdictions to exercise the national discretion of applying either the actual ILM or ILM = 1. Given that researchers cannot easily estimate the benefits from the incremental increase of financial stability without supervisors' intelligence, the analysis of this book assumes that the incremental benefit of financial stability from the application of the strictest option is zero. The supervisor would choose the option that produces the lowest SMA capital requirements.

2.11   The Final Basel III: Leverage Ratio

The latest BCBS proposals on LR (BCBS, 2016d) introduce a revised framework for the calculation of the LR, based on an amendment to the definition of the total exposure measure (denominator of the LR). Moreover, the BCBS revised the methodology for the estimation of minimum LR capital requirement for G-SIBs. The changes in the LR definition include the amendment of the standardised approach for measuring counterparty credit risk (SA-CCR) for derivative exposures and changes in the treatment of written credit derivatives. The new LR framework also seeks to provide clarity regarding the use of trade-date and settlement-date accounting relating to the purchase of securities. It also revises the treatment of accounting provisions and cash pooling products, that is, products, which net out positive and negative outstanding cash balances with international subsidiaries. The impact of implementing the revisions in the calculation of the LR could be either positive or negative depending on the distribution of the exposures.

Apart from the changes which affect the basis for the calculation, that is, the total exposure measure, the BCBS increases the minimum capital required for G-SIBs as a percentage of the total exposure measure. The BCBS sets the G-SIBs add-on at 50% of the G-SIBs surcharge, which applies to the risk-based minimum capital requirements (Chap. 9).

2.12   Conclusions

The present chapter presents the evolution of the international banking regulation from its inception (1988) up to the development of the final Basel III banking standards (2015–), along with the most critical alterations that characterised each of them. In describing each of the steps of the regulatory evolution, the reader realises the caveats of each piece of regulatory standards which triggered the final Basel III agreement and the direction of the impact they imply.

The reader can also spot the specific elements in several risk categories where the final Basel III aims to enhance the current framework (Basel III). The analysis in the current chapter distinguishes amongst credit, market, and operational risk. It also describes the significant alterations in the CVA and LR frameworks.

Notes

1. Comprising Argentina, Australia, Brazil, Canada, China, France, Germany, India, Indonesia, Italy, Japan, Mexico, the Republic of Korea, Russia, Saudi Arabia, South Africa, Turkey, the UK, the US, and the EU.
2. The international institutions which have participated in G20 meetings are the United Nations, the International Monetary Fund, the World Bank, the World Trade Organization, the Financial Stability Board, the International Labour Organisation, the Organisation for Economic Co-operation and Development (OECD).

3. The G7 consists of the seven major advanced economies: Canada, France, Germany, Italy, Japan, the UK, and the US. In the last years, the EU is also represented within the G7.
4. In fact, the G10 consists of 11 industrial countries, that is, Belgium, Canada, France, Germany, Italy, Japan, the Netherlands, Sweden, Switzerland, the UK, and the US.
5. Henceforth, references to "BCBS" cite either BCBS or its predecessor (CBRSP).
6. Argentina, Australia, Belgium, Brazil, Canada, China, the EU (as represented by the Single Supervisory Mechanism of the European Central Bank), France, Germany, Hong Kong SAR, India, Indonesia, Italy, Luxembourg, Mexico, the Netherlands, Russia, Saudi Arabia, Singapore, South Africa, Spain, Switzerland, Turkey, the UK, and the US.
7. Chile, Malaysia, and the United Arab Emirates.
8. Bank for International Settlements, Basel Consultative Group, EBA, European Commission, and the International Monetary Fund.
9. The market risk framework has been developed in close cooperation between the BCBS and International Organisation of Securities Commissions (IOSCO).
10. According to the BIS, the G-SIB surcharges span from 0% (for non-G-SIBs) to 3.5% (for the most systemically important G-SIB). As of now, none of the G-SIBs has been assigned to the highest surcharge level of 3.5%. The following G-SIBs are subject surcharges (the level of which is shown in parenthesis): HSBC (2.5%), JP Morgan Chase (2.5%), Barclays (2.0%), BNP Paribas (2.0%), Citigroup (2.0%), Deutsche Bank (2.0%), Bank of America (1.5%), Credit Suisse (1.5%), Goldman Sachs (1.5%), Mitsubishi UFJ FG (1.5%), Morgan Stanley(1.5%), the Royal Bank of Scotland (1.5%), Agricultural Bank of China (1.0%), Bank of China (1.0%), Bank of New York Mellon (1.0%), BBVA (1.0%), Groupe BCPE (1.0%), Group Crédit Agricole (1.0%), Industrial and Commercial Bank of China Limited (1.0%), ING Bank (1.0%), Mizuho FG (1.0%), Nordea (1.0%), Santander (1.0%), Société Générale (1.0%), Standard Chartered (1.0%), State Street (1.0%), Sumitomo Mitsui FG (1.0%), UBS (1.0%), Unicredit Group (1.0%), and Wells Fargo (1.0%).
11. A common example of "buy-to-let" arrangement is the purchase of a residential real estate with a mortgage whose repayment relies on the letting of the residential real estate.
12. The BIS press release on capital treatment for bilateral counterparty credit risk (1 June 2011) https://www.bis.org/press/p110601.htm is reflected in the consolidated document of Basel III: https://www.bis.org/publ/bcbs189.pdf. Accessed 14 November 2017.

References

Bank for International Settlements (BIS). (2016a). Press release: Revised market risk framework and work programme for Basel Committee is endorsed by its governing body. Retrieved January 11, 2016, from http://www.bis.org/press/p160111.htm

Bank for International Settlements (BIS). (2016b). Press release: Governors and Heads of Supervision announce progress in finalising post-crisis regulatory reforms. Retrieved September 11, 2016, from http://www.bis.org/press/p160911.htm

Basel Committee on Banking Supervision (BCBS). (1988, July). International convergence of capital measurement and capital standards. Retrieved September 19, 2017, from http://www.bis.org/publ/bcbs04a.pdf

Basel Committee on Banking Supervision (BCBS). (1991, November). Amendment of the Basle Capital Accord in respect of the inclusion of general provisions/general loan-loss reserves in capital. Retrieved September 20, 2017, from http://www.bis.org/publ/bcbs09.pdf

Basel Committee on Banking Supervision (BCBS). (1995, April). Treatment of potential exposure for off-balance sheet items. Retrieved September 20, 2017, from http://www.bis.org/publ/bcbs18.pdf

Basel Committee on Banking Supervision (BCBS). (1996, April). Interpretation of the capital accord for the multilateral netting of forward value foreign exchange transactions. Retrieved September 21, 2017, from http://www.bis.org/publ/bcbs25.pdf

Basel Committee on Banking Supervision. (2006, June). Basel II: International convergence of capital measurement and capital standards: A revised framework – comprehensive version. June 2006. Retrieved December 2016, from http://www.bis.org/publ/bcbs128.pdf

Basel Committee on Banking Supervision. (2011, June). Basel III: A global regulatory framework for more resilient banks and banking systems – revised version. Retrieved December 2016, from http://www.bis.org/publ/bcbs189.pdf

Basel Committee on Banking Supervision. (2013, January). Basel III: The Liquidity Coverage Ratio and liquidity risk monitoring tools. Retrieved December 2016, from http://www.bis.org/publ/bcbs238.pdf

Basel Committee on Banking Supervision. (2014, December). Revisions to the Standardised Approach for credit risk – consultative document. Retrieved December 2016, from http://www.bis.org/bcbs/publ/d307.pdf

Basel Committee on Banking Supervision (BCBS). (2015a, July). Review of the Credit Valuation Adjustment (CVA) risk framework – consultative document. Retrieved July 2015, from http://www.bis.org/bcbs/publ/d325.pdf

Basel Committee on Banking Supervision (BCBS). (2015b, December). Revisions to the Standardised Approach for credit risk – second consultative document. Retrieved December 2015, from http://www.bis.org/bcbs/publ/d347.pdf

Basel Committee on Banking Supervision (BCBS). (2016a, January). Minimum capital requirements for market risk – Standards. Retrieved January 2016, from http://www.bis.org/bcbs/publ/d352.pdf

Basel Committee on Banking Supervision (BCBS). (2016b, March). Standardised Measurement Approach for operational risk – consultative document. Retrieved March 2016, from http://www.bis.org/bcbs/publ/d355.pdf

Basel Committee on Banking Supervision (BCBS). (2016c, March). Reducing variation in credit risk-weighted assets – constraints on the use of internal model approaches – consultative document. Retrieved March 2016, from http://www.bis.org/bcbs/publ/d362.pdf

Basel Committee on Banking Supervision (BCBS). (2016d, April). Revisions to the Basel III leverage ratio framework – consultative document. Retrieved March 2016, from http://www.bis.org/bcbs/publ/d365.pdf

Basel Committee on Banking Supervision (BCBS). (2016e, December). History of the Basel Committee. Retrieved September 19, 2017, from http://www.bis.org/bcbs/history.htm

Basel Committee on Banking Supervision (BCBS). (2017a, June). Simplified alternative to the standardised approach to market risk capital requirements – consultative document. Retrieved June 2017, from http://www.bis.org/bcbs/publ/d408.pdf

Basel Committee on Banking Supervision (BCBS). (2017b, December). Basel III: Finalising post-crisis reforms. Retrieved December 2017, from https://www.bis.org/bcbs/publ/d424.pdf

Basel Committee on Banking Supervision (BCBS). (March 2018). Revisions to the minimum capital requirements for market risk. Retrieved March 2018, from https://www.bis.org/bcbs/publ/d436.pdf

Devlin, R., & Ffrench-Davis, R. (1995). The great Latin America debt-crisis, a decade of asymmetric adjustment. *Revista de Economia Politica, 15*(3), 117–142.

Draghi, M., Chairman of the Financial Stability Forum. (2009, April). Re-establishment of the FSF as the Financial Stability Board: Remarks at the conclusion of London Summit. Retrieved September 19, 2017, from http://www.fsb.org/wp-content/uploads/r_090402.pdf

European Banking Authority (EBA). (2017, December). Ad hoc cumulative impact assessment of the Basel reform package. https://www.eba.europa.eu/documents/10180/1720738/Ad+Hoc+Cumulative+Impact+Assessment+of+the+Basel+reform+package.pdf/76c00d7d-3ae3-445e-9e8a-8c397e02e465

(The) European Parliament and the Council. (2013a, June). Regulation (EU) No. 575/2013 (Capital Requirements Regulation). http://eur-lex.europa.eu/legal-content/EN/TXT/PDF/?uri=CELEX:32013R0575&from=EN

(The) European Parliament and the Council. (2013b, June). Directive 2013/36/EU (Capital Requirements Directive). http://eur-lex.europa.eu/LexUriServ/LexUriServ.do?uri=OJ:L:2013:176:0338:0436:En:PDF

Financial Stability Board (FSB). (2012). Report to the G20 Los Cabos summit on strengthening FSB capacity, resources and governance. Retrieved September 19, 2017, from http://www.fsb.org/wp-content/uploads/r_120619c.pdf

Financial Stability Board (FSB). (2017). Our history. Retrieved September 19, 2017, from http://www.fsb.org/about/history/

Sarbanes–Oxley Act (SOA). (2002). Public law 107–204. *107th Congress.* Retrieved September 19, 2017, from https://www.sec.gov/about/laws/soa2002.pdf

3

Impact Assessment Methodology

The current chapter describes the formulae that quantify the impact of the transition from the current to the final Basel III framework. First, it presents the core regulatory ratios that banks need to comply with their minimum capital requirements, that is, the risk-based capital ratio and the leverage ratio (LR). Then, it presents the typology for assessing the impact of the implementation of the final Basel III framework, at the level of the minimum required capital (MRC). It also suggests the formulation for the evaluation of the capital shortfall (SFL) that the new framework implies, assuming that the current actual regulatory capital is entirely assigned to Pillar I capital requirements.

3.1 Calculation of Capital Ratios

The actual capital ratios show the level of compliance of banks with the minimum Pillar I requirement, being a central indicator of the degree of banks' resilience against economic downturns which could harm the quality of the assets held in their portfolio. The current framework separates between risk-based and leverage capital ratios. The risk-based capital ratios are simply the division of a measure of capital over the risk-weighted assets (RWAs). The MRC, being the necessary capital considered as adequate to absorb any adverse financial conditions, is set out in the Pillar I minimum capital requirements for various types of capital. The competent authorities could also impose bank-specific capital add-ons, aka Pillar II capital, to restore any anticipated vulnerabilities arising from idiosyncratic risk factors. However, the analysis targets the assessment of the impact on Pillar I capital requirements

© The Author(s) 2018
I. Akkizidis, L. Kalyvas, *Final Basel III Modelling*,
https://doi.org/10.1007/978-3-319-70425-8_3

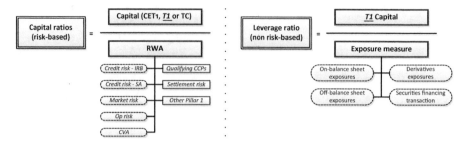

Fig. 3.1 Graphical presentation of the calculation of risk-based capital ratios and leverage ratio

only, as the level of Pillar II capital depends on the bank's characteristics and the competent authority's expert judgement. Figure 3.1 illustrates the general formula for the estimation of Pillar I capital and LRs.

The nominator in the risk-based capital ratios could be either the CET1, Tier1, or the total capital, while for the LR it is only the Tier1 capital which is the relevant type of capital for the estimation of LR. The RWA is always the denominator for all types of risk-based capital ratios, that is, CET1, Tier1, and total capital, while a measure of total exposures[1] is the denominator of the LR.

Also, the analysis distinguishes between the actual and minimum capital required for both risk-based and LRs. Actual capital ratios take into account the actual regulatory capital held by a bank, while the minimum ratio accounts for the capital that would have fulfilled the relevant provisions for the capital ratio in the Basel framework.[2] The actual capital ratio should always be higher or equal to the minimum capital ratio.

Figure 3.1 brakes down the RWA by risk type and method of estimation. The parts of the RWA which correspond to the entire credit risk (IRB and standardised approach [SA]), market risk, operational risk, and CVA framework are subject to changes due to the implementation of the new framework. The analysis does not consider the rest of the RWA categories as they are not subject to changes and will not influence the overall impact (see boxes with solid frames in Fig. 3.1).

3.2   Overview of the Proposed Changes

As mentioned, the conceptual variations in the current regulatory framework are quite extensive and extend from credit (BCBS, 2017c) and operational risk (BCBS, 2017c) to CVA and FRTB (BCBS, 2016a; BCBS, 2017a). The proposal of implementing input floors, applied to the parameters of credit risk, and the output floor on the cumulative RWA are probably the most radical revisions of the existing framework. Its application by international banks caused controversy as to whether this particular revision renders ineffective the IRBA models. The formulation of this part of the final framework could trigger a debate amongst supervisors of different jurisdictions,[3] but also between supervisors and IRBA banks, as well as amongst international banks in various jurisdictions which apply different national discretions as to the application of IRBA models. Although the debate focuses on whether a potential increase would hit international banks, the real issue is whether the increased capital is sufficient to safeguard banks from the actual risk of their exposures and, thus, from a potential financial crisis. In any case, the new set of capital requirements is more transparent, which could enhance the competitiveness amongst banks and stimulate consumers' benefits.

The debate especially involves the discussion as to whether the output floor puts some international banks into comparative disadvantage vis-à-vis their smaller or vis-à-vis their peers coming from other countries where the application of IRBA models is less widespread.

Before estimating the output floor add-on RWA, banks should apply a set of other amendments at the risk-category level, which changes the landscape of banking supervision. These changes imply the deeper involvement of banks' quantitative experts in the implementation of the integrated mechanism for estimating the risk-specific RWA and engage the competent authorities to closely monitor the rightful implementation of the rules and take corrective actions if and where needed.

As shown in Fig. 3.1, the revisions to credit risk framework are the most predominant, equally because they introduce a new philosophy in the calculation of RWA and the impact caused by its broad participation of credit risk in the portfolios of international banks. The new credit risk framework comprises revisions to the methodology of supervisory risk quantification in five distinct asset classes, that is, corporate exposures, bank exposures, retail exposures, specialised lending exposures, and equity exposures.

Given their weighting in the formulation of RWA, corporate and retail exposures are the asset classes which the analysis will mostly focus on. Examining the attributes of the final Basel III capital requirements related to corporate exposures is imperative due to the size of corporates' exposures in banks' portfolios. On the other hand, the analysis of retail exposures is necessary to mine potential implications that the construction of the new framework may have in the provision of retail lending. Also, the analysis of retail exposures under the new framework is essential for advising smaller banks on how to estimate the new capital requirements and what would be the impact on their daily conduct of business. Likewise, all banks will make the necessary preparations for the implementation of the new framework.

The impact from the SA to credit risk arises from the changes in the definition and treatment of asset classes as well as from changes in risk weights and credit conversion factors (CCFs) assigned, respectively, to the balance and off-balance sheet exposures. The book assesses only the differences stemming from changes in CCFs and risk weights.

The estimation of capital requirements takes into account the on-balance sheet-equivalent exposure of the off-balance sheet original exposure by using the relevant CCF. It then assigns the CCF to the relevant asset category where the original off-balance sheet exposure is attributed to, for example, a balance sheet equivalent of a bank exposure derived from the original credit line (off-balance sheet exposure) to the same bank after applying the relevant CCF. Thus, the methodology assigns to the specific asset category the impact of the changes in the regulatory framework. The same applies to the off-balance sheet exposures under the IRBA.

Regarding on-balance sheet exposures which are currently subject to the SA, the new framework suggests a new set of risk weights for a few asset categories (see Sect. 4.3.5). The main impact arises from the change in the categorisation of residential real estate (RRE) exposures (changes related to the definition of RREs) and the reduction in risk weights of A-rated bank exposures. The direction of the impact from the first part of the modifications depends exclusively on the average LTV of the current portfolio. If the current weighted LTV of a given bank is higher than 80%, then it will face an increase in its capital requirements for RRE. On the contrary, if the same LTV lies below 80% then it will see its capital requirements from RRE dropping. On the other hand, the direction of the impact, due to the reduction in the risk weights of A-rated bank exposures, is obviously negative (decline in RWA and capital requirements) (see Table 3.1).

Table 3.1 The various metrics for expressing the impact from the implementation of the final Basel III

Impact on	MRC	TRC	SFL
Changes of RWA (dRWA)	n.a.	n.a.	n.a.
Changes of capital expressed as ratio of RWA:			
(a) CET1 (4.5%) plus G-SIBs buffer (0% to 3.5%)	√	√	√
(b) T1 (6.0%) plus G-SIBs buffer (0% to 3.5%)	√	√	√
(c) TC (8.0%) plus G-SIBs buffer (0% to 3.5%)	√	√	√
(d) CET1 (4.5%) plus G-SIBs buffer (0% to 3.5%) plus CCB (2.5%)	√	√	√
(e) T1 (6.0%) plus G-SIBs buffer (0% to 3.5%) plus CCB (2.5%)	√	√	√
(f) TC (8.0%) plus G-SIBs buffer (0% to 3.5%) plus CCB (2.5%)	√	√	√
Changes of LR T1 expressed as ratio of total exposures	√	√	√

As to the IRBA models, the Basel proposals introduce changes that demand the radical change of the treatment of the underlined exposures. The most notable changes are the implementation of input and output floors, the migration of several exposures from the AIRBA to FIRBA or SA, and some changes in the definition of certain exposures which modify their current treatment and implicitly the level of capital requirements. The analysis presents the case where the same exposures migrate to FIRBA and SA to facilitate the reader to observe the impact of the changes in the eligibility of some asset categories and the impact of the output floor.

The implementation of input floors implies a positive or no shift in cases where the internal models' estimations of risk parameters are above the relevant floors. This implementation is one factor that drives the impact attributed to the switch from the current to the new IRBA model of the same nature, that is, from the current AIRBA to the new AIRBA and from the current FIRBA to the new FIRBA. In addition, the analysis examines the impact of removing the "1.06 scaling factor" as an add-on to all IRBA models.

Although the new framework allows specialised lending exposures to be assessed under the AIRBA, the book examines the impact stemming from the corporate-type specialised lending exposures to anticipate the impact of potential future revisions of the treatment of specialised lending (SL) exposures.

Figure 3.2 designates the mechanism for the estimation of the completed Basel III capital requirements, including all high-level modelling specifications and interactions amongst risk-based capital requirements, output floor, and the LR.

The aggregation of the asset-specific amendments in the calculation of capital requirements formulates the new credit risk framework (element A in Fig. 3.2), which constitutes the majority of RWAs in an average international bank. The rest of the elements for the calculation of total RWA are the operational risk (element B), the CVA RWA equivalent (element C), the market risk RWA equivalent (element D), the output floor impact (element E), and the LR add-on (element F).

The CVA and market risk account for less than 6% of the total MRC of a sample of international banks (BCBS, 2017b: 30). However, its complexity and the anticipated high impact demand a separate and extensive analysis on these two subject areas. As announced by the GHoS on 7 December 2017, the overall market risk framework is not yet final.

Thus, the analyses in the book focus on the existing provisions (BCBS, 2015) without making any additional assumptions or examining alternative options. Also, the book conducts a comparative analysis of the FRTB-SA initially proposed (BCBS, 2016a) vis-à-vis the so-called reduced-form FRTB-SA, which applies to small, non-systemic banks (BCBS, 2017a).

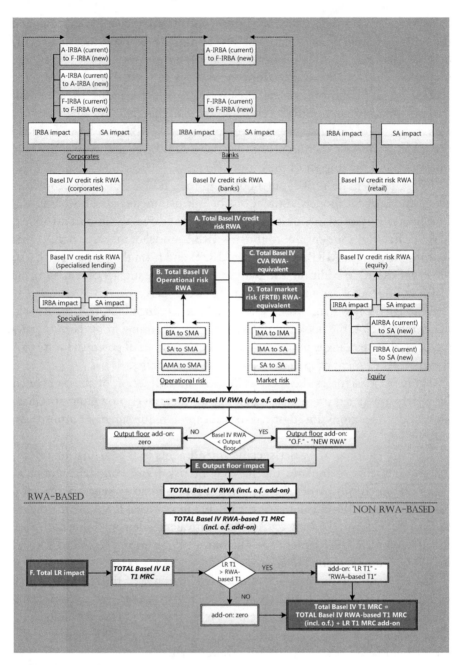

Fig. 3.2 The mechanism for the implementation of the finalised risk-specific, output floor, and LR Basel III capital requirements

Regarding operational risk, the final framework attempts, and to some extent succeeds, to harmonise the operational risk regulatory risk assessment by suggesting a unified approach for the estimation of operational risk capital requirements, that is, the standardised measurement approach (SMA). Its implementation implies that small banks, which currently apply the basic indicator approach (BIA), will face significant operational costs for the implementation of the SMA framework. The same banks will most probably benefit from reduced operational risk capital requirements. Contrariwise, large international banks which currently benefit from lower capital requirements due to the application of the advanced measurement approach (AMA) will most likely experience an increase in the amounts relating to operational risk although at the same time they will save resources due to the abolition of AMA, which is resource-intensive. The book examines the impact of migrating from AMA to SMA.

The constituents of credit, CVA, and market and operational risk comprise the part of the final Basel III implementation that relates to *risk-sensitive RWA estimation*, that is, the impact that arises from the direct application of ' and internal models' risk weights. This part of the RWA excludes the RWA add-on amid the application of the output floor (element E). The latter does not relate to risk-sensitive factors and addresses model-error risks inherent in the internal models.

Contrary to the above stand-alone asset-specific elements (Fig. 3.2, A–E), which require the estimation of RWA, the LR assumes the estimation of regulatory capital as a percentage of total exposures (BCBS, 2016d). Hence, it is a pre-requisite to transform the RWA of elements A–E into MRC, which then becomes the basis for evaluating whether the LR designates a capital add-on to that already estimated by the risk-based framework (including the output floor).

Both current and final frameworks imply that a bank should set aside the highest of the MRC arising from the risk-based and LR MRC in view to comply with the Basel framework.[4]

3.3   Estimation of the Impact

The impact of implementing the risk-based Basel III capital requirements could be expressed in terms of RWA, CET1, T1, and total capital. For each of the capital components, the impact could be expressed in terms of MRC, the "targeted required capital" (TRC), and "shortfall" (SFL). The (theoretical) impact on MRC assumes that a bank is currently holding capital equal to the current minimum capital requirements (BCBS, 2006; BCBS, 2011). The same bank is expected to hold the minimum capital to meet the final Basel III requirements.

The impact on TRC terms assumes that a bank would like to retain its current actual level of capital ratio after full implementation of Basel III. Finally, the "SFL indicates what would be the deficit of capital assuming that a bank uses the current actual capital to comply with the new minimum capital requirements.

The credit risk formulae produce RWA amounts (see Chap. 4), which in turn are the basis for the estimation of capital requirements, while the formulae for market, operational, and CVA produce the minimum capital requirements directly. To express every single risk component in RWA, the banks should convert capital requirements into their RWA equivalent and then calculate the MRC. To produce the RWA-equivalent, banks will divide by the required capital ratio in question; for example, to achieve the minimum required total capital ratio of 8%, the banks derive the RWA-equivalent by dividing the MRC by 0.08 or multiplying it by 12.5 (1/0.08).

As mentioned, there are various measures to express the impact of implementing the risk-based minimum requirements, while the LR impact translates only to Tier1 capital. Thus, to assess the impact from the joint implementation of risk-based capital requirements and LR, it is inevitable to express the impact only in terms of Tier1 capital.

The remaining part of the chapter presents the capital impact measures which refer to joint compliance with the risk-based and LR Tier1 capital requirements. Setting aside the changes in the definition of asset classes, there are explicit changes in risk weights, CCF, input floors, output floors, and migration from one method to another which directly affect the level of RWA. Albeit the direction of these changes depends on the business model and portfolio composition of banks, the change will generally alter the level of MRC, TRC, and possibly SFL through an increase in the RWA. The general formula for the estimation of the impact in terms of RWA is given below:

$$dRWA = RWA_{proposed} - RWA_{current} \qquad (3.1)$$

3.3.1 "Minimum Required Capital" (MRC) Impact Measure

The change in MRC (ΔMRC) is an impact measure aiming at assessing the differences between the current and final Basel III MRC. As, in practice, banks hold capital which is somewhat higher[5] than the required minimum, the MRC measure is a theoretical measure. Banks usually hold capital above the minimum as an initiative to hold add-on capital, which would serve as "management buffer", that is, an add-on that would allow for small fluctuations of the RWA between reporting dates without regular interventions by the management of the banks. The formulae for the estimation of impact in terms of T1 MRC are given below:

$$\Delta MRC^{T1} = MRC^{T1}_{proposed} - MRC^{T1}_{current} \tag{3.2}$$

$$\Delta MRC^{T1+CCB} = MRC^{T1+CCB}_{proposed} - MRC^{T1+CCB}_{current} \tag{3.3}$$

These equations define the current and proposed Tier1 MRC, with and without the capital conservation buffer (CCB). Henceforth, the analysis focuses only on the impact measures which include the CCB. The *mrr* and *ddr* variables refer, respectively, to the minimum required ratio and deduction rate of the surplus of provisions.[6] The *T1 mrr$_i$* corresponds to 6.0% (without the CCB) and 8.5% (with the CCB), that is, *mrr$_i$* = 6.0% or 8.5%. The *ddr$_j$* is the deduction rate of the surplus of provisions that applies to Tier1,[7] which currently equals one. The deficit of provisions is deductible from Tier1 capital (BCBS, 2011: 22, para 73) to set the level of the actual disposable capital used as the basis for the estimation of capital ratios. Analogically, for the calculation of MRC, the deficit of provisions should be added to the MRC as it would increase the minimum amount of *T1* MRC needed to comply with Basel requirements.

$$MRC^{T1(+CCB)}_{proposed} = \left\{ mrr_i + \max\left(G - SIBs, D - SIBs \right) \right\} \times RWA_{proposed}$$
$$- ddr_j \times \max\left(0, provisions_{proposed} - EL_{proposed} \right) \tag{3.4}$$

$$MRC^{T1(+CCB)}_{current} = \left\{ mrr_i + \max\left(G - SIBs, D - SIBs \right) \right\} \times RWA_{current}$$
$$- ddr_j \times \max\left(0, provisions_{current} - EL_{current} \right) \tag{3.5}$$

where G-SIBs represent the G-SIB surcharge (see Chap. 2); and domestic systemically important banks (D-SIBs) are the D-SIBs surcharge.[8]

As given below, the above set of equations can be further specified by using the values for the calculation of Tier1 MRC:

$$MRC^{T1(+CCB)}_{proposed} = \left\{ \sum_{\lambda=1}^{8} \left[0.06 + 0.025 + \max\left(G - SIBs, D - SIBs \right) \right] \times RWA^{\lambda}_{proposed} \right\}$$
$$- \min\left\{ 0, provisions^{IRB}_{proposed} - EL^{IRB}_{proposed} \right\} \tag{3.6}$$

$$MRC_{\text{current}}^{T1(+CCB)} = \left\{ \sum_{\lambda=1}^{8} \left[0.06 + 0.025 + \max\left(G - SIBs, D - SIBs\right) \right] \times RWA_{\text{current}}^{\lambda} \right\} - \min\left\{ 0, \text{provisions}_{\text{current}}^{IRB} - EL_{\text{current}}^{IRB} \right\}$$

(3.7)

where

$$\lambda = \begin{cases} 1 : \text{internal ratings} - \text{based approach}\left(IRBA\right) \\ 2 : \text{standardised approach}\left(SA\right) \text{to credit risk} \\ 3 : \text{operational risk}\left(OpRisk\right) \\ 4 : \text{market risk}\left(MR\right) \\ 5 : \text{credit valuation adjustments}\left(CVA\right) \\ 6 : \text{aualified central counterparties}\left(QCCP\right) \\ 7 : \text{settlement risk}\left(SR\right) \\ 8 : \text{other Pillar I} \end{cases}$$

3.3.2 "Target Required Capital" (TRC) Impact Measure

An alternative measure of the impact is the difference in terms of the targeted Tier1 capital (ΔTRC), which is the impact of the final Basel III framework assuming that the current actual capital ratio will continue to be the target ratio after the full implementation of Basel III. This measure addresses the need of banking supervisors and banks to retain the same resilience of banks and thus the same level of financial stability under the final Basel III. This measure is proportional to the MRC but it is a better approximation should banks desire to maintain the same external credit rating by retaining the same capital ratio. Thus, it is a better approximation of the impact for the banks that would like to sustain their creditworthiness.

$$\Delta TRC^{T1(+CCB)} = TRC_{\text{proposed}}^{T1(+CCB)} - TRC_{\text{current}}^{T1(+CCB)}$$

(3.8)

$$TRC_{\text{proposed}}^{T1(+CCB)} = \left\{ trr_i + \max\left(G - SIBs, D - SIBs\right) \right\} \times RWA_{\text{proposed}} - ddr_j \times \max\left(0, \text{provisions}_{\text{proposed}} - EL_{\text{proposed}}\right)$$

(3.9)

$$TRC_{\text{current}}^{T1(+CCB)} = \left\{ trr_i + \max\left(G - SIBs, D - SIBs\right)\right\} \times RWA_{\text{current}}$$
$$- ddr_j \times \max\left(0, \text{provisions}_{\text{current}} - EL_{\text{current}}\right) \quad (3.10)$$

Proportionally to the estimation of MRC, the trr_i indicates the target required ratio without the add-ons. Therefore, the trr corresponds to target $T1$ capital requirement rates; for example, for the estimation of $T1$ without CCB, the trr_i would simply be the current actual $T1$ ratio while for $T1$ with CCB, the trr_i would be the current actual $T1$ ratio plus 2.5% CCB.[9] As with $T1$ MRC, the ddr_j corresponds to 1 for $T1$.

$$TRC_{\text{proposed}}^{T1(+CCB)} = \left\{ \sum_{\lambda=1}^{8} \left[trr_i + \max\left(G - SIBs, D - SIBs\right)\right] \times RWA_{\text{proposed}}^{\lambda} \right\}$$
$$- \max\left\{ 0, \text{provisions}_{\text{proposed}}^{IRB} - EL_{\text{proposed}}^{IRB}\right\} \quad (3.11)$$

$$TRC_{\text{current}}^{T1(+CCB)} = \left\{ \sum_{\lambda=1}^{8} \left[trr_i + \max\left(G - SIBs, D - SIBs\right)\right] \times RWA_{\text{current}}^{\lambda} \right\}$$
$$- \max\left\{ 0, \text{provisions}_{\text{current}}^{IRB} - EL_{\text{current}}^{IRB}\right\} \quad (3.12)$$

3.3.3 "Shortfall" Impact Measure

The Tier1 SFL measure (ΔSFL^{T1}) measure aims at assessing what would be the Tier1 capital that a bank would need for the transition from the current actual Tier1 capital ratio (Basel III) to the minimum Tier1 ratio under the final Basel III. The formulae for ΔSFL measure are given below:

$$\Delta SFL^{T1(+CCB)} = MRC_{\text{proposed}}^{T1(+CCB)} - TRC_{\text{current}}^{T1(+CCB)} \quad (3.13)$$

The current TRC, that is, the current actual capital, and the MRC, that is, the final Basel III MRC, are defined in Eqs. (3.6) and (3.10) while the analysis implies that the entire actual capital held aside by the banks corresponds to Pillar I requirements.

3.3.4   Joint Impact Measure

3.3.4.1   Theoretical Background

According to Basel III, banks must comply with both risk-weighted capital requirements and the non-risk-weighted framework, that is, the LR. Tier1 is a common nominator for calculating both ratios (see Fig. 3.1). By showing the impact arising from the compliance with risk-weighted ratios, one could miss the add-on that the compliance with LR requirements would imply or vice versa. To ensure that a bank fully complies with both sets of requirements, it should simply comply with the higher of the two Tier1 requirements. The joint compliance criterion must hold under both current and final Basel III frameworks. The formulae from Eqs. (3.14), (3.15), (3.16), (3.17), (3.18), (3.19), (3.20), (3.21), (3.22), and (3.23) provide the framework for the evaluation of the joint impact by focusing only on Tier1 MRC including CCB, as the other forms of MRC are not relevant for the estimation of the joint impact.

To comply with both Basel III risk-based and LR requirements, any given bank should make sure that it currently holds capital equal to $JMRC_{proposed}^{T1(+CCB)}$.

$$JMRC_{current}^{T1(+CCB)} = \max\left(MRC_{current}^{T1(+CCB)}, MRC_{current}^{LR}\right) \qquad (3.14)$$

$$MRC_{current}^{LR} = 3.0\% \times \text{total Basel III exposures} \qquad (3.15)$$

Similarly, the same bank should comply with the final Basel III framework by holding capital equal to $JMRC_{proposed}^{T1(+CCB)}$.

$$JMRC_{proposed}^{T1(+CCB)} = \max\left(MRC_{proposed}^{T1(+CCB)}, MRC_{proposed}^{LR}\right) \qquad (3.16)$$

$$MRC_{proposed}^{LR} = \left(3.0\% + G - SIBs \text{ add} - \text{on}\right) \times \text{total Basel IV exposures} \qquad (3.17)$$

Hence, the joint impact measure can be written as given below:

$$\Delta JMRC^{T1(+CCB)} = JMRC_{proposed}^{T1(+CCB)} - JMRC_{current}^{T1(+CCB)} \qquad (3.18)$$

As shown in Fig. 3.1, the RWA comprises different elements, some of which are subject to changes from the current to final Basel III (credit, operational, market, and risk) while the rest remain (or considered to remain) unaffected by the transition (qualifying Central counterparties (CCPs), settlement risk, and other Pillar 1 RWA).

$$\Delta MRC^{T1+CCB} = \sum_{\lambda=1}^{8} \Delta MRC^{T1+CCB,\lambda} =$$

$$\left\{0.085 + \max\left(G - SIBs, D - SIBs\right)\right\} \times \left\{ \sum_{\lambda=1}^{8} RWA^{\lambda}_{proposed} - RWA^{\lambda}_{current} \right\}$$

$$- \min\left\{0, provisions^{IRB}_{proposed} - EL^{IRB}_{proposed}\right\}$$

$$+ \min\left\{0, provisions^{IRB}_{current} - EL^{IRB}_{current}\right\} \tag{3.19}$$

Given that the level of provisions often depends on managerial decisions which are difficult to predict, the analysis assumes that the current level of provisions remains the same under the fully implemented Basel III. In this case, Eq. (3.19) could be simplified to the following form:

$$\Delta MRC^{T1(+CCB)} = \sum_{\lambda=1}^{8} \Delta MRC^{T1+CCB,\lambda} =$$

$$\left\{0.085 + \max\left(G - SIBs, D - SIBs\right)\right\} \times \left\{ \sum_{\lambda=1}^{8} RWA^{\lambda}_{proposed} - RWA^{\lambda}_{current} \right\}$$

$$+ \min\left\{0, provisions^{IRB}_{current} - EL^{IRB}_{proposed}\right\}$$

$$+ \min\left\{0, provisions^{IRB}_{current} - EL^{IRB}_{current}\right\} \tag{3.20}$$

As shown in Fig. 3.2, the estimation of the output floor impact follows the estimation of the impact of the risk-based components. The output floor impact is simply the difference between the total RWA including the use of internal models, where there is relevant permission by the national supervisor, and a percentage of the total SA-equivalent RWA, should the latter be higher than the former. The SA equivalent arises from the estimation of RWA according to the relevant SA that would be applicable in the absence of internal models. The methodology for the calculation of output floor impact is given in detail in Chap. 9. For the sake of completeness, the high-level properties for estimating the output floor impact are also given below:

$$\Delta MRC^{OF} = \left\{0.085 + \max\left(G - SIBs, D - SIBs\right)\right\} \times$$
$$\left\{\sum_{\lambda=1}^{8} \max\left(0, \left[OFR \times RWA^{\lambda}_{\text{proposed}(SA-eq)} - RWA^{\lambda}_{\text{proposed}}\right]\right)\right\} \quad (3.21)$$

where the output floor rate (OFR) is set at 72.5% as of the full implementation date but takes any value between 50% and 72.5% to cope with the phase-in provisions from 2022 to 2027 (see BCBS, 2017c) on the final calibration of the final Basel III framework; and $RWA^{\lambda}_{\text{proposed}(SA-eq)}$ is the SA equivalent (see Fig. 3.2).

Although the BCBS has not yet proposed any treatment of the excess provisions when calculating the output floor add-on, Chap. 9 proposes an approach for the beneficial treatment of banks which exhibit surplus of provisions.

The impact from the joint compliance with the risk-weighted and non-risk-weighted minimum requirements under the current and final ("proposed") Basel III is given below:

$$\Delta JMRC^{T1(+CCB)} = JMRC^{T1(+CCB)}_{\text{proposed}} - JMRC^{T1(+CCB)}_{\text{current}}$$
$$= \Delta MRC^{T1+CCB} + \Delta MRC^{OF} + \Delta MRC^{LR} - JMRC^{T1+CCB}_{\text{current}} \quad (3.22)$$

The logic behind the implementation of the joint impact measure derives from the fact that either the Tier1 risk-weighted ratio or the LR Tier1 requirement is the binding factor, that is, the requirement which produces the highest capital under the current framework. Thus, to comply with both, a bank should comply with the highest of risk-based and non-risk-based requirements. However, the binding factor under the current Basel III is not necessarily binding under the final Basel III. This interchange as to the binding factor could underestimate or overestimate the impact if the risk-based requirement or the LR impact measures are considered in isolation.

To eliminate the noise that the implementation of the new LR framework could imply, the following formula provides an unbiased predictor of the stand-alone LR impact:

$$\Delta MRC^{LR} = \max\left(0, \left[MRC^{LR}_{\text{proposed}} - MRC^{T1(+CCB)}_{\text{proposed}}\right]\right)$$
$$- \max\left(0, \left[MRC^{LR}_{\text{current}} - MRC^{T1(+CCB)}_{\text{current}}\right]\right) \quad (3.23)$$

The logic behind the formula for the quantification of the impact from implementing the final Basel III LR framework is to assess whether there is less or more additional Tier1 MRC arising from the implementation of the new LR Tier1 MRC, as opposed to the current implementation of Tier1 MRC. The last "max" expression of the second part of Eq. (3.23) shows whether there is an add-on arising from the $T1$ MRC and, if yes, its level for the *current* framework. If $MRC_{\text{current}}^{T1(+CCB)} \geq MRC_{\text{current}}^{LR}$ there is no contribution of the LR MRC in the formulation of the joint total current Tier1 MRC, whereas if $MRC_{\text{current}}^{T1(+CCB)} < MRC_{\text{current}}^{LR}$, the LR MRC would be the constraining factor for the formulation of the joint total current Tier1 MRC.

Analogously, the first "max" expression of the second part of Eq. (3.23) shows whether there is an add-on arising from the $T1$ LR MRC and, if yes, its level for the proposed framework. If $MRC_{\text{proposed}}^{T1(+CCB)} \geq MRC_{\text{proposed}}^{LR}$ there is no contribution of the LR MRC in the formulation of joint total proposed Tier1 MRC, whereas if $MRC_{\text{proposed}}^{T1(+CCB)} < MRC_{\text{proposed}}^{LR}$, the LR MRC would be a constraining factor for the formulation of the joint total proposed Tier1 MRC.

The second part of Eq. (3.23) shows whether the magnitude of LR of being a constraining factor for the formulation of joint total Tier1 MRC has been exacerbated or soothed between the current and the proposed frameworks.

The contribution of Tier1 LR MRC in the change of joint Tier1 could be positive only if it is higher than the risk-based Tier1 MRC under the current framework, while its contribution would be zero or negative in any other case. The negative contribution of $T1$ LR MRC to the change of joint $T1$ MRC is capped at $MRC_{\text{current}}^{T1(+CCB)} - MRC_{\text{current}}^{LR}$ whereas its positive contribution could be unlimited.

Box 3.1   Examples for the Calculation of the Joint Impact Measure

The examples below intend to elucidate the calculation of the joint impact measure and show its universal applicability. To this end, four distinct cases are provided including changes in the factor binding under the current framework and the one binding under the proposed framework; for example, while risk-based capital is currently the binding factor, the LR $T1$ MRC could be the binding factor under the final Basel III or vice versa.

Risk-Based Tier1 MRC Constraints Under Current and Final Basel III

Suppose that the current risk-based Tier1 MRC, that is, the minimum risk-based Tier1 requirement after including CCB is EUR 100 billion, while the Tier1 LR MRC produced by the application of the current minimum LR requirements on total LR exposures is EUR 98 billion. The risk-based Tier1 MRC and the LR Tier1 MRC amount to EUR 105 billion and EUR 101 billion, respectively, under the final framework.

(continued)

Box 3.1   (continued)

The joint impact is EUR 5 billion (see Eqs. (3.14), (3.16), and (3.18)), which is entirely attributed to changes in the risk-based Tier1 MRC given that it is the constraining factor under both current and final Basel III frameworks. The contribution of LR Tier1 MRC is zero under the current framework and zero under the final Basel III (Eq. (3.23)).

LR Tier1 MRC Constraints Under the Current and Final Basel III

Suppose now that the current risk-based Tier1 MRC, after including CCB, is EUR 90 billion while the current LR Tier1 MRC is EUR 98 billion. The risk-based Tier1 MRC and the LR Tier1 MRC amount to EUR 97 billion and EUR 101 billion, respectively, under the final framework.

The joint impact from the full implementation of Basel III is EUR 3 billion (see Eqs. (3.14), (3.16), and (3.18)) as capital of the joint compliance increased from EUR 98 billion under Basel III to EUR 101 billion under the final Basel III. Since the proposed risk-based Tier1 MRC has not reached the level of the proposed LR Tier1 MRC which would ensure full compliance, the full increase of EUR 3 billion is attributed to the LR Tier1 MRC add-on.

When looking at the LR Tier1 MRC in isolation, one can observe that it is the constraining factor under the current framework, being EUR 8 billion higher than the current risk-based Tier1 MRC. When switching to the proposed framework, albeit the LR Tier1 MRC remains the constraining factor, its margin from the risk-based Tier1 MRC is lower by EUR 4 billion. This implies that the impact of LR Tier1 MRC in the joint $T1$ MRC is negative (by EUR 4 billion).

Conversely, when observing in isolation the changes in risk-based Tier1 MRC, one observes that its level has increased by EUR 7 billion. Nonetheless, it is not the constraining factor for the formulation of the joint Tier1 MRC under any of the current or proposed frameworks.

Taking into account the above-mentioned changes, the impact of the transition from the current to final Basel III on the joint Tier1 MRC is composed by a positive change in the risk-based Tier1 MRC (EUR 7 billion) and a negative change of the add-on of the LR Tier1 MRC (EUR 4 billion). All in all, this leads to an overall change of EUR 3 billion in the joint Tier1 MRC (see Eq. (3.23)).

LR Tier1 MRC Constraints Under Basel III/Risk-Based Tier1 MRC Constraints Under the Final Basel III

Suppose that the current risk-based Tier1 MRC, after including CCB, is EUR 90 billion while the LR Tier1 MRC is EUR 98 billion. The risk-based Tier1 MRC and the LR Tier1 MRC amount to EUR 103 billion and EUR 101 billion, respectively, under the final framework.

The joint impact is EUR 5 billion (see Eqs. (3.14), (3.16), and (3.18)) as the Tier1 MRC which would ensure full compliance increased from EUR 98 billion under Basel III to EUR 103 billion under the final Basel III. The risk-based Tier1 MRC increased from EUR 90 billion to EUR 103 billion (+EUR 13 billion) and became the constraining factor, that is, compliance with it would ensure joint compliance with both risk-based and LR requirements under the final framework. On the other hand, the LR Tier1 MRC, albeit being the constraining factor by EUR 8 billion (= EUR 98 billion − EUR 90 billion) under Basel III, is not constraining any more under the final Basel III as it has been surpassed by risk-based Tier1 MRC by EUR 2 billion (= EUR 103 billion − EUR 101 billion). Thus, the binding factor for full compliance has changed sides from the LR in Basel III to risk-based requirement in the final Basel III.

(continued)

Box 3.1   (continued)

When looking at LR Tier1 MRC in isolation, one observes that it is the constraining factor under the current framework as it is EUR 8 billion higher than the current risk-based Tier1 MRC. When switching to the proposed framework, the LR is not constraining any more as it is not contributing to the formulation of joint $T1$ MRC under the final Basel III. This implies that the impact of $T1$ LR MRC in the joint $T1$ MRC impact was reduced by EUR 8 billion, that is, from EUR 8 billion to EUR 0.

Conversely, when observing the changes in the risk-based Tier1 MRC in isolation, one observes that its level has increased by EUR 7 billion and has now become the constraining factor for the formulation of the joint Tier1 MRC under the new provisions given that it is higher than the proposed LR Tier1 MRC by EUR 2 billion.

Taking into account the above-mentioned changes, the impact on the joint Tier1 MRC is composed of a positive change of EUR 13 billion in the risk-based Tier1 MRC and a reduction of the LR add-on by EUR 8 billion due to the implementation of the final Basel III. All in all, this leads to an overall change of EUR 5 billion in the joint $T1$ MRC (see Eq. (3.23)).

Risk-Based Tier1 MRC Constraints Under Basel III/LR Tier1 MRC Constraints Under the Final Basel III

Suppose now that the current risk-based Tier1 MRC, after including CCB, is EUR 100 billion while the LR Tier1 MRC is EUR 98 billion. The risk-based Tier1 MRC and the LR Tier1 MRC amount to EUR 100 billion and EUR 101 billion, respectively, under the final Basel III framework.

The joint impact is EUR 1 billion (see Eqs. (3.14), (3.16), and (3.18)) as the Tier1 MRC which would ensure full compliance increased from EUR 100 billion under Basel III to EUR 101 billion under the final Basel III. The risk-based Tier1 MRC remains unchanged at EUR 100 billion. On the other hand, the LR Tier1 MRC becomes the constraining factor by a margin of EUR 1 billion (= EUR 101 billion − EUR 100 billion) under the final Basel III as it has overcome the risk-based measure. Thus, the constraining factor for full compliance has changed sides from the risk-based in Basel III to the LR measure of Tier1 MRC in the final framework.

When looking at LR Tier1 MRC in isolation, one observes that it was not the constraining factor under the current framework as it is lower than the respective risk-based measure. When switching to the proposed framework, LR becomes the constraint as it contributes to the formulation of the joint Tier1 MRC under the final Basel III by an add-on of EUR 1 billion. This implies that the impact of the LR has been increased by EUR 1 billion, that is, from EUR 0 to EUR 1 billion.

Conversely, when observing the changes in the risk-based MRC in isolation, one observes that, despite its level remaining the same, it is not any more the constraining factor for the formulation of joint $T1$ MRC under the final Basel III, as it is lower than the proposed LR metric.

The impact on the joint Tier1 MRC is only composed of an increase of EUR 1 billion in the leverage add-on between the current and final Basel III. All in all, this leads to an overall change of EUR 1 billion in the joint Tier1 MRC (see Eq. (3.23)).

Box 3.2   Comprehensive Example on the Total Joint Impact

Assume that a G-SIB, with a supervisory G-SIBs surcharge of 1%, has estimated the current total RWA at EUR 100. The total current and proposed RWA, respectively, consist of the following elements:

Risk category	Current/proposed (in billion)
IRBA RWA	EUR 53.0/EUR 57.0
SA RWA	EUR 23.0/EUR 24.0
OpRisk RWA	EUR 16.0/EUR 15.5
MR RWA	EUR 5.0/EUR 6.0
QCCP RWA	EUR 1.5/EUR 1.5
Settlement risk RWA	EUR 1.0/EUR 1.0
Other Pillar I RWA	EUR 0.5/EUR 0.5
Total RWA	EUR 100/EUR 105.5
Provisions	EUR 3.0/EUR 3.0
Expected losses (ELs)	EUR 5.0/EUR 3.8575
LR exposure	EUR 330/EUR 330

The credit and market risk RWA are calculated according to internal models, that is, IRB and the IMA, respectively, under the current framework. It is also assumed that the national supervisory authority will extend the approval of the internal models under the new regime. The bank's current provisions against credit losses arising from the IRBA credit portfolio are EUR 3 billion while the current EL from the IRBA credit portfolio is estimated at EUR 5 billion. The current total LR exposures are EUR 330 billion.

As discussed above, the bank's estimates, conducted on a best-effort basis, show that under the finalised framework the total RWA would become EUR 106 billion.

The total LR exposures under the final proposals would remain unchanged at EUR 330 billion. The provisions also remain at the same level (EUR 3 billion), whereas the future ELs is estimated slightly increased to EUR 3.8575.

According to the calculation in Eq. (3.5) the current $T1$ MRC including CCB is EUR 10 billion and will become EUR 10.5 billion under the proposed framework. After substituting the market and credit internal models' RWA with their SA-equivalent RWA, the SA equivalent would become EUR 159.31 billion. By applying an OFR of 72.5% on the SA equivalent, the RWA output floor would become EUR 115.5 billion. Based on the output floor, the calculations depicted in Eq. (3.21) produce a $T1$ MRC risk-based add-on of EUR 0.95 billion (=(115.5 − 105.5) × (0.085 + 0.01)). All in all, the risk-based $T1$ MRC according to the new framework becomes EUR 11.45 billion (=10.5 + 0.95).

To comply with both risk-based and LR requirements, the banks should also calculate the $T1$ LR MRC. According to the new framework this is estimated at EUR 11.55 billion (=330 × (0.03 + 0.5 × 0.01)), which means that the LR minimum requirement will contribute an additional EUR 0.10 billion atop risk-based minimum requirements.

Analytically, the $T1$ MRC (including CCB) impact (in EUR billion) from the implementation of the final Basel III standards is the following:

(continued)

Box 3.2   (continued)

Risk category	Change (EUR billion/% change)
IRBA RWA	0.3575/3.6%
SA RWA	0.0950/1.0%
OpRisk RWA	−0.0475/−0.5%
MR RWA	0.0950/1.0%
QCCP RWA	0/0.0%
Settlement risk RWA	0/0.0%
Other Pillar I RWA	0/0.0%
Risk-based *T1* MRC	0.5000/5.0%
Output floor add-on *T1* MRC	0.9500/9.5%
Total risk-based T1 MRC	*1.4500/14.5%*
Total LR T1 MRC add-on	*0.1000/1.0%*
Total impact of the final Basel III	*1.5500/15.5%*

3.4   Conclusions

Chapter 3 provides the reader with an overview of the current (Basel III) and proposed frameworks for the calculation of the minimum requirements assigned to the risk-based and LR metrics of capital. It presents the methodology for the estimation of the anticipated impact by converting the provisions in the current and final Basel III frameworks into formulae. Likewise, it renders the impact assessment clearer to the average reader and makes the analyses that follow in Chaps. 5, 6, 7, 8, and 9 more understandable and easier to interpret.

The presentation of the typology focuses on the impact relating to the MRC, that is, the change in the MRC implied by the transition to the final Basel III. It also touches briefly upon the impact relating to the TRC and the capital SFL.

Notes

1. A measure close but not identical to accounting total assets.
2. For example, the minimum required total capital ratio under Basel III is 8% of the RWA while the minimum required Tier1 capital ratio is 6% of the RWA.
3. Hence, the delay in the BCBS agreement.
4. To fully comply with the final Basel III framework one should take into account the TLAC requirement which is not covered in the book.
5. Mainly due to Pillar II add-ons.

6. For details on the definition of provisions and the detailed calculation of the surplus and deficit of provisions compared to the expected losses, see BCBS (2011).
7. According to the BCBS provisions (BCBS, 2011: 22, para 73) the deficit of provisions is deductible from the CET1 capital. Given that the CET1 is a subset of Tier1, the one-to-one deduction from CET1 has the same effect.
8. The D-SIBs are set by the national competent authorities after expert judgement. In Europe, the list of other systematically important institutions (the equivalent of D-SIBs) is set out by the European Banking Authority under the following link: http://www.eba.europa.eu/risk-analysis-and-data/other-systemically-important-institutions-o-siis-/2016
9. The analysis does not take into account the partial implementation of the capital conservation buffer which some jurisdictions may apply for a transitional period until the full implementation of Basel III.

References

Basel Committee on Banking Supervision. (2006, June). Basel II: International convergence of capital measurement and capital standards: A revised framework – comprehensive version. Retrieved December 2016, from http://www.bis.org/publ/bcbs128.pdf

Basel Committee on Banking Supervision. (2011, June). Basel III: A global regulatory framework for more resilient banks and banking systems – revised version. Retrieved December 2016, from http://www.bis.org/publ/bcbs189.pdf

Basel Committee on Banking Supervision (BCBS). (2015, July). Review of the Credit Valuation Adjustment (CVA) risk framework – consultative document. Retrieved July 2015, from http://www.bis.org/bcbs/publ/d325.pdf

Basel Committee on Banking Supervision (BCBS). (2016a, January). Minimum capital requirements for market risk – Standards. Retrieved January 2016, from http://www.bis.org/bcbs/publ/d352.pdf

Basel Committee on Banking Supervision (BCBS). (2016d, April). Revisions to the Basel III leverage ratio framework – consultative document. Retrieved March 2016, from http://www.bis.org/bcbs/publ/d365.pdf

Basel Committee on Banking Supervision (BCBS). (2017a, June). Simplified alternative to the standardised approach to market risk capital requirements – consultative document. Retrieved June 2017, from http://www.bis.org/bcbs/publ/d408.pdf

Basel Committee on Banking Supervision (BCBS). (2017b, June). Basel III monitoring report. Retrieved September 2017, from https://www.bis.org/bcbs/publ/d416.pdf

Basel Committee on Banking Supervision (BCBS). (2017c, December). Basel III: Finalising post-crisis reforms – Standards. Retrieved December 7, 2017, from https://www.bis.org/bcbs/publ/d424.pdf

4

Credit Risk: Aspects of Implementation

The impact of the credit risk-related changes on the total RWA and capital requirements is important primarily due to the share of the current share of credit risk to the total RWA and capital requirements (almost two-thirds of the total minimum required regulatory capital of the major international banks [BCBS, 2017]).

The scope of this chapter is to provide the reader with the necessary background for the evaluation of the current and final Basel III. The comparison between the current and revised frameworks focuses on the assessment of the migration from the current to the revised standardised approach (SA) and from the current to the revised internal ratings-based approach (IRBA). Also, it aims at discussing the properties of such horizontal migration and introduces the reader to the properties of credit risk modelling.

This chapter discusses Basel III (BCBS, 2006, 2011) and the newly revised framework (BCBS, 2014, 2015, 2016a, 2017) regarding the SA (Sect. 4.3) and the IRBA (Sect. 4.4) for credit risk, with a view towards assessing the conceptual differences between the two under the two versions of Basel supervisory standards. It examines alternative specifications as to the parameter values and the modelling of final Basel III to cover a wider spectrum of choices from which the Basel Committee on Banking Supervision (BCBS) could have selected when finalising the framework.

The analysis presents the basic background information on (a) the categorisation of asset classes under the IRBA and SA, (b) the current and proposed framework for the estimation of RWA under the IRBA and SA, respectively,

© The Author(s) 2018
I. Akkizidis, L. Kalyvas, *Final Basel III Modelling*,
https://doi.org/10.1007/978-3-319-70425-8_4

and (c) the methodology for the estimation of the impact of implementing the new proposals. Finally, this chapter highlights intuitive examples to enhance the understanding of the final framework.

4.1   Asset Classes Categorisation Under the SA

The second consultative paper on the "Revisions to the standardised approach for credit risk" (BCBS, 2015) aims at finding a balance between simplicity and risk sensitivity and, at the same time, increasing the harmonisation of the treatment of international banks. Ultimately, the BCBS targets at rendering the SA a credible substitute of the IRBA but also makes it directly comparable to the IRBA. The new framework does not touch upon sovereign exposures where the BCBS intends to revise their treatment in a separate proposal outside the current package of Basel reforms.

In general, the revised SA keeps the same categorisation for the vast majority of asset classes except for the real estate exposure class, where the taxonomy is different. As to the real estate exposures, the proposals assign both retail and commercial real estate (CRE) exposures under the real estate exposure asset class. In addition, they introduce two specialised lending categories, that is, income-producing real estate (IPRE) and land acquisition, development, and construction (ADC) under the real estate exposure class. The rest of specialised lending exposure classes have remained under corporate exposures.

The definition and naming of the previously called "past-due" exposures (Basel II and Basel III) changes to align with the "defaulted" exposures used under the IRBA. So far, the "past-due" exposures contain loans, which are past due for more than 90 days. On the other hand, the IRBA definition of "defaulted" includes those loans which are 90 days past due or it is unlikely that the obligor will pay its obligations.

According to the final Basel III, a residential real estate (RRE) exposure is an "exposure secured by immovable property that has the nature of dwelling" (BCBS, 2015: 36, para 53), while a CRE is an "exposure secured by any immovable property that is not a residential property" (BCBS, 2015: 36, para 57). The new framework assigns different risk weights (RWs) according to loan-to-value (LTV) ratios and differentiates between the RRE and CRE exposures. It also distinguishes the treatment of RRE and CRE whose repayment ability is materially dependent on whether cash flows are generated by the property or not. Section 4.3.2 shows this treatment analytically.

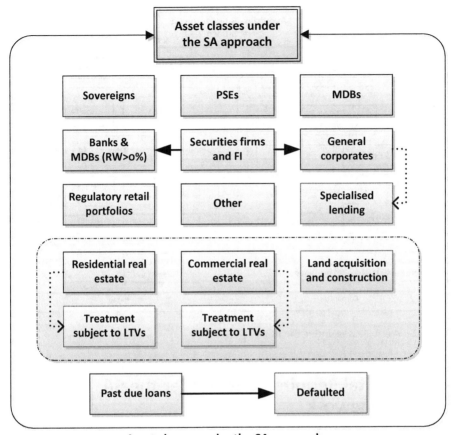

Asset classes under the SA approach

Fig. 4.1 Asset classes under the revised SA to credit risk

Figure 4.2 exhibits the classification of asset classes under the IRBA. The categorisation of IRBA asset classes remained broadly the same under the new framework. On the other hand, there was an effort from the BCBS to align the taxonomy of the standardised approach asset classes with the IRBA asset classes to make possible the comparison between the two. However, the alignment in the mapping does not necessarily imply that the respective RWs coincide or converge.

Sections 4.3 and 4.4 present the methodology for the estimation of capital requirements under the SA and the IRBA approach for both current and final Basel III.

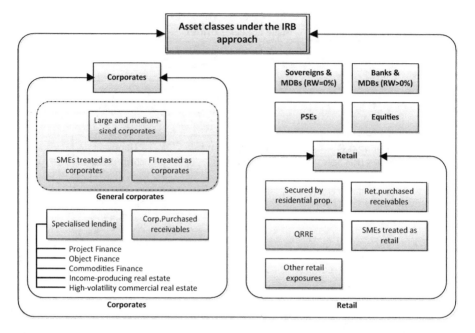

Fig. 4.2   Asset classes under the IRBA

4.2   Capital Requirements Under the SA Framework

4.2.1   Overview of the Changes Under the Final Basel III

The RWs under the SA for credit risk aim at differentiating the treatment of asset classes with different risk profiles, but also amongst subcategories of the same asset class. Up to December 2014, the Basel framework had been differentiating amongst asset classes and credit quality by making use of external ratings, that is, credit ratings provided by External Credit Assessment Institutions (ECAIs[1]) (Bindseil, Corsi, Sahel, & Visser, 2017; ECB, 2015; BIS, 2013), aka "rating agencies". The BCBS (2014) published a consultative document whose main proposal was to reduce the reliance on credit ratings as a response to increasing public pressure but mainly to tackle the influence of the external ratings in the volatility of the markets and the cost of funding. The BCBS proposals originally suggested assigning RWs to asset classes according to a set of risk drivers.

Nonetheless, the international banking sector, that is, banks and investors, expressed their opposition as they expected that the proposals could discontinue the credit assessments at the time when they did not have in place a reliable substitute or the expertise to create one at short notice. In addition, the exclusive reliance on a non-ratings-based assessment would disrupt the central banks' monetary policy transactions, which use the same ratings to assess the collateral posted for monetary operations, and subsequently could disorder the flow of central bank funding.

Hence, the BCBS reintroduced the use of external ratings in a non-mechanistic manner in the revised consultative document published in December 2015 (BCBS, 2015). The amended proposals allow the assessment under two alternative methods: the method relying on external ratings and an alternative method in jurisdictions which do not permit the use of external ratings. Moreover, it changes the treatment of off-balance sheet (OffBS) items, the exposures to Multinational Development Banks (MDBs), and the retail and defaulted exposures (labelled as "past-due" under Basel II and Basel III).

However, the major change of the final Basel III SA framework refers to the treatment of real estate exposures. The revisions to the treatment of the real estate exposures suggest their grouping under the same category, the application of higher RWs for real estate exposures whose "repayment is materially dependent on cash flows (i.e. rent/sale) generated by the property" (BCBS, 2015: 2), and the modification of the risk-weighting scheme which now derives from the categorisation according to LTV ratios.

4.2.2 The Risk-Weighting Scheme of On-Balance Sheet Items

Since the majority of the SA framework remains unchanged, Table 4.1 shows the treatment of various asset classes under the Basel III SA to credit risk. Albeit not identical, the classification of assets (Figs. 4.1 and 4.2) in SA and IRBA is not as divergent as it used to be in Basel II and Basel III. The MDB and sovereign (and central bank) exposures are still treated more favourably than other asset classes due to their lower risk bearing. In addition, banks still receive lower RWs than the standard RWs to sovereign exposures (and central banks), if the exposures are denominated and funded in the domestic currency. More specifically, the existing framework allows national supervisory authorities (NSAs) to "permit their banks to apply the same risk weight to domestic currency exposures to this sovereign (or central bank) funded in that currency" (BCBS, 2006: 20, para 54). The EU-specific implementation of the above treatment permits all EU member states of the Euro area to apply a 0% RW to all EU-area sovereign exposures issues denominated in euros.

Table 4.1 Risk weights under the current and final Basel III for long-term ratings of on-balance sheet assets (Source: BCBS, 2011, 2017)

Exposures	AAA to AA−	A+ to A−	BBB+toBBB−	BB+toBB−	B+ to B−	Below B−	Unrated
Sovereigns and central banks	0%	20%	50%	100%	100%	150%	100%
Banks, regulated FI, MDB (not eligible for 0% RW), and PSEs	20%	50% (30%)[2]	50%[3]	100%	100%	150%	100% (40%/75%/150%)—(50% for MDBs and PSEs)
Covered bonds (new)	10%	20%	20%	50%	50%	100%	Linked to the rating of the issuing bank
Corporates, FIs, and SMEs treated as corporate and issue-specific specialised lending	20% (or 20%)	50%	100% (75%)[4]	100%	150%	150%	100% (or 85% if SME treated as corp.)[5]
Securitisation (unchanged throughout rating classes)	20%	50%	100%	350%	Deduction from capital[6]		
MDB (eligible for 0% RW)	0% (or 20%)	n.a. (50%)	n.a. (50%)	n.a. (100%)	n.a. (100%)	n.a. (150%)	n.a. (50%)
Retail portfolios and SMEs treated as retail	75%						
Secured by residential property	35% (for the final Basel III RW see Table 4.2)						
Secured by CRE	100% (for the final Basel III RW see Table 4.2)						
Past due (provisions <20%)	150% (150%)						
Past due (20% < provisions < 50%)	100% (150%)						
Past due (provisions > 50%)	100% (or 50%[7]) (150%)						
QRRE past due (provisions < 20%)	100% (100%)						
QRRE past due (provisions > 20%)	50% (100%)						
Subordinated debt and equity	100%–150% (100%–400%)						

Table 4.2 Risk weights assigned to real estate exposures which meet the eligibility criteria under the final Basel III (Source: BCBS, 2017)

Real estate exposures under the final Basel III[8]	LTV ≤ 50%	50% < LTV ≤ 60%	60% < LTV ≤ 80%	80% < LTV ≤ 90%	90% < LTV ≤ 100%	LTV > 100%
RRE exposures (whole-loan approach)	20%	25%	30%	40%	50%	70%
CRE exposures (whole-loan approach)	Min (60%, $RW_{counterparty}$)			$RW_{counterparty}$		
Income-producing RRE (IPRRE)	30%	35%	45%	60%	75%	105%
Income-producing CRE (IPCRE)	70%		90%		110%	

As shown in Table 4.1, the treatment of sovereign and securitisation exposures remains unchanged between the two frameworks. Nonetheless, the final Basel III lowered the RWs assigned to certain ratings of investment-grade corporate and bank exposures, leaving the rest of the categories broadly unchanged.

As mentioned, the final framework differentiates the treatment of real estate exposures by introducing the LTV as a distinguishing factor for assigning different RWs. The analysis in Chap. 9 shows the implicit impact that a potential shift in the SA RWs may have on the level of RWs in conjunction with the implementation of the input and output floors on RRE under the AIRBA. The motivation behind the additional analysis is to provide the reader with a sensitivity analysis of the SA and the AIRBA RWs.

Basel III assigns an RW of 150% to the unsecured part of past-due *non-QRRE loans* (more than 90 days in arrears), with attached credit provisions of less than 20% of the outstanding amount. The *past-due QRRE loans* with provisions of more than 50% receive the most favourable RWs amongst the categories of past-due loans (50%). The final Basel III framework unifies the treatment of all past-due loans, irrespective of the level of provisions, by assigning an RW of 150%.

The standard RW for all other equity-like assets is 100%. The category of "all other assets" includes, among others, investments in equity or regulatory capital instruments issued by banks or securities firms (financial institutions). These investments also receive a 100% RW unless they are deducted from the regulatory capital.

The unsecured, or not guaranteed, portion of the defaulted exposures (except for real estate) net of provisions and partial write-offs are risk-weighted with 150%. The defaulted real estate exposures "where repayments do not materially depend on cash flows generated by the property securing the loan" (BCBS, 2015) are risk-weighted with 100%, while all other defaulted real estate exposures are risk-weighted with 150%.

4.2.3   Revisions to the Treatment of Exposures to Banks and Corporates

As already mentioned, sovereign exposures are not subject to changes in this round of the BCBS reforms. On the other hand, the exposures to banks and corporates, which receive external rating assessments, are subject to changes that affect the minimum capital required under the SA. However, apart from the corporates with external rating assessments, the new framework introduces RWs to exposures for jurisdictions which do not allow external rating assessments, that is, assessments from rating agencies. Hence, latest changes introduced the standardised credit risk assessment (SCRA) approach (BCBS, 2015), which assigns bank and corporate exposures to grades specified by the expert judgement of the national competent authorities.

4.2.3.1   Exposures to Banks

The revised framework reduces the RWs for bank exposures for A+ to A− rated banks only.

The revised framework (BCBS, 2017) assigns a 40% RW to Grade A bank exposures under SCRA, 75% to Grade B, and 150% to Grade C. Grade A bank exposures are those attributed to bank counterparties which have the capability to fulfil their obligations timely until the maturity of the asset irrespective of the external economic or financial conditions and they exceed the minimum regulatory capital requirements (including but not limited to the national and international add-ons like CCB and G-SIBs and domestic significantly important banks (D-SIBs) surcharges). Grade B bank exposures are those to bank counterparties which are subject to substantial credit risk and their capability to fulfil their obligations depends on favourable economic or financial conditions but, nonetheless, they meet the minimum regulatory capital requirements imposed by the national supervisor. Grade C bank exposures are those to bank counterparties which do not meet the conditions for classification under Grade A and Grade B or an external auditor publishes an opinion that the financial condition of the bank counterparty (borrowing bank) is likely to deteriorate, something which would affect its ability to fulfil its obligations.

4.2.3.2   Exposures to Corporates

The main difference that the final framework implements is that bank exposures rated from BBB+ to BBB− under the ECRA receive an RW of 75%

(instead of 100% in Basel III) if they comply with certain qualitative criteria (BCBS, 2015: 31, para 36). According to the consultative document (BCBS, 2015), the unrated bank exposures are further assessed according to quantitative and qualitative criteria to receive an RW which will be more representative of the credit risk they bear. The unrated exposures to SMEs treated as corporates receive an 85% RW while the exposures to SMEs treated as retail exposures receive a 75% RW.

Corporate exposures rated as "investment grade" receive an RW of 65% (not shown in Table 4.1) in jurisdictions which do not allow the use of external ratings.

4.2.4   Provisioning Under the Standardised Approach

Before proceeding to describing the treatment of provisions under the Basel framework, it would be useful to ensure that readers of this book have the same high-level understanding of the term "credit provisions" as defined by banking regulators, banking supervisors, and supervised banks. General provisions according to the Basel framework and international accounting standards is a form of capital[9] set aside by the bank to pay future losses which are likely to appear. The regulatory treatment of provisions is somewhat different from the accounting treatment (BCBS, 2016b), although lately there is an effort from the BCBS to bridge the gap between the two.

The provisions are distinguished into general and specific provisions and constitute balance sheet items, which are intended and, if needed, will be directed to cover losses that arise from adverse general economic conditions or from impaired or defaulted loans or trades which are likely to fail. The general provisions are not assigned to specific exposures but are rather a backup for a general impairment of the bank's assets.

Specific provisions are assigned to assets with high risk or trades, which for various reasons (economic, legal, etc.) are likely to fail. Specific provisions are loan-specific or portfolio-specific. In principle, banks could assign specific provisions to a part of the loan or portfolio of loans or other receivables of low quality. Furthermore, specific provisions could be provided on the basis of the likelihood of an asset to fail; for example, a 70% probability of default (PD) could lead a bank to hold provisions of 70% of the exposure.

To estimate the appropriate level of specific provisions, banks should carry out regular asset quality review to estimate the recovery rates and the resilience of the balance sheet assets, rather than relying on past trends and observations.[10]

As to the treatment of provisions for supervisory purposes, the Basel II framework still applies under the final Basel III framework. The existing framework requires clear separation of general provisions between the SA and IRBA, on a pro rata basis, according to the proportion of the RWA, which are subject to each method. General provisions could be included in Tier2 capital up to a ceiling of 1.25% of the RWA.

4.2.5   Credit Conversion Factors for Off-Balance Sheet Items

Under the standardised approach, the off-balance sheet items[11] are converted into the equivalent balance sheet exposures by multiplying their nominal amount with the credit conversion factors (CCFs). The standard CCF, and the ceiling for the off-balance sheet items, is 100%. Only OTC derivative transactions are not subject to any ceiling.

According to Basel II and Basel III, the commitments with a maturity of less than one year receive a CCF of 20%, while those with a maturity of more than one year will receive a CCF of 50%. The unconditionally cancellable credit line (UCC), that is, those cancellable at any time without prior notice or are subject to an automatic cancellation mechanism which triggers upon the deterioration of borrower's creditworthiness, receive a 0% CCF.

Implying that all off-balance sheet items bear a risk, the new regulatory framework has assigned a non-zero RW to all off-balance sheet items. To this end, it eliminates the 0% CCF for the eligible UCC under Basel II and III and increases it to 10%. The rationale behind this increase is that the majority of those UCCs are cancellable subject to certain contractual conditions, which in practice may not render them as unconditionally cancelled and consequently does not make them eligible for 0% CCF. The final Basel III framework does not only increase CCF (from 0% to 10%) but also narrows down the definition of UCCs, which are eligible for the lower CCF to those UCCs which are unconditionally cancellable in practice. Moreover, the final framework aligns the treatment of the remaining commitments, that is, those which are not eligible for 10% CCF, by assigning them to a CCF of 40%.

The treatment of short-term self-liquidating trade letters of credit arising from the movement of goods, as well as note issuance facilities (NIFs) and revolving underwriting facilities (RUFs), remains unchanged under the final Basel III, that is, trade letters still receive 20%[12] and NIF and RUF a 50% CCF.

4.3   Capital Requirements Under IRBA

The generic formula for the calculation of RWA under the IRBA is:

$$RW = K \times 12.5 \times 1.06^{13} \tag{4.1}$$

$$RWA = RW \times EAD \tag{4.2}$$

where
    RW denotes the risk weight;
    K denotes the capital;
    EAD denotes the exposure-at-default; and
    RWA denotes the risk-weighted asset.

The set of formulae for the estimation of IRBA RWs remains broadly the same from Basel II to the final Basel III. The Basel regulation implicitly recognises the existence of model-error risk in the final RW output by scaling up the output of the IRBA RW by a factor of 1.06 (4.1).[13] On the input side, Basel II and Basel III set a floor on the estimations of PD (0.03%), recognising the lack of adequate data for low PD exposures, and subsequently the embedded model-error risk.

The final Basel III moves beyond by proposing the increase of the input floor on PDs and the implementation of input floors on loss-given default (LGD) and exposure-at-default (EAD)[14] estimates. Moreover, the new framework introduces an output floor on the estimation of the total RWA for all exposure classes and risk categories under the internal models (and thus the IRBA). All the amendments above address the issue of model-error risk in the estimation of RWs under the IRBA. To this end, the application of the 1.06 scaling factor is redundant under the new framework. Chapter 9 discusses extensively the interaction between input and output floor and the impact of abolishing the IRBA scaling factor.

The IRBA RW depends on the estimation of PD, LGD, asset correlation (ρ), and maturity (M), which deviate across assets classes. The following sections will describe these differences at a high level as well as the differences between the existing and proposed framework, where applicable.

4.3.1   Exposures to Corporates, Financial Institutions, Sovereigns, and Banks

The analysis throughout the book considers the EAD, which is one of the input parameters in (4.2), as given. Thus, the only input parameter subject to estimation is the capital requirement (K). The K for non-defaulted exposures to corporates, sovereigns, and banks under the current and revised framework is given below.

$$K = LGD \times \left[N \left(\frac{G(PD) + \sqrt{\rho} \times G(0.999)}{\sqrt{1-\rho}} \right) - PD \right]$$
$$\times \frac{1 + (M - 2.5) \times b}{1 - 1.5 \times b} \tag{4.3}$$

$$\rho_{C,S,B} = 0.12 \times \left[\frac{1 - e^{-50 \times PD}}{1 - e^{-50}} \right] + 0.24 \times \left[1 - \frac{1 - e^{-50 \times PD}}{1 - e^{-50}} \right] \tag{4.4}$$

$$\rho_{FLI} = 1.25 \times 0.12 \times \left[\frac{1 - e^{-50 \times PD}}{1 - e^{-50}} \right] + 0.24 \times \left[1 - \frac{1 - e^{-50 \times PD}}{1 - e^{-50}} \right] \tag{4.5}$$

$$b = \left(0.11852 - 0.05478 \times \ln(PD) \right)^2 \tag{4.6}$$

where

ρ in (4.3) takes values from $\rho_{C,S,B}$ (4.4), ρ_{LFI} (4.5), ρ_{SME} (4.7), or ρ_{SL} (4.8); $\rho_{C,S,B}$ is the correlation for corporates, sovereigns, and banks; ρ_{LFI} is the correlation for large regulated financial institutions with total assets greater than US $100 billion or unregulated financial institutions of any size; ρ_{SME} is the correlation for SME; ρ_{SL} is the correlation for specialised lending; PD is the probability of default; LGD is the loss-given default, which for the FIRBA banks is set by the supervisor (45% for the senior unsecured exposures and 75% for the subordinated unsecured exposures); the reform package reduces the LGD for the former category to 40%, while it keeps the supervisory LGD for the latter stable; M is the maturity of the exposure; and b is the adjustment factor for the maturity.

Although the analysis in the book does not consider the input floor on EAD estimation, its application could imply a detrimental impact for those banks which currently benefit from low CCFs of the off-balance sheet positions. In turn, the increase in the EAD could affect the level of K, and thus the level of RW and RWA. The holistic assessment of the final Basel III impact should always account for all three input floors, that is, PD, LGD, and EAD. The book examines the impact assessment of PD and LGD floors in Chap. 5.

4.3.2   Firm-Size Adjustments for Small- and Medium-Sized Entities (SME)

Exposures to SMEs, that is, corporates with annual sales below EUR 50 million, are subject to a more favourable regime than the treatment of general corporates by setting a lower correlation factor. The correlation measure differentiates amongst SMEs with different sizes (from EUR 5 to EUR 50 million).

In principle, the formula for the calculation of capital requirements and RWA for general corporate exposures remains the same for SMEs. The only difference is the application of a correlation factor that reduces the RWA for SMEs with sales of less than EUR 50 million. The following formula provides the correlation estimate for SMEs:

$$\rho_{SME} = \rho_{C,S,B} - 0.04 \times \left(1 - \frac{\min\left[\max\left[S,5\right],50\right] - 5}{45} \right) \tag{4.7}$$

The term S denotes the sales of the SME. The correlation function for the SMEs is preferential compared to the general corporate and is bound between EUR 5 million and EUR 50 million. The above mathematical expression treats the SMEs equivalently to general corporates when sales are equal to or higher than EUR 50 million a year. In such cases, for example, a company with sales of EUR 70 million, the formula ensures that the treatment will fall into the RW of the general corporates.

Under the current framework banks should use a minimum PD of 0.03% (current PD floor) if the internal estimation of the one-year PD associated with the borrower's internal risk grade falls below this level (see Jacobson et al., 2004). The final Basel III framework suggested the implementation of an increased floor of 0.05% for general corporates, which also applies to the SME exposures treated as corporates (BCBS, 2016a); nonetheless, the book also conducts a broader sensitivity analysis by examining alternative levels of input floors and their impact on RWs and the minimum required capital (MRC).

4.3.3   Specialised Lending

Banks that meet the requirements for the estimation of the PD of non-defaulted specialised lending exposures are able to use the formula of risk weighting the general corporates to derive the RWs for SL subclasses under the AIRBA. The same applies under the revised framework.

For High Volatility Commercial Real Estate (HVCRE) exposures, the supervisors allow banks that meet the qualitative requirements for the estimation of PD/LGD/EAD to use the AIRBA, while those which comply only with the qualitative requirements for the estimation of PD should use the FIRBA specification (supervisory LGD) for corporate exposures to derive RWs for SL subclasses.

Banks which apply the FIRBA should use the formula applicable for general corporates by substituting ρ with the following expression:

$$\rho_{SL} = 0.12 \times \left[\frac{1 - e^{-50 \times PD}}{1 - e^{-50}} \right] + 0.30 \times \left[1 - \frac{1 - e^{-50 \times PD}}{1 - e^{-50}} \right] \qquad (4.8)$$

Banks which do not meet the qualitative requirements for the estimation of PD should use the RWs shown in Table 4.3, by using slotting criteria approach (SCA). The SCA, also considered as a "bridging" approach, lies between the SA and the FIRBA approach.

4.3.4   Exposures Subject to Double Default

According to Basel III, a bank may decide to apply either the substitution approach or the double-default framework for each exposure subject to a double default of the originator and guarantor. For the covered part of the exposure, Basel III recognises an RW that derives from the application of (4.3) by using the PD and LGD of the guarantor. As the guarantor is usually a corporate (large corporate or SME), bank, or sovereign, the capital requirements for exposures to double default is given after substituting risk parameters of the obligor with those of the guarantor in the relevant formula. However, the BCBS, as part of the completed Basel III framework, proposes "the removal of the double default approach due to its complexity and the lack of evidence of its use by banks" (BCBS, 2016a: 12) rendering obsolete the discussion on the double-default treatment in detail.

4.3.5   Collateralised Corporate Exposures Under IRBA

The presentation below focuses on the treatment and attributes of the collateralised corporate exposures which are subject to the FIRBA for the assessment of credit risk. The analysis will focus only on the quantification of the effective LGD (LGD*) under the FIRBA and AIRBA, given that the completed framework does implement changes in the modelling and input values of the LGD under both approaches.

Table 4.3 Risk weights for positions of different ratings under slotting criteria approach

Rating	SL category	BBB– or better	BB+ or BB	BB– or B+	B to C–	Default
RW	PF, OF, CF, IPRE	70%	90%	115%	250%	0%
	HVCRE	95%	120%	140%	250%	0%

The current framework differentiates between the treatment of financial and non-financial collateral for corporate exposures by providing an exhaustive set of supervisory haircuts, which are applicable to different asset classes, that is, sovereigns, non-sovereigns, and securitisation exposures, as well as for equities and convertible bonds. The new framework changes the majority of the haircut structure, which is applicable to jurisdictions which allow the use of external ratings (Table 4.4).

In general, the supervisory haircuts under the final Basel III became more stringent compared to Basel III for exposures with long maturity (above ten years), equities of main indices, other equities, and convertible bonds. Instead, the new framework is more lenient for short-term (below ten years) exposures to non-sovereign investment-grade exposures. The revised structure of haircuts implicitly promotes the acceptance of collateral with higher credit ratings. This could lead to a "flight to quality" by internationally active banks, diminishing the demand for lower-rated corporate issuances. This could subsequently imply that the non-investment-grade corporates may face difficulties in borrowing from banks, as their exposures would be less preferable.

The supervisory haircuts presented in Table 4.4 are applicable to exposures subject to either the SA or the IRBA only for the determination of effective exposure (E^*) with a view to estimate the LGD*.[15] Banks must continue calculating the EAD without accounting for the presence of any collateral. This section[16] presents the haircut structure of the SA to provide the reader with a clearer flow of the steps for the estimation of LGD* under the FIRBA.

According to the existing framework (BCBS, 2006: 68, para 291), the estimation of the LGD* applicable to the collateralised transactions backed by financial collateral is expressed as follows:

$$LGD^* = LGD \times \left(\frac{E^*}{E} \right) \tag{4.9}$$

where

LGD is that of the unsecured exposure before the recognition of collateral;

E is the current value of the exposure (i.e. cash or securities lent or posted);

Table 4.4 Supervisory haircuts (in %) of the comprehensive approach for jurisdictions that allow the use of external ratings for regulatory purposes (Source: BCBS, 2006, 2015), ten business days

Issue rating for debt securities	Residual maturity	Sovereigns	Other issuer	Securitisation exposures
AAA to AA−	≤1 year	0.5	1	2
	>1 years, ≤3 years	2	4 (3)	8
	>3 years, ≤5 years		4	
	>5 years, ≤10 years	4	8 (6)	16
	>10 years		8 (12)	
A+ to BBB− and unrated bank securities	≤1 year	1	2	4
	>1 years, ≤3 years	3	6 (4)	12
	>3 years, ≤5 years		6	
	>5 years, ≤10 years	6	12	24
	>10 years		12 (20)	
BB+ to BBB−	All	15	Not eligible	Not eligible
Main index equities (including convertible bonds) and gold		15 (20)		
Other equities and convertible bonds listed on a recognised exchange		25 (30)		
Undertakings for Collective Investment in Transferable Securities (UCITS)/mutual funds		Highest haircut applicable to any security the fund can invest, unless the bank can apply the look-through approach (LTA) for equity investments in funds, in which case the bank may use a weighted average of haircuts applicable to instruments held by the fund		
Cash in the same currency		0		

E^* is the exposure value after risk mitigation as determined by the comprehensive approach for the recognition of collateral under the standardised approach.

To calculate the effective exposure (E^*) for positions mitigated by posting financial collateral Basel III provides the following equation:

$$E^* = \max\left\{0,\left[E\times\left(1+H_e\right)-C\times\left(1-H_c-H_{fx}\right)\right]\right\} \qquad (4.10)$$

where

E is the current value of the exposure;

H_e is the haircut appropriate to the exposure;

C is the current value of the collateral received;

H_c is the haircut applicable to the collateral; and

H_{fx} is the haircut applicable to the currency mismatch between the collateral and exposure.

The haircut for currency risk (H_{fx}), assuming a ten-business-day holding period, remained unchanged at 8% under the new framework. The minimum holding period for repo-style transactions is set at 5 business days, for other capital market transactions it is set at 10 business days, and for secured lending at 20 business days. Generally, the minimum condition for collateral relating to capital market transactions (inclusive repo-style transactions) is the daily remargining of collateral while for secured lending it is the daily revaluation of collateral.

In cases where the actual holding and/or remargining (revaluation) period of haircuts does not correspond to the ten-business-day period the supervisory haircuts in Table 4.4 and the haircut for currency mismatch should adjust according to the formula below:

$$H = H_{10} \times \sqrt{\frac{N_R + (T_M - 1)}{10}} \qquad (4.11)$$

where

H denotes the haircut;

H_{10} is the ten-business-day haircut for investment;

N_R is the actual number of business days between remargining for capital market transactions or revaluation for secured transactions; and

T_M is the minimum holding period for the type of transaction.

Beyond the financial collateral, the FIRBA recognises additional types of non-financial collateral which are not eligible under the SA. The additional types embrace the non-financial collateral for which the BCBS provides a different haircut structure. The non-financial IRBA-eligible collateral includes four additional categories: "receivables", "CRE", "RRE", and "other physical" collateral. The new framework uses the level of overcollateralisation as a guide for the partial or full recognition of the collateral for the reduction of LGD.

The Basel III proposal (BCBS, 2011) suggests the application of a fixed supervisory LGD under the FIRBA approach and differentiates between the senior and subordinated unsecured exposures for the level of this LGD, that is, 45% and 75%, respectively. The latest revisions reduced the supervisory LGD for senior unsecured exposures to 40%.

Under Basel II and Basel III, a C' lower than a threshold (C^*) for the recognition of LGD reduction did not allow for a reduction, that is, the effective LGD remained at the initial level of supervisory LGD. Instead, if the C' is higher than the upper threshold (C^{**}), the LGD reduction is fully recognised according to Table 4.5, that is, the LGD is 0% for exposures secured by financial collateral, 35% (final Basel III: 10%) for the exposures secured by receivables, CRE, and RRE, and 40% (final Basel III: 15%) for the exposures secured by other collateral.

The final Basel III changes the framework for the recognition of the FIRBA collateral (for fully and partially secured exposures) for corporate exposures not secured by financial collateral. The new framework reduces the minimum percentage of collateral in relation to the exposure, that is, $C' = C/E$, above which the collateral is eligible for the reduction of the effective LGD. Under the revised framework, the minimum LGDs for eligible financial collateral, receivables, CRE/RRE, and other eligible collateral become 0%, 10%, 10%, and 15%, respectively. According to the BCBS, "the minimum collateralisation requirement has been removed to: (a) align the treatment with the recognition of financial collateral, where no such minimum collateral requirement exists; and (b) increase risk-sensitivity through greater recognition of the presence of collateral" (BCBS, 2016a).

The increased minimum required level of collateralisation (from 140% to 166.67%), for the full recognition of LGD reduction, implies that the Basel III framework increases the haircut for receivables from 20% (=1−100%/125%) to 40% (=1−100%/166.67%).

Table 4.5 Minimum LGD for the secured portion of senior exposures (Source: BCBS, 2006: 69, para 295, 2016a: 9)

	Minimum LGD	Required minimum collateralisation level of the exposure for eligibility (C^*)	Required level of overcollateralisation for full recognition of LGD reduction (C^{**})
Eligible financial collateral	0%	0%	n.a.
Receivables	35% (10%)	0%	125% (166.67%)
CRE/RRE	35% (10%)	30% (0%)	140% (166.67%)
Other collateral	40% (15%)	30% (0%)	140% (166.67%)

Any level of collateralisation which is lower than the revised threshold for the full recognition ($C' < 166.67\%$) leaves an unsecured part of the exposure without any LGD reduction ($1-C'/C^{**}$). The unsecured part of exposures remains subject to the LGD for senior unsecured exposures (40% according to the revisions). For the fully secured part of the exposure (C'/C^{**} or $C'/166.67\%$) there is full recognition of LGD reductions. Tables 4.4 and 4.5 provide a comparison of the current and final Basel III supervisory haircuts applicable to the estimation of financial collateral and IRBA-eligible collateral (BCBS, 2006, 2016a).

Assuming that the bank does not estimate haircuts with the internal models used, the steps for the calculation of the reduced LGD (LGD*), when eligible financial collateral is considered, are the following:

- Calculation of E^* by applying the current collateral values on the relevant exposures as well as the supervisory haircuts H_e, H_c, and H_{fx} (Table 4.4);
- Calculation of the LGD* by substituting the E^* produced by Eq. (4.9);

Similarly, for the IRBA-eligible collateral, the calculation of the LGD* should follow the steps below:

- Calculation of the current collateralisation level (C') with the use of the current exposures and collateral values;
- Comparison of the C' with the minimum level of collateral recognition of any LGD reduction (C') (current Basel III: 35%, final Basel III: 0%) and the minimum level of collateralisation for the full recognition of LGD reduction (C^{**}) (current Basel III: 140%, final Basel III: 166.67%), as shown in Table 4.5;
- Calculation of the part of the exposure which receives the minimum LGD allowed under the specific type of collateral, and of the remaining exposure attributed to the senior unsecured exposures (current Basel III: 45%, final Basel III: 40%) or the subordinated unsecured exposures (75%).

The final framework unifies the two approaches above to provide a unique approach for the estimation of the effective LGD.

$$LGD^* = LGD_U \times \frac{E_U}{E \times (1 + H_E)} \times LGD_S \times \frac{E_S}{E \times (1 + H_E)} \qquad (4.12)$$

where:

E is the current value of exposure;

H_E is the percentage increase in exposure values that banks are required to assume when the formula is being used to calculate the counterparty credit risk to gross up the requirement to non-cash exposures (e.g. securities lending) secured by non-financial collateral;

$E_S = \min (E \times (1 + H_E), C' \times * (1 - H_C))$ or C'/C^*, which represents the amount of the exposure that is collateralised;

$E_U = E \times (1 + H_E) - E_U$ or $1 - C'/C^*$, which is the amount of exposure that has not been collateralised;

LGD$_U$ is the relevant supervisory downturn LGD for unsecured exposures; and

LGD$_S$ is the relevant supervisory downturn LGD on a fully secured exposure, that is, the floors of the downturn LGD for secured exposures.

4.3.6   Retail Exposures

The IRBA formula for the estimation of the MRC (K) of retail exposures (Eq. (4.13)) remains the same again between the current and the revised framework, while AIRBA is the only eligible method if a bank decides to follow the IRBA. However, the PD and LGD inputs for retail exposures under the revised framework are subject to higher floors than those applied under the current framework, and thus higher capital (K).

$$K = LGD \times \left[N \left(\frac{G(PD) + \sqrt{\rho_{RTL}} \times G(0.999)}{\sqrt{1-\rho}} \right) - PD \right] \quad (4.13)$$

The Basel III correlation (ρ_{RTL}) for *residential mortgage exposures* is set at 0.15; the same parameter for qualifying revolving retail exposures equals 0.04, while for *other retail exposures* it should be calculated as follows:

$$\rho_{RTL} = 0.03 \times \left[\frac{1 - e^{-35 \times PD}}{1 - e^{-35}} \right] + 0.16 \times \left[1 - \frac{1 - e^{-35 \times PD}}{1 - e^{-35}} \right] \quad (4.14)$$

The retail exposures are subject to a PD floor of 0.03% under the current Basel III, while the final Basel III increases it to 0.05%–0.10%, depending on the retail asset class (qualifying revolving retail exposures [revolvers] receive 0.10%). In addition, the latest revisions impose an LGD floor which ranges from 30% to 50% depending on the retail asset class (see Table 4.6).

Table 4.6 PD and LGD floors of unsecured exposures and non-financial IRBA-eligible collateral under the current and final Basel III

Risk parameters	Asset class	PD/LGD floors and supervisory LGD of unsecured exposures, in %		LGD floor of the full recognition of non-financial IRBA-eligible collateral (CRE and RRE/other), in %	
(1)	(2)	Current (3)	Proposed[17] (4)	Current (5)	Proposed (6)
Part 1: PD floors applicable to IRBA	Corporate	0.03	0.05		
	Retail (Mortgages)	0.03	0.05		
	Retail (QRRE transactors)	0.03	0.05		
	Retail (QRRE revolvers)	0.03	0.10		
	Retail (other)	0.03	0.05		
Part 2: LGD floors applicable to AIRBA	Corporate		25		15/20
	Retail (mortgages)		5		
	Retail (QRRE transactors)		50		
	Retail (QRRE revolvers)		50		
	Retail (other)		30		15/20
Part 3: Supervisory LGD applicable to FIRBA	Corporate	45	40	35/40	10/15
	Retail (mortgages)				
	Retail (QRRE transactors)				
	Retail (QRRE revolvers)				
	Retail (other)				

4.3.7 Equity Exposures

The unexpected losses (K) stemming from equity exposures not held in the trading book are calculated by using either the market-based approach or the PD/LGD approach. For consistency with the previous sections, the basis for the conduct of the comparative analysis (see Chap. 5) is the PD/LGD approach. This approach uses the formula for calculating the RWs for general corporates, and scales up the resulting RWs by 1.5 to come up with the RWs for equity exposures (Eqs. (4.15) and (4.16)). Nonetheless, all equity exposures migrate to the SA for credit risk under the final Basel III.

$$RW = K \times 12.5 \times 1.06 \times 1.5 \qquad (4.15)$$

$$K = LGD \times \left[N\left(\frac{G(PD) + \sqrt{\rho} \times G(0.999)}{\sqrt{1-\rho}} \right) - PD \right]$$
$$\times \frac{1 + (M - 2.5) \times b}{1 - 1.5 \times b} \tag{4.16}$$

In addition, equity exposures under the FIRBA are subject to a regulatory LGD of 90% and regulatory maturity (M) of five years. The public and private equity portfolios are subject to a 100% RW, as far as they are part of a long-term consumer relationship and produce regular and periodic cash flows. Analytically, Eqs. (4.17),[18] (4.18), and (4.19) outline the RWs for equity exposures.

$$RW = \min\left(\max\left(\frac{(K + PD \times LGD)}{\times 12.5 \times 1.5}, 100\% \right), 1250\% \right) \tag{4.17}$$

For publicly traded equity holdings:

$$RW = \min\left(\max\left(\frac{(K + PD \times LGD)}{\times 12.5 \times 1.5}, 200\% \right), 1250\% \right) \tag{4.18}$$

For all other equity holdings:

$$RW = \min\left(\max\left(\frac{(K + PD \times LGD)}{\times 12.5 \times 1.5}, 300\% \right), 1250\% \right) \tag{4.19}$$

The increased levels of LGD and M inputs indicate that the RWs assigned to equities are higher than those the debt exposure to the same entity (corporate) would receive. The reason behind the lower RWs of debt-related exposures is the preferential treatment of debt-related compared to the equity-related exposures, which stems from the different loss-absorbing capacity of these asset classes.

The equity-related RW under the current framework is higher than that of subordinated debt exposures (90% vs. 75%), as the latter is liquidated after the equity in the case of a bank default. Overall, equity exposures serve as the highest absorbing bail-in financial instrument in the event of a default, and thus bear the highest risk and thus RW compared to all debt-related exposures.

4.3.8   Defaulted Exposures

For defaulted exposures the capital requirement is calculated as follows:

$$K = \max\left(0, LGD - EL\right) \qquad (4.20)$$

In theory, the expected loss (EL) of a defaulted exposure cannot exceed 100%, that is, the loss is limited to the amount of the exposure. Nonetheless, there could be additional costs (litigation, monitoring, and other operational costs) which could increase the loss from a defaulted exposure to an amount that is higher than the EL. Thus, the exposed bank should regularly assess whether the LGD at any time is higher than the ELs estimated at the time of the initiation of the exposure and keep aside capital for the maximum amount of the two.

4.3.9   Treatment of the Surplus (Deficit) of Provisions to Expected Losses

When calculating the MRC according to IRBA, the deficit of provisions in relation to the ELs, estimated by the IRBA, should be added to the *MRC* after having estimated the MRC that arises from the application of the minimum required CET1 ratio on RWA. This adjustment complies with the provision of Basel III (Basel, 2011: para 73) which requires the deduction of the deficit of provisions from the *actual capital*. In other words, the deficit of provisions implicitly means that the MRC, before accounting for provisions, should increase by the amount of the deficit of provisions to cope with the part of the ELs not covered by the provisions. The new framework does not take into account the positive difference between provisions and ELs.

Provisions or write-offs for equity exposures under the PD/LGD approach are not used in the EL provision calculation. Similarly, any specific provisions against securitisation exposures should not be included in the measurement.

The generic formula for the calculation of ELs is the following:

$$EL \text{ amount} = PD \times LGD \times EAD \qquad (4.21)$$

In principle, the formulation of capital after adjusting for EL amounts and provisions follows the following steps:

$$T1\,MRC^* = RWA \times CET\,1\,\text{ratio} + \max\left(EL - \text{Provisions}, 0\right) \qquad (4.22)$$

where $T1\ MRC^*$ is the adjusted Tier1 MRC after taking into account the deficit of provisions and the CET1 ratio is 4.5%.

According to Basel III, the EL amount for SL, subject to the supervisory slotting criteria, is determined by the following formula:

$$T1\ MRC^* = 8\% \times RW\ SL\ \text{slotting} \times EAD \qquad (4.23)$$

Subject to certain qualitative criteria which are not within the scope of the book, the SL exposures are assigned to five different categories according to their quality, that is, "strong", "good", "satisfactory", "weak", and "default". For the HVCRE, these categories receive RWs equal to 5%, 5%, 35%, 100%, and 625%, respectively. The RWs for SL, other than HVCRE, receive 5%, 10%, 35%, 100%, and 625%, respectively, for the same categories.

The total eligible amount of provisions under the IRBA is given below:

$$TEP = SpPro + ParWriteOffs + PorGenPro + GenPro \qquad (4.24)$$

The amount of provisions should not include any specific provisions stemming from equity and securitisation exposures. Should the EL amount be lower than the provisions, the national competent authority judges whether the EL corresponds to the market conditions and thus whether the difference should be added to Tier2 capital.

4.3.10   Comparison of Input Floors Between the Current and Final Basel III

The current BCBS framework assumes a PD floor of 0.03% for corporates, banks, and retail exposures under the IRBA. The final Basel III proposals for the revision of IRBA framework increase the input floor for corporate and retail exposures to 0.05% (0.10% for "revolving retail exposures"). However, the impact assessment (Chap. 5) will also examine two additional scenarios to examine the sensitivity of the RW to changes in the input floor. The alternative scenarios include the parallel shift of the PD floors for both corporates and retail by 0.05% and 0.10%.

4.3.11   Detailed Revisions of the IRBA Under the Final Basel III

As mentioned before, the retail exposures under the IRBA should be assessed by the AIRBA. Banking supervisors do not impose any supervisory values for the PD or LGD, as, by definition, the AIRBA produces its own estimates. However, the proposed framework imposes input floors on the own estimations of PD and LGD. The PD estimations arising from the application of the FIRBA are also subject to input floors (see Table 4.6).

As regulators impose them, these floors are considered as "regulatory restrictions" (RRs) which limit the free floating of RW estimation and thus the risk sensitivity of the IRBA.

Another "regulatory restriction" is the fixed regulatory LGD for senior unsecured (current Basel III: 45%, final Basel III: 40%) and subordinated unsecured (75%) corporate, bank, and sovereign exposures under the FIRBA and equity exposures (current Basel III: 90%, final Basel III: not applicable as equities migrate to the SA).

The RWs provided in Table 4.6 account for the restrictions on PD for various asset classes under the AIRBA and FIRBA as well as the restrictions on LGD, where applicable. The assessment of the impact estimates the difference between the final and current Basel III RW, conditional to the RRs applied to both regimes. The analysis uses the minimum PD and LGD values allowed by the current regulation for each asset class as the baseline framework and calculates the impact arising from the final proposals (BCBS, 2017) to estimate the impact.[19] In addition, the analysis will examine the impact of alternative scenarios to provide evidence on the sensitivity of the floors. Overall, the impact is assessed by the following equation.

$$\%dRWs = \frac{\begin{array}{c} f\left(PD,,,|LGD,,,|M,,,|\rho,,,|RR_{prop}\right) \\ -f\left(PD,,,|LGD,,,|M,,,|\rho,,,|RR_{cur}\right) \end{array}}{f\left(PD,,,|LGD,,,|M,,,|\rho,,,|RR_{cur}\right)} \qquad (4.25)$$

While the challenge related to the SA for credit risk is to apply sufficient differentiation to the treatment of asset classes, the revised IRBA aims at reducing the excess variability of RWA outputs over time and across banks. Moreover, the unwarranted deviation of the IRBA RW from the SA RW, stemming from assets with the same risk characteristics, raised concerns that IRBA banks underestimate their risks to the point that they create a competitive advantage in the conduct of business. Any evidence indicating that IRBA banks are prone to the above deficiencies could undermine the level playing field in the competition amongst international banks under the revised framework.

The final documentation of Basel reforms (BCBS, 2017) removes the option to use the AIRBA for the following portfolios:

- banks and other financial institutions (migrate to FIRBA);
- large corporates, defined as corporates belonging to consolidated groups with total assets exceeding EUR 50 billion or corporates which are part of consolidated groups that have annual revenues greater than EUR 500 million (migrate to FIRBA); and
- equities (migrate to SA).

In principle, the migration of the above exposures to any non-AIRBA increases the RWA and capital requirements.

Table 4.6 shows the full set of PD and LGD floors under the current and proposed Basel frameworks. In general, the PD floors increase from 0.03% to 0.05% with the exception of retail revolving exposures whose output floor becomes 0.10%. Moreover, the final Basel III introduces LGD floors for the unsecured exposures, which range from 5% (mortgages) to 50% (retail revolvers), and for secured (collateralised) corporate and retail exposures, which span from 0% (financial) to 15% (other physical collateral), depending on the type of eligible collateral (Table 4.6).

The new framework also introduces an input floor for the EAD which equals the total amount of balance sheet items augmented by the half of the balance sheet equivalent of the off-balance sheet exposures using the CCF of the standardised approach, that is, "balance sheet amount + 50% × off-balance sheet exposures × SA–CCF".

Table 4.6 illustrates the current set of PD floors (Part 1, column 3) which is the baseline for assessing the impact of implementing the revised Basel III set of PD (Part 1, column 4). The same table shows the final Basel III LGD floors applicable to the unsecured exposures under the AIRBA (Part 2, column 4) and those that would apply to the fully secured part of collateralised exposures (Part 2, column 6). Finally, Table 4.6 presents the supervisory LGDs as formulated under the current and new frameworks for both unsecured and fully collateralised exposures (Part 3).

Following the BCBS to "test a higher LGD floor for mortgage exposures" (BCBS, 2016a: 6) and "also consider the appropriateness of the 0% LGD floor on exposures fully secured by eligible financial collateral (together with the corresponding zero exposure value that can be obtained under the standardised approach)" (BCBS, 2016a: 6), Chap. 5 empirically tests the impact of the LGD floor.

The LGD and EAD floors are only applicable to AIRBA approaches. The LGD floors separately apply to the fully secured and the fully unsecured parts of the exposure in question. For partly secured exposures, the following formula applies:

$$LGDfloor^* = LGDfloor_{sec} \times \%Exposures_{sec} + LGDfloor_{unsec}$$
$$\times \%Exposures_{unsec} \qquad (4.26)$$

where

$LGDfloor^*$ is the effective LGD floor assigned to a specific proportion of secured and unsecured exposures held by a bank which applies the AIRBA,

$LGDfloor_{sec}$ is the LGD assigned to the fully covered portion of the exposure,

$LGDfloor_{unsec}$ is the LGD assigned to the fully uncovered portion of the exposure,

$\%Exposures_{sec}$ is the proportion of the exposure deemed as fully secured,

$\%Exposures_{unsec}$ is the proportion of the exposure deemed as fully unsecured.

4.3.11.1   Probability of Default

The bespoke estimation of PD has contributed to the variability of RWs amongst banks over time. The variability is also apparent when switching from the accession to the recession phase of a business cycle, as the PDs are affected accordingly. To reduce the variability and facilitate the comparability of IRBA models across banks, the BCBS introduces the following requirements as to the estimation of PDs:

- The rating categories of internal systems should remain stable over time;
- Any migration across them should be due to idiosyncratic or industry-specific changes in credit quality, and not by switching between recession and accession phases of business cycles, that is, due to systemic factors, which could temporarily affect the classification of a specific entity or exposure;
- PD modelling should rely on the "observed historical average one-year default rate" which should include observations from the full spectrum of the business cycle, that is, recessions and accessions. Amongst them, at least one out of ten years should represent a downturn PD observation;
- PD estimations are specific to rating category; and
- Banks should consider the seasoning effect as a risk factor when estimating PDs.

In addition to the above revisions, the PD is subject to asset-specific floors (Table 4.6), before being used as an input in the supervisory formula for the calculation of RW.

The analysis in Chap. 5 uses the observed default rates as the basis for the estimation of the impact of changes in PD modelling. The data on default rates include a representative mix of good and bad performing years (low and high PDs), with a minimum of one of high PD. The PD used in the analysis is a simple ten-year average of default rates.

In addition to the changes above, which will apply to corporate exposures and, where relevant, retail exposures, the BCBS proposes the incorporation of seasoning in the models for the estimation of PDs for retail exposures. The analysis treats the PD estimation as known (by substituting it with historical default rates) and focuses on the impact of PD floors on RWs (see Chap. 5, Sects. 5.4, 5.6, and 5.7). It also investigates the modelling properties and sensitivities of different levels using the revised provisions, that is, including input and output floors, and the impact of different modelling specifications, that is, proposed modelling versus current modelling specifications, on the level of RWs.

4.3.11.2   Loss-Given Default

As depicted in Eq. (4.26), the AIRBA LGD input in the supervisory formulae (4.1) and (4.3) depends on the participation (portion) of secured and unsecured in the total exposure. The methodology for the estimation of AIRBA capital requirements, according to the final framework, is applicable only to corporate and retail exposures, as these are the types of exposures subject to LGD input floors. This methodology should also consider the downturn LGDs, which reduces the RWA variability.

To address the issues relating to the AIRBA, and to facilitate the comparability of this approach with the SA, the BCBS requires banks to separately estimate (1) a long-run average LGD for each exposure; and (2) an add-on to reflect the impact of downturn conditions for all non-defaulted assets. Thus, the LGD parameter will be the sum of these two components. To limit the extent to which the component leads to undue variation in LGD estimates, the BCBS will also consider applying a floor to the downturn add-on. This floor would be in addition to the floor on the overall LGD set out in Table 4.6.

In effect, the BCBS allows the AIRBA banks to estimate the part of the exposure that corresponds to the fully secured exposures (corporate and retail) and subsequently estimates the effective LGD floor by using Eq. (4.26). Hence, the supervisory-determined floor is the weighted average of the floor that applies to the unsecured exposures and a floor applicable to the fully secured exposures, with the weightings being the proportion of the exposure that is unsecured and the proportion of the secured exposure. The proposed calibration of the floors will vary with the type of collateral that secures the exposure.

The final Basel III allows banks to apply the formula for fully or partially secured exposures under the AIRBA to determine the collateral effect, as far as the collateral is eligible under the IRBA and the bank's LGD estimate does not account for any effects of collateral recoveries.

Box 4.1   Examples for the Calculation of the Effective LGD (LGD*) of Collateralised Exposures

Calculation of the Effective LGD (LGD*) for Eligible Financial Collateral Under the IRBA

An EU bank has an exposure of EUR 100,000 to a BBB+ corporate bond with a 15-year maturity, which is collateralised by FTSE 100[20] equities worth EUR 120,000. According to the current framework, a haircut of 12% applies to the exposure and a haircut of 15% to the collateral. According to the final provisions, these haircuts increase to 20% and 20%, respectively. Given that the denomination of both exposure and collateral is in the same currency, there is no haircut for currency mismatch.

After applying Eq. (4.10) for the calculation of E^*, the uncovered amount (E^*) under the current framework is EUR 10,000 while under the final Basel III it is EUR 24,000. In turn, the formula for the calculation of the reduced LGD (Eq. (4.12)) produces an LGD* of 4.5% under the current framework and 10.8% under the final Basel III. The new collateral framework designates a positive impact due to the increase in the haircuts for corporate exposures with maturity of more than ten years and the respective increase of the haircut for collateral denominated in main index equities.

Calculation of Effective LGD (LGD*) for Non-financial IRBA-eligible Collateral: The Case of FIRBA

The current value of an exposure to a BBB-rated corporate is EUR 100,000 and the collateral, which backs this exposure, is an RRE, currently valued at EUR 120,000. The collateralisation level, that is, C' ratio, is 120%, which is above the minimum collateralisation level (30%) for the recognition of an LGD reduction under the current framework, but below the collateralisation level for the full recognition of LGD reduction (140%).

According to Basel III, there is full recognition of LGD reduction for the part of the exposure considered as fully collateralised 85.7% (see Eq. (4.12)), while there will be no recognition for the remaining 14.3%. In other words, the minimum LGD (35%) for fully recognising the effect of eligible collateral applies on EUR 85,714.29 while the remaining amount of EUR 14,285.71 will receive the supervisory LGD of senior unsecured exposures (45%) under the current regime. The above calculation results in a weighted average effective LGD (LGD*) of 36.4% (=[EUR 85,714.29 × 35% + EUR 14,285.71 × 45%]/EUR 100,000).

The consideration of the same case under the final Basel III implies that the current collateralisation level is compared to a higher threshold for the full recognition of LGD reduction, which under the new rules has gone up to 166.67%. This level of collateralisation implies a 40% haircut to recognise full coverage of

(continued)

Box 4.1   (continued)

the exposure. The changes arising from the implementation of the final Basel III result in the reduction of the exposure that will receive full recognition (EUR 72,000) compared to the respective amount under the current framework (EUR 85,714.29). The amount, which will receive no recognition, increases to EUR 28,000 (from EUR 14,285.71 under the current framework). The part of covered exposure (EUR 72,000) will receive an LGD of 20% (instead of 35% as under the current framework), whereas the remaining part will receive an LGD of 40% (instead of 45% under the current framework). This produces a weighted average LGD* of 25.6% which is 10.8 percentage points less than the LGD* produced by the current framework. Thus, the application of the final Basel III has a negative impact on the effective LGD and thus the RW. This negative impact will counterbalance the positive impact generated by the implementation of the input floors on LGD.

Calculation of LGD* for Non-financial IRBA-eligible Collateral: The Case of AIRBA

Another bank applies the AIRBA and that its internal estimate happens to coincide with the supervisory LGD of 45% used in the previous example for the FIRBA bank. This bank has the same exposure of EUR 100,000 to a BBB-rated corporate while the collateral attached to this exposure is again an RRE, currently valued at EUR 120,000.

As shown in Table 4.6, the new LGD estimate is subject to an LGD input floor of 25%, that is, the bank's internal LGD estimate cannot be lower than 25%, which is the floor applicable to the unsecured part of the exposures. Since the RRE exposure collateralises the original corporate exposure, the covered part is subject to a floor of 10% (see also Table 4.6). Similar to the FIRBA, the effective LGD is the weighted average of the internal estimation of the LGD (in this case it happens to coincide with the supervisory LGD) and the floored LGD of the specific type of exposures (10%). The estimated effective LGD floor would lie somewhere between 10% and the internal AIRBA estimation, depending on the collateralisation level.

According to the new AIRBA framework, the current collateralisation level compares to the threshold of 166.67% for the full recognition of LGD reduction. The increase of this threshold implies that the exposure amount that gets the full recognition is EUR 72,000, whereas the amount that receives no recognition is EUR 28,000. Thus, the effective LGD is the weighted average of the internal estimate (40%) and the estimation of the LGD floor (10%). Again, according to the composition of covered and uncovered exposure, the effective LGD becomes 18.4%, reduced by (7.2%) compared to the final Basel III FIRBA estimation.

The examples above illustrate the relationship between the effective LGD produced by the FIRBA and AIRBA for the specific example only. The relationship between the FIRBA and AIRBA effective LGD does not always produce results in favour of the AIRBA, assuming the same level of internally estimated LGD. Instead, their relationship is a function of the level of collateralisation across the spectrum of different collateralisation ratios (see Table 4.5). Chapter 5 provides detailed description of the effects of the new collateralisation framework.

4.4   Conclusions

Chapter 4 presents the methodology for the estimation of the current and revised Basel framework under the SA and IRBA for credit risk, and sets the field for the comparison of the two approaches applied in Chap. 5. The description of the methodology assists banks to assess the bank-specific impact of the final provisions on their portfolios. It also shows the correspondence between the SA and IRBA asset classes which could be used as the basis for banks to assess the migration dynamics from one approach to another.

Finally, this chapter articulated the new collateralisation framework under the IRBA to provide the reader with a solid understanding of the methodology and subsequently of the analysis that follows in Chap. 5. The examples provide clarifications on the application of the new framework, as well as evidence on the impact of the final rules on the collateralised exposures to enhance further the understanding of the new framework.

Notes

1. This term is adopted by the ECB's European Credit Assessment Framework (ECB, 2015).
2. RW in italics refer to the final Basel III.
3. This RW corresponds to "option 2" of the two alternative sets of ratings available for banks under Basel II (BCBS, 2006a: para 63) and Basel III.
4. BCBS, 2015: 31, para 36.
5. SMEs treated as corporates.
6. The one-to-one deduction from capital is generally deemed equivalent to an RW of 1250%, where the actual capital ratio of a bank is exactly at the minimum required total capital ratio (8%). However, for highly capitalised banks (well above 8%), the deduction from capital is more favourable than an RW of 1250% as it reduces the capital ratio less than the RW of 1250%.
7. The values in parenthesis refer to national discretions that would result in a different RW.
8. The content of this table refers exclusively to the final Basel III framework.
9. According to the Basel framework, provisions are items additive to TC.
10. According to the International Financial Accounting Standards (IFRS), it is prohibited to rely on past experience to form current provisions.
11. Off-balance sheet (OffBS) items are assets which the bank is not the recognised as legal owner of, or liabilities which the bank does not have direct legal responsibility for. However, since there could be direct or indirect recourse to the bank, OffBS items bear a certain level of risk which should be translated to the equivalent risk of assets or liabilities of the balance sheet.

12. The CCF of 20% applies to both issuing and confirming banks.
13. The scaling factor is not explicitly included in the typology of formulae for the calculation of RW and RWA, but it is mentioned as an additional requirement of Basel II (BCBS, 2006: para 14).
14. The book will not examine the formulation and impact of the EAD as it depends on the nature of banks' portfolios.
15. The illustrations and the examples presented in this book consider the LGD input as given.
16. Instead of presenting it in the SA section.
17. The impact assessment will test additional scenarios.
18. Basel II framework (BCBS, 2006) sets out a lower floor of 100% for public and private equities with certain characteristics, that is, investment in public equities should be part of long-term customer lending or general banking relationship with the issuing corporate while the capital gains are expected in the long term; investments in private equity should be based on regular and periodic cash flows not derived from capital gains. This lower floor would result in the overestimation of the current RWA corresponding to equities and consequently to underestimation of the impact from the implementation of the final Basel III.
19. It disregards asset classes where the floors remained the same.
20. FTSE 100 Index (UKX) comprises the 100 most highly capitalised "blue-chip" companies listed on the London Stock Exchange. For more information see http://www.ftse.com/products/indices/uk

References

Bank for International Settlements (BIS). (2013). Central bank collateral frameworks and practices. Retrieved September 2017, from http://www.bis.org/publ/mktc06.pdf

Basel Committee on Banking Supervision (BCBS). (2006, June). Basel II: International convergence of capital measurement and capital standards: A revised framework – comprehensive version. Retrieved from http://www.bis.org/publ/bcbs128.pdf

Basel Committee on Banking Supervision (BCBS). (2011, June). Basel III: A global regulatory framework for more resilient banks and banking systems – revised version. Retrieved from http://www.bis.org/publ/bcbs189.pdf

Basel Committee on Banking Supervision (BCBS). (2014, December). Revisions to the Standardised Approach for credit risk – consultative document. Retrieved from http://www.bis.org/bcbs/publ/d307.pdf

Basel Committee on Banking Supervision (BCBS). (2015, December). Revisions to the Standardised Approach for credit risk – second consultative document. Retrieved from http://www.bis.org/bcbs/publ/d347.pdf

Basel Committee on Banking Supervision (BCBS). (2016a, March). Reducing variation in credit risk-weighted assets – constraints on the use of internal model approaches – consultative document. Retrieved from http://www.bis.org/bcbs/publ/d362.pdf

Basel Committee on Banking Supervision (BCBS). (2016b, October). Regulatory treatment of accounting provisions – interim approach and transitional arrangements – consultative document. Retrieved from http://www.bis.org/bcbs/publ/d386.pdf

Basel Committee on Banking Supervision (BCBS). (2017, December). Basel III: Finalising post-crisis reforms – Standards. Retrieved December 7, 2017, from https://www.bis.org/bcbs/publ/d424.pdf

Bindseil, U., Corsi, M., Sahel, B., & Visser, A. (2017). *The Eurosystem collateral framework explained.* Occasional Paper, No 189. Retrieved September 2017, from https://www.ecb.europa.eu/pub/pdf/scpops/ecb.op189.en.pdf

European Central Bank (ECB). (2015). The financial risk management of the Eurosystem's monetary policy operations. Retrieved September 2017, from https://www.ecb.europa.eu/pub/pdf/other/financial_risk_management_of_eurosystem_monetary_policy_operations_201507.en.pdf

Jacobson, T., Lindé, J., & Roszbach, K. (2004). *Credit risk versus capital requirements under Basel II: Are SME loans and retail credit really different?* Sveriges Riksbank. Working Papers Series No. 162. April. Retrieved March 2017, from http://www.riksbank.se/Upload/WorkingPapers/WP_162.pdf

5

Credit Risk: Quantitative Impact

The new credit risk specifications include, inter alia, the implementation of higher floors for the probability of default (PD), LGD, and EAD in the internal ratings-based approach (IRBA) models, which allow banks to estimate these parameters internally. It also requires the migration of certain exposures from the AIRBA to the FIRBA and the standardised approach (SA). However, the utmost goal of the Basel reform package is the reduction of the variability of RWAs across time. These revisions target the reduction of the variability of RWAs across time, and implicitly amongst banks with similar portfolio risk profiles.

The current chapter examines the quantitative impact of the structural changes that Basel introduces in the calculation of capital requirements under the FIRBA and AIRBA. Also, the analysis investigates the differences in RWA between the SA and IRBA and the dynamic evolution of these differences if the banks find it necessary to switch risk assessment approaches due to the transition from the current to final Basel III. It also identifies whether the new framework maintains the intended risk sensitivity of the IRBA and whether input and output floors facilitate this goal.

The analysis of RWA variability involves a comparison of the evolution of differences between FIRBA and SA over time. To facilitate this goal, the analysis uses weighted averages of all publicly available default rates over the last ten years, as well as available LGDs cited in empirical studies (Bonsall, Koharki, Muller, & Sikochi, 2017; Elizondo-Flores, Lemus-Basualdo, & Quintana-Sordo, 2010; Johnston-Ross & Shibut, 2015) to represent the actual values used as inputs in the formulae of the IRBA. The authors estimated the default rates as weighted averages of all publicly available data to

© The Author(s) 2018
I. Akkizidis, L. Kalyvas, *Final Basel III Modelling*,
https://doi.org/10.1007/978-3-319-70425-8_5

the best of their knowledge.[1] The empirical study provides an indication as to whether the final Basel III reduces the differences between SA and IRBA RWs, in view to assess whether the new framework reduces regulatory arbitrage opportunities.

5.1   Mapping of SA Asset Classes on IRBA Asset Classes

The present chapter provides evidence on the impact of migrating from the current to the final Basel III, without changing approaches of credit risk estimation, that is, from AIRBA to AIRBA and from FIRBA to FIRBA. It also assesses the impact of the new framework from the "diagonal" transition, that is, from the AIRBA to the FIRBA or from the AIRBA to the SA. In doing so, the analysis estimated the impact of two components of migration: the horizontal transition from the current Basel III to the respective approach under the final Basel III and the vertical migration, that is, from the one approach to another within the final Basel III framework, that is, from the AIRBA to the FIRBA.[2]

Before estimating the impact of the asset classes under different approaches, one should map the exposures to make the impact comparable. Table 5.1

Table 5.1 Alignment of SA to IRBA asset classes and migration patterns under the final Basel III

SA asset class	IRBA asset classes	Migrating to:
Banks	Senior exposures to banks and financial institutions (FI) subject to equivalent prudential supervision	FIRBA
Real estate	Specialised lending: income-producing real estate (IPRE), HVCRE	FIRBA
	Retail exposures secured by real estate	AIRBA
	Corporate and FI exposures secured by real estate	FIRBA for corporates with revenue > EUR 500 million
Corporates	Unsecured general corporate (non-SME) and FI exposures or exposures secured with anything other than real estate	
	Non-regulatory retail SME exposures	
	Purchased corporate receivables	AIRBA or FIRBA according to obligor
Specialised lending	Specialised lending: PF, ObF, CF	AIRBA
Retail	Regulatory retail SME loans	AIRBA
	Purchased retail receivables	
Subordinated debt, equity, other capital instruments	Equity exposures, subordinated debt, or other capital instruments (to banks and corporates)	SA

provides the definition of asset classes, which are subject to migration from the AIRBA under Basel III to the FIRBA or SA under the final Basel III (BCBS, 2016, 2017).

However, it is out of the scope of the analysis to cover asset classes whose framework is still under review (sovereign exposures) or those whose treatment is not subject to change public sector entities (PSEs) or where the changes are immaterial multinational development banks (MDBs). The credit risk analysis should use the mapping, below to estimate the potential impact of the migration from the AIRBA to FIRBA or SA. The estimation of the output floor impact (see Chap. 9) uses the same mapping for the estimation of the SA equivalent, which is the basis for the calculation of the newly implemented output floor, while the sensitivity analysis per each asset class relies on the same mapping. Table 5.1 provides the mapping of the IRBA to SA exposures, as well as the migration dynamics assuming that all exposures are currently under the AIRBA.

5.2 Input Parameters of IRBA Models

When estimating PDs, banks use their own internal models and thus come up with an estimate of the future default rates on a best-effort basis. No matter how robust an IRBA model is, the PD is likely to deviate from the actual default rates of the portfolios to be observed in the future. Given the diversity of model specifications, each bank produces its own estimate of PD for a certain asset class, which is also likely to deviate among banks, even if they have similar exposures. Even if it was feasible to align banks' estimations, they will not coincide with the actual default rates. To this end, the bank should back-test the accuracy of its internal model to ensure its robustness estimations and to adjust its specifications if it deviates from the actual default rates.

As it is not possible to collect banks' own estimates of PDs per asset class, the analysis below relies on authors' own estimations based on publicly available sources of default rates observed over the last ten years and observed LGDs from various empirical studies. The reliance of the analysis on observed values implies that the study assumes that default rates coincide with banks' PD estimates. The analysis presents the current and final Basel III behavioural statistics, assuming that the last ten years represent a full economic cycle. The reliance on (observed) default rates bypasses the subjectivity embedded in PD estimations and thus avoids any model-error risk that bank-specific PD models will additionally introduce in the estimation of RW.

To come up with the structure of corporate RW, the analysis uses the respective default rates as inputs in the IRBA formula for the calculation of RW for corporates. In other words, the book considers that observed default rates are the best estimations of the future PD for the analysis below.

Under the current framework, the default rates are subject to a 0.03% PD floor, while the final Basel III raises it to 0.05%. On the other hand, the supervisory LGD for senior unsecured exposures under the FIRBA is 45% (40% under the final Basel III). The own estimate of LGD under the AIRBA stems from a range of alternative LGD model specifications, depending on banks' modelling properties. To test the impact of different LGDs on the final RW output, the analysis will assume different levels of corporate LGD on the one side and the revised set of LGD floors on the other. The impact assessment will test alternative LGD floors to contribute to the sensitivity analysis of input floor parameters.

The 1.06 scaling factor is an essential element embedded in the current RW framework. The final Basel III does not anymore require banks to scale up their RWA with the 1.06 scaling factor. Thus, the impact discussed throughout this chapter embeds the reduction of RW due to the removal of the 1.06 scaling factor.

Unless otherwise stated, the analysis assumes that a bank applies the FIRBA on senior unsecured corporate exposures by applying the supervisory LGD (current Basel III: 45%, final Basel III: 40%), without covering the analysis of the impact stemming from the implementation of output floor on the total RWA. Chapter 9 elaborates the impact of the output floor.

One of the main drivers of the categorisation of RWs across different asset classes is the different specification of correlation (ρ). The ρ is a function of PD for all asset classes except for residential mortgages and other retail exposures where the correlation is constant and provided by the supervisors. Even though the PD (default rate) is assumed to be the same across all corporate-related asset classes, the differences in the model specification of ρ, alone, lead to different RWs.

The ρ of corporate-related assets classes are lower for exposure with lower ratings. The correlation (ρ) of CCC/C-rated corporate and specialised lending (HVCRE) exposures converges to 0.12, for medium-sized SMEs to 0.10, for small SMEs to 0.08, and for other retail to 0.03 (see Annex). The levels of correlation for residential mortgages remain stable across all ratings, as it is not subject to any modelling. In the end, ρ influences the level of RWs through the normal distribution function producing different RWs across asset classes.

5.3   The Impact of PD Floors

The use of supervisory LGDs in the FIRBA leaves the PD as the only factor for which the bank should provide estimations. The increased PD floors under the final Basel III imply that the impact stems only from the change in modelling specifications. The use of the suggested input floors on the (observed) default rates, which the analyses use as proxies for the own estimated PDs, provides a mixed picture when different rating notches are involved. While the increased floors raise the RW for AAA and AA rating classes, the rest of the rating classes remain unaffected by the PD floors, as the associated default rates are above the relevant floor. The picture is different when the analysis excludes the scaling factor of 1.06 from the estimation of RW. Again, AAA and AA rating classes show increased RW, albeit at a lower level, while the RWs corresponding to the rest of the ratings appear reduced in relation to Basel III RW, after accounting for the scaling factor.

5.3.1   FIRBA Horizontal Migration

The revisions (BCBS, 2017) abolish the 1.06 scaling factor applicable to all IRBA exposures under the current framework.

Figure 5.1 presents the final Basel III RW (Eqs. (4.1) and (4.3)) of each of the rating notches, gross and net of the 1.06 scaling factor, by utilising the supervisory LGD for senior unsecured corporate exposures (current Basel III: 45%, final Basel III: 40%) and the ten-year average (observed) default rate assigned to each rating notch. As mentioned, the PDs of AAA and AA rating classes are currently constrained by the current floor of 0.03%, as they lie below it and thus they are constrained by it. Thus, the impact of full implementation on RWs, for these rating classes, embeds a PD increase of 0.02%, that is, from 0.03% (current) to 0.05% (final).

Translating the PD increase of AAA to AA– exposures into RW impact on the same exposures, the latter equals 2.2 pp, net of the 1.06 scaling factor, and 3.2 pp, gross of scaling factor. The horizontal FIRBA transition/migration (from the current to final Basel III) has a negative effect on RWs attributed to all other rating notches. The removal of the 1.06 scaling factor and the reduction of the supervisory LGD (from 45% to 40%) are the factors of the impact on the rest of the rating notches (A-CCC). The PD floors do not affect the PD input in the supervisory formula, that is, the default rates are already above the PD floors for these asset classes. The impact on these rating classes spans from −2.7 (A) to 41.9 (CCC) percentage points.

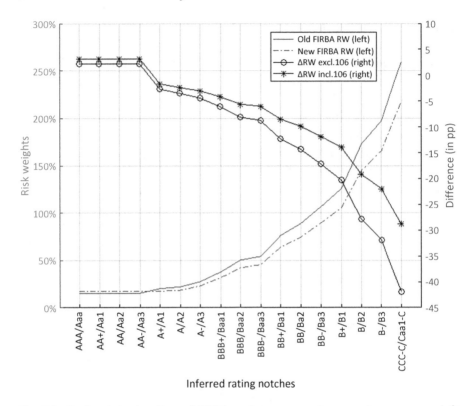

Fig. 5.1 Horizontal migration of FIRBA senior unsecured corporate exposures, left y-axis: RW in %, right y-axis: impact in percentage points

Figure 5.2 presents the new RW of each of the rating notches, gross and net of the 1.06 scaling factor, by utilising the supervisory LGD for subordinated unsecured corporate exposures (75%) and the ten-year average (observed) default rate assigned to the specified rating notch. The PDs of AAA and AA rating classes are constrained by both the current and revised floors, that is, 0.03% and 0.05%, respectively, which results in an increase in the PD input by 0.02%.

The impact, net of the 1.06 scaling factor, AAA to AA–risk weights is 7.2 pp, whereas it increases to 9.2 pp when the estimations are gross of scaling factor (Fig. 5.2). The horizontal FIRBA migration also affects the RW attributed to the A+ rating notch. The impact on A+ RW is also positive (1.1 pp) when the 1.06 is included, as the PD assigned to A+ is above the current floor and constrained only by the increased floor under the final Basel III. The removal of the 1.06 scaling factor is the sole factor of the reduction on the rest of the rating notches (A–CCC). This reduction spans from 2.1 (A) to 24.5 (CCC) percentage points.

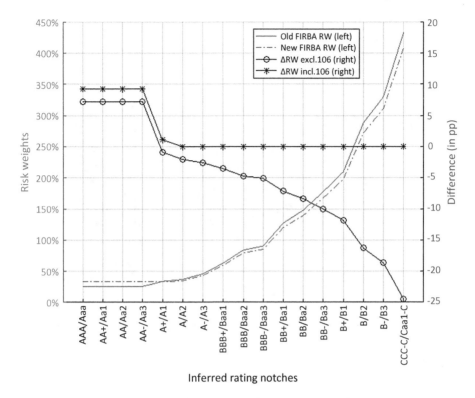

Fig. 5.2 Horizontal migration of FIRBA subordinated unsecured corporate exposures, left y-axis: RW in %, right y-axis: impact in percentage points

The PD floor affects not only the general corporate exposures but also the remaining exposures linked to corporate default rates (SME, SL, equity exposures), as well as all types of retail exposures. The analysis considers only the corporate default-related exposures,[3] given that there are no publicly available data for the retail exposures' LGD and PD.

Assuming all corporate default-related exposures bear the same PD, the analysis below uses the ten-year average (observed) default rate to assess the impact on corporate exposures, SMEs, and SL for three different levels of PD floors on A-rated corporates.

Figure 5.3 designates the incremental impact of input floors on the current RWs assigned to general corporates, SMEs with sales of EUR 5 million and EUR 27.5 million, as well as specialised lending exposures. The current RW (including 1.06 scaling factor) is 15.3%, 12.0%, 13.6% and 20.8%, respectively. The incremental impact of implementing a PD floor of 0.05% exhibits incremental RW which ranges from 3.4 pp (small SMEs) to 5.8 pp (SL), assuming that the AIRBA LGD coincides with the supervisory LGD for the FIRBA. The incremental RW impact of an increase in PD floors, from 0.05%

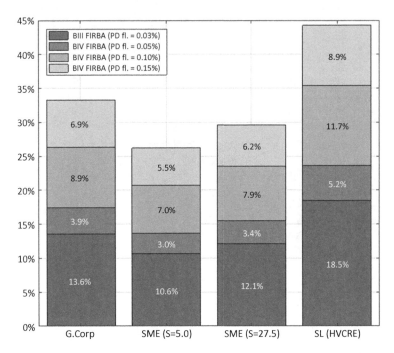

Fig. 5.3 The impact of the FIRBA horizontal migration assuming the adaptation of alternative PD floors, inferred rating: A

to 0.10%, spans from 7.9 pp to 13.2 pp while an additional increase of the PD floors by 0.05% (from 0.10% to 0.15%) would imply an RW add-on between 6.2 pp and 10 pp. The total impact from the implementation of the highest examined PD floor (0.15%) would be 29 (5.8 + 13.2 + 10.0) percentage points for SL, 22.1 (4.3 + 10.0 + 7.8) percentage points for general corporates, 19.7 (3.9 + 8.9 + 6.9) for medium-sized corporates, and 17.5 (3.4 + 7.9 + 6.2) for small corporates.

5.4   The Difference Between Economic and Regulatory Capital

The sections below focus on the potential over- or underestimation of economic capital by the regulatory capital. The forthcoming investigation adopts the RW as a proxy for the economic capital, that is, the amount of capital that would suffice to absorb observed losses. To approximate the exact level of past losses we use the (observed) default rates and realised LGD as inputs in the formula for the estimation of the RW under the AIRBA. In turn, the analysis considers the RW that uses the supervisory LGD as the best proxy for the regulatory capital.

The comparison of RWs that corresponds to the economic and regulatory capital provides evidence on how the final Basel III affects the assessment of senior unsecured and subordinated unsecured corporate exposures.

5.4.1 The Supervisory LGD, the Realised LGD, and the LGD Floors

Both FIRBA and AIRBA use their own PD estimates to feed the corporate exposures formula for the estimation of RW, while only AIRBA uses its own estimations for the LGD. The FIRBA banks use the supervisory LGD as input in the RW formula. As mentioned, the supervisory LGD currently equals 45% for senior unsecured exposures (final Basel III: 40%), while it is 75% for subordinated unsecured exposures under both regimes. On the other hand, the realised average LGD varies according to different studies (see Table 5.2) for senior unsecured and subordinated unsecured exposures, respectively. Bonsall et al. (2017) showed that the exposures to corporates show LGDs that span from 38.12% (1st quartile) to 78.75% (3rd quartile). Assuming that the lowest LGD value corresponds to "high-recovery priority" and the highest to "low-recovery priority", the analysis assigns the former to senior unsecured exposures and the later to subordinated unsecured exposures.

The evaluation of the differences between the supervisory LGD vis-à-vis the realised LGD provides useful insights as to the direction which the supervisory LGD could take in the future. As shown in Table 5.2, if the realised LGD were representative of the population of corporate exposures held by banks, the supervisory LGD overestimates the realised values (40% vs. 38.12%) that correspond to the senior unsecured exposures. In contrast to this evidence, the supervisory LGD for subordinated unsecured exposures underestimates the realised LGD (75% vs. 78.75%).

Table 5.2 LGD rates of corporate, commercial real estate, and retail (credit card) exposures provided by different studies

Type of exposure	Metric	Value (in %)	Paper
Corporates	1st/3rd quartile	38.12/78.75	Bonsall et al. (2017: 13)
Commercial real estate	Median	59.00	Johnston-Ross and Shibut (2015: 8)
Retail: credit cards	Portfolio average	81.00	Elizondo-Flores et al. (2010: 12)

The comparison between the realised LGD and the revised LGD floors, related to the AIRBA estimates, reveals useful information about the role of LGD floors as an impact factor for the formulation of the new RW. The realised LGDs for all asset categories are above the designated LGD floors. This implies that the LGD floor assigned to the AIRBA portfolios will only have a marginal impact, if any, on the final RW, and thus on the capital requirements.

5.5   The Vertical Migration from AIRBA to FIRBA: The Impact on RW

The use of internal PD estimates by both the FIRBA and the AIRBA renders the LGD input as the only differentiating factor for the estimation of RWs between the two approaches. The analysis utilises the (observed) default rates considering them as the best estimate of the banks' own estimated PD. By using the actual loss derived from the (observed) default rates and realised LGDs, one could come up with an estimate of the expected loss (EL). The combination of default rates/realised LGDs could also provide an unbiased predictor of the unexpected loss (UL), if used as an input in the IRBA formula for the estimation of RW. Thus, the analysis considers the EL and UL that arise from the (observed) default rates and realised LGDs as the best estimate of economic capital. The economic capital would render the bank capitalised enough to confront all the losses that may occur due to a financial crisis.

Since the use of the AIRBA models, based on actual observations, provides an unbiased estimation of the RW (and economic capital), one could use it as the basis for testing whether the FIRBA RW, based on the supervisory LGD input, overvalues or undervalues the RW that would correspond to the economic capital (actual LGD). This could lead to useful conclusions as to whether the current level of the FIRBA supervisory LGD refers to an accurate and up-to-date calibration.

Figure 5.4 shows the relationship between the AIRBA and FIRBA and the differences in percentage points. As expected from the comparison of the supervisory and realised LGDs[4] (Table 5.2), the supervisory LGD causes the FIRBA RW to overestimate the actual risk as represented by the AIRBA output using the observed default rates and LGDs.

The difference between the two approaches spans from 0.8 to 10.2 percentage points depending on the rating notch examined, assuming that the 1.06 scaling factor is not included. All other factors being equal, this difference

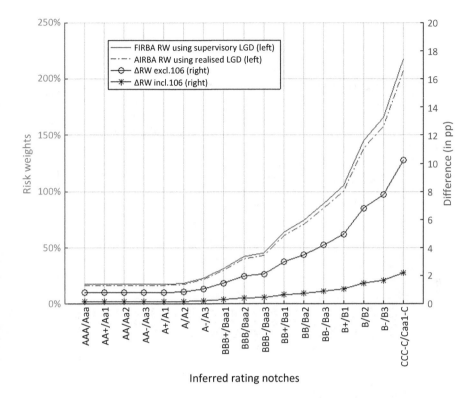

Fig. 5.4 The final Basel III FIRBA and AIRBA RW for senior unsecured corporate exposures, left y-axis: RW in %, right y-axis: impact in percentage points

indicates that the international supervisors could recalibrate downwards the supervisory LGD for senior unsecured exposures.

When examining the subordinated unsecured corporate exposures (Fig. 5.5), the analysis comes across the inverse picture, that is, the FIRBA underestimates the AIRBA RW by 1.6 to 20.4 percentage points, with the difference being higher at the lower end of the rating scale. This difference is due to the lower realised LGD observations, as compared to the supervisory LGD.

To assess the impact of the diagonal migration from the current AIRBA to the proposed FIRBA, one should add up the impact of the migration from the current to the revised AIRBA and the impact of the migration from the revised AIRBA to the revised FIRBA. Given that the analysis has already quantified the impact of the vertical migration from AIRBA to FIRBA, the only missing part is the impact of the horizontal migration from the current to the revised AIRBA.

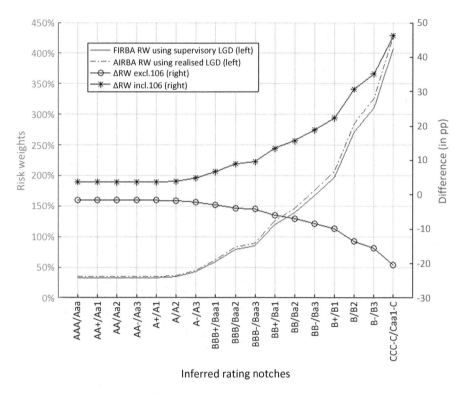

Fig. 5.5 The final Basel III FIRBA and AIRBA for subordinated unsecured corporate exposures, left y-axis: RW in %, right y-axis: impact in percentage points

5.6   The Impact of the Horizontal Migration of AIRBA

The final proposals suggest that the corporate exposure is subject to PD and LGD floors, which are 0.05% and 25%, respectively. Figure 5.6 examines the impact of setting higher input PD/LGD floors by shifting upwards the PD floor by 0.05% and 0.10% and the LGD floor by 5% and 10%, respectively. To assess the impact of the various combinations of floors, the analysis uses the current estimation of the AIRBA based on the default rates and realised LGDs. Once again, the default rates are subject to the current PD floor (0.03%), while the realised LGD is not subject to any floor under the current regime. In the absence of LGDs for all rating notches, Fig. 5.6 shows only the impact per rating class, that is, AAA, AA, and so on, where AA-rated corporates exhibit the lowest impact.

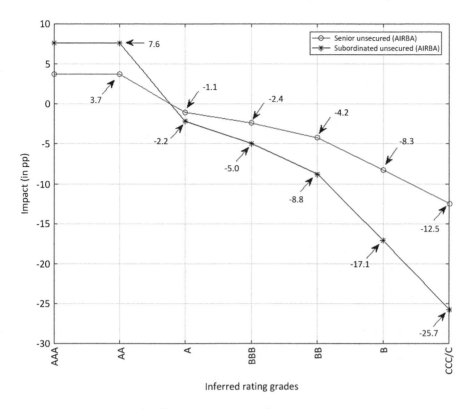

Fig. 5.6   Impact of PD/LGD floors on AIRBA RW for corporate exposures

Figure 5.6 shows the impact of the adopted combination of PD/LGD floors in the final document of the final Basel III. The combined impact of the implementation of the revised PD/LGD floors ranges from 2.2 pp (AA) to 23.2 pp (for CCC).

Moving beyond the estimation of the impact for corporate exposures, Fig. 5.7 investigates the impact per asset class subject to the AIRBA input floors, assuming that the current LGD of all asset classes is 5 percentage points lower than the relevant LGD floor. It also assumes that the current PD estimation, as approximated by the relevant default rate, ranges from 0.03% to 0.15% according to six different scenarios (current PD = 0.030%, 0.050%, 0.075%, 0.100%, 0.125%, and 0.150%) for four asset classes (fully unsecured corporate exposures, fully unsecured retail exposures, mortgages, and revolving retail exposures). Finally, the analysis examines the impact in the absence of the 1.06 scaling factor under the new framework.

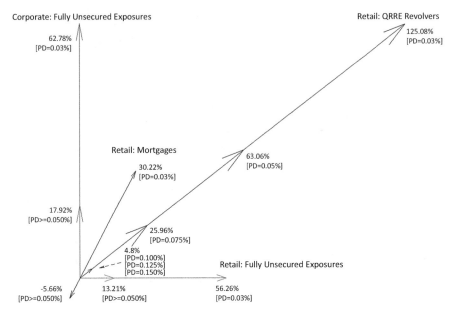

Fig. 5.7 The impact of the horizontal migration of AIRBA on different asset classes net of the 1.06 scaling factor, LGD internal estimate 5% lower than the relevant floor, PD internal estimate: 0.00% to 0.15%

The results show that the most heavily affected asset class is the retail revolving exposures. Under the scenario of a current PD estimation of 0.03%, the impact exceeds 125 percentage points. The fully unsecured corporate exposure is the asset class with the second highest impact which in the case of PD = 0.03% reaches 63 percentage points. The fully unsecured retail exposures exhibit the second lowest impact for a current PD = 0.03% (56 pp) while retail fully unsecured exposures show lowest impact amongst the four asset classes examined (31 pp).

The examination of the scenarios with the highest current PD (0.15%) shows that three out of four asset classes are affected by the AIRBA transition, that is, they show higher RWs, while mortgages benefit from the lower RWs due to the removal of the 1.06 scaling factor.

Notwithstanding the analysis above, the total impact from the modified specifications depends on the composition of banks' portfolios. However, the new rules could force a part of the banking system to change the composition and the risk profile of their portfolios.

5.7   The Vertical Migration from FIRBA to SA: The Impact on RW

Basel II motivated the implementation of IRBA models, by assuring that they will always produce RWs lower than the SA. However, the IRBA models have recently received criticism that they produce RWs which are significantly and unjustifiably lower than the SA RWs, and that they fail to represent the real risk of banks' exposures.

The current section examines the changes in the RW difference between SA and IRBA RWs before and after the full implementation of the new rules, that is, the "difference of the difference", to assess whether the new framework leads to the convergence of the approaches.

There has been some time since national supervisors and market participants (banks) have started to debate on whether the SA for credit risk penalises banks or whether the IRBA underestimates the credit risk of the banks which apply it. To provide further input to this debate, the book compares the RWs of the SA with those of the IRBA models.

By construction, the SA and IRBA frameworks provide different RWs for exposures rated with the same external rating. Initially, the SA RW factored in this difference as an add-on to address risks that SA banks were not in the position to assess. Irrespective of whether the SA overvalues or the IRBA undervalues the RW attributed to certain exposures, it is worth examining whether the final Basel III proposals widens or narrows the gap between the two approaches.

Following are the relevant provisions of Basel II,

Table 5.3 presents through-the-cycle (TTC) RW estimations by using the ten-year average default rates. The PD approximations are conducted per rating grade (e.g. AAA, AA, A, BBB, etc.) and assigned accordingly to allow the distinction amongst RWs. The ten-year averaging horizon shown in Table 5.3 includes one bad year (2009), when PDs appeared significantly increased for all rating grades in relation to their long-term average (especially for investment-grade ratings). Thus, the composition of the ten-year averaging is compatible with the requirements of BCBS which suggest that at least the ten-year average PD contain at least one bad year (of an increased PD).[5]

The IRBA RWs for corporates are generally lower, and in some cases significantly lower, than the respective SA RWs. When comparing the SA and FIRBA approximations of RW for senior unsecured exposures (45%) there is a significant convergence stemming from the transition to the final Basel III. This convergence is apparent for all rating classes except for BB and B-rated corporates.

Table 5.3 Comparison of SA and FIRBA prior and after the full implementation of the final Basel III

Inferred rating grade	10-year average B3 RW	10-year average B4 RW (net of 1.06)	SA RW (BIII)	SA RW (BIV)	Δ: IRBA–SA based on 10-year DR avg.		Change in the difference
					BIII	BIV (net of 1.06)	
1	3	4	5	6	7 (= 3 – 6)	9 (= 4 – 6)	10 = (abs(9)– abs (7))
AAA/ AAA	15.3	17.5	20.0	20	–4.7	–2.5	↓
AA/Aa	15.8	17.5	20.0	20	–4.2	–2.5	↓
A	17.0	17.5	50.0	50	–33.0	–32.5	↓
BBB/Baa	45.7	40.6	100.0	75	–54.3	–34.4	↓
BB/Ba	92.7	82.4	100.0	100	–7.3	–17.6	↑
B	149.9	133.3	150.0	150	–0.1	–16.7	↑
CCC/ Caa–C	236.1	209.8	150.0	150	86.1	59.8	↓

Source of default rates: authors' own estimations

The calculation of RW under the Basel III relies on the general IRBA formulae (4.1, 4.3, 4.4, 4.6) after substituting the LGD for 45%, M for 2.5 years, and the relevant TTC PD, while the new set of rules assumes an LGD of 40% and the removal of the 1.06 scaling factor. Under the current framework, the ratio of FIRBA to SA RWs is below 100% (second column of Table 5.4), complying with the provisions in Basel II that the IRBA RW should be lower than the SA. This provision does not hold for CCC ratings where the FIRBA-to-SA ratio is approximately 1.57 of the respective SA. The low ratios for A (0.34) and BBB ratings (0.46) signifies the preferential treatment of these exposures under the FIRBA compared to the same exposures treated under the SA. The observation above should be subject to further investigation to identify whether there is need for adjustment to the SA and/ or IRBA RW framework.

When considering the new FIRBA RW, net of the scaling factor, (Table 5.4), the FIRBA-to-SA ratio remains below unity for AAA and AA, being consistent with the principle described above.

The analysis in Table 5.4 indicates that the removal of the scaling factor makes the FIRBA RW of BBB, BB, and B-rated exposures more favourable, as their distance from the SA RW is wider under final Basel III. On the other side, the difference between the FIRBA and SA RW of AAA, AA, A, and CCC ratings becomes less apparent.

Table 5.4 The ratio of FIRBA to SA RW for different rating grades under current and final Basel III

Inferred rating grades	IRBA versus SA (B3)	IRBA versus SA (B4 net of 1.06)	Implied output floor (OF: 72.5%) impact	Convergence between FIRBA and SA under the final Basel III (Yes/No)
AAA/AAA	−23%	−13%	0%	Yes
AA/Aa	−21%	−13%	0%	Yes
A	−66%	−65%	108%	Yes
BBB/Baa	−54%	−59%	78%	No
BB/Ba	−7%	−18%	0%	No
B	0%	−11%	0%	No
CCC/Caa1-C	57%	40%	0%	Yes

5.8   The Dynamics of the New Collateralisation Framework Under the IRBA

Both current and final Basel III frameworks allow the recognition of a lower LGD, where the collateral pledged intends to mitigate the risk of credit exposures. The difference between the two frameworks is that Basel III allows the partial recognition of LGD reduction only if the collateral exceeds 35% of the exposure value, whereas the final framework allows the recognition of any level of collateralisation for the reduction of the applicable LGD. Another difference is the overcollateralisation threshold for the full recognition of LGD reduction, which is set at 140% under the current Basel III and at 200% under the final Basel III. Finally, the completed framework reduces the minimum level of the applicable effective LGD in cases where the collateralization exceeds the upper threshold for the full recognition of the IRBA-eligible collateral.

The above amendments imply a more favourable treatment of collateralised FIRBA exposures under the new framework for all levels of collateralisation. The black area in Fig. 5.8 shows the difference in the effective LGD between the current and final Basel III FIRBA frameworks. Nonetheless, the magnitude of the improved treatment differs for different levels of collateralisation. In general, there are three values of collateralisation (35%, 140% and 166.67%), which define four ranges (0–35%, 35%–140%, 140%–166.67%, and above 166.67%), where there is differences exhibits a structure change between Basel II and Basel III.

The global maximum benefit from the application of the final Basel III is observed for all collateralisation values above 166.67% where the LGD reduction is 20 percentage points, when considering the FIRBA and collateral that consist of receivables, CRE, and RRE. Figure 5.8 also shows the combinations

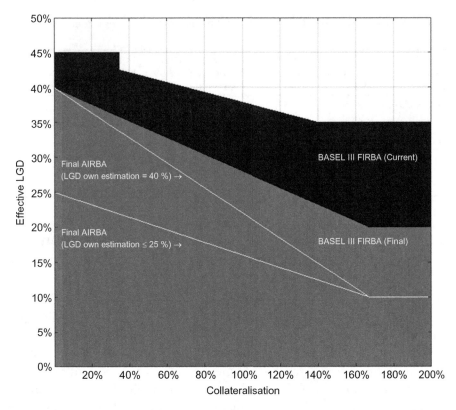

Fig. 5.8 Effective LGD for various levels of collateralisation according to FIRBA (current and final Basel III) and the AIRBA under the final Basel III

of collateralisation and effective LGDs for the AIRBA under the final set of rules. Assuming the internal LGD estimate coincides with the supervisory LGD (40%), the AIRBA framework is more favourable that the FIRBA under the final Basel III framework, as it shows a reduction of 30 pp, all others being equal. The new framework for both FIRBA and AIRBA is more favourable than the same approaches under the current Basel III. Thus, the new collateralisation framework will mitigate the impact caused by the increase in the input floors.

5.9   RWA Variability

Table 5.5 shows the minimum, maximum, median, and standard deviation of FIRBA RWs per rating grade, using the floored ten-year average default rates. The final Basel III RW estimate does not include the 1.06 scaling factor.

Table 5.5 Changes in RW variability between the current and final Basel III

Inferred rating grades	Current Basel III					Final Basel III, net of 1.06				
	Min	Median	Max	IQR	Std	Min	Median	Max	IQR	Std
AAA/AAA	15.3	15.3	15.3	0.0	0.0	17.5	17.5	17.5	0.0	0.0
AA/Aa	15.3	15.3	45.3	0.0	10.7	17.5	17.5	38.0	0.0	6.5
A	15.3	17.4	43.3	17.1	9.4	17.5	17.5	36.3	0.0	5.5
BBB/Baa	15.3	51.8	77.3	18.8	15.1	17.5	41.2	64.8	17.3	12.5
BB/Ba	46.3	91.4	144.5	34.5	23.5	38.8	77.4	121.2	28.9	19.4
B	92.6	138.5	240.6	46.5	37.4	77.6	121.8	201.8	35.8	32.4
CCC/Caa1-C	225.9	247.7	256.7	4.6	7.3	189.4	206.8	215.3	7.8	6.2

As observed in Table 5.5, the transition to the final Basel III implies an increase in median RWs of investment-grade corporates, which is due to the increased input floor (0.05%) of corporate exposures.

The absence of the 1.06 scaling factor does not have any explicit effect on the RWs of investment-grade exposures, as the increase in input floors is predominant in the increase of the RW. The upward shift in the descriptive statistics is due to the implementation of a higher PD floor. Conversely, the median RWs of non-investment-grade corporates drops due to the removal of the scaling factor, while the input floor has no effect on RWs, as the PDs (default rates) were already above the level of the input floor.

Box 5.1   Expected and Unexpected Loss of the Current and Revised Frameworks

Figure 5.9 shows the relationship amongst default rates corresponding to each rating class, EL, UL, and RW for every rating class ranging from "AAA" to "defaulted". For each of the credit ratings, the calculations rely on the ELs by using the floored PD estimates and the supervisory LGD of the FIRBA.

The EL and UL amounts represent the capital estimated under the FIRBA, which covers the ELs and ULs that the credit risk portfolio may experience. The IRBA formulae produce the RW which represents the UL for a given credit risk exposure and risk parameters.

In the absence of data on PD, the example below uses the default rates observed for each credit rating grade for the calculation of RW together with the LGD of 40% assigned to the senior unsecured exposures. The UL amount intends to cover credit losses at 99.9% confidence level minus the EL, that is, $EL = PD \times LGD \times$ maturity adjustment. In other words, the formulae for the FIRBA capital requirements cover the excess of the EL up to a certain extreme credit loss, which in the case of credit risk formulae represents the 99.9th percentile. The relationship between PD and UL is, by the construction of the formula, non-linear, while the relationship between the PD and EL is linear using the LGD as scalar for the transformation of PD to EL. All in all, the relationship between the PD and the total estimated loss at 99.9% is non-linear.

Moving from AAA-rated to "defaulted" corporates, the ten-year average annual rate (not shown) increases the EL proportionally. In general, the increase

(continued)

Box 5.1   (continued)

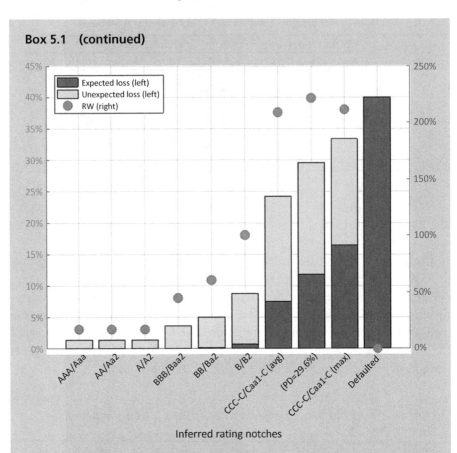

Fig. 5.9 Expected loss, unexpected loss, and RW per rating class under the final Basel III based on authors' own estimation default rates, LGD of 40%, and maturity of 2.5 years

in the default rates translates also into increases in UL. However, the UL (RW) reaches its global maximum when the PD is 26.2% while the RW for this PD becomes 248.8%. The UL (RW) starts descending for PD inputs higher than 26.2% while, above this level, the EL increases. The EL of defaulted exposures is better approximated by the LGD (=40%) while the UL becomes zero since the exposure has defaulted and the loss is "absolutely (i.e. 100%) expected".

The increase in default rates causes a linear increase in the EL across all rating classes. At the lower end of the rating scale, the EL-to-UL differential is predominant for default rates which correspond to ratings between Caa1-C and "defaulted". The EL is less visible for high-rated corporates as they are not likely to default on its obligations, and thus the EL is close to zero.

The EL becomes more apparent towards the lower ratings as the default becomes gradually expected and thus the EL is high too. On the other hand, the UL drops as we move closer to default since it becomes "less unexpected" for the

(continued)

Box 5.1   (continued)

specific corporate to default and thus the capital which should be set aside for UL is less.

Overall, the UL amount is the RW applicable to the exposure, while the estimated EL corresponds to the provisions and is deductible from the disposable capital before calculating the relevant capital ratio.

Box 5.2   Illustration of the Consecutive Steps for the Estimation of Expected and Unexpected Loss and RW for Various Asset Classes

To isolate the impact of model specification, the example uses the ten-year average corporate default rates of A-rated asset classes after applying the PD floors, where applicable. In other words, the analysis assumes that all asset classes of the same rating or equivalent ratings exhibit the same default rates, which, in our analysis, coincide with the bank's PD estimation. Although this assumption does not necessarily correspond to reality, it is a necessary compromise to isolate the effect of model specification.

Table 5.6 compares the minimum RW, constrained by the PD and/or LGD floors or the supervisory LGD. It presents the RWs of all A-rated types of exposures as described by the latest Basel proposals (BCBS, 2017), that is, PD floors of 0.10% for revolvers and 0.05% for all corporate and retail exposures. In the case of A-rated exposures, the PD floor has no impact as the average (observed) default rate is already above the PD floor.

It also uses standard regulatory inputs for LGD, that is, 40% for debt-related corporates exposures and 90% for equity-related corporate exposures, and maturity of 2.5 years for debt-related corporate exposures and 5 years for equity-related corporate exposures, to estimate the RW for various asset classes.

5.10   Conclusions

The current chapter examined empirically the dynamics of the horizontal transition, that is, to final Basel III assuming the same approach, and the vertical migration, that is, from the final Basel III AIRBA to the final Basel III FIRBA or SA, as well as the diagonal migration, that is, the combination of vertical and horizontal migration. The observed default rates and actual LGD values approximate the input parameters (PD and LGD), rendering the RWs of AIRBA as resembling the economic capital, that is, the capital that could absorb actual losses.

The empirical study showed that the FIRBA underestimates the economic capital of senior unsecured corporate exposures and overestimates the economic capital of the subordinated unsecured corporate exposures. Assuming

Table 5.6 The process of estimating minimum risk weights and comparison of the RW output of different asset classes under the FIRBA (corporate-related) and AIRBA (retail)

Parameter estimation	Corporates and Bank exposures	SME exposures		Specialised Lending (HVCRE)	Retail		
		SME (sales EUR 5.0 million)	SME (sales EUR 27.5 million)		Res. Mortgage	QRRE (reveolvers)	Other retail
Default rates	0.05	0.05	0.05	0.05	0.05	0.10	0.05
Min LGD	0.40	0.40	0.40	0.40	0.40	0.40	0.40
Maturity (M)	2.5	2.5	2.5	2.5	2.5	2.5	2.5
G(0.999)	3.09	3.09	3.09	3.09	3.09	3.09	3.09
G(PD)	−3.29	−3.29	−3.29	−3.29	−3.29	−3.29	−3.29
Correlation—ρ	0.24	0.20	0.22	0.30	0.15	0.04	0.16
SQRT(ρ)	0.49	0.44	0.47	0.54	0.39	0.20	0.40
SQRT(1–ρ)	0.87	0.90	0.88	0.84	0.92	0.98	0.92
N ()	0.02	0.02	0.02	0.03	0.01	0.01	0.01
Maturity adjustment (b)	0.29	0.29	0.29	0.29	0.29	0.25	0.29
f(M)	1.75	1.75	1.75	1.75	1.75	1.59	1.75
UL (K)	0.01	0.01	0.01	0.02	0.00	0.00	0.01
EL	0.00	0.00	0.00	0.00	0.00	0.00	0.00
RW	17.5	13.7	15.5	23.7	1.2	4.8	7.7

that the sample used for observing the default rates and realised LGD is representative of the population, there is evidence that the supervisory LGD for senior unsecured exposures could be revised downwards, while that of the subordinated exposures could be revised upwards.

Moreover, the evolution of the effective LGD of various levels of collateralisation showed that the new collateralisation framework of the FIRBA is more favourable than the respective framework under current Basel III and the final Basel III collateralisation framework that applies to the AIRBA.

Finally, the simulated evolution of the current and final Basel III RWs over time exhibited a significant reduction of the RW variability while the difference between SA and FIRBA appeared reduced under the new set of rules.

Notes

1. The reader could contact the authors to request details on the exact methodology for the estimation of the default rates and LGD inputs.
2. The analysis does not consider the impact of the transition of equity exposures from AIRBA to SA, as it is straightforward and it depends exclusively on banks' individual exposures.
3. Excluding equities which are currently subject to a different regime and migrate to the SA under the final Basel III.
4. The results are subject to the quality of data used but they are indicative of the impact of the structural changes between AIRBA and FIRBA.
5. The data used in this analysis are supposed to be robust enough to reflect the actual impact.

References

Basel Committee on Banking Supervision (BCBS). (2016, March). Reducing variation in credit risk-weighted assets – Constraints on the use of internal model approaches – Consultative document. Retrieved from http://www.bis.org/bcbs/publ/d362.pdf

Basel Committee on Banking Supervision (BCBS). (2017, December). Basel III: Finalising post-crisis reforms – Standards. Retrieved December 7, 2017, from https://www.bis.org/bcbs/publ/d424.pdf

Bonsall, S., Koharki, K., Muller, K., & Sikochi, A. (2017). Credit rating adjustments prior to default and recovery rates. Harvard Business School. Retrieved from http://www.hbs.edu/faculty/conferences/2017-imo/Documents/Siko_BKMS_03_07_17.pdf

Elizondo-Flores, J. A., Lemus-Basualdo, T., & Quintana-Sordo, A. R. (2010). *Regulatory use of system-wide estimations of PD, LGD and EAD 2010.* Financial Stability Institute (FSI) Award 2010 Winning Paper, Bank for International Settlements. Retrieved from http://www.bis.org/fsi/awp2010.pdf

Johnston-Ross, E., & Shibut, L. (2015). *What drives loss given default? Evidence from commercial real estate loans at failed banks.* Federal Deposit Insurance Corporation (FDIC). Centre for Financial Research. Working Paper Series. FDIC CFR WP 2015-03. Retrieved September 2017, from https://www.fdic.gov/bank/analytical/cfr/2015/wp2015/2015-03.pdf

6

Market Risk: Fundamental Review of the Trading Book (FRTB)

The trading book (TB) consists of actively traded positions which are facing financial losses due to the fluctuation of the underlying market risk factors (RFs). Since the latest market risk framework did not adequately capture the severity of such losses, the BCBS proposed a new framework for the estimation of the minimum capital requirements for market risk, also known as the Fundamental Review of the Trading Book (FRTB) framework (BCBS, 2013, 2016a, 2017). The Basel Committee is monitoring the pace of implementation of the market risk standard proposing revisions to address related issues (BCBS, 2018).

The FRTB proposals revise the changes the philosophy for the valuation of market risk under both the standardised approach (SA) and the internal model approach (IMA). The new framework considers market liquidity risk under both approaches, whereas under the advanced IMA it introduces the estimation of the expected shortfall (ES) substituting the value at risk (VaR) as a measure for the assessment of market risk. Furthermore, for the trading desk to be qualified for using IMA, it must pass a profit and loss attribution (PLA) test defined by the new framework. In addition to capital against the exposure to modellable risk factors, the framework recognises an additional capital requirement dedicated to non-modellable risk factors (NMRFs). Also, the new framework fills in the gaps between the treatment of trading and banking book exposures which create regulatory arbitrage, that is, cherry-picking of an approach and interchange of the characterisation of financial instruments with the sole aim to reduce the capital charges arising from market risk exposures. To this end BCBS proposes updated revisions to the boundary between the two books (BCBS, 2018: 35 paras Annex E.2).

© The Author(s) 2018
I. Akkizidis, L. Kalyvas, *Final Basel III Modelling*,
https://doi.org/10.1007/978-3-319-70425-8_6

6.1 The Standardised Approach to Market Risk

The BCBS emphasises on the revisions and implementation of the SA for the TB. Under this approach, banks employ the *sensitivities-based method (SbM)*, the *default risk charge (DRC)*, and the *residual risks add-on (RRAO)* methods for certain risk classes (Fig. 6.1). The SbM framework suggests banks use sensitivity analysis for the estimation of capital charges against *delta*, *vega*, and *curvature risks*.

However, many small banks cannot apply the requirements of the SbM under the SA as it may be difficult or even unnecessary to implement for their portfolios. For those banks, the amount and complexity of classification rules, the requirements for IT resources, and infrastructure for the calculation of the sensitivities, as well as the low degree of TB activities, are factors that prohibit the application of the SbM. Against this background, the BCBS suggested a simpler version of the SbM, based on a list of the fulfilment of a set of criteria (BCBS, 2017: 7 paras 204–207). Once the supervisors verify that banks follow these criteria, the latter could put forward the application of the alternative method (see BCBS, 2017).

For the *DRC*, banks should capture the *jump-to-default (JTD) risk*, based on the instruments' value and the relevant LGD, and the *net JTD*, based on given offsetting rules. They should then weigh and allocate the resulting amount into buckets for the estimation of the end value of the DRC for non-securitisations and securitisations of trading portfolios which are subject to correlations and those which are not subject to correlations.

Also, there is additional capital requirement assigned to the residual risks, that is, the risks beyond the main RFs already taken into account in the SbM and DRC. To this end, banking supervisors should use a simple, but rather conservative, capital treatment which applies to sophisticated trading instruments under residual risks.

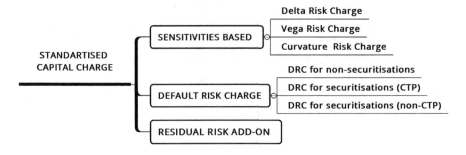

Fig. 6.1 FRTB standardised approaches

All banks should estimate, at least monthly, the regulatory capital requirements of their trading portfolios based on, at least, the SA. The total SA capital charge is simply the aggregation of the capital charge assigned to the SbM, the DRC, and the RRAO. The SA charge is also used as a fall-back, as well as a floor, charge in case any of the desks fail to meet the eligibility criteria to apply the IMA model, outlined in Sect. 6.8; furthermore, banks may monitor the relative calibration and apply the necessary adjustments in the standardised and modelled approaches (BCBS, 2016a: 1 and 58).

6.1.1   Sensitivities-Based Method

The SbM uses the main elements of the former standardised measurement method for market risk, which allowed for the use of sensitivities in some risk treatments within a risk class. Thus, banks should estimate the capital charge by measuring delta and vega sensitivities, as well as calculating curvature risk via *stress scenarios*. The new framework has specified (BCBS, 2016a: 6–8 paras 8–17) the instruments which are subject to delta and vega risks.

Banks could also apply a simplified alternative to the standardised approach (hereafter "the simplified alternative"), which is a reduced version of the sensitivities-based method (R-SbM) depending on the fulfilment of certain eligibility criteria. The R-SbM provides a less demanding framework for those banks that have simpler business models, infrastructures, and TBs. Proportionally to the nature of their portfolios, banks do not need to estimate vega and curvature risks under this method, whereas they have to consider less RFs and correlation scenarios. Furthermore, in addition to the R-SbA the committee proposes a second option of employing the simplified alternative by using a recalibrated version of the Basel II standardised approach (BCBS, 2018). To this end, the bank is recalibrating the Basel II standardised approach by using four multiplication scaling factors applied respectively to the capital requirements in the four risk classes: 1) general and specific interest rate risk, 2) general and specific equity risk, 3) commodity risk, and 4) FX risk.[1] By aggregating the recalibrated capital requirements, banks can estimate the capital requirement under the proposed simplified alternative approach (BCBS, 2018, Annex F: 39 para 3).

6.1.2   Default Risk and Residual Risk Add-On Charges

The DRC refers to the counterparty credit risk of the TB. The exposed banks should estimate DRC separately from the general market risk. The DRC estimation applies to non-securitised and securitised positions in the correlated and non-correlated part of the trading portfolios. To avoid inconsistencies in capital requirements with similar risk exposures across the banking and TB, the SA-DRC aligns with the respective treatment of the banking book. Banks should estimate the DRC for three different risk classes, that is, for non-securitisation positions, securitisation positions subject to correlations, and securitisation positions not subject to correlations.

Also, the new framework imposes an additional capital charge to cope with RFs not captured by the SbM and DRC, which is the RRAO.

6.1.3 Instruments, Valuation, and Hedging

The final Basel III framework defines the new standards relating to the instruments (BCBS, 2016a: 7 paras 12–17) that banks should assign to their trading and banking books. It also sets out the rules which define which of the instruments should or are deemed to be included in or excluded from the TB, as well as the rules governing the switching of instruments from one portfolio to the other. In case banks opt to switch books for an instrument or sets of instruments, then they have to calculate the capital charge before and immediately after the transitions across banking and TBs to evaluate potential capital benefits that would result from such transition. The calculation of the capital charges should also account for adverse economic circumstances to better evaluate whether the banks would benefit from such transitions. The restrictions in the transition between trading and banking books will influence the hedging strategies, as well as the level and composition of exposures of TB portfolios.

On the other hand, banks should value their trading portfolios on a daily basis. The daily valuation of the TB instruments should rely on fair valuation of the TB, rendering any change in the valuation to be reflected in the "profit and loss" (P&L) accounts. Moreover, the calculation of the market risk capital charge allows the use of eligible hedges in the estimation of the credit valuation adjustment capital charge (see Chap. 7).

6.2 Sensitivities-Based Method

The SbM distinguishes the estimation of delta, vega, and curvature sensitivities for the following *risk classes*:

1. General interest rate risk (GIRR),
2. Credit spread risk (CSR) on non-securitisation

3. CSR securitisations correlation trading portfolio (CTP)
4. CSR securitisations (non-CTP)
5. Equity risk (large and small cap)
6. Foreign exchange (FX) risk, and
7. Commodity

As mentioned above, the calculation of SbM capital charge for the TB uses sensitivity measures. Figure 6.2 illustrates the main steps for the estimation of capital charges according to the FRTB framework.

6.2.1 Principles of Sensitivity Measurements

The sensitivity analysis aims at estimating the future value of market RFs when applying certain shocks to their current values. In mathematical terms, as defined in Eq. (6.1), the sensitivity is the first derivative of the value V of a financial instrument with respect to changes of the underlying RF, for example, interest rate.

$$\frac{\partial V^{(\beta)}}{\partial RF} \tag{6.1}$$

The valuation of a financial instrument should, beforehand, take into assumption a valuation method, indicated as factor β (Eq. (6.1)). However, not all

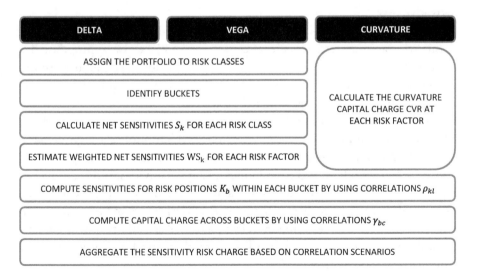

Fig. 6.2 Main steps for the estimation of SbM capital charge

valuation methods are sensitive to RFs only, for example, methods based on time-dependent valuation principles. The appropriate valuation principle for the calculation of a first-order derivative is the mark-to-market (MTM) on a fair value basis.

In the absence of analytical derivatives, banks can measure sensitivities by applying the numerical derivative defined in Eq. (6.2), where the shock on the RF is deterministic applied on two directions, that is, upward and downward shock, which will impact the value depending on the positions against these factors, that is, long or short. The dual shock is particularly useful when used for complex portfolios as it assists banks to evaluate the direction of the impact of a set of shocks which would not be observable with the "naked eye". Also, such method does not require many computational resources.

$$\frac{\Delta V}{\Delta RF_i} = \frac{V\left(FR^+\right) - V\left(FR^-\right)}{RF^+ - RF^-} \qquad (6.2)$$

The first derivative in the sensitivity analysis considers a linear type of relation between the instrument value and RFs. Therefore, an aggregation of all first-order sensitivities for all individual instruments is enough to obtain the sensitivity of the entire portfolio. However, there are cases where the relation between the value and the underlying RF is highly non-linear. Thus, banks should use the second-order derivative to enhance the estimation of the first derivative.

The risk management, in general, assigns a pivotal role to the estimation of sensitivities as they retroactively assess what would be the appropriate TB position that would result in a loss that is affordable for the bank in question. Therefore, the estimation of sensitivities assists banks in setting their trading and position limits. However, banks should strike a balance between precision and performance. To achieve high accuracy, banks have to repeatedly perform a full re-evaluation of their trading portfolio, which implies a high demand for computational resources. Alternatively, less costly in computational resources, but with high precision in measuring sensitivities, is the conduct of an approximate revaluation by using higher-order derivatives, if applicable. The use of a very high order of mathematical derivatives increases the complexity without always resulting in a clear picture of sensitivity measurements. Typically, the use of first- and second-order mathematical derivatives provides a sufficiently good approximation.

6.2.2 Delta and Vega Risks Charge for Trading Books

The SA suggests the estimation of delta and vega risk charges of the TB for the seven *risk classes* mentioned above. For each of these risk classes, banks have to initially aggregate the capital charges within each bucket and then compute the capital requirements across those buckets. Both the weighted delta and vega sensitivities on RFs, as well as the correlation factors, drive the capital charge, albeit in different proportions due to the nature of each TB portfolio.

The estimation of delta (for both SbM and R-SbM) and vega (for SbM only) risk capital charges implies that banks have to perform the following step-by-step identification and calculation methodology:

Step 1. *Assign the instruments to risk classes:* The bank should identify the risk classes associated with the portfolio's instruments. For instance, a portfolio that solely contains financial instruments sensitive to interest rates is entirely assigned to the GIRR risk class.

Step 2. *Identify the buckets:* The bank should specify the buckets associated with the underlying counterparties or exposures of portfolio's instruments. For instance, as explained in Sect. 6.3.1, the underlying currency for the instruments sensitive to interest rates defines the bucket where the counterparties or exposures should be assigned to.

Step 3. *Calculate the net sensitivities S_k for each risk class:* Banks should calculate the net sensitivities (S_k) for each risk class and underlying *RFs* (k) based on the BCBS framework formulae (Sect. 6.2.6).

Step 4. *Estimate the weighted net sensitivities WS_k for each RF:* Banks should calculate the risk weights (RW_k), based on certain classification rules as discussed in Sect. 6.3. The risk-weighted sensitivity (WS_k) is the result of the product of risk weights RW_k and net sensitivities S_k as shown in Eq. (6.3).

$$WS_k = RW_k \cdot S_k \qquad (6.3)$$

Step 5. *Compute sensitivities delta (and vega) risk positions of each bucket:* At each bucket b, the correlation (ρ_{kl}) between two RFs k and l and weighted sensitivities WS_k and WS_l are set by the new framework. Thus, the weighted sensitivities WS_k and correlations ρ_{kl} are used as pre-set elements for the estimation of delta (and vega) risk positions K_b for each bucket b. The formula, shown in Eq. (6.4), calculates the delta (and vega) risk positions K_b of bucket b, which is floored at zero.

$$K_b = \sqrt{\sum_k WS_k^2 + \sum_k \sum_{k \neq l} \rho_{kl} \cdot WS_k \cdot WS_l} \qquad (6.4)$$

Step 6. *Calculate delta (and vega) risk capital charge across all buckets:* Equation (6.5) estimates the total delta capital charge. This formula suggests that the bank has to aggregate the squares of risk positions K for all buckets as computed in step 2. Moreover, the product of all pairs of sensitivities, that is, S_b and S_c, for all RFs in each of the buckets (b and c), is weighted by the correlation across buckets γ_{bc}.

$$\text{Delta}\left(\text{Vega}\right) = \sqrt{\sum_b k_b^2 + \sum_b \sum_{c \neq b} \gamma_{bc} \cdot S_b \cdot S_c} \qquad (6.5)$$

where the sensitivities S_b and S_c of all RFs at bucket levels b and c are estimated[2] by aggregating their corresponding weighted sensitivities, as shown in Eq. (6.6).

$$S_b = \sum_k WS_k \qquad (6.6)$$

The above formulae imply that all of the risk weights (RWs), sensitivities, correlations between weighted sensitivities, and the correlation between sensitivities of different buckets drive the delta and vega risks and thus the capital charge.

6.2.3   Curvature Risk Charge

Apart from delta risk, banks need to capture risks assigned to non-linear instruments, for example, bonds and options. The final Basel III framework approximates the second-order sensitivity of non-linear instruments with the curvature risk. The curvature risk addresses any changes in the price of an option not identified by delta. Regarding capital charges, the curvature is the incremental capital charge atop delta capital charge.

Based on the FRTB framework, banks should estimate the curvature risk charge CVR at each RF level, compute the curvature risk positions at each bucket level, and calculate the risk charge across all buckets using the exact order.

6.2.3.1 Step 1: The Curvature Risk Capital Charge (*CVR*)

In the estimation of curvature risk capital charge of RF k (CVR_k), banks have to take into account the following:

- Calculate the stress prices $V_i\left(x_k^{\left(RW^{(Up)}\right)}\right)$ and $V_i\left(x_k^{\left(RW^{Down}\right)}\right)$ for each instrument *i* and RF *k* starting from the current level of price $V_i(x_k)$, for example, the current spot price of the underlying equity, and apply both upward and downward shocks;
- Subtract from each of the two stressed prices of instrument *i*:
  - The price of the instrument $V_i(x_k)$ resulting from the current level of a single RF *k*; and
  - The curvature risk-weighted $RW_k^{(Base)}$ sensitivity s_{ik} of the instrument *i* for the curvature RF *k*;
- Aggregate the above results for all financial instruments based on the two stress scenarios;
- Obtain the curvature risk capital charges for the two shocks scenarios.

Equation (6.7) illustrates, in mathematical terms, the formula of CVR_k under upward and downward shocks:

$$CVR_k^{Up} = -\left[\sum_i\left\{V_i\left(x_k^{\left(RW^{Up}\right)}\right) - V_i(x_k) - RW_k^{Base} \cdot s_{ik}\right\}\right]$$

$$CVR_k^{Down} = -\left[\sum_i\left\{V_i\left(x_k^{\left(RW^{Down}\right)}\right) - V_i(x_k) - RW_k^{Base} \cdot s_{ik}\right\}\right] \quad (6.7)$$

where $RW_k^{(Base)}$ and s_{ik} are based on the RWs, sensitivities, and correlations applicable to delta sensitivity analysis described in Sect. 6.3.

Specifically, for curvature RF *k* and for instrument *i*:

- s_{ik} is, for FX and equity curvature risk classes, the delta sensitivity of instrument *i* with respect to delta RF that corresponds to curvature RF *k*; while, for other risk classes, it is the sum of delta sensitivities of all tenors of the relevant curve of the instrument *i* with respect to curvature RF *k*.
- $RW_k^{(Base)}$, as defined in Sect. 6.3, equals the respective delta RWs, when considering equity and FX curvature RFs, while it corresponds to the highest delta RW, when considering GIRR, CSR, and commodity curvature RFs and for each risk class.

In case the price depends on several risks factors, banks should estimate the curvature risk charge (CVR_k) for each RF individually.

Equation (6.7) shows that a combined high level of sensitivities, stressed RWs, and the current level of the instrument prices linearly reduces the curvature risk charge. On the other hand, the upward or downward shock in the current level of a price increases or decreases the risk capital charge depending on the underlying position.

6.2.3.2   Step 2: The Curvature Risk Positions Within Each Bucket

The curvature risk position K at each particular bucket[3] b, obtained under the shock scenarios, is estimated (based on the formula defined in Eq. (6.8)) as the root square applied to the greater of:

- The sum of the squared curvature risk charge CVR_k for all curvature RFs k, floored at zero, and the sum of the products or curvature risk charges, correlations, and functions that ensure non-negativity for all pairs of RFs, that is, k and l. Specifically, the above-mentioned product takes into consideration the:

  (a) Curvature risk charges CVR_k and CVR_l,
  (b) Correlations[4] between CVR level for all combinations of RFs, ρ_{kl}, and ρ_{lk},
  (c) Functions $\psi(CVR_k, CVR_l)$ and $\psi(CVR_l, CVR_k)$ which ensure that this aggregation is invalid in cases where both CVRs are negative, that is, the function takes the value 0 when both CVR_k and CVR_l are negative, or 1 in all other cases;

  or
- Zero.

$$\left\{ K_b^{Up} = \sqrt{\max\left(0, \sum_k \max\left[\left(CVR_k^{Up}, 0\right)^2\right] + \sum_k \sum_{k \neq l} \rho_{kl} CVR_k^{Up} CVR_l^{Up} \psi\left(CVR_k^{Up}, CVR_l^{Up}\right)\right)} \right.$$

$$\left\{ K_b^{Down} = \sqrt{\max\left(0, \sum_k \max\left[\left(CVR_k^{Down}, 0\right)^2\right] + \sum_k \sum_{k \neq l} \rho_{kl} CVR_k^{Down} CVR_l^{Down} \psi\left(CVR_k^{Down}, CVR_l^{Down}\right)\right)} \right.$$

$$(6.8)$$

The outer maximum expression of Eq. (6.8) implies that negative aggregations of curvature risk exposures are ignored unless they hedge a positive curvature exposure or vice versa. In case the net curvature risk exposure from an option is negative, the risk charge is zero.

The curvature risk position K at each particular bucket b is the best-case position, that is, the maximum value, of the two scenarios:

$$K_b = \max\left(K_b^{Up}, K_b^{Down}\right)$$

In case, under both scenarios, the curvature risk position K resulting zero, i.e., $K_b^{Up} = K_b^{Down} = 0$, the bank must consider the downward scenario, unless $\sum_k CVR_k^{Up} > \sum_k CVR_k^{Down}$ where the upward scenario is chosen.

6.2.3.3 Step 3: The Curvature Risk Charge Across All Buckets

Similarly, for the delta and vega risks, curvature risk charge must be calculated across all buckets. In the formula provided by the final Basel III framework, as shown in Eq. (6.9), one has to apply the root square of the sum of:

- Squared curvature risk positions summed across all buckets, for example, for two buckets K_b and K_c; and
- Sum within all buckets of the product of:

  (a) Pair sensitivities across buckets, S_b and S_c
  (b) Correlations of sensitivities across buckets, γ_{bc} and γ_{cb}; and
  (c) Functions ψ, that is, $\psi(S_b, S_c)$ and $\psi(S_c, S_b)$, which produce zero in the case where both S_k and S_l are negative, or 1 in all other cases.
  or
  Zero.

$$Curvature\ risk = \sqrt{\max\left(0, + \sum_b K_b^2 + \sum_b \sum_{c \neq b} \gamma_{bc} S_b S_c \psi\left(S_b, S_c\right)\right)} \quad (6.9)$$

The new framework defines the sensitivities of all RFs, at bucket level (b), which is conditionally[5] defined by aggregating their corresponding RF k curvature risk charge (CVR_k) conditional to selected scenarios (Eq. (6.10)).

$$\begin{cases} S_b = \sum_k CVR_k^{Up} & \text{if upward scenario has been selected} \\ S_b = \sum_k CVR_k^{Down} & \text{otherwise} \end{cases} \quad (6.10)$$

As already mentioned, the R-SbM simplifies the SbM described above by excluding the calculation of capital charges relating to curvature risks.

6.2.4 Sensitivity Risk Charge Aggregation Based on Correlation Scenarios

The estimation of delta, vega, and curvature sensitivity risk capital charges (Eqs. (6.5) and (6.9)) uses three scenarios of shocks on the correlations (ρ_{kl}) between RFs within a bucket and cross-bucket correlations (γ_{bc}) within a risk class. The three scenarios, henceforth labelled as high, medium, and low, are the following:

Scenario 1. A shock of high level of correlation parameters ρ_{kl} and γ_{bc} by 25%, that is, applying a multiplication factor of 1.25, with both correlations subject to cup at 100%;

Scenario 2. No shock, that is, unchanged correlation, that is, applying a multiplication factor of 1; and

Scenario 3. A shock of low level of correlation parameters ρ_{kl} and γ_{bc} by 25%, that is, applying a multiplication factor of 0.75. However, based on the Committee's proposed amendments (BCBS, 2018: 15 paras 54(c)) the scenario of low correlations defined by the formulae $\rho_{kl}^{low} = \max(2 \times \rho_{kl} - 100\%; 75\% \times \rho_{kl})$ and $\gamma_{bc}^{low} = \max(2 \times \gamma_{bc} - 100\%; 75\% \times \gamma_{bc})$.

The estimation of the sensitivity risk charge at the portfolio level takes into account the following three steps:

Step 1. The bank has to implement the above three scenarios individually for each risk class to calculate the risk charges accordingly, that is, it should calculate three risk charges for each risk class;

Step 2. A portfolio exposed to risk classes must aggregate the associated risk charges. Thus, the three scenario-based risk charges result in three values of the aggregated portfolio;

Step 3. The highest of the three aggregated values corresponding to the three different scenarios is the recognised capital charge at the portfolio level.

6.2.5 Sensitivity Risk Factors

The SbM provides the following definitions of the RFs.

6.2.5.1   General Interest Rate Risk

For the GIRR

- The GIRR delta risk refers to

    (a) The risk-free yield curves[6] assigned to time vertices[7];
    (b) The flat curve of market-implied inflation rates; and
    (c) The cross-currency basis RFs for each currency.

- The vega risk refers to the implied volatilities of options linked to the GIRR-sensitive underlying instruments. The new framework maps implied volatility to vertices[8] that correspond to the maturity of the option residual maturity of the underlying instruments.
- The curvature risk considers only[9] per currency, risk-free yield curves. Thus, banks should first identify all curves that belong to the same currency and should conduct a parallel shift of the yield curves for all time vertices.

6.2.5.2   Credit Spread Risk Non-Securitisation

The RFs of the CSR of non-securitisation positions are the following:

- In delta risk, the sensitivity to credit spread curves and the vertex which are assigned to;
- In vega risk, the implied volatilities of options exposed to the underlying credit issuer and the vertices which the maturity of the option(s) is assigned to;
- In curvature risk, the underlying issuer credit spread of all instruments linked to the specific issuer. If several instruments link to the same issuer, the same parallel shifts (upward and downward shocks) are applied to all spreads.

6.2.5.3   CSR Securitisation (Non-Correlation Trading Portfolio)

The RFs of securitisation CSR of the non-correlation TB portfolio (non-CTP) are the following:

- The delta RFs are the tranche-specific credit spread curves assigned to time vertex;

- The vega RFs refer to the implied volatilities of options linked to the underlying tranche of non-CTP credit spreads. The new methodology assigns the implied volatilities to the option's maturity vertex[10];
- The curvature RFs refer to the underlying tranche-specific credit spread curves. These credit spread curves are subject to parallel shifts (upward and downward shocks) for all vertices.

6.2.5.4   CSR Securitisation (Correlation Trading Portfolio)

The RFs of the securitisation CSR of the CTP are the following:

- The delta RFs consider the underlying credit spread curves assigned to different time vertices;
- The vega RFs refer to the implied volatilities of options mapped to maturity vertices which link to the CTP credit spreads of the underlying instrument; and
- The curvature RFs refer to the underlying credit spread curves, all the vertices of which are subject to a parallel shift.

6.2.5.5   Equity Risk

Respectively, the equity RFs are the following:

- The estimation of equity delta sensitivity considers the equity spot prices and equity repo rates (only for the SbM);
- The estimation of equity vega refers to the implied volatilities of options of the underlying equity spot prices only.[11] It also assumes the mapping of implied volatilities to the maturity vertices of the option.
- The estimation of the equity curvature risk refers to the equity spot prices only.

6.2.5.6   Commodity Risk

The calculation of commodity RFs takes into consideration the following:

- The delta of commodities RFs refers to the commodity spot prices. Such prices are conditional to the commodity's contract grade,[12] legal terms on the delivery location, and time to maturity[13] of the trade.

- The vega of commodity risk refers to the underlying RF used for the measurement of options' implied volatilities. The new method maps options' implied volatilities to maturity vertices.
- The curvature of commodity risk refers to the spread curve of commodity prices. These curves are subject to a parallel shift of all vertices they are assigned to.

6.2.5.7 Foreign Exchange Risk

Based on the proposed amendments (BCBS, 2018), the delta, vega, and curvature risks of the FX RFs refer to FX rates between the reported currency and the currency of denomination of the instrument as well as any currencies referenced by the instrument. The committee is proposing the allowance for banks to combine two currency liquid pairs resulting in a new FX liquid pair. Thus, a bank can create a liquid instrument that references, for instance, the currency pair EUR/BRL by combining the liquid instruments that reference, in this instance, to currency pairs USD/EUR and USD/BRL. The vega of FX RFs are the implied volatilities of options that reference exchange rates between currency pairs. The method maps options' implied volatilities to one or several maturity vertices.

6.2.6 The Estimation of Sensitivities

6.2.6.1 Delta Sensitivities

The GIRR and CSR deltas consider the change in the market value of the instrument as a result of changes in the risk-free interest rate curve and credit spread curve. Based on the formula provided by the Basel proposals, the GIRR delta includes counterparty credit risk. Similarly, the interest rate is also a parameter in the estimation of CSR delta. Thus, both interest rate and counterparty credit risk drive, at the same time, the level of sensitivity value. Moreover, a deterministic shock is applied as an absolute additive quantity, that is, a change of 0.01% on the risk-free yield curve and credit spread curve applies to the estimation of GIRR and CSR delta.

A similar approach applies for the estimation of the delta of equity delta equity repos where a 0.01% applies to the term structure of equity repo rates. On the other hand, the estimation of the sensitivity of deltas on equity spot, commodity, and FX refers to the value change in equity spot price, commodity spot price, and FX rates, respectively, due to a change in the underlying risk. All sensitivity formulae for the calculation of deltas assume the application of the same shock to shift the RFs, that is, 1%.

6.2.6.2   Vega Sensitivities

The vega risk sensitivity of options is the product of the implied volatility and vega of the option. At the portfolio level, the vega sensitivity is the sum of the above-mentioned vega risk sensitivities across all options of the TB portfolio. Moreover, it is noteworthy that banks are expected to assign the options with no explicit maturity to the vertex with longest prescribed maturity and the add-on for residual risks. Furthermore, the new framework assigns options which have no strike prices and multiple strike prices or are subject to barriers to the add-on for residual risks. In the absence of explicit strike prices and maturities, banks should use the ones applied internally for the valuation of such options. The new framework poses additional requirements for the calculation of vega sensitivities. These requirements refer to the use of the lognormal or normal assumptions for the estimation of GIRR or CSR vega and the use of lognormal assumption for the estimation of equity, commodity, or FX vega.

6.2.6.3   Curvature Sensitivities

Delta sensitivities are the main drivers of the curvature risk. Particularly, as mentioned earlier, the calculation of FX rates and equity spot prices curvature RFs take into account the respective delta sensitivities. The sum of deltas applies to all tenors in respect to (a) the risk-free yield curve for the GIRR risk class, (b) the credit spread curves of the issuer for the CSR non-securitisation risk class, (c) the tranche-specific credit spread curves for the securitisation CSR of non-CTR risk class, (d) the underlying credit spread curves for the securitisation CSR of CTP risk class, and (e) the constructed curve per commodity spot prices for the commodity risk class. As mentioned above, the curvature sensitivity analysis does not apply to FX and equity positions while all vertices of the above risk classes, except for FX and equity risk classes, are shifted in parallel to get the curvature sensitivity. It is noteworthy that the definitions and methodology for the calculation of sensitivities are the same under both SbM and R-SbM.

Table 6.1 shows the parameters and formulae for estimating sensitivities to all risk classes.

Table 6.1 Parameters and formulae for estimating sensitivities of different risk classes (BCBS, 2016a)

Risk class	Parameters	Formulae
GIRR	PV01 r_t risk-free yield curve at vertex t cs_t credit spread curve V_i market value of the instrument as a function of cs_t and r_t	$s_{k,r_t} = \dfrac{V_i(r_t+0.0001,cs_t)-V_i(r_t,cs_t)}{0.0001}$
CSR non-securitisation	CS01	
CSR securitisation (non-CTP, CTP) and nth-to-default		$s_{k,c_t} = \dfrac{V_i(r_t,cs_t+0.0001)-V_i(r_t,cs_t)}{0.0001}$
Delta equity repos	RTS_k repo term structure of equity k V_i market value of the instrument as a function of RTS_k	$s_k = \dfrac{V_i(RTS_k+0.0001)-V_i(RTS_k)}{0.0001}$
Delta equity spot	EQ_k market value of equity k $V_i(EQ_k)$ market value of the instrument as a function of EQ_k	$s_k = \dfrac{V_i(1.01EQ_k)-V_i(EQ_k)}{0.01}$
Delta commodity	CTY_k market value of commodity k $V_i(CTY_k)$ market value of the instrument as a function of CTY_k	$s_k = \dfrac{V_i(1.01CTY_k)-V_i(CTY_k)}{0.01}$
Delta FX	FX_k exchange rate between currency k and the reporting currency $V_i(FX_k)$ market value of the instrument as a function of FX_k	$s_k = \dfrac{V_i(1.01FX_k)-V_i(FX_k)}{0.01}$
Vega RF	Vega v Implied volatility σ_i	$s_k = \left(\dfrac{\partial V}{\partial \sigma}\right)\sigma_i$

6.3   Risk Weights and Correlations on Delta Sensitivities in SbM and R-SbM

The FRTB defines the buckets, the rules and RWs, the correlations between weighted sensitivities, and the correlations on aggregating cross-buckets under both SbM and R-SbM.

6.3.1   Delta GIRR

The FRTB uses the same buckets under both SbM and R-SbM and assigns them to individual currencies. However, there are differences in the applicable elements of RWs and correlations under the SbM and R-SbM. The following section presents these elements under both methods.

6.3.1.1   SbM

The RWs that correspond to GIRR delta refer to the risk-free yield curves which are set along ten different vertices.[14] In view of the proposed amendments (BCBS, 2018), as the vertex increases from a quarter of a year to three years, the RW decreases accordingly (from the range of [1.5–1.9%] to [1.0–1.4%]). On the other hand, the same RW applies to vertex from 5 to 30 years (0.9–1.2%). Moreover, the RW for the inflation risk and the cross-currency basis RFs is set at [1.4–1.8%]. However, the RW can be reduced[15] by up to 30% for selected currencies.[16]

The definition of correlation ρ_{kl} between weighted sensitivities WS_k and WS_l derives from the rules for buckets, vertices, and curves, as illustrated in Table 6.2. The application of the second and third rules of correlation ρ_{kl} is driven by the difference in the vertex that relates to WS_k and WS_l. High differences between weighted sensitivities result in high correlations ρ_{kl}, and vice versa. However, correlation ρ_{kl} is subject to a floor of 40%.

Table 6.2 Correlation (ρ_{kl}) between sensitivities WS_k and WS_l per vertices and risk curves, GIRR delta

Rule	Vertexes T	Curves	Correlation ρ_{kl}
1	Same	Different	99.90%
2	Different T_k and T_l	Same	$\max\left[e^{\left(-3\%\frac{\|T_k-T_l\|}{\min(T_k;T_l)}\right)};40\%\right]$
3	Different	Different	$\max\left[e^{\left(-3\%\frac{\|T_k-T_l\|}{\min(T_k;T_l)}\right)};40\%\right]\times 99.90\%$

6.3.1.2   R-SbM

The RWs that correspond to the GIRR delta under the alternative R-SbM refer to the risk-free yield curves. However, a RW of 5% applies to all vertices. Thus, the RW under this approach is twice as high as the highest RW used in the SbM which implies that the impact from the application of the R-SbM would be at least twice as much as the impact implied by the SbM. Accordingly, the RW for the inflation risk and the cross-currency basis RFs is set at 3%, which implies an increase of 33% arising from the application of the R-SbM in relation to the SbM.

The correlation ρ_{kl} between the weighted sensitivities WS_k and WS_l that refer to yield curves is set at 20%, reducing the recognition of diversification benefits.

6.3.1.3   Provisions Applicable to Both SbM and R-SbM

SbM and R-SbM are subject to the following provisions which are common for both. These provisions are the following:

- The correlations ρ_{kl} between the weighted sensitivities of inflation and yield curves is set at 40%;
- A zero correlation $\rho_{kl} = 0\%$ is applicable between a weighted sensitivity (WS_k) of cross-currency basis curve and the weighted sensitivity (WS_k) to any other GIRR RF;
- The correlation γ_{bc} on aggregating cross-bucket currencies is set at 50%.

Box 6.1   Example of the Estimation of Capital Charge

The current section applies the estimation of capital charges according to the SbM and R-SbM methodologies described earlier. The following example considers a bank which is based in the Euro area and holds a portfolio comprising three assets:

Asset 1. a three-year maturity corporate bond with a modified duration of 2.8, denominated in USD;

Asset 2. a one-year maturity government bond with a modified duration of 0.999, denominated in USD; and

Asset 3. a six-year maturity corporate bond with a modified duration of 5.7, denominated in EUR.

(continued)

Box 6.1   (continued)

The bank would like to estimate the capital charges which result from the new FRTB-SA for market risk by using SbM and the reduced-form SA by applying the R-SbM. The estimation of delta and vega risks capital charges follow the steps discussed in Sect. 6.2.2 as analytically presented below.

1. The first three assets are interest rate sensitive, and therefore they fall under the GIRR risk class.
2. Based on bucket definition of GIRR delta, the two currencies, that is, USD and EUR, define two buckets, b_1 and b_2, respectively.
3. Considering the modified duration of the instruments, the bank identifies the sensitivities S_k denominated to USD and EUR.
4. By knowing the instruments' maturity, the bank identifies the risk weights RW_k using the combination of vertices and RWs defined by the framework for both SbM[14] and R-SbM (5%). The weighted sensitivities WS_k for each S_k is estimated by using Eq. (6.3).
5. For each of the buckets

   - the correlations ρ_{kl} and ρ_{lk} between the two weighted sensitivities WS_k and WS_l, derive from the rules defined in Table 6.2;
   - the calculation of the products of the weighted sensitivities, that is, $WS_k \times WS_l$ and $WS_l \times WS_k$, follows; and
   - the aggregation of all combinations of the product between correlation and corresponding weighted sensitivities, that is, $\sum_k \sum_{k \neq l} \rho_{kl} \times WS_k \times WS_l$, should be calculated.

The weighted sensitivities of both buckets, b_1 and b_2 should be first squared and then aggregated, that is, $\sum_k WS_k^2$. The above estimations enable the bank to calculate delta (and vega) risk positions K_{b1} and K_{b2}, for each bucket b_1 and b_2, as defined in Eq. (6.4).

6. All delta risk positions K_{b1} and K_{b2} should then be squared and aggregated, that is, $\sum_b k_b^2$.

The use of Eq. (6.6) enables the bank to estimate[17] the sensitivities of all RFs for both buckets b_2 and b_2. Under both SbM and R-SbM, in delta GIRR, the correlation across buckets γ_{bc} is set at 50%. The product of all sensitivities, that is, $S_b \times S_c$, must be weighted by the bucket correlation (γ_{bc}) and then aggregated for all buckets, that is, $\sum_b \sum_{c \neq b} \gamma_{bc} \times S_b \times S_c$.

The bank calculates the delta (and vega) risk capital charge across all buckets by applying the formula defined in Eq. (6.5).

Table 6.3 illustrates the results of the estimation of the parameters described in the example above. The resulting risk capital charge of the three-asset portfolio above is four to five times higher when applying the R-SbM in relation to the SbM. Notably, using the RW of the current framework (BCBS, 2016), the capital charge is 0.105. In this example, however, the new proposed amendments (BCBS, 2018) of RWs are taken into account, resulting in a delta capital charge within the range of 0.062 to 0.084 allowing, therefore, reduction benefit in capital charge from 40% to 20%.

Table 6.3 Results on different parameters used for estimating capital charge

		Asset 1	Asset 2	Asset 3
Risk class		GIRR		
Bucket		b_1(USD)		b_2(EUR)
Sensitivities		$S_k = 2.8$	$S_l = 0.999$	$S_m = 5.7$
Vertex		3Y	1Y	10Y
RWs[a]	SbM	$RW_k = [1.0–1.4\%]$	$RW_l = [1.4–1.8\%]$	$RW_m = [0.9–1.2\%]$
	R-SbM	$RW_k = 5\%$	$RW_l = 5\%$	$RW_m = 5\%$
Weighted sensitivities	SbM	$WS_k = [0.028–0.039]$	$WS_l = [0.014–0.018]$	$WS_m = [0.051–0.068]$
	R-SbM	$WS_k = 0.14$	$WS_l = 0.0499$	$WS_m = 0.285$
Corrections[b] ρ	SbM	$\rho_{kl} = 0.9408$	$\rho_{lk} = 0.9408$	N/A
	R-SbM	$\rho_{kl} = 0.2$	$\rho_{lk} = 0.2$	N/A
Product of weighted sensitivities	SbM	$WS_k \cdot WS_l = [0.0004–0.0007]$	$WS_l \cdot WS_k = [0.0004–0.0007]$	N/A
	R-SbM	$WS_k \cdot WS_l = 0.007$	$WS_l \cdot WS_k = 0.007$	N/A
Aggregated squared weighted sensitivities $\sum_k WS_k^2$	SbM	$WS_k^2 + WS_l^2 = [0.00098–0.00186]$		$WS_m^2 = [0.0026–0.0047]$
	R-SbM	$WS_k^2 + WS_l^2 = 0.0221$		$WS_m^2 = 0.0812$
Risk positions of a bucket	SbM	$k_{b1} = [0.041–0.057]$		$k_{b2} = [0.0026–0.0047]$
	R-SbM	$k_{b1} = 0.1577$		$k_{b2} = 0.0812$
Aggregated risk positions $\sum_b k_b^2$	SbM	$k_{b1} + k_{b2} = [0.044–0.061]$		
	R-SbM	$k_{b1} + k_{b2} = 0.239$		
Sensitivities of all RFs	SbM	$S_{b1} = [0.042–0.057]$		$S_{b2} = [0.051–0.068]$
	R-SbM	$S_{b1} = 0.19$		$S_{b2} = 0.285$
Product of sensitivities	SbM	$S_{b1} \cdot S_{b2} = [0.0022–0.0039]$		$S_{b2} \cdot S_{b1} = [0.0022–0.0039]$
	R-SbM	$S_{b1} \cdot S_{b2} = [0.054]$		$S_{b2} \cdot S_{b1} = [0.054]$
Buckets' correlation γ_{bc}		$\gamma_{b1b2} = 0.5$		
Capital charge	SbM	Delta Capital Charge = [0.062–0.084]		
	R-SbM	Delta Capital Charge = 0.29		

[a]RW for the SbM as proposed by the amendments of BCBS, 2018
[b]Based on rule number 3, defined in Table 6.2

6.3.2   Delta CSR Non-Securitisations

6.3.2.1   SbM

The new framework assigns the RWs[18] of CSR delta of non-securitisations to one of the 16 buckets[19] that correspond to investment grade (IG) and high-yield and non-rated (HY&NR) categories of the various sectors of the economy. The first eight buckets refer to exposures to sectors with IG credit quality. The additional seven buckets refer to exposures to the same sectors[20] which have HY&NR. The last bucket is allocated to "other sectors" irrespective of their credit quality.

The correlation parameter among sensitivities WS_k and WS_l, ρ_{kl}, within the same sector bucket, is defined as the product of three sub-correlation parameters, that is, $\rho_{kl} = \rho_{kl}^{(\text{name})} \times \rho_{kl}^{(\text{tenor})} \times \rho_{kl}^{(\text{basis})}$, and their values are based on definitions provided by the BCBS (Table 6.4). It is worth noting that curvature risk and the delta of exposures belonging to the last bucket ("other sectors" not explicitly defined) do not account for the correlation parameter (ρ_{kl}).

The cross-bucket correlation of sensitivities is the product of the two sub-correlation parameters, that is, $\gamma_{bc} = \gamma_{bc}^{(\text{rating})} \times \gamma_{bc}^{(\text{sector})}$, where their values rely on whether the buckets belong or not to the same rating category, sector, or combination of buckets[21] set by the new framework (Table 6.5).

6.3.2.2   R-SbM

The new framework reduces the buckets assigned to sensitivities or risk exposures to six under the R-SbM, and thus the sectors are explicitly assigned to a bucket,[22] while sectors are still allocated between two credit quality categories, that is, IG and HY&NR. The first three buckets are assigned to IG while the last three to HY&NR. The RWs set to those buckets depend on the sectors'[23] classification and range between 1% and 15% for IG and 5% and 30% for HY&NR.

When considering exposures within the same bucket, the new proposals assign a 100% correlation $(\rho_{kl} = 1)$ between sensitivities WS_k and WS_l. However, in case that either the sector or the rating of sensitivities is the same then the correlation is set at 35%. The degree of correlation (γ_{bc}) between different buckets depends on the pair of bucket combination.[24]

Table 6.4 The level of sub-correlation for the estimation of correlation between sensitivities of k and l, of CSR delta of securitisations and non-securitisations, CSR delta of securitisation (non-CTP), commodity risks, applied under SbM

Risk	Correlation	Degree	Condition
Delta CSR securitisations and non-securitisations	$\rho_{kl}^{(name)}$	1	Names of sensitivities k and l are identical
		35%	Otherwise
	$\rho_{kl}^{(tenor)}$	1	Vertices of sensitivities k and l are identical
		65%	Otherwise
	$\rho_{kl}^{(basis)}$	1	Sensitivities k and l are related to same curves
		99, 90%	Otherwise
Delta CSR securitisation (non-CTP)	$\rho_{kl}^{(tranche)}$	1	Names of sensitivities k and l related to the same securitisation tranche
		40%	Otherwise
	$\rho_{kl}^{(tenor)}$	1	Vertices of sensitivities k and l are identical
		80%	Otherwise
	$\rho_{kl}^{(basis)}$	1	Sensitivities k and l are related to same curves
		99, 90%	Otherwise
Commodity	$\rho_{kl}^{(cty)}$	1	Two commodities of sensitivities k and l are identical
		Based on assigned bucket[a]	Intra-bucket correlations
	$\rho_{kl}^{(tenor)}$	1	Vertices of sensitivities k and l are identical
		99%	Otherwise
	$\rho_{kl}^{(basis)}$	1	Sensitivities k and l are identical[b]
		99, 90%	Otherwise

[a]The degrees of sensitivities correlation parameter assigned to the 11 buckets {1, ..., 11} are 55%, 95%, 40%, 80%, 60%, 65%, 55%, 45%, 15%, 40%, and 15%, respectively
[b]Identical in both (1) contract grade of the commodity and (2) delivery location of a commodity

Table 6.5 The sub-correlations for the estimation of cross-bucket correlation (γ_{bc}) (CSR non-securitisations delta)

	Degree	Condition
$\gamma_{bc}^{(rating)}$	1	Buckets b and c having same rating category
	50%	Otherwise
$\gamma_{bc}^{(sector)}$	1	Buckets b and c having same sector
	Matrix defining buckets' combination	Otherwise

6.3.3   CSR Delta of Securitisations (CTP)

The FRTB defines the buckets, RWs, and correlations of the CSR delta of securitisations in the same way as for non-securitisations. However, it suggests the adjustment of RWs and correlations to align them with longer liquidity horizons and larger basis risk.

The RWs are again assigned to 16 buckets,[25] while for estimating the correlation between sensitivities (ρ_{kl}) banks have to follow the same approach as in CSR delta of non-securitisations. In case, however, that the two sensitivities do not refer to identical curves the correlation of the basis risk ($\rho_{kl}^{(\text{basis})}$) equals 99.9%, while in any other case it equals unity. For the definition of correlation between buckets, γ_{bc}, the CSR deltas follow exactly the same approach followed under the CSR delta of non-securitisations.

6.3.4   Delta CSR Securitisations (Non-CTP)

6.3.4.1   SbM

For the CSR delta of securitisations of the non-CTP, the FRTB defines 24 buckets, divided into three groups differentiated by the credit quality, plus one more bucket, and assigns each of the 8 buckets of the three groups to a specific sector bucket.[26] Moreover, banks have to assign each tranche of the securitisation products to one of the sector buckets. However, should they not be able to assign some tranches to sectors they should assign them to the 25th bucket ("other sector") that acts as the pool of all unassigned exposures.

As briefly mentioned above, the credit quality differentiates the three groups of buckets. These groups are flagged as "senior investment grade" (SIG), "non-senior investment grade" (NSIG), and HY&NR, respectively, while the 25th bucket is not assigned or characterised by any credit quality attributes. As indicated above, the first group (SIG) has the highest credit quality amongst the three and thus receives the lowest RWs, spanning from 0.9% to 1.4%.[27] The scaling up of the same RWs by multiplication factors of 1.25 and 1.75 produces the buckets assigned to the second and third groups, respectively. The last bucket receives a RW of 3.5%.

The correlation between sensitivities WS_k and WS_l of the same sector bucket (ρ_{kl}) is the product of three sub-correlation parameters, that is, $\rho_{kl} = \rho_{kl}^{(\text{tranche})} \times \rho_{kl}^{(\text{tenor})} \times \rho_{kl}^{(\text{basis})}$, which are respectively the correlations assigned between the tranches, between the tenors, and between different basis risks. The correlation assigned to the "other sectors" bucket is zero while there is no diversification or hedging effects recognised between this bucket and any of the others. The full set of correlations is shown in Table 6.4.

6.3.4.2 R-SbM

The R-SbM reduces the number of the buckets to 12, divided into three groups based on their credit quality.[28] As in the SbM, a sector[29] is assigned to each of the four buckets of the three-bucket groups. Each tranche must be assigned to one of these sector buckets. For all 12 buckets, the FRTB sets a specific RW ranging from 2% to 17.5%.[30] In cases where two names of sensitivities k and l are associated with the same bucket and securitisation tranche, the correlation (ρ_{kl}) between the corresponding weighted sensitivities WS_k and WS_l is set at 100%, whereas in any other case it is set at 40%. The correlation (γ_{bc}) of integrating sensitivities between different buckets is set at 0% under both SbM and R-SbM.

6.3.5 Equity Risk

6.3.5.1 SbM

The equity risk refers to equity spot prices and equity repo rates. The SbM defines ten buckets classified according to:

- Size: there are two different categories of sizes,[31] defined according to the market capitalisation, that is, large market capitalisation and small market capitalisation. The large market capitalisation categories are split into eight buckets (1–8) while the small market capitalisation categories into two buckets (9–10).
- Types of economy: there are two types of economy, allocated according to their strength: emerging markets and advanced markets.[32] In turn, there are five buckets assigned to each type of the economy, that is, emerging markets associate with buckets 1–4 and 9 and advanced economies with buckets 5–8 and 10 (see the allocation of sectors below).
- Sector: there are four sector groups[33] associated with the buckets, that is, sectors that belong to the same bucket, which are allocated to different combinations of market capitalisation and economy.

There is also an 11th bucket ("other sector") which acts as a pool of unassigned exposures, that is, risk positions that are not assigned to the first 10 buckets/sectors. All 11 buckets are classified according to market capitalisations, types of economies, and sectors' groups. There are two scales of RWs, based on the sensitivities to equity spot prices and equity repo rates, assigned[34] to these buckets.

Within the same bucket, the correlation between two weighted sensitivities WS_k and WS_l is shown in Table 6.6. In case where both sensitivities are correlated to equity spot price (ρ_{kl}^s) or to equity repo rate (ρ_{kl}^r), the bucket drives the level of correlation. The buckets allocated to large market capitalisation of advanced economies have the highest correlation $\rho_{kl}^s = \rho_{kl}^r = 25\%$, whereas bucket 9 allocated to small market cap of emerging market economies has the lowest correlation ($\rho_{kl}^s = \rho_{kl}^r = 7.5\%$). However, if sensitivity of k is correlated to equity spot price and l to equity repo and the equity issuer name is the same in both, the correlation is 99.90 ($\rho_{kl}^{sr} = 99.90$); whereas if the equity issuer name is different the correlation is $\rho_{kl}^{sr} = \rho_{kl}^s \times 99.90\%$ or $\rho_{kl}^{sr} = \rho_{kl}^r \times 99.90\%$. Finally, the correlation is zero for the bucket of "other sector".

6.3.5.2   R-SbM

The R-SbM considers only the equity spot price and a reduced number of buckets to six. As in the case of SbM, the six buckets are classified according to their market capitalisation (large market cap: buckets 1–4; small market caps: buckets 5 and 6), type of the economy (emerging markets:

Table 6.6 The correlation between sensitivities k and l (ρ_{kl}) of equity risks

Risk	Correlation	Degree	Condition
Equity			Sensitivity k correlated to equity spot price AND l to equity repo rate
	ρ_{kl}^{sr}	99, 90%	Names of equity issuer is identical
		$\rho_{kl}^s \times 99.90\%$	Names of equity issuers are different
	$\rho_{kl}^s,\ \rho_{kl}^r$	Otherwise	Both sensitivities k and l are correlated to equity spot price OR to equity repo rate
		15%	Falling under large market cap, emerging market economy (buckets {1,..,4})
		25%	Falling under large market cap, advanced economy (buckets {5,..,8})
		7.5%	Falling under small market cap, emerging market economy (bucket {9})
		12.5%	Falling under small market cap, advanced economy (bucket {10})

buckets 1, 2, and 5; advanced economy: 3, 4, and 6), and group of sectors[35] associated to buckets. Each of the six buckets is associated to the RWs for equity spot price, ranging from 40% to 70%.[36] The correlation ρ_{kl} among two weighted sensitivities WS_k and WS_l, where the two names of sensitivities k and l are associated to the same bucket, is set[37] based on the bucket number.

6.3.5.3 SbM and R-SbM

The SbM and R-SbM necessitate banks to use the sector where the equity issuer (or grouping issuers) operates in. If, however, an issuer belongs to a multinational group of companies that holds other companies which operate in several sectors, the allocation should reflect the region and sector that the group operates the most. Finally, the correlation of integrating sensitivities amongst all buckets (γ_{bc}) is set at 15%.

6.3.6 Commodity Risk

6.3.6.1 SbM

The RWs of commodity risk[38] are assigned to 11 commodity bucket categories according to the related sector.[39] The correlation ρ_{kl} between sensitivities WS_k and WS_l within the same sector bucket is the product of three sub-correlation parameters, that is, $\rho_{kl} = \rho_{kl}^{(\text{cty})} \times \rho_{kl}^{(\text{tenor})} \times \rho_{kl}^{(\text{basis})}$. The value of such sub-correlations is set according to conditions shown in Table 6.4.

6.3.6.2 R-SbM

As in the case of SbM, there are 11 commodity buckets associated with commodity categories, according to the industry they belong to, which receive RWs ranging from 30% to 90%.[40]

When the correlated commodities are identical, the correlation between their weighted sensitivities WS_k and WS_l is 1 (ρ_{kl}). On the other hand, when commodities are not the same, the correlation ρ_{kl} is set according to the bucket that it belongs to, ranging from 15% to 95%.[41]

Under both SbM and R-SbM, the cross-bucket correlation (γ_{bc}) between buckets belonging to the 1st to 10th is set at 20%, while the correlation of any of the first 10 buckets with the 11th bucket is assumed to be zero.

6.3.7   Foreign Exchange Risk

The RW assigned to FX sensitivities or risk exposures under the SbM is modified from 30% (BCBS, 2016a), to the range of [15–22%] based on the later proposed amendments (BCBS, 2018) except for the currency pairs specified by the BCBS[42] as well as those establishing first-order crosses across the specified currency pairs (BCBS, 2018), for which the RW becomes $(15-22)\% / \sqrt{2}$. The respective RW assigned under the R-SbM is 45%, which applies to all FX net sensitivities. Again, the RW for specific FX currency pairs is reduced to 32%. The cross-bucket correlation (γ_{bc}), under both SbM and R-SbM, is set at 60%.

Box 6.2   Example of the Estimation of Capital Charge for the Foreign Exchange Risk

The following example considers a Euro area reporting bank that holds a portfolio comprising two foreign currency-exposed assets:

Asset 1. a corporate bond with a market value of 300, denominated in USD; and
Asset 2. a government bond with a market value of 150, denominated in GBP.

Let us assume that at time t the EUR/USD and EUR/GBP rates equal to 0.81 and 1.14, respectively.

The capital charges against FX risk at time t are estimated as presented below:

1. Both asset 1 and asset 2 fall under the FX risk class. The delta sensitivities for the EUR/USD and EUR/GBP FX risk classes are denoted as $S_{k,\,USD}$ and $S_{k,\,GBP}$ and are computed as defined in Table 6.1, by taking the value of a 1 percentage point change in exchange rate, divided by 1%, that is,

$$S_{k,\,EUR} = \frac{300\times(1.01\times0.81)-300\times0.81}{0.01} = 243\,EUR \quad \text{and}$$

$$S_{k,\,GBP} = \frac{150\times(1.01\times1.14)-150\times1.14}{0.01} = 171\,EUR.$$

2. A risk weight RW_k of [15–22%] and 45% under the SbM and the R-SbM apply, respectively, to all FX sensitivities. However, for the specified EUR/USD and EUR/GBP liquid currency pairs, the RW_k may, at the discretion of the bank, be divided by the square root of 2. Applying Eq. (6.3) the weighted sensitivities WS_k under SbM are $WS_{k,\,USD} = RW_k \times S_{k,\,USD} = \dfrac{15\%}{\sqrt{2}} \times 243 = 25.8\,EUR$,

---

(continued)

> **Box 6.2   (continued)**
>
> and $WS_{k, GBP}$ = 18.1 *EUR* when *RW* = 15%, whereas $WS_{k, USD}$ = 37.8 *EUR*, and $WS_{k, GBP}$ = 26.6 *EUR* when *RW* = 22%; moreover under R-SbM they are $WS_{k, USD} = RW_k \cdot S_{k, USD}$ = 32 % · 243 = 77.8 *EUR*, and $WS_{k, GBP}$ = 54.7 *EUR*.
> 3. The risk positions K_b equals to WS_k should then be squared and aggregated, that is, $\sum_b K_b^2$, and used in the risk charge as defined in Eq. (6.5). In both SbM and R-SbM, a uniform correlation parameter γ_{bc} = 60% applies to the product of sensitivities, that is, $S_{k, USD} \cdot S_{k, GBP}$ and it is then aggregated for all buckets, that is, $\sum_b \sum_{c \neq b} \gamma_{bc} \cdot S_b \cdot S_c$. Under SbM the
>
> $$Risk\ charge = \sqrt{25.8^2 + 18.1^2 + 2 \times 0.6 \times 25.8 \times 18.1} = 39.4\ EUR, \text{ and } Risk\ charge = 57.8$$
>
> *EUR* when the *RW* of 15% and 22% apply respectively whereas based on R-SbM the *Risk charge* = 118.9 *EUR*.

6.4   Risk Weights and Correlations Assigned to Vega

The assessment of vega risk uses the same buckets as delta risk. For a vega RF k, the risk weight RW_k is expressed by Eq. (6.11) as the lower of:

- the volatility risk weight (RW_σ) multiplied by the ratio of the square root of liquidity horizon (LH) applied to the particular risk class ($LH_{\text{risk class}}$) and divided by the root square of 10; or
- 100%.

$$RW_k = \min \left[RW_\sigma \times \frac{\sqrt{LH_{\text{risk class}}}}{\sqrt{10}}; 100\% \right] \qquad (6.11)$$

The new framework sets the volatility RW at 55%, that is, RW_σ = 55 %, and uses the ten-day liquidity horizon as a scaling factor to ensure that the capital is in line with the granularity of liquidity horizons specified in internal models. It also assigns eight liquidity horizons[43] to the respective number of different risk classes ($LH_{\text{risk class}}$). The risk classes are identical to the ones used in delta sensitivity analysis.

The above formulation implies that a high *LH* that corresponds to a RF results in a high RW. The highest LH is attributed to all kinds of credit risk spread and commodity risks classes whilst the lowest *LH* is assigned to equity risk class with small market capitalisations. Notably, only the lowest market liquidity risk horizon, that is, $LH_{\text{Equity (large cap)}} = 20$, results in a RW below 100%, that is, $RW_k = 77.7\%$. All other liquidity horizons associated with the remaining risk classes exceed the floor of 100% defined in Eq. (6.11). In fact, any market liquidity risk horizon beyond 33 days ($LH > 33$) will result in a vega RW above 100%.

Under the new framework, banks should estimate two vega risk correlation parameters: the correlations between vega risk sensitivities within the same bucket for the GIRR risk class and the non-GIRR risk classes. The former is shown by Eq. (6.12) and is the lower of:

- The product of two sub-correlations $\rho_{kl}^{(\text{option maturity})}$ and $\rho_{kl}^{(\text{underlying maturity})}$; or
- One.

$$\rho_{kl} = \min\left[\rho_{kl}^{(\text{option maturity})} \times \rho_{kl}^{(\text{underlying maturity})}; 1\right] \tag{6.12}$$

where

$$\rho_{kl}^{(\text{option maturity})} = e^{-a \cdot \frac{|T_k - T_l|}{\min\{T_k;\, T_l\}}} \qquad \rho_{kl}^{(\text{underlying maturity})} = e^{-a \cdot \frac{|T_k^U - T_l^U|}{\min\{T_k^U;\, T_l^U\}}} \tag{6.13}$$

The latter is shown by Eq. (6.14) and is the lower of:

- The product of two sub-correlations $\rho_{kl}^{(\text{delta})}$ and $\rho_{kl}^{(\text{option maturity})}$; or
- One.

$$\rho_{kl} = \min\left[\rho_{kl}^{(\text{delta})} \times \rho_{kl}^{(\text{underlying maturity})}; 1\right] \tag{6.14}$$

It is obvious that the three sub-correlations drive the formulation of correlation ρ_{kl}. The $\rho_{kl}^{(\text{option maturity})}$ rely on an exponential function e of a weighting factor $a = 1\%$ and the maturities (in years) of the options T_k and T_l. Similarly, the $\rho_{kl}^{(\text{underlying maturity})}$ rely on an exponential function e of a weighting factor $a = 1\%$ and the maturities of the underlying asset T_k^U and T_l^U. This implies that when maturities match, both sub-correlations equal 100%; otherwise, the sub-correlations reduce exponentially with the increase of the mismatch. Hence, maturity mismatches increase the correlation factor and, thus, the capital charge exponentially.

The third correlation corresponds to delta correlation, that is, $\rho_{kl}^{(\text{delta})}$, and provides evidence on the link between the vega of the underlying RFs k and l

of the options in question. The level of this correlation equals that of the respective delta RF. For instance, an equity option of an advanced economy and small market capitalisation, which is assigned to bucket 10, has a delta correlation of 50%, that is, $\rho_{kl}^{(DELTA)} = 50\%$. The cross-bucket correlation (γ_{bc}), used for the integration of vega risk sensitivities across buckets within the same risk class, is exactly the same as the delta correlations of the risk class in question.

Box 6.3   Example for Vega Correlations of a Portfolio Exposed to GIRR Risk

The present example refers to vega correlations of a portfolio exposed to GIRR risk. Banks should use Eq. (6.13) to estimate the correlations $\left(\rho_{kl}^{(option\ maturity)}\right)$ between weighted vega risk sensitivities that refer to seven different option maturities, i.e., 0.2, 0.3, 0.5, 0.75, 0.8, 0.9 and 1Y; moreover, to estimate the weighted vega risk sensitivities $\left(\rho_{kl}^{(underlying\ maturity)}\right)$ that refer to seven different maturities, i.e., 0.3, 0.5, 1.2, 1.5, 2, 2.7 and 3Y, for the underlying asset maturities of the options. Table 6.7 presents the results of these calculations.

The covariance matrix (ρ_{kl}) of correlations referring to maturities of options and maturities of the underlying assets of options (Eq. (6.12)) are illustrated in Table 6.7. Assuming $RW_k = 100\%$, the matrix of ρ_{kl}, and the vega sensitivities for the different maturities (Table 6.8) banks can estimate (using Eq. (6.4)) the vega risk positions K_b for each bucket as illustrated in Table 6.8. It is noteworthy that under the SA, vega and delta risk charges are aggregated without considering any diversification or hedging benefits between vega and delta RFs.

6.5   Building Blocks for Analysing the Impact of Parameters on Capital Charge

The main elements that affect the level of capital charge are the value of sensitivities, the buckets where the assets belong to, the correlations between weighted sensitivities (ρ_{kl}), and the cross-bucket correlations (γ_{bc}). The optimisation of the above elements would optimise the minimum capital charges that a bank is subject to, but would also affect the portfolio structure. The following paragraphs discuss the evolution of capital charge that results from the performance of the above-mentioned elements.

Assume a portfolio that contains assets that belong to either bucket 1 (b_1) or bucket 2 (b_2) and that 50% of assets of this portfolio has high sensitivities and corresponds to b_1, whereas the remaining 50% has low sensitivities and corresponds to b_2. Banks can estimate the impact on a capital charge, resulting from the combinations of buckets, sensitivities, and correlation, as defined under the different risk classes.

Table 6.7 Correlation matrix of weighted vega sensitivities for seven different option maturities ($T_{k(1)}$ to $T_{k(7)}$), $\rho_{kl}^{(option\,maturity)}$, and of weighted vega sensitivities for seven underlying maturities, ($T_{k(1)}^U$, $T_{k(7)}^U$), $\rho_{kl}^{(underlying\,maturity)}$, and the matrix of correlations ρ_{kl} for different combinations of the above mentioned seven maturities

$\rho_{kl}^{(option\,maturity)}$

	$T_{k(1)}$ 0.2	$T_{k(2)}$ 0.3	$T_{k(3)}$ 0.5	$T_{k(4)}$ 0.75	$T_{k(5)}$ 0.8	$T_{k(6)}$ 0.9	$T_{k(7)}$ 1
$T_{l(1)}$ 0.1	99.00%	98.02%	96.08%	93.71%	93.24%	92.31%	91.39%
$T_{l(2)}$ 0.25	99.75%	99.80%	99.00%	98.02%	97.82%	97.43%	97.04%
$T_{l(3)}$ 0.4	99.00%	99.67%	99.80%	99.53%	99.50%	99.45%	99.40%
$T_{l(4)}$ 0.65	97.78%	98.84%	99.70%	99.87%	99.81%	99.72%	99.65%
$T_{l(5)}$ 0.7	97.53%	98.68%	99.60%	99.93%	99.86%	99.71%	99.57%
$T_{l(6)}$ 0.82	96.95%	98.28%	99.36%	99.91%	99.98%	99.90%	99.78%
$T_{l(7)}$ 0.9	96.56%	98.02%	99.20%	99.80%	99.88%	100.00%	99.89%

$\rho_{kl}^{(underlying\,maturity)}$

	$T_{k(1)}^U$ 0.3	$T_{k(2)}^U$ 0.5	$T_{k(3)}^U$ 1.2	$T_{k(4)}^U$ 1.5	$T_{k(5)}^U$ 2	$T_{k(6)}^U$ 2.7	$T_{k(7)}^U$ 3
$T_{k(1)}^U$ 0.2	99.50%	98.51%	95.12%	93.71%	91.39%	88.25%	86.94%
$T_{k(2)}^U$ 0.27	99.89%	99.15%	96.61%	95.55%	93.79%	91.39%	90.38%
$T_{k(3)}^U$ 0.9	98.02%	99.20%	99.70%	99.40%	98.90%	98.21%	97.91%
$T_{k(4)}^U$ 1.3	96.72%	98.41%	99.90%	99.80%	99.30%	98.61%	98.31%
$T_{k(5)}^U$ 1.8	95.12%	97.43%	99.50%	99.80%	99.89%	99.50%	99.34%
$T_{k(6)}^U$ 2.2	93.86%	96.66%	99.17%	99.53%	99.90%	99.77%	99.64%
$T_{k(7)}^U$ 2.5	92.93%	96.08%	98.92%	99.34%	99.75%	99.92%	99.80%

$$\rho_{kl} = \min\left[\rho_{kl}^{(option\,maturity)} \times \rho_{kl}^{(underlying\,maturity)},\ 1\right]$$

	$T_{l(1)}, T_{k(1)}^U$	$T_{l(2)}, T_{k(2)}^U$	$T_{l(3)}, T_{k(3)}^U$	$T_{l(4)}, T_{k(4)}^U$	$T_{l(5)}, T_{k(5)}^U$	$T_{l(6)}, T_{k(6)}^U$	$T_{l(7)}, T_{k(7)}^U$
$T_{l(1)}, T_{k(1)}^U$	98.51%	96.56%	91.39%	87.81%	85.21%	81.46%	79.45%
$T_{l(2)}, T_{k(2)}^U$	99.64%	98.95%	95.65%	93.65%	91.75%	89.05%	87.71%
$T_{l(3)}, T_{k(3)}^U$	97.04%	98.87%	99.50%	98.94%	98.41%	97.66%	97.32%
$T_{l(4)}, T_{k(4)}^U$	94.57%	97.27%	99.60%	99.67%	99.12%	98.33%	97.97%
$T_{l(5)}, T_{k(5)}^U$	92.77%	96.14%	99.10%	99.73%	99.75%	99.22%	98.91%
$T_{l(6)}, T_{k(6)}^U$	91.00%	95.00%	98.54%	99.44%	99.88%	99.68%	99.42%
$T_{l(7)}, T_{k(7)}^U$	89.73%	94.18%	98.13%	99.14%	99.63%	99.92%	99.69%

Table 6.8 Vega sensitivities for the seven maturities defined and the resulting vega risk positions K_b

	Vegas (sensitivities)						
	$T_{(1)}$	$T_{(2)}$	$T_{(3)}$	$T_{(4)}$	$T_{(5)}$	$T_{(6)}$	$T_{(7)}$
Option A	6.8	5.5	4	3.1	2.5	1.8	0.7
Option B	9.8	8.4	7.4	6.5	5.6	3.2	2.5
K_b							
$T_{(1)}$	16.540	13.785	11.174	9.341	7.840	4.782	3.086
$T_{(2)}$	16.586	13.865	11.287	9.466	7.956	4.872	3.132
$T_{(3)}$	16.481	13.862	11.387	9.578	8.072	4.973	3.185
$T_{(4)}$	16.381	13.809	11.390	9.593	8.085	4.981	3.189
$T_{(5)}$	16.307	13.771	11.377	9.594	8.096	4.991	3.194
$T_{(6)}$	16.235	13.733	11.362	9.588	8.098	4.996	3.197
$T_{(7)}$	16.183	13.705	11.351	9.582	8.094	4.999	3.198

A bank would like to construct the portfolio mentioned above with assets that are assigned to EUR and USD currencies. Under the analysis of GIRR risk class (Sect. 6.3.1), the exposure to two major currencies indicates the assignment of the portfolio to two different buckets. Moreover, the SbM indicates that there are ten possible vertices (with the associated RWs), three possible delta risk correlations (ρ_{kl}), and one cross-bucket correlation (γ_{bc}).

The bank could apply all combinations of these parameters to estimate, by using Eqs. (6.4) and (6.5), and the corresponding evolution of the risk positions K_b and capital charges. As illustrated in Fig. 6.3, the level of K_b drops when RWs, which refer to the corresponding vertices, decrease. Moreover, a higher correlation (ρ_{kl}) results in higher K_b and capital charges, as shown in Fig. 6.3. Figure 6.4 shows that the capital charge is highly correlated with the vertex, the associated RWs, and the sensitivity of the assets. Figure 6.5 shows that the parallel shift of different correlations (ρ_{kl}) does not modify the entire surface of capital evolution.

In the banks with non-securitisation portfolio, the CSR delta of non-securitisations applies under both SbM and R-SbM (Sect. 6.3.2). Given the existence of only two different sectors, the application of all possible combinations of buckets and correlations would be an easy task which simplifies the quantification of the impact of these parameters on the capital charge. The exposure type of a specific sector and credit quality, which are assigned to one of the 16 buckets of the SbM or one of the 6 buckets of the R-SbM, are associated to a specific RW. Table 6.4 shows all the possible combinations of correlation (ρ_{kl}) under the SbM. Table 6.5 shows all cross-bucket correlations based on the rules applied to the combinations of the buckets of exposures, while Fig. 6.6 illustrates the evolution of the SbM capital charges based on the

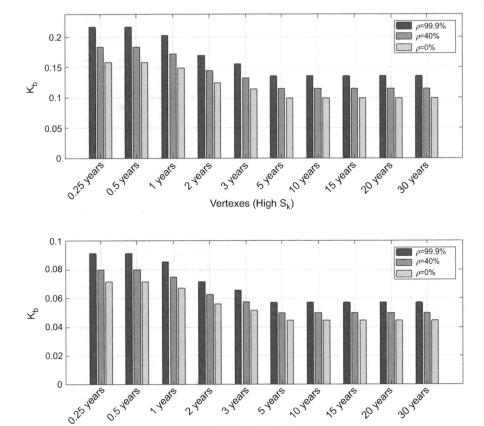

Fig. 6.3 GIRR delta (SbM) of risk positions K_b (all vertices and three possible correlations $[\rho_{kl}]$). The upper and lower figures refer to assets with high and low sensitivities, respectively

combination of buckets and the corresponding RWs. The exposures are supposed to belong to the bucket indicated by the combination of the corresponding sector and credit quality. The highest capital charges appear in buckets 11 and 16 and in assets with high sensitivities. The application of the R-SbM to the same portfolio designates that the capital charge increases significantly (Fig. 6.7).

The bank may follow the same approach, as described in the above paragraphs, to estimate the capital charge of all types of risk classes of both sensitivity-based methods. Therefore, banks can identify the possible combinations and classifications of parameters that optimise the minimum capital charge and the structure of a portfolio.

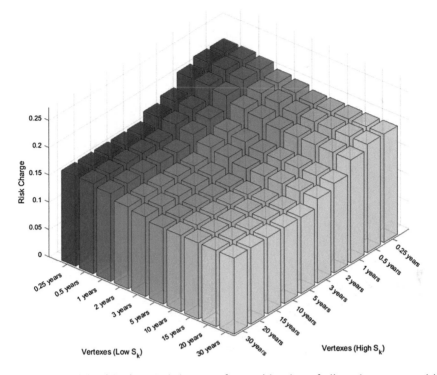

Fig. 6.4 GIRR delta (SbM) capital charges of a combination of all vertices; assets with different currencies are assigned to all vertices—cross-bucket correlation across all vertices

6.6   Standardised Default Risk Charge

A long credit position entails both MTM and JTD risks. The former refers to daily fluctuations of the credit spreads, whereas the latter to a default event that may occur over time. The JTD risk is more detrimental for held-to-maturity exposure, as a default event has more time to unfold. A default credit event for a long credit position may result in severe, sudden JTD risk losses. The use of MTM risk with credit spread sensitivities, where only deterministic shocks applied to credit spread, may underestimate the loss arising from a JTD event.

The final Basel III framework intends to capture such sudden and stress events in the tail of the default distribution, which may not have been encapsulated in credit spread shocks when using the MTM method. To do so, a bank should apply the JTD analysis to the tail of the distribution, where extreme events and corresponding losses appear, instead of applying

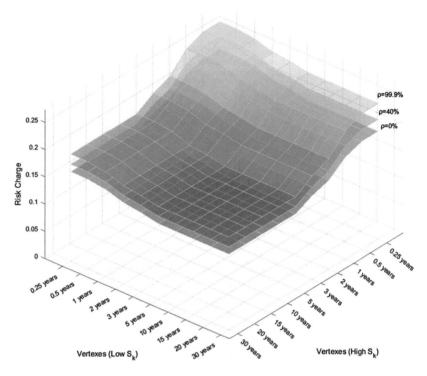

Fig. 6.5 Risk capital charges, under delta GIRR (SbM), along all vertices using different correlations between weighted sensitivities, ρ_{kl}

the shocks to the entire loss distribution, which may underestimate severe default loss.

The results of such simulation may lead to hedging of such positions. To hedge JTD risks, banks need to identify and measure how the credit event affects the exposure. A default event is unlikely to result in a loss that equals the amount of the exposure given that recoveries would compensate part of the losses. Thus, the analysis should account for recovery rate when estimating the JTD risk. In turn, the expected recovery relates to the seniority of the specific credit instrument. Therefore, it is crucial to stress the impact of default risk on both the value and expected recovery of the defaulted position.

According to the new framework, banks should estimate the DRC against extreme losses that they may face due to the severity of a default event. They also have to follow a four-step process to estimate the standardised default risk capital charge of the trading portfolios which contain both securitisation and non-securitisation instruments. These steps are the following:

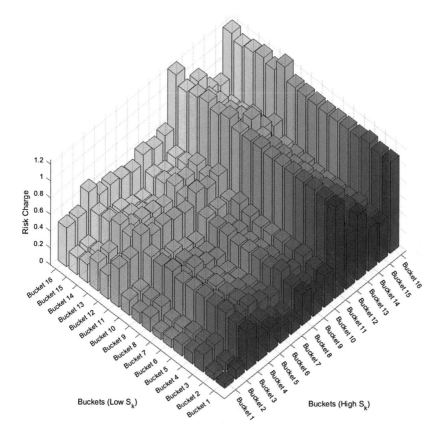

Fig. 6.6 Capital charges of a non-securitisation *portfolio* (SbM), 16 buckets

1. Estimation of JTD loss amounts for each instrument exposed to counter-party risk;
2. Netting of the JTD risk amounts that refer to long and short exposures of the same obligor. This netting will produce the net long or net short JTD amount which coincides with the net exposure to JTD risk;
3. Calculation of the discounted hedge benefit ratio applied to net short exposures; and
4. Application of the default RWs to get the final capital charge.

This capital charge is independent of any other capital charges of the SA for market risk. The new framework discriminates between the estimation of DRC of a trading portfolio with non-securitisations and securitisations, assuming the existence and absence of correlation.

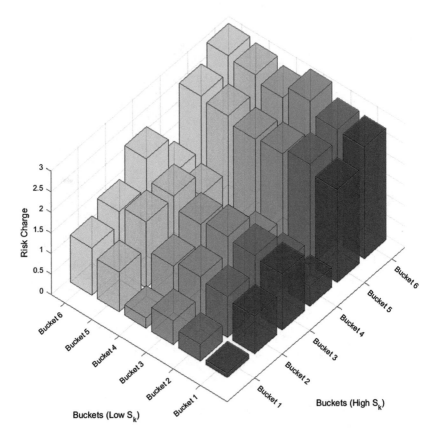

Fig. 6.7 Capital charges of a non-securitisation portfolio (R-SbM), eight buckets

6.6.1   Default Risk Charge of Non-Securitisations

6.6.1.1   Estimating Gross *JTD*

The proposed formula, as shown in Eq. (6.15), determines the gross JTD loss amounts of non-securitisation default risk as the higher of (a) the product of LGD and long notional amount of the exposure plus the P&L amount and (b) zero, or the lower of the (c) product of LGD and short notional amount of the exposures plus the P&L amount, and (d) zero.

$$JTD_{long} = \max\left(LGD \times \text{notional} + P \& L; 0\right)$$

$$JTD_{short} = \min\left(LGD \times \text{notional} + P \& L; 0\right) \tag{6.15}$$

The notional amount coincides with the security's nominal (or face) value of the position; for example, upon a default event, the bonds credit default swaps (CDSs) are accounted at the original value of the issuance, whereas the nominal value of a bought call option, on the underlying bond, is zero. The P&L is the cumulative MTM profit (or loss) already embedded in the exposure, that is, P&L = current market value—notional value. The level of LGD depends on the type of instrument and its level of seniority (see Chaps. 4 and 5).[44]

Scaling of JTD Maturity

The JTD refers to exposures with an assumed time horizon of one year. Thus, banks should scale up exposures with maturities (M) shorter than a year to reach the one-year maturity. Exposures with less than three-month maturity are assumed to have a maturity of three months, while securities related to cash equity positions are supposed to have a maturity of either three months or more than one year.

6.6.1.2   Net Jump-To-Default Risk Positions (Net JTD)

After estimating the gross JTD, banks have to approximate the net JTD exposures to the same obligor by applying the following rules:

- *Maturity longer than one year*: In cases where a bank holds both long and short positions the offset applies only if the short exposures have equal or lower seniority relative to the long exposures;
- *Maturity shorter than one year*: Subject to the same restrictions applied above, if maturities of the *long or short exposures* are less than the one-year horizon, banks should weigh the corresponding exposures with the ratio of their maturity to the one-year horizon.

The net JTD risk exposure that results after the application of the offsetting rules described above is weighted according to their credit quality and allocated to buckets according to the type of exposure to estimate the default risk capital charges, as shown in Eq. (6.17).

6.6.1.3   Estimation of the Default Risk Capital Charge for Non-Securitisations

In the process of estimating the DRCs for non-securitisation exposures, banks have to assign the associated net JTD to RWs. These RWs take values from 0.5% to 100% depending on their credit quality and the type of exposure. The new framework assigns the types of exposures to three different buckets, that is, corporates, sovereigns, and local governments/municipalities. The credit rating scale defines the credit quality ranges from AAA (Aaa) to default, reflecting the classification of RWs.[45]

Then banks have to estimate the possible hedging benefit between long and short positions within the same bucket. The hedge benefit ratio, henceforth, the weighted-to-short (WtS) ratio, is given by Eq. (6.16).

$$WtS = \frac{\sum net\ JTD_{long}}{\sum net\ JTD_{long} - \sum net\ JTD_{short}} \tag{6.16}$$

where

$\sum net\ JTD_{long}$ and $\sum net\ JTD_{short}$ are the sums of unweighted net long JTD and net short JTD amounts across the credit quality categories (i.e. rating bands). The WtS is a discount factor of the function that estimates the DRC. This capital charge, at the level of a bucket b and instrument i, is the greater of:

- the difference between the sum (across the credit quality categories) of (a) the risk-weighted long net JTD, that is, $\sum_{i \in Long} RW_i \cdot net\ JTD_i$, and (b) the risk-weighted short net JTD, that is, $\sum_{i \in Short} RW_i \cdot net\ JTD_i$, multiplied by the WtS discounting factor; or
- zero.

Equation (6.17) illustrates the formula for estimating the default risk charge DRC_b at the level of bucket b.

$$DRC_b = \max\left[\left(\sum_{i \in Long} RW_i \times net\ JTD_i\right) - WtS \times \left(\sum_{i \in Short} RW_i \times net\ JTD_i\right); 0\right]$$

$$\tag{6.17}$$

After taking into consideration that the new framework does not allow hedging between different buckets, the total capital charge for default risk of non-securitisations is as simple as adding up the capital charges of individual buckets.

Box 6.4 Example for Estimating DRC for Non-Securitisations Products

The present example refers to a bank which holds a TB portfolio with the following exposures:

- A long senior IT corporate bond position (P_1) with notional of EUR 20 million and 3 years of maturity, hedged by a EUR 25 million short position of IT corporate equity position (P_2) of the same issuer with a maturity of 9 months. The rating of the issuer is set to B while the level of LGD for P_1 and P_2 is set at 75% and 100%, respectively;
- A long CDS position (P_3), which relates to selling three-month protection of EUR 10 million against the default of a B-rated oil-refining corporate, whose expected LGD is 100%;
- A short position (P_4) of EUR 5 million on a B-rated pharmaceutical company for three months;
- A long senior industrial corporate bond position (P_5) with notional of EUR 10 million, with credit quality A, maturity of two years, and expected LGD of 75%;
- A long senior telecom corporate bond position (P_6) with notional of EUR 100 million duration of 1.5 years, hedged by a EUR 100 million short position (P_7) of bought protection against the default of the same issuer for a duration of nine months. The credit quality of the issuer is A. Based on the seniority of the instruments, the LGDs of P_6 and P_7 are 75% and 100%, respectively.

Based on rating grades, the RW of P_1 to P_4 is set at 30% while the RW of P_5 to P_7 is set at 3%. The maturity weight assigned to P_3 and P_4 is 25% (3 months/12 months), whereas for the maturity weight of P_2 is 75% (9 months/12 months).

Table 6.9 contains the information of the above-mentioned portfolio including the assumed P&L. After taking into account the information shown in Table 6.9 and applying Eq. (6.15), the bank can estimate the gross and net amounts of long and short positions (JTD_{long} or JTD_{short}) as illustrated in the last four columns of Table 6.9 For instance, if the prices of the IT corporate bond and equity dropped the long and short positions (P_1 and P_2) would result in losses and profits, respectively. Thus, for P_1, the $JTD_{long} = max\ (LGD \times notional + P\ \&\ L;\ 0) = max\ (75\ \% \times 20 + 0.5) = 14.5\ 0$ and for P_2, the $JTD_{short} = min\ (LGD \times notional + P\ \&\ L;\ 0) \times MaturityWeight = min\ (-(100\ \% \times 25 + 0.75);\ 0) \times 75\ \% = -19.88$. Note that the maturity weighting factors are applicable only on the positions P_2, P_3, and P_4.

The estimation of WtS considers two different credit quality grades, that is, A-rated and B-rated, in the application of Eq. (6.16), as all exposures are assumed to belong to one of the two grades. Thus, for P_1 to P_4, which are B-rated, the $WtS = 2.54/(2.54 + |-6.59|) = 0.28$. Similarly, for P_5 to P_7, which are A-rated, the $WtS = 8.2/(8.2 + |-7.1|) = 0.54$.

(continued)

Box 6.4 (continued)

The bank in question calculates the default risk capital charge (DRC_b) on the basis of the "corporate" bucket and the ratings that the portfolio positions belong to. Equation (6.17) uses the parameters of $netJTD$, WtS, and RW to calculate the DRC. The RWs derive their values from A and B ratings of RWs which are 3% and 30%, respectively (see Table 6.9).

The first part of Eq. (6.17) estimates the sum of risk-weighted net JTD for the long positions. Thus, this part, for the A rating, becomes $\sum_{i\epsilon Long} RW_i \times net\ JTD_i =$ 3 % × 8.2 = 0.25, while, for B rating, it becomes $\sum_{i\epsilon Long} RW_i \times net\ JTD_i =$ 30 % × 2. 54 = 0.76. Similarly, the results in the second part of Eq. (6.17), which refers to short positions, is $WtS \times (\sum_{i\epsilon Short} RW_i \times net\ JTD_i) = 0.54 \times 3\ \% \times 7.1 = 0.11$, for A rating, and $WtS \times (\sum_{i\epsilon Short} RW_i \times net\ JTD_i) = 0.28 \times (30\ \% \times (-1.21) + 30\ \% \times (-5.3$ 8)) = $-$ 0.55 for B rating.

In turn, the DRC of the corporate bucket for each of the ratings is $DRC_b^{Rating\ A} = \left[(0.25-0.11);0\right] = 0.13$ and $DRC_b^{Rating\ B} = \left[(0.76-0.55);0\right] = 0.21$, which result in a total default risk capital charge of $DRC_b = 0.13 + 0.21 = $ EUR 0.34 million.

6.6.2 Default Risk Charge of Securitisations in the Non-Correlation Trading Portfolio

6.6.2.1 The Estimation of Gross and Net JTD

Unlike the relevant process in non-securitisation positions, the estimation of gross JTD of securitisations embeds the LGD ratio in the default RWs. Thus, the JTD of the securitisation exposures is, in fact, the market value of these exposures.

Offsetting rule of securitisation exposures[46] applies to tranches of different positions (long and short) with the same underlying pool of assets. Also, under certain conditions, banks could decompose the securitised exposures to each component and offset them with opposite positions within the same securitised portfolio. Offsetting may also apply to identical securitisation exposures with an exception to positions of less than one year which are subject to the same restriction of *maturity shorter than one year* described above for non-securitisations.

Table 6.9 Description of portfolio characteristics used for the calculation of the capital charge

Position	Notional (in MM)	Maturity	Credit quality (issuer)	RW	LGD	P&L (in MM)	Gross JTD_{Long}	Gross JTD_{Short}	Net JTD_{Long}	Net JTD_{Short}
P_1: IT corporate bond—[long]	20	3Y	B	30%	75%	−0.5	14.5			−5.38
P_2: IT Corp equity—[short]	25	9 M	B	30%	100%	0.75		−19.88		
P_3: CDS (protection to OilCom corporate)—[long]	10	3 M	B	30%	100%	0.15	2.54		2.54	
P_4: Pharma stock—[short]	5	3 M	B	30%	100%	−0.15		−1.21		−1.21
P_5: Industrial corporate bond—[long]	10	2Y	A	3%	75%	0.7	8.2		8.2	
P_6: Telecom corporate bond—[long]	120	1.5Y	A	3%	75%	2,4	92.4			7.10
P_7: CDS (protection to telecom corporate)—[short]	100	1Y	A	3%	100%	−0.5		−99.5		

6.6.2.2   Estimating Default Risk Charge for Securitisations in Non-CTP

Aligned to the provisions related to non-securitisation positions (Sect. 6.6.1), securitisations exposures also correspond to specific RWs based on the tranches they refer to. The RWs of securitisation positions follow the rules of the banking book (BCBS, 2014, 2016a).

Thus, securitisation exposures are assigned to two types of buckets which refer to (1) corporates, also linked to regions, or (2) combination of asset classes[47] and regions.[48] Any exposure that does not fall under the above categories should be assigned to the "other" bucket. Equation (6.17) provides the default risk capital charge against securitisation exposures following the equivalent steps described in Sect. 6.6.1.

6.6.3   Default Risk Charge of Securitisations in the Correlation Trading Portfolio

6.6.3.1   Estimating Gross and Net JTD

According to the new provisions, banks should estimate the gross JTD in the CTP following the same approach as for default risk securitisations in non-CTP. The only additional element is the treatment of nth-to-default products. When dealing with these products (contracts) banks should estimate the borderline between the "attachment" and "detachment" points, that is, the borderline which defines activation of a contract due to a default event. The attachment point is given by $(N - 1)/TN$, while the detachment point is given by N/TN, where TN is the total number of names in the underlying pool of assets.

Banks should apply full offsetting of exposures where these have maturities longer than a year. Exposures maturing in less than a year are partially recognised (BCBS, 2016a: 48, para 169), whereas offsetting is not allowed for different tranches, series of the same index, and index families.

Estimating Default Risk Charge for Securitisations in CTP

Securitisations tranches of the TB are subject to the same default RWs as defined in the treatment of the banking book (BCBS, 2014). The rules of the banking book rules provide RWs for non-tranched products too. Also, securitisations of a recognised index[49] are treated as one bucket.

The estimation of the DRC of securitised exposures follows a similar approach to the one applied for non-securitisations (Sect. 6.6.1). Equation (6.18) estimates the default risk capital charges, at the bucket level. This equation is similar to the estimation of DRC of non-securitisations (see Eq. (6.17)) without applying, at the bucket level, the floor of 0. The absence of such a floor may result in a negative DRC at the index level DRC_b. The hedge benefit ratios WtS_{ctp}, applied to net short positions in the bucket, are calculated using the combined long and short positions across the entire CTP and not just the positions in the particular index/bucket.

$$DRC_b = \left[\left(\sum_{i \in \text{Long}} RW_i \times \text{net } JTD_i \right) - WtS_{ctp} \times \left(\sum_{i \in \text{Short}} RW_i \times \text{net } JTD_i \right) \right] \quad (6.18)$$

The bucket-specific capital charge (Eq. (6.19)) is aggregated by the maximum of:

- the sum of the higher of (a) the DRC at the bucket level b or (b) zero; and half of the amount of the lower of (a) the DRC at bucket level b or (b) zero; or
- zero.

$$DRC_{CTP} = \max \left[\sum_b \left(\max[DRC_b, 0] + 0.5 \times \min[DRC_b, 0], 0 \right) \right] \quad (6.19)$$

Thus, the DRC_{CTP} is the aggregation of the bucket-specific capital charges, floored to zero.

6.7   Residual Risk

On top of the other two components, the SA introduces the estimation of the RRAO intended to capture the risks that remain uncovered. The RRAO capital charges intend to capture the residual risk, known as the gap, correlation, and behaviour risks,[50] which instruments of the TB portfolios are exposed to. For instance, instruments associated with a market-driven behavioural risk of embedded prepayment options of securitised portfolios are subject to RRAO. The new SA proposals include clear definitions of the types of risk included in or excluded from the calculation of RRAO (BCBS, 2016a: 20, paras 58 [g] and [h]).

Thus, the RRAO ensures the coverage of the remaining market risks. The calculation of the RRAO also involves RWs, as a multiplication factor, on the gross notional amounts of the exposures to residual RFs. The RW assigned to exotic underlying instruments is 1.0%, whereas exposures to the remaining instruments bear other residual risks, whose RW is 0.1%. The SA also defines the rules for identifying the TB instruments where RW for residual risks is applied (BCBS, 2016a: 19, paras 58 [d] and [e]), as well as a list of rules for excluding instruments from the residual risk, for example, central clearing eligible instruments (BCBS, 2016a: 19, para 58 (f)).

6.8   Internal Models Approach

A bank that has the capability to develop sophisticated models for the internal estimation of market risk capital charges, and has these models approved[51] by the pertinent supervisors, is eligible to apply the internal models approach (IMA) under the FRTB framework. The IMA aims to identify market and liquidity risks attributed to stress conditions, be consistent with the SA treatment, and be prudent in the estimation of market risk losses. In doing so, it applies constraints on the capital-reducing effects of hedging and diversification. Also, the IMA introduces a change in the risk assessment measure, switching from the VaR to the expected shortfall (ES) for capturing risks arising during periods of significant financial market stress. Likewise, it embeds "tail risk" events in the calculation of capital adequacy. Moreover, banks must perform back-testing, as well as the P&L attribution test, at the level of individual trading desks.

As illustrated in Fig. 6.8, the IMA comprises three discrete parts for the estimation of capital charges against market risk: the ES, the DRC, and the stressed capital add-on (SCAO) for "non-modellable" risks. The IMA defines qualitative and quantitative standards, as well as specific methods for the estimation of the capital charges.

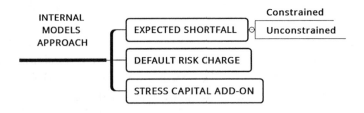

Fig. 6.8 FRTB internal model approaches

6.8.1 Qualitative Standards

The new framework suggests that supervisors request banks to have in place, independent from the business lines, a control unit to measure and report, on a daily basis, the risk of TB exposures vis-à-vis the TB limits. The unit should also conduct back-testing and P&L analysis against portfolio value changes over a long period. Moreover, internal models used for the estimation of capital and profitability management should be consistent and aligned, for example, share and stress the same RFs, and apply similar valuation models.

The aforementioned internal models must be validated internally (annually) by the internal auditors and top management, and externally (regularly) by external auditory and the competent supervisory authorities.

The application of regulatory stress-testing should influence the processes for the formulation of capital and the conduct of risk management. Responding to this requirement, banks should produce documentation on the best practices of the risk management processes and systems. The internal and external auditors should verify and approve the main elements of risk management processes and systems, such as data, RFs, valuation models. Last, but not the least, high-level[52] management should maintain an active role in the risk control process.

6.8.2 Quantitative Standards and Capitalisation

Except for the qualitative requirements, there are also minimum quantitative standards which banks' internal models should align with. These quantitative standards refer mainly to addressing the market and liquidity risks when calculating the capital charge of the TB exposures. "Basel II.5", that is, the amendment to Basel II that refers to market risk (see BCBS, 2010, 2011), introduced the stress VaR for the market risk which was an addition to the "plain vanilla" VaR framework. Stress VaR narrowed the gap between the projected capital and the capital which should have been held against historical stress but did not factor in the losses arising from market liquidity during those periods. Thus, before the introductions of the FRTB, the framework of market risk capital charge assumed that, regardless of the type of position, it would be feasible for banks to liquidate their positions within ten days[53] under stress conditions.

However, during the financial crisis, the market revealed the weakness of this assumption, which necessitated the changes introduced by the FRTB. According to the FRTB, different types of instruments can be liquidated in different periods. Thus, according to the new framework, the liquidity horizons range from 10 to 120 days depending on the type of RF (BCBS, 2016a: 54–55, para 181 [k]).

Also, the new framework provides additional requirements for the estimation of the ES, the setting of liquidity horizons, the eligibility of trading activities, the model validation, the interaction between the IMA and the SA, the specification of market RFs, the estimation of default risk, the estimation of capital charge, as well as stress-testing, back-testing, and P&L attribution.

6.8.2.1   Expected Shortfall

The measurement of VaR is positively homogeneous, as a scaling in the quantile leads to a scaling in the VaR-estimated loss amount, which is also monotonic, as the quantiles preserve monotonicity. However, the VaR fails to be a coherent measurement.

Assuming a set V_{rand} of real-valued random variables, the function $\rho : V \to R$ represents a capital measure. For having a coherent risk measure, the model should satisfy four conditions, if it is:

1. *Monotonic:* $\forall X, Y \in V$ with $X \leq Y \Rightarrow \rho(X) \leq \rho(Y)$
   The natural property of monotonicity is defined as follows: the portfolios A and B have expected losses of XA and XB, respectively. If the losses of portfolio A are lower than the losses of portfolio B, that is, $XA \leq XB$, then the required risk capital $\gamma(XA)$ for portfolio A should be less than the required risk capital $\gamma(XB)$ for portfolio B.
2. *Sub-additive:* $\forall X, Y \in V \Rightarrow \rho(X + Y) \leq \rho(X) + \rho(Y)$
   That is, the risk inherent in the additive union of two portfolios should be less than the sum of risks of the two individual separate portfolios; such axiom of sub-additivity results in a portfolio diversification effect.
3. *Positively homogeneous,* $\forall X \in V, \forall h > 0,$ *and* $h X \in V \Rightarrow \rho(h X) = h \rho(X)$
   This axiom implies that a scaling of a loss variable results in a scaling of the corresponding quantile. For instance, the scaling of a credit portfolio exposure by a factor h results in scaling the expected loss X by the same factor, that is, h X. As a result, the original capital requirement $\rho(X)$ will also be scaled to $h \rho(X)$.
4. *Translation invariant,* $X \in V, q \in R \Rightarrow \rho(X + q) = \rho(X) + q$
   This axiom describes the case where a shift, by a fixed amount, in P&L distribution with a specific horizon results in a corresponding change of in the quantile. Hence, the capital requirement against losses of the portfolio increases or decreases accordingly.

The VaR measurement of a portfolio consisting of sub-portfolios results in an amount which is at most equal to the sum of the discrete amounts of VaR of the sub-portfolios. However, under the composition/addition of portfolios, the risk measure should be based on the axiom that "the overall size of a portfolio risk is equal to the sum of its risks only in the case when the latter results in simultaneous events; that is, all risks are combined and act simultaneously". In all other situations, the overall size of a portfolio risk is strictly less than the sum of its risks due to risk diversifications. Sub-additivity also implies a convex portfolio risk surface, facilitating the optimisation of the risk profile of the portfolio, due to the diversification effect. Sub-additivity is an essential characteristic for the estimation of risk metrics of a large bank which holds several entities/subsidiaries. In such cases, the sum of the subentities' risk measure is less than the respective risk measure estimated at a consolidated level. Also, the exposure limits at the consolidated level can be estimated accordingly.

To resolve the problem of the non-coherence of VaR, Artzner et al. (1999)[54] proposed a coherent measure of risk known as expected shortfall (ES). Equation (6.20) defines the general formula for the calculation of ES at the confidence level (CL) q (ES_q). Instead of providing a point estimation that coincides with a quantile at a particular CL, the ES formula estimates the number of events that exceed the CL $u \geq q$ for $q \in (0, 1)$, focusing on the tail of the loss distribution (L). In fact, the ES depends on the VaR estimation, moving though one step beyond by estimating the average losses that exceed the VaR estimation of a particular CL. Having employed the tail distribution, the model is much more sensitive to scenarios resulting in tail events. It is also worth mentioning that VaR is a sensitive measure in cases of portfolios with discontinuous distributions (e.g. a portfolio of derivatives where mixtures of continuous and discrete distributions may occur). As the VaR measure considers only a single quantile defined by the CL q, a portfolio having discontinuous distributions would yield a VaR which is sensitive to small changes in the CL q. On the other hand, the ES_q is continuously changing with respect to q, regardless of the nature of the underlying distributions,[55] which means that it is less sensitive to changes in q.

$$ES_q = \frac{1}{1-q} \int_q^1 \mathrm{VaR}_u (L)\, du \qquad (6.20)$$

The ES is, by definition, a more conservative measure than the VaR. To this end, instead of only calculating a ten-day horizon VaR with a 99% CL, proposed by the Basel I framework, and the stressed VaR, proposed by Basel II.5, the FRTB framework proposes the estimation of ES (aka conditional VaR) at the 97.5th percentile one-tailed confidence interval. Likewise, the supervisors achieve a dual objective: first, to reduce the conservatism of the new metric and, second, to attain sufficient observations of extreme events that would render the estimation of ES robust.

For Basel risk measurement purposes, banks should compute, on a daily basis, the more coherent risk measurement measure of the shortfalls, rather than the naked *VaR* and stress *VaR* measures. The ES can be interpreted as the expected loss to be incurred if VaR is exceeded, which mainly occurs during periods of stress. In other words, it reflects the capital charge needed to cope with risks which may arise under periods of stress of the relevant RFs. The ES calculation involves instantaneous shocks to those factors which would impact the liquidity characteristics of the instruments. Therefore, the ES measure focuses on possible extreme risk losses and liquidity shortages that may occur[56] in excess of the set quantile.

The longer liquidity horizons, adopted by the new framework, depend on the RF category.[57] In fact, the IMA defines five lengths, defined as j, of liquidity horizons that the RFs are associated with. Moreover, the base liquidity horizon is set at $T = 10$ days.

On the one hand, banks should calculate the base ES ($ES_T(P)$), at base horizon T, by applying shocks on the set of RFs that the TB positions ($P = (p_i)$) are exposed to. These shocks would affect the value and the sensitivity of the portfolio that contains these positions. On the other hand, in the absence of a long history of data, the analysis could rely only on the liquidity horizon of a subset[58] of RFs ($Q(p, j)$), linked to the TB portfolio positions ($P = (p_i)$). In this case, banks should apply the above-mentioned shocks on each of the positions p_i to estimate the corresponding series of $ES_T(P, j)$ for the base case horizon T, considering only the subsets of RFs $Q(p, j)$.

The estimated $ES_T(P, j)$ should be adjusted by multiplying it with the factor $\sqrt{LH_j - LH_{j-1}/T}$, which takes into consideration the actual length j of the liquidity horizon (LH_j) of the RF category. For example, an RF category on *interest rate: volatility* corresponds to liquidity length of $j = 4$ with liquidity horizon $LH_j = LH_4 = 60$ days, whereas LH_{j-1} corresponds to the length $j - 1$ of liquidity horizon which is one level below j, that is, $j - 1 = 3$, which implies that $LH_{j-1} = LH_3 = 40$ days. It is noteworthy that this liquidity adjustment uses the factor $\sqrt{LH_j - LH_{j-1}/T}$ as far as the lengths of the liquidity horizons are higher than ten days $LH_j > 10$, where $j > 2$.

The ES is equal to the square root of the squares of the base $ES_T(P)^2$ and the sum of the $ES_T(P, j)$ for the subsets of the RFs whose LH_j is longer than ten days.

$$ES = \sqrt{ES_T\left(P\right)^2 + \sum_{j \geq 2}\left(ES_T\left(P,j\right)\sqrt{\frac{LH_j - LH_{j-1}}{T}}\right)^2} \qquad (6.21)$$

The bank should also simulate the evolution of the set and subset of RFs to obtain extreme loss events in the tail of the distribution which will be used as inputs in the ES model for the estimation of the respective capital charges. To capture the effect of the reduced liquidity during market stress, banks should repeat the simulation process for all trading positions. For each subset, the simulated 97.5th percentile ES is scaled up by the associated liquidity horizon. Banks are not explicitly restricted to use a particular type of ES model[59]: they can use a stochastic Monte Carlo simulation, historical simulation, or other analytical methods. The framework, however, provides principles concerning the data used for expected shortfall models (BCBS, 2018: 31–33 paras Annex D).

Unlike VaR, which uses the most current one-year period, the ES calibration uses the relevant RFs of a one-year historical horizon of severe stress, irrespective of the vicinity of this horizon to the time of the estimation. This historical horizon should also capture stressed correlations[60] among RFs. When relying on the reduced set of RFs, the estimation of the reduced ES is subject to model-error risk which could arise from the mapping of the subset of factors to the actual RFs which should have been used by the ES model. The reduction of RFs used by the reduced ES model should capture at least 75% of the variation of the full ES model, measured as the average variability over 12 weeks preceding the estimation. As described in Eq. (6.22), the ES capital charge requires the scaling of the reduced ES $ES_{R,S}$, based on a stressed observation period using a reduced set of RFs, by the ratio of the current (most recent) ES ($ES_{F,C}$), based on a 12-month observation period using the full set of RFs, to the reduced ES ($ES_{R,C}$) calculated with the reduced set of RFs over the same current (most recent) period. The adjustment ratio $ES_{F,C}/ES_{R,C}$ is subject to a floor of 1.

$$ES = ES_{R,S} \times \max\left(\frac{ES_{F,C}}{ES_{R,C}}, 1\right) \qquad (6.22)$$

Banks which use the IMA should calculate the ES capital charge on a daily basis for each trading desk.

6.8.2.2 Default Risk Charge

The assessment of default risk[61] of all TB positions should employ, on a weekly basis, the estimation of a credit default base VaR model by setting a one-tail 99.9% CL and a one-year time horizon (BCBS, 2016a: 61 para 186 (b)). The VaR model should include all positions exposed to default risk, for example, sovereign exposures, equity, and defaulted debt positions, which are not subject to SA capital charges. Amongst other parameters, banks estimate default correlations over a period of ten years, which includes a subperiod of at least one year. Default correlations are retrieved by either credit spreads or the corresponding equity market prices.

As shown in Eq. (6.23), the DRC is the greater of (a) the average DRC over the last 12-week period or (b) the measurement of the most recent default risk capital charge.

$$DRC = \max\left\{ \frac{\sum_{week=1}^{12} DRC_{week}}{12}; DRC_{recent} \right\} \qquad (6.23)$$

In addition to the above-mentioned provision, banks are not allowed to use any market-implied PDs to estimate the probability of default (PD) risk, whereas the minimum acceptable PD is subject to a regulatory floor of 0.03%. This floor is consistent with the current floor of the IRBA capital requirements framework (see Chaps. 4 and 5) but not consistent with the regulatory PD of 0.05% proposed in the latest consultative document relating to the credit risk framework (BCBS, 2016b). The latest proposals include additional guidance on the treatment of mismatch between a position and its hedge, the treatment of market concentration, the dependency of recoveries on the systemic RFs, the validation by using back-testing and stress-testing techniques, the sensitivity and scenario analyses, as well as PD and LGD estimations.

6.8.2.3 Stressed Capital Add-on

In the new framework, banks must also measure an additional capital requirement against the exposure of trading positions to non-modellable risk factors (NMRFs). The NMRFs are the ones that do not satisfy the risk factor eligibility test (RFET), set by the framework (BSBS, 2016a and BCBS, 2018: 11 paras 183c). Trading positions can be subject to an amount I of non-modellable idiosyncratic CSR factors, an amount J of non-modellable idiosyncratic equity spread risk factors and an amount K of NMRFs included in the model-eligible desks. To address the NMRFs, banks have to calculate capital charges assigned to stress scenarios,[62] which are applied to these risk factors without benefiting from any correlation or diversification effects. However, based on the committee proposal (BCBS, 2018: 10 paras 2.2.3), permission to recognise diversification benefits apply to NMRFs associated with idiosyncratic credit spread risk. Equation (6.24) shows the formula (BCBS, 2018: 11 box 3) to aggregate regulatory capital measure (SES) against the exposures to an amount of I, J and K non-modellable risk factors. The resulting capital defines the SCAO.

$$SES = \sqrt{\sum_{i=1}^{L} ISES_{NM,i}^{2}} + \sqrt{\sum_{j=1}^{j} ISES_{NM,j}^{2}} + \sum_{j=1}^{K} SES_{NM,K} \qquad (6.24)$$

As mentioned above, banks must capitalise every non-modellable risk factor by using a stress scenario. Thus, the estimation of individual stress scenario capital charges ($ISES_{NM,i}$) and ($ISES_{NM,j}$) are assigned to each idiosyncratic non-modellable CSR factor i and each idiosyncratic non-modellable equity risk j factor, respectively. As illustrated in Eq. (6.24), banks must aggregate both ($ISES_{NM,i}$) and ($ISES_{NM,j}$) based on the associated amounts I and L of NMRFs. Notably, in both aggregations, there is not recognition of correlation effect among NMRFs. Finally, the bank must aggregate the stress scenario capital charges $SES_{NM,j}$ assigned to the amount K of each NMRFs k.

6.8.2.4   Aggregate Capital Charges

The ES estimation relies on two measures of the TB capital charge: the diversified and undiversified ES capital charges. In particular, banks should estimate these measures as follows:

1. The *diversified ES capital charge* ($IMCC(C)$) is the unconstrained internal model estimation of the ES capital charge, where banks perform the estimation of ES without applying any supervisory constrains as to the correlation between different risk classes; and

2. The *undiversified ES charge* $\left(\sum_{i=1}^{R} IMCC(C_i) \right)$ is the constrained internal model estimation of the ES capital charge, where banks, after estimating the individual ES for each of the five different R risk classes,[63] aggregate the partial ES without taking into consideration the estimated correlations.

All in all, the total *ES charge* is the weighted average of the diversified ES and undiversified ES capital charges, as illustrated in Eq. (6.25).

$$IMCC = \rho\big(IMCC(C)\big) + (1-\rho)\left(\sum_{i=1}^{R} IMCC(C_i)\right) \qquad (6.25)$$

where following Eq. (6.26):

$$IMCC(C) = ES_{R,S} \times \max \frac{ES_{F,C}}{ES_{R,C}}$$
$$IMCC(C) = ES_{R,S,i} \times \max \frac{ES_{F,C,i}}{ES_{R,C,i}} \qquad (6.26)$$

and the assigned weighting factor $\rho = 0.5$.

The period of stress used for calibrating the reduced ES of risk class i ($ES_{R,S,i}$) and reduced portfolio-wide ES ($ES_{R,S}$) should be identical, due to the absence of correlation.

As defined in Eq. (6.27) (BCBS, 2018: 24 paras 192), the aggregated capital requirement (C_A), estimated on a daily basis, is the higher of (a) the aggregate capital charge for market risk that refers to the most resent observation[64]; and (b) the average capital charges of the preceding 60 business days scaled up by a multiplier[65] m_c (BCBS, 2016a: 64, para 189), which depends on the predictive capacity of the internal model (number of exceptions). Moreover, SES is referring to the aggregated regulatory capital measure for the amount NMRFs which are included in the model-eligible desks, as shown in Eq. (6.24).

$$C_A = \max\big\{IMCC_{t-1} + SES_{t-1}; m_c \times IMCC_{avg} + SES_{avg}\big\} \qquad (6.27)$$

As already highlighted, banks should calculate the capital charge or market risk based on the SA as a fall-back charge of non-eligible that is, disapproved, trading desks. They should also calculate the capital charge per each regulatory trading desk, that is, the desks which are eligible for the application of the IMA.

All in all, the aggregate capital charge ($C_{A,M}$) of IMA-eligible treading desks includes both modellable and NMRFs as estimated in Eq. (6.27). Moreover, the regulatory capital charge ($C_{A,U}$) of non-eligible trading desks is given by the aggregation of all associated risks under the SA capital charge. Finally, using credit default base VaR model, the bank estimates the *DRC* as in Eq. (6.23). Summing all of the above, the aggregate capital charge *ACC*, for the market risk where the trading desks is exposed, is calculated as shown in Eq. (6.28).

$$ACC = C_{A,M} + C_{A,U} + DRC \tag{6.28}$$

In case that in the PLA test, discussed in the following section, at least one eligible trading desk falls into the "amber zone" the bank must add a capital surcharge. Thus, the enhanced aggregate capital charge ACC is calculated as shown in Eq. (6.29) (BCBS, 2018: 25 paras 194).

$$ACC = C_{A,M} + C_{A,U} + DRC + Capital\ surcharge \tag{6.29}$$

Equation (6.30) defines the calculation of capital surcharge where the bank has to estimate the delta between the aggregated capital charges resulted from the standardised approach ($SA_{G,A}$) and the internal model-based approach ($IMA_{G,A} = C_A + DRC$) multiplied by a factor k. The capital surcharge is subject to a floor of zero. Given that all of the desks' positions in the PLA are within the "green" or "amber" zones, the bank estimates the aggregated capital charges.

$$Capital\ surcharge = k \times \max\{0, SA_{G,A} - IMA_{G,A}\} \tag{6.30}$$

The factor k is given by Eq. (6.31)

$$k = 0.5 \times \frac{\sum_{i \in A} SA_i}{\sum_{i \in G,A} SA_i}; \tag{6.31}$$

In Eq. (6.31), the multiplier factor of 0.5 implies that the Capital surcharge is subject to a floor of 50% of the abovementioned delta aggregated capital charges.

Given the positions of the desk "i", the standardised capital charge, denoted as SA_i, is aggregated for all the approved desks in the "amber zone," i.e., $i \in A$, as well as for all the approved desks in the "green zone" or "amber zone," i.e., $i \in G, A$. The former aggregation is allocated in the nominator and then later in the denominator in the formula for estimating the k factor (Eq. 6.31).

The new BCBS framework states that *for an institution to remain eligible for capitalisation under the IMA, a minimum of 10% of the bank's aggregated market risk charges must be based on positions held in desks that qualify for inclusion in the bank's internal model for regulatory capital* (BCBS, 2016a: 57, para 183 [b]).

The internal models-based capital charge estimation does not include securitised products whose capital charge is exclusively calculated under the SA (BCBS, 2016a: 60, para 185 (f)). As a result of their ineligibility, securitised instruments, such as mortgage-backed securities, asset-backed securities, and other types of securitised products, imply a higher capital charge relative to non-securitised types of traded instruments. Thus, banks' business models, which rely on securitised products investment, bear higher capital charges under the final Basel III framework. In turn, this may affect their overall business strategy on the grounds described above.

6.8.3   Back-Testing and P&L Attribution Requirements

Since internal models need the supervisory approval at the level of individual trading desks, banks should perform back-testing and the so-called, P&L attribution (PLA) test for each trading desk. Likewise, they could prove to the supervisors the eligibility of their trading desks. Unlike back-testing, the requirement to pass the PLA test is newly introduced. Such test checks the incompleteness of modelling and hedges material risk. The fundamental principle of applying both back-testing and PLA is the comparison between the model-generated risk measures and the actual profit or loss, defined as the "trading outcome".

To test whether the estimated risk measures adequately capture the volatility of TB exposures, the new framework suggests the use of both back-testing and the attribution of P&L not only to determine the robustness of the internal model but also to determine the eligibility of the trading desk involved in the IMA. Banks should use both hypothetical and actual trading outcomes to enhance the understanding of the connection, relevance, and equivalence between trading outcomes and risk measures.

According to the final Basel provisions, national supervisors should ensure that banks maintain "an independent risk control unit [which] must regularly perform backtesting and PLA programmes, to compare the measures generated by the model risk and P&L values against actual daily changes in portfolio values over longer periods of time, as well as hypothetical changes based on static positions" (BCBS, 2016a: 50, para 180 (b)). Complementing the above qualitative standards, the final Basel framework also provides guidance on the regulatory quantitative standards of measuring ES, by suggesting that "banks may employ historical or Monte Carlo simulations or any other analytical methods as long as such models capture the risks confirmed by backtesting and PLA" (BCBS, 2016a: 54, para 181 [g]). In case a trading desk fails to satisfy the minimum back-testing and PLA requirements, banks are not eligible to produce capital charges based on the IMA.

6.8.3.1   P&L Attribution Requirements

The risk management system framework should consider all necessary RFs which drive the regulatory trading desks' daily P&L, as well as those used by the front-office systems.

The risk management model of banks uses a set of RFs to value the portfolios of regulatory trading desk, which exclusively[66] define the Risk-theoretical daily

P&L ($P \& L_{\text{RiskTheo}}$). On the other hand, for the same desk's portfolio considered in the theoretical P&L the front desk estimates the hypothetical daily trading desk P&L ($P \& L_{\text{Hypo}}$) independently. In $P \& L_{\text{Hypo}}$ analysis the trading desk's portfolio remains static during the day as it excludes the consideration of intra-day risks, similar to the portfolio applied in risk management analysis. The hypothetical portfolio is generally more precise as the front desk considers more RFs[67] than in the valuation of $P \& L_{\text{RiskTheo}}$. The bank should calculate and com-pare the last year's outcome of theoretical and hypothetical P&L to assess whether, and at what level, the two measurements are related to each other over time. Banks should perform PLA tests that rely on two metrics:

1. The average of the unexplained daily P&L, defined as the difference between the $P \& L_{\text{RiskTheo}}$ and $P \& L_{\text{Hypo}}$, divided by the standard deviation of the $P \& L_{\text{Hypo}}$ (Eq. (6.32))

$$\frac{\frac{1}{n}\sum_{1}^{n}\left(P \& L_{\text{RiskTheo}} - P \& L_{\text{Hypo}}\right)}{\sigma\left(P \& L_{\text{Hypo}}\right)} \quad (6.32)$$

where n is the number of trading days within a month; and

2. The ratio of variances (σ) of the unexplained daily P&L and the hypotheti-cal daily P&L (Eq. (6.33))

$$\frac{\sigma^2\left(P \& L_{\text{RiskTheo}} - P \& L_{\text{Hypo}}\right)}{\sigma^2\left(P \& L_{\text{Hypo}}\right)} \quad (6.33)$$

According to the new framework, banks can apply the IMA to specific trading desks only if, over the course of one year, the ratio of Eq. (6.32) is within a range of -10% to 10%, and the ratio of Eq. (6.33) is below 20%. The above thresholds set in the PLA test ensure that the internal models esti-mate risk with high precision. In case the trading desk faces four or more breaches in the prior 12 months, the approach used to calculate capital must fall back to the standardised one i.e., the model fall back from the "green zone," to the "red zone." Given the likelihood, however, that an immediate change from IMA to SA may cause significant volatility in the capital require-ments, the committee is proposing for those models that although unable to pass the PAL test are still performing sufficiently well, to belong in the "amber zone." For the trading desk that belongs to this intermediate zone, an additional formula-based capital requirement integrated into the trading desk's IMA-based capital requirements.

The committee is revising a) the frequency of conducting the PLA test together with the length of the data time series, and b) the design of the test metrics. In the design of the PLA test metrics, the committee is proposing methods for assessing the level of dependencies and correlation of Hypothetical and Risk-theoretical P&L based on the statistical distributions of the time series of their values (BCBS, 2018: 6–7 paras 2.1.2).

Base on the proposed amendments by the committee, a trading desk identifies to what zone it belongs based on the outputs of the distributional test metric. Thus, in case both (i) the correlation metric is above 0.825, and (ii) the distributional test metric is below [0.083 (p-value = 0.35)/14], the trading desk belongs to the green zone. In case the correlation metric is less than 0.75; or the distributional test metric is [above 0.095 (p-value = 0.20)/above 18] the trading desk is assigned to the green zone. When however the trading desk is allocated neither to the green zone nor to the red zone, it is then allocated to the amber zone (BCBS, 2018: 10–30 paras Annex B).

6.8.3.2 Back-Testing Requirements

The Need and Challenges of Back-Testing

Both regulators and banks must ensure that the internal models, as well as the resulting P&L values generated by these models, reflect the evolution of the markets over time by applying back-testing techniques. The term "back-testing" implies that banks take a backward look to compare the estimations of their internal models with what would be the P&L of the assessed portfolio. Thus, banks should always keep track of the history of data, for example, actual values of RFs and ES estimations, P&Ls, the trading activities, and so on. Thus, back-testing confirms or rejects the assumption of the bank that the IMA is robust, by testing whether the observed actual trading outcomes are in line with the estimations of the risk measurement models. To this end, back-testing applied in actual and hypothetical trading portfolios judges the ES estimations concentrating on the tail part of the loss distribution, by counting the number of times actual losses exceed the ES risk measure. Back-testing is unable, however, to capture missing risks that may not be included in the model.

Banks should measure the cases of potential underestimations of model predictions, that is, the underestimations of model predictions and real trading outcomes, aka outliers. When the number of the differences is small, the model is accepted by the supervisors. Despite the resources and efforts spent by banks, the internal model may still fail to generate predictions which are aligned with the actual events.

As mentioned above, the VaR and ES estimates assume 99% and 97.5% CLs, respectively. The back-testing model could produce different results as to its predictive power, as shown below:

1. Rejection of the model. According to this case, the results indicate that the model should be rejected due to the high number of exceptions, aka outliers. Albeit the rejection of the model relies on a high level of confidence, there is always the possibility that the model is rejected due to the existence of "Type I" error which is attributed to the bias of the data used. Thus, a decision to reject a model could be "unfair" or "fair" according to the following:

   (a) the model is correct but erroneously rejected (Type I [or α] error); or
   (b) the model is incorrect and correctly rejected ("True negative" decision).

2. Acceptance of the model: According to this case, the results indicate that the model should be accepted following the low number of exceptions. Albeit the acceptance of the model relies on a high level of confidence, there is always the possibility that the model is erroneously accepted due to the existence of the "Type II" error, which is attributed to the bias of the sample of data used. Thus, a decision to accept a model could be "unfair" or "fair" according to the following:

   (a) the model is incorrect, but it is erroneously accepted (Type II [or β] error); or
   (b) the model is correct and, therefore, correctly accepted ("True positive" decision).

Naturally, supervisors have to minimise the above two possible errors (Type I and Type II). In this respect, the BCBS states that "when comparing the actual trading results with model-generated risk measures and such comparison uncovers sufficient differences that problems almost certainly must exist, either with the model or with the assumptions of the backtesting. In between these two cases is a grey area where the test results are, on their own, inconclusive" (BCBS, 2016a: 74) (see Table 6.10).

Back-Testing Based on Hypothetical and Actual Trading Outcomes

Internal models' measurements conduct the calculations of sensitivities assuming a static portfolio to avoid any inconsistencies that may arise from changes in portfolio composition. Based on the recent revision of supervisory standards and regulations, banks should perform daily back-testing to compare each desk's one-day static ES estimations against P&Ls (trading outcomes) which result from (a) the actual daily performance of the portfolio (actual P&L) and (b) from the hypothetical changes of the portfolio that could have occurred (hypothetical P&L).

Applying Back-Testing

Assuming that a bank faces a left tail p which is 1% of the entire loss distribution for a total of T days. Given that the total number of trading is time horizon of T = 250 days, one has to estimate the number of days the actual losses exceed those estimated by the model, that is, the estimation of the number of outliers. The distribution of the number of outliers, aka exceptions, follows a binomial probability distribution, as defined in Eq. (6.34).

$$f(x) = \binom{T}{x} \times p^x \cdot (1-p)^{250-x} \qquad (6.34)$$

Based on this Eq. (6.34), Table 6.11 illustrates the exact probabilities arising from a number of observed outliers out of 250 observations (one year) for a model that is assumed to be accurate by 99%. Setting $p = 0.01$, the second column of Table 6.11 indicates the exact probability (8.1%) of a model, with an assumed 99% predictive ability, producing zero outliers, while the probability of it producing one outlier is 20.5%.

The above means that the acceptance of a 99% CL internal model which produces zero outliers is subject to Type II error only by 8.11%, or, otherwise, the rejection of the same internal model is subject to Tier I error with 91.89% certainty. In practice, this means that a 99% CL internal model can be accepted with 91.89% certainty. Moving towards a higher number of exceptions, the possibility of Type II error increases, that is, the possibility of accepting a model although it should have been rejected. This possibility reaches 99.99% when the internal models produce ten exceptions in relation to the actual losses, which implies that the model can be rejected with 99.99% certainty. Supervisors should deem this level of confidence as sufficient to safely reject a model. Thus, any model that produces more than ten exceptions should be rejected.

Table 6.11 shows the probabilities of Type I and Type II errors under internal models with lower CLs, that is, 98% and 97%, respectively. As observed, under these alternative model specifications, the supervisors would need more exceptions to reach the level of certainty implied in the 99% CL internal model. According to the 98% CL internal model, the supervisors should observe at least 15 exceptions to safely reject the model, while under the 97% CL internal model they would need 19 observations. The aforementioned evidence implies that one of the reasons to select the 99% CL is the easiest means of monitoring that it provides to both banks and supervisors.

Despite the 99.99% certainty of model rejection that ten exceptions would provide, the back-testing could provide evidence (but not certainty) that the model is not appropriate for implementation. To cope with the uncertainty that a model may or may not be appropriate for implementation, the Basel framework assesses the quality and accuracy of the models according to the following three zones: (a) green, (b) yellow, and (c) red, where green represents a robust model, red indicates a model that should be rejected, and yellow designates a model which is not definitely appropriate or inappropriate for application.

The Basel framework defines the boundaries of these zones based on the cumulative probabilities set for the number of exceptions. Thus, as illustrated in Table 6.10, the boundaries of the yellow zone range from 95.88% to 99.9%, that is, the cumulative distribution of Type II error. To cope with this uncertainty and protect banks from potential misspecifications of the internal model, supervisors should request them to apply a multiplication factor which will further the capital charge.

The green zone, which is attributed to zero to four exceptions, receives a multiplication factor of 1.5 on the estimated capital charge that arises from the application of IMA. The yellow zone, which extends from five to nine exceptions, receives a somewhat increased multiplication factor reflecting the increased model-error risk incorporated in the IMA. In this critical zone the degree of Type I error is rather low; however, the acceptable degree of Type II error risk is rather significant. Thus, the additional capital charge is between 70% and 92% in relation to the output produced by the IMA, and 20 to 42 percentage points in relation to what the multiplication factor of the green zone indicates. Finally, the red zone (above nine exceptions) indicates that the internal model cannot adequately capture the loss events which result in the rejection of the model. The possibility of confronting with a Type I error is minor, whereas the chances of Type II errors, arising from a potential

Table 6.10 Supervisory green, yellow, and red zones use to assess back-testing results

Zone	Number of exceptions	Multiplier	Cumulative probability
Green zone	0	1.5	8.11%
	1	1.5	28.58%
	2	1.5	54.32%
	3	1.5	75.81%
	4	1.5	89.22%
Yellow zone	5	1.7	95.88%
	6	1.76	98.63%
	7	1.83	99.60%
	8	1.88	99.89%
	9	1.92	99.97%
Red zone	10	2	99.99%

acceptance of this model, are significantly high. Internal models that fall under the red zone should review the failures to improve the predictability of the model immediately. Moreover, as defined in Table 6.10, the additional capital charge for such models is 200% of the value estimated by the internal model. Internal models that fail to align with the back-testing and P&L attribution requirements are not eligible for the estimation of capital charges under the IMA and they, henceforth, use the SA.

6.9   Conclusion

The FRTB framework addresses a set of various financial risks, that is, market, counterparty, credit, and other behavioural risks. As discussed in this chapter, all banks, irrespective of the approach they use, should calculate the capital charge according to the SA. The SA capital charges arise from the application of the SbM, the DRC, and the RRAO.

Under the SbM, delta, vega, and curvature sensitivities are assigned to eight risk classes. The estimation of delta risk derives from the classification rules which govern the buckets, RWs, and correlations. On the other hand, the buckets and cross-bucket correlations are aligned to delta risk, while RWs are driven by the liquidity horizons assigned to each risk class. Moreover, the new framework estimates the correlations of the options' and their underlying assets' maturities. Finally, the buckets and correlations of curvature risk align with the delta risk after providing for some adjustments, whereas RWs result from the application of deterministic shifts.

The risk position under the SA uses the risk-weighted sensitivities and correlations for each bucket and then considers the cross-bucket correlations to estimate the aggregated sensitivity capital charge. Subject to additional requirements, some banks may also apply a reduced, simplified, sensitivity-based (R-SbM) approach, which considers only the delta risk. However, the use of R-SbM produces higher RWs which increase the capital charge in relation to the SbM.

The standardised DRC against JTD risk losses applies to both securitisation and non-securitisation instruments. For non-securitisations, the bank estimates and then offsets the obligor-specific JTD loss amounts that refer to long and short exposures. The JTD estimation relies on the LGD, the notional, and the P&L amounts and, subsequently, is the input for the estimation of the hedge benefit ratio which, in turn, discounts the net short exposures. The final capital charge is estimated based on the values of JTD, RWs, and hedge benefit ratios. For securitisations in a non-CTP, the bank follows the same approach as for the default risk when estimating JTDs and default risk capital charge. Equivalently, banks offset RWs at the level of tranches. For the securitisations in the CTP, the JTD estimation follows the same approach with the estimation of default risk securitisations in non-CTP. Regarding the default RWs, banks should consider those applied in the banking books according to the securitisation framework. The estimation of default risk capital charge follows the principles of non-securitisations.

Banks should also estimate a capital add-on against residual risks (RRAO), such as losses attributed to behavioural risks. The Basel framework estimates the RRAO capital charge is the product of the RW to the gross notional amounts of the exposures linked to residual RFs.

As an alternative to the SA, banks may also apply the IMA, subject to certain qualitative and quantitative standards. Under the IMA, banks should estimate the ES, the DRC, and the SCAO for non-modellable risks. The major innovation that the IMA introduces is the shift from the VaR framework to liquidity-adjusted ES estimation, which focuses on extreme events resulting from liquidity risk. Banks have to estimate the base ES considering either the full or a subset of RFs, including the appropriate adjustment to liquidity horizons. The model is calibrated by using historical observations of severe stresses. Moreover, the default risk takes into consideration the simulation of default events according to a VaR model while the bank estimates the capital charge of NMRFs based on stress scenarios.

Finally, the Basel III framework, except for the application of the amended back-testing technique, introduces P&L attribution requirements to test the eligibility of trading desks. The primary purpose of applying PLA test is to measure possible inconsistencies between the Hypothetical and Risk-theoretical P&L measures that indicate "missing risks" which are excluded in the risk management model. The framework defines a limit of acceptance for such inconsistency before a trading desk is no longer permitted to use the IMA.

Table 6.11 Type I and II errors for different outliers and confidence intervals of a sample of 250 independent observations

Number of exceptions	Coverage = 99%			Coverage = 98%			Coverage = 97%		
	Exact (%)	Type I (%)	Type II (%)	Exact (%)	Type I (%)	Type II (%)	Exact (%)	Type I (%)	Type II (%)
0	8.1	100.0	0.0	0.6	100.0	0.0	0.0	100.0	0.0
1	20.5	91.9	8.1	3.3	99.4	0.6	0.4	100.0	0.0
2	25.7	71.4	28.6	8.3	96.1	3.9	1.5	99.6	0.4
3	21.5	45.7	54.3	14.0	87.8	12.2	3.8	98.1	1.9
4	13.4	24.2	75.8	17.7	73.8	26.2	7.2	94.3	5.7
5	6.7	10.8	89.2	17.7	56.1	43.9	10.9	87.2	12.8
6	2.8	4.1	95.9	14.8	38.4	61.6	13.8	76.3	23.7
7	1.0	1.4	98.6	10.5	23.6	76.4	14.9	62.5	37.5
8	0.3	0.4	99.6	6.5	13.1	86.9	14.0	47.6	52.4
9	0.1	0.1	99.9	3.6	6.6	93.4	11.6	33.7	66.3
10	0.0	0.0	100.0	1.8	3.0	97.0	8.6	22.1	77.9
11	0.0	0.0	100.0	0.8	1.3	98.7	5.8	13.4	86.6
12	0.0	0.0	100.0	0.3	0.5	99.5	3.6	7.6	92.4
13	0.0	0.0	100.0	0.1	0.2	99.8	2.0	4.0	96.0
14	0.0	0.0	100.0	0.0	0.1	99.9	1.1	2.0	98.0
15	0.0	0.0	100.0	0.0	0.0	100.0	0.5	0.9	99.1
16	0.0	0.0	100.0	0.0	0.0	100.0	0.2	0.4	99.6
17	0.0	0.0	100.0	0.0	0.0	100.0	0.1	0.2	99.8
18	0.0	0.0	100.0	0.0	0.0	100.0	0.0	0.1	99.9
19	0.0	0.0	100.0	0.0	0.0	100.0	0.0	0.0	100.0
20	0.0	0.0	100.0	0.0	0.0	100.0	0.0	0.0	100.0

Notes

1. The proposed four scaling factors are [1.50–2.00], [3.00–3.50], [1.50–2.50] and [1.25–1.50] (BCBS, 2018: 13 table 1).
2. As shown in Eq. (6.6) for bucket b, $S_b = \sum_k WS_k$ and bucket c, $S_C = \sum_k WS_k$; however, if $\sum_b k_b^2 + \sum_b \sum_{c \neq b} \gamma_{bc} S_b S_c < 0$ then $S_b = \max [\min(\sum_k WS_k, k_b), -k_b]$ for all risk factors in bucket b. This rule is not applicable under the R-SbA.
3. The same buckets used in in delta sensitivities.
4. The curvature correlation parameters ρ_{kl} and γ_{bc} are the same as defined in delta sensitivities; however, the values in both parameters ρ_{kl} and γ_{bc} should be squared.
5. As illustrated in Eq. (6.10), the formulae which estimate the sensitivities for all risk factors in bucket b and c are given by $S_b = \sum_k CVR_k$ and $S_c = \sum_k CVR_k$, respectively; however, if the value under square root in Eq. (6.9) is negative, sensitivities are defined as $S_b = \max [\min(\sum_k CVR_k, k_b), -k_b]$ and $S_C = \max [\min(\sum_k CVR_k, k_c), -k_c]$ for all risk factors in corresponding buckets b and c.

6. The rules for identifying such curves are set out in the Basel framework for the SbM (BCBS, 2016a: 20 para 59) and R-SbM (BCBS, 2017: 4, para 211).

7. The new framework distinguishes vertices amongst periods of a quarter of a year, half a year, 1, 2, 3, 5, 10, 15, 20, and 30 years. For assigning risk factors to the above vertices, banks may use linear interpolation or a method consistent to pricing functions used internally.

8. The vertices are 0.5, 1, 3, 5, and 10 years.

9. The curvature risk charge does not include inflation and cross-currency basis risks.

10. The maturity vertices are set to 0.5, 1, 3, 5, and 10 years.

11. Vega risk capital charge does not apply to equity repo rates.

12. Contract grade of the commodity is the minimum accepted standard that a commodity must meet to be accepted as the actual physical deliverable against the contract (also known as the "basis grade" or "par grade") (BCBS, 2016a: 24, para 65).

13. The time vertices are 0, 0.25, 0.5, 1, 2, 3, 5, 10, 15, and 20 years.

14. The ten vertices are 0.25, 0.5, 1, 2, 3, 5, 10, 15, 20, and 30 years. Based on the proposed amendments the RWs correspondingly assigned to the five vertices modified and set from 2.4%, 2.25%, 1.88%, and 1.73% (BCBS, 2016a), to the ranges of [1.5–1.9%], [1.4–1.8%], [1.1–1.5%], [1.0–1.4%] (BCBS, 2018) respectively, while the RW assigned to the last five vertices is modified and set from 1.5% (BCBS, 2016a) to the range of [0.9–1.2%] (BCBS, 2018).

15. The RWs may at the discretion of the bank be divided by $\sqrt{2}$.

16. EUR, USD, GBP, AUD, JPY, SEK, CAD, and domestic reporting currency of a bank.

17. Note that in reference to endnote number $\sum_b k_b^2 + \sum_b \sum_{c \neq b} \gamma_{bc} S_b S_c > 0$.

18. The RWs for the 16 buckets {1, …, 16} are 0.5%, 1.0%, 5.0%, 3.0%, 3.0%, 2.0%, 1.5%, 4.0%, 3.0%, 4.0%, 12.0%, 7.0%, 8.5%, 5.5%, 5.0%, and 12.0%, respectively.

19. Sectors' allocation on buckets 1 (IG) and 9 (HY&NR) to sovereigns include central banks, multilateral development banks; buckets 2 (IG) and 10 (HY&NR) to local government, government-backed non-financials, education, public administration; buckets 3 (IG) and 11 (HY&NR) to financials including government-backed financials; buckets 4 (IG) and 12 (HY&NR) to basic materials, energy, industrials, agriculture, manufacturing, mining and quarrying; buckets 5 (IG) and 13 (HY&NR) to consumer goods and services, transportation and storage, administrative and support service activities; buckets 6 (IG) and 14 (HY&NR) to technology, telecommunications; buckets 7 (IG) and 15 (HY&NR) to health care, utilities, professional and technical activities; bucket 8 (IG) to covered bonds; and bucket 16 to other sectors.

20. Excluding covered bonds.

21. The correlations between buckets having different sectors are defined as in the table below:

Bucket	1/9	2/10	3/11	4/12	5/13	6/14	7/15	8
1/9		75%	10%	20%	25%	20%	15%	10%
2/10			5%	15%	20%	15%	10%	10%
3/11				5%	15%	20%	5%	20%
4/12					20%	25%	5%	5%
5/13						25%	5%	15%
6/14							5%	20%
7/15								5%
8								

22. Sectors' allocation on buckets 1 (IG) and 4 (HY&NR) to sovereigns include central banks, multilateral development banks, local government, government-backed non-financials, education, public administration; buckets 2 (IG) and 5 (HY&NR) to financials including government-backed financials; buckets 3 (IG) and 6 (HY&NR) to other sectors.

23. For the sectors sovereigns including central banks, multilateral development banks' RWs, associated with buckets 1 and 4 (HY&NR) the RWs are set to 1.0% and 5.0%, respectively, to these buckets; whereas for the sectors local government, government-backed non-financials, education, public administration, also associated with buckets 1 and 4 (HY&NR), the RWs are set to 1.0% and 5.0%, respectively, to these buckets. The RWs for buckets 2, 3, 5, and 6 are 10%, 15.0%, 25.0%, and 30.0%, respectively.

24. The correlation parameter γ_{bc} defined as in the table below:

Bucket	1	2	3	4	5	6
1		10%	0%	50%	5%	0%
2			0%	5%	50%	0%
3				0%	0%	50%
4					10%	0%
5						0%
6						

25. The RWs for the 16 buckets {1, ..., 16} are 4.0%, 4.0%, 8.0%, 5.0%, 4.0%, 3.0%, 2.0%, 6.0%, 13.0%, 13.0%, 16.0%, 10.0%, 12.5%, 12.0%, 12.0%, 13.0%, respectively.

26. The sectors assigned to each of the eight buckets of all three groups of the non-correlation trading portfolio are residential mortgage-backed securities (RMBS)—prime, RMBS—mid-prime, RMBS—subprime, commercial mortgage-backed securities (CMBS), asset-backed securities (ABS)—student loans, asset-backed securities (ABS)—credit cards, asset-backed securities (ABS)—auto, and collateralised loan obligations (CLO).

27. The RWs for the eight buckets are 0.9%, 1.5%, 2.0%, 2.0%, 0.8%, 1.2%, 1.2%, and 1.4%, respectively.
28. The credit quality for the three groups of buckets is defined identically for both SbM and R-SbM, that is, as SIG, NSIG, and HY&NR, respectively.
29. The sectors assigned to the three groups of four buckets {1, …, 4} are RMBS, non-mortgage retail securitisations, CMBS, other.
30. The risk weights for the 12 buckets {1, …, 12} are set at 2.0%, 5.0%, 5.0%, 10.0%, 5.0%, 6.25%, 6.25%, 12.5%, 3.5%, 8.75%, 8.75%, 17.5%, respectively.
31. Defined as the sum of the global market capitalisations (across all stock markets) of the same legal entity or group of legal entities: small market cap < US $2 billion and large market cap ≥ US $2 billion.
32. Advanced economies: Canada, the US, Mexico, the Euro area, the non-Euro area Western European countries (the UK, Norway, Sweden, Denmark, and Switzerland), Japan, Oceania (Australia and New Zealand), Singapore, and Hong Kong SAR.
33. Sectors of consumer goods and services, transportation and storage, administrative and support service activities, health care, and utilities are allocated to buckets 1, 5, 9, and 10; sectors of telecommunications and industrials are allocated to buckets 2, 6, 9, and 10; sectors of basic materials, energy, agriculture, manufacturing, mining and quarrying are allocated to buckets 3, 7, 9, and 10; and sectors of financials including government-backed financials, real estate activities, and technology are allocated to buckets 4, 8, 9, and 10.
34. Based on the proposed amendments for the 11 buckets {1, …, 11} the RWs for equity spot price modified and set from 55%, 60%, 45%, 55%, 30%, 35%, 40%, 50%, 70%, 50%, and 70% (BCBS 2016a), to the ranges of [27.5–41.25%], [30–45%], [22.5–33.75%], [27.5–41.25%], [15–22.5%], [17.5–26.25%], [20–30%], [25–37.5%], [35–52.5%], [25–37.5%] and [35–52.5%] (BCBS, 2018); whereas the RWs for equity repo rate modified and set from 0.55%, 0.60%, 0.45%, 0.55%, 0.30%, 0.35%, 0.40%, 0.50%, 0.70%, 0.50%, and 0.70% (BCBS 2016a), to the ranges of [0.275–0.4125%], [0.30–0.45%], [0.225–0.3375%], [0.275–0.4125%], [0.15–0.225%], [0.175–0.2625%], [0.20–0.30%], [0.25–0.375%], [0.35–0.525%], [0.25–0.375%] and [0.35–0.525%] (BCBS, 2018), respectively.
35. Sectors of financials including government-backed financials, real estate activities, technology are allocated to buckets 1 and 3, other sectors are allocated to buckets 2 and 4, and finally all sectors are allocated to buckets 5 and 6.
36. For the six buckets {1, …, 6}, the RWs for equity spot price are 60%, 60%, 50%, 40%, 70%, and 60%, respectively.
37. For the six buckets {1, …, 6} the correlation ρ_{kl} is set to 15%, 15%, 25%, 25%, 7.5%, and 12.5% accordingly.
38. The RWs for the 11 buckets {1, …, 11} are 30%, 35%, 60%, 80%, 40%, 45%, 20%, 35%, 25%, 35%, and 55%, respectively.

39. For the 11 buckets {1, ..., 11} the corresponding commodity categories are defined by the regulators as: (1) energy—solid combustibles, (2) energy—liquid combustibles, (3) energy—electricity and carbon trading, (4) freight, (5) metals—non-precious, (6) gaseous combustibles, (7) precious metals (including gold), (8) grains and oilseed, (9) livestock and dairy, (10) softs and other agriculturals, and (11) other commodity.

40. The risk weights for the 11 buckets {1, ..., 11} are 40%, 45%, 70%, 90%, 50%, 55%, 30%, 45%, 35%, 45%, and 60%, respectively.

41. The correlation ρ_{kl} between non-identical commodities for each of the 11 buckets is set at 55%, 95%, 40%, 80%, 60%, 65%, 55%, 45%, 15%, 40%, and 15%, respectively.

42. The following currency pairs have been selected by the Basel Committee: USD/EUR, USD/JPY, USD/GBP, SD/AUD, USD/CAD, USD/CHF, USD/MXN, USD/CNY, USD/NZD, USD/RUB, USD/HKD, USD/SGD, USD/TRY, USD/KRW, USD/SEK, USD/ZAR, USD/INR, USD/NOK, USD/BRL, EUR/JPY, EUR/GBP, EUR/CHF, and JPY/AUD and based on the proposed amendments (BCBS, 2018) currency pairs forming first-order crosses across these specified currency pairs.

43. The liquidity horizon assigned to risk class is set for GIRR at 60 days, CSR non-securitisations at 120 days, CSR securitisations (CTP) at 120 days, CSR securitisations (non-CTP) at 120 days, equity (large cap) at 20 days, equity (small cap) at 60 days, commodity at 120 days, and FX at 40 days.

44. The Basel framework assigns LGD = 100% to non-senior debt instruments, LGD = 75% to senior debt instruments, and LGD = 25% to covered bond.

45. The proposed classification of the credit quality assigns rating grades AAA (Aaa), AA (Aa), A (A), BBB (Baa), BB (Ba), B (B), CCC (Caa), unrated, and defaulted to the following default RWs: 0.5%, 2%, 3%, 6%, 15%, 30%, 50%, 15%, and 100%, respectively.

46. Offsetting is not allowed among securitisation exposures with different underlying securitised portfolios as well as exposures arising from different tranches with the same securitised portfolio (see: BCBS, 2016a: 46 para 159).

47. The asset classes are asset-backed commercial paper (ABCP), auto loans/leases, residential mortgage-backed securities (RMBS), credit cards, commercial mortgage-backed securities (CMBS), collateralised loan obligations (CLOs), collateralised debt obligations (CDOs)-squared, small and medium corporate entities (SMEs), student loans, other retail, and other wholesale.

48. Asia, Europe, North America, and all others.

49. CDX North America IG, iTraxx Europe IG, CDX HY, iTraxx XO, LCDX (loan index), iTraxx LevX (loan index), Asia Corp, Latin America Corp, Other Regions Corp, Major Sovereign (G7 and Western Europe), other Sovereign.

50. But excluding smile, dividend, cheapest-to-deliver option and some types of correlation risks.

51. In trading, risk control, auditing, back-office areas.
52. For example, board of directors and senior management.
53. Or could be unwound hedged.
54. Artzner (1997) describes sub-additivity based on the idea that "merging assets will not create extra risk"; otherwise, if risk were not sub-additive, then one could be exposed to two assets 1 and 2 and would be better off opening a separate account for each of them due to the fact that the risk-based margin requirement would be lower than if both are held in the same account.
55. In fact, most definitions of ES lead to same results when applied to continuous loss distributions. Differences may appear when the underlying loss distributions have discontinuities. In this case, even the coherence property of ES could cease to exist, unless the bank carefully calibrates the confidence levels of VaR and ES to the right degree.
56. In case no extreme tail event is expected to emerge, the ES would be equal to the *VaR*.
57. The new framework (BSBS, 2016a: 55, para 181 (k)) assigns one out of the five liquidity horizons $\{1, …5\}$, that is, $LH = \{10,20,40,60,120\}$, to each of the risk factor categories: interest rates—widespread currencies: EUR, USD, GBP, AUD, JPY, SEK, CAD, and the domestic currency of a bank have $LH = 10$ days, interest rate—other currencies—$LH = 20$ days, interest rate volatility: $LH = 60$ days, interest rate—other types: $LH = 60$ days, credit spread—sovereign (IG): $LH = 20$ days, credit spread—sovereign (HY), $LH = 40$ days, credit spread—corporate (IG): $LH = 40$ days, credit spread—corporate (HY): $LH = 60$ days, credit spread—volatility: $LH = 120$ days, credit spread—other types: $LH = 120$ days, equity price (large cap): $LH = 10$ days, equity price (small cap): $LH = 20$ days, equity price (large cap)—volatility: $LH = 20$ days, equity price (small cap)—volatility: $LH = 60$ days, equity—other types: $LH = 60$ days, FX rate—specified currency pairs: $LH = 20$ days, FX rate other currency pairs: $LH = 20$ days, FX volatility: $LH = 40$ days, FX—other types: $LH = 40$ days, energy and carbon emissions trading price: $LH = 20$ days, precious metals and non-ferrous metals price: $LH = 20$ days, other commodities price: $LH = 60$ days, energy and carbon emissions trading price—volatility: $LH = 60$ days, precious metals and non-ferrous metals price—volatility: $LH = 60$ days, other commodities price—volatility: $LH = 120$ days, commodity—other types: $LH = 120$ days.
58. Banks may use a subset of risk factors as far as they do not have at their disposal a sufficiently long history of good-quality data.
59. As long as the supervisor judges that the ES model captures, through the P&L attribution and back-testing, all material risks which the bank is exposed to.
60. Empirical correlations between risk factors can also be used.
61. Default risk is the risk of direct loss due to an obligor's failure to fulfil his or her contractual obligations.

62. The framework provides guides on the scenario definition and capital estimation, e.g., stress scenarios used liquidity horizons similar to the ones applied in the ES calibration assigned to modelled risks (BSBS, 2018 and BCBS, 2016a: 64 paras 190).

63. Interest rate risk, equity risk, foreign exchange risk, commodity risk, and credit spread risk.

64. Notably, according to (BCBS, 2016a: 63 paras 189), the aggregate capital charge for market risk refers to the previous day's observation.

65. The standard level of multiplication factor m_c is set at 1.5; however, supervisory authorities may increase this level depending on the assessed quality of risk management system; they may also increase it by 0 to 0.5 depending on the performance of back-testing results against hypothetical and actual P&L as described in Sect. 6.8.3.

66. Any risk factor that is not included in the risk management model of the trading desk cannot be considered in the estimation of the risk-theoretical P&L which is the P&L that would be produced by the bank's pricing models for the desk (BCBS, 2016a: 71).

67. The hypothetical P&L of the trading desk's instruments is estimated daily at the desk level and is based on the MTM value of the instruments derived from the bank's pricing models, for the desk, including all risk factors (BCBS, 2016a: 71). In hypothetical P&L bank must remove the commissions, fees, the impact of intraday trading and certain valuation adjustments.

References

Artzner, P., Delbaen, F., Eber, J., & Heath, D. (1997). Thinking coherently. *Risk, 10*(11), 68–71.

Artzner, P., Delbaen, F., Eber, J., & Heath, D. (1999). Coherent measures of risk. *Mathematical Finance, 9*(3), 203–228.

Basel Committee on Banking Supervision (BCBS). (2010, December). Basel III: A global regulatory framework for more resilient banks and banking systems. https://www.bis.org/publ/bcbs189.pdf. Accessed December 2010.

Basel Committee on Banking Supervision (BCBS). (2011, February). Revisions to the Basel II market risk framework. Retrieved February 2011, from https://www.bis.org/publ/bcbs193.pdf

Basel Committee on Banking Supervision (BCBS). (2013, October). Fundamental review of the trading book: A revised market risk framework. Retrieved October 2013, from https://www.bis.org/publ/bcbs265.pdf

Basel Committee on Banking Supervision (BCBS). (2014, December). Basel III Document Revisions to the securitisation framework. Retrieved December 2014, from https://www.bis.org/bcbs/publ/d303.pdf

Basel Committee on Banking Supervision (BCBS). (2016a, January). Minimum capital requirements for market risk. Retrieved January 2016, from https://www.bis.org/bcbs/publ/d352.pdf

Basel Committee on Banking Supervision (BCBS). (2016b, March). Reducing variation in credit risk-weighted assets – Constraints on the use of internal model approaches. Retrieved March 2016, from https://www.bis.org/bcbs/publ/d362.pdf

Basel Committee on Banking Supervision (BCBS). (2017, June). Simplified alternative to the standardised approach to market risk capital requirements. Retrieved June 2017, from https://www.bis.org/bcbs/publ/d408.pdf

Basel Committee on Banking Supervision (BCBS). (March 2018). Revisions to the minimum capital requirements for market risk. Retrieved March 2018, from https://www.bis.org/bcbs/publ/d436.pdf

7

Credit Valuation Adjustments

The derivative positions are subject to changes due to market volatility which changes the exposure to counterparty risk and the credit quality of the counterparty. Against this background, banks should keep aside additional capital, known as credit valuation adjustments (CVAs) capital charge, which stands for the difference between the risk-free and actual portfolio values which takes into account the default probability of a counterparty.

The CVA analysis is a critical element in pricing over-the-counter (OTC) derivatives. Since the changes in CVA are due to the market pricing of counterparty risk, the variability of the counterparty risk over time could be potentially more significant than the credit risk of the underlying position. Hence, the fair value of a financial derivative depends on the counterparty credit risk (CCR) of the traded derivative. The current chapter examines the properties of the CVA.

7.1 Fundamentals of CVA Estimation

The estimation of the CVA relies on the potential movements in the underlying market variables as well as the counterparty default probabilities and corresponding credit spreads. Moreover, the expected recovery and the duration of the exposure are also essential factors in CVA estimation. The general formula (Eq. (7.1)) expresses the CVA for a particular counterparty as the sum over all n points in time of the discounted expected exposure $EE(t_i)$ at each time point i multiplied by the probability of default (PD) assigned to the specific counterparty in the interval between t_{i-1} and t_i. The output of the

© The Author(s) 2018
I. Akkizidis, L. Kalyvas, *Final Basel III Modelling*,
https://doi.org/10.1007/978-3-319-70425-8_7

above is multiplied by the expected losses likely to occur after the default of the counterparty. The dependency of exposure on the counterparty's credit quality may be excluded, where possible, to avoid increasing the degree of the models' complexity and additional effort in the calibration process.

$$CVA \approx \left(1-\bar{\delta}\right)\sum_{i=1}^{n}D\left(t_i\right)EE\left(t_i\right)PD\left(t_{i-1}, t_i\right) \qquad (7.1)$$

where $PD(t_{i-1}, t_i)$ is the cumulative risk-neutral probability of the counterparty's default from t_{i-1} to t_i, $EE(t_i)$ is the risk-neutral discounted expected exposure (EE) at time t_i, and δ is the recovery rate.

In the existence of correlation between the exposure and the PD, the above general CVA formula should include the correlation factor ρ, as defined in Eq. (7.2).

$$CVA \approx \left(1-\bar{\delta}\right)\sum_{i=1}^{n}D\left(t_i\right)\cdot\rho\cdot EE\left(t_i\right)\cdot PD\left(t_{i-1}, t_i\right) \qquad (7.2)$$

The application of scenarios and deterministic shock in both market and market-implied counterparty spread risk results in a corresponding distribution of CVAs. Both scenarios and shocks are the basis of the CVA value at risk (VaR), the CVA sensitivity analysis. The generation of market risk factors which drive the evolution of the exposures used is discussed in Sect. 7.2. Moreover, in Sect. 7.3, the generation of counterparty credit spreads and default probabilities based on intensity-based credit risk models are applied in CVA (VaR) analysis. Section 7.4 covers the approaches proposed by BCBS related to the estimation of CVA capital charges.

7.2   Exposure Analysis

The valuation adjustment process includes the adjustment of market value for a derivative contract at future times due to probable default events. The actual market value of a contract trade i, linked to a specific counterparty, is known only for the current date, that is, $t = 0$. For any future date t, this value $V_i(t)$ is unknown as it is driven by market risk factors and possible uncertainties, whose properties are random. Thus, there is a need for simulating a number of scenarios to estimate the evolution of market conditions.

Let us assume that at future time τ a derivative is out of money due to market conditions and default of the underlying asset prior to the contract's maturity. For the bank, the credit exposure to derivative counterparty is the maximum of the contract's market value V_i and zero. Thus, for a particular trade i, the stand-alone exposure E_i at any future time t is defined as $E_i(t) = \max\{V_i(t), 0\}$ whereas at default time τ it is $E_i(\tau) = \max\{V_i(\tau), 0\}$.

This counterparty exposure indicates the degree of loss that a bank faces, and partially or fully absorbs in case of a default event. After such an event, banks may have to deal with losses due to defaulted contract's replacement cost, determined by the market value of the contract i at the time $V_i(\tau)$. In brief, if the contract value is positive, that is, $V_i(\tau) > 0$ at the time of default τ, the institution closes out the position at the then current market value $V_i(\tau)$, replacing the defaulted counterparty with another. If the contract value is negative, that is, $V_i(\tau) < 0$, at the time of default τ, the institution closes out the position by paying the defaulting counterparty the market value $V_i(\tau)$ of the contract; this results in a net loss of zero (i.e. neither loss nor gain) assigned to counterparty credit. Then, the bank has to enter into a similar contract with another counterparty to receive its market value $V_i(\tau)$.

In cases of collateralised exposure, the mechanism of margin agreements is applied for reducing the net exposure and credit losses from counterparty risks. In cases where more than one trade is linked to the defaulted counterparty, the bank's maximum loss equals the sum of all stand-alone individual derivative contract exposures. Thus, the role of netting, where applicable, plays a significant role in the exposure analysis. When applying netting agreements, the value of contacts is offset; that is, at the time of default, positions with negative values offset the ones with positive values, whereas only the net positive value is assigned to counterparty credit exposure.

Thus, the total exposure of all contracts in a netting agreement is reduced to the maximum of the net portfolio value and zero, that is, $E_{CP}(t) = \max \sum_i \{V_i(t), 0\}$. However, in cases where netting is not applicable, the trades with negative values cannot offset the ones with positive values, that is, $E_{CP}(t) = \sum_i E_i(t) = \sum_i \max\{V_i(t), 0\}$. In some cases, for example, due to operational constraints, there is a mix of netting and non-netting agreements applied to defaulted counterparties. In such instances, multiple netting agreements that cover non-overlapping subsets of the portfolio are applied. A general formula for multiple netting agreements is given by Eq. (7.3), which includes both netting and non-netting agreements.

$$E_{multiple}(t) = \sum_n \max\left[\sum_{i \in NA_n} \{V_i(t), 0\}\right] + \sum_{i \notin NA} \max\{V_i(t), 0\} \quad (7.3)$$

In the first term of the above formula, the inner sum of values refers to all trades covered only by the nth netting agreement, that is, $i \in NA_n$, whereas in the second term the sum of values refers to all trades that do not belong to any netting agreement, that is, $i \notin NA$.

Note that CVA considers only the positive exposure profile[1] of the derivative, that is, the derivative is in the money; on the other hand, the so-called debt valuation adjustments[2] (DVAs) refer to the negative exposure profile, that is, the derivative is out of money. In other words, the bank faces three possible situations due to the default of the counterparty: a positive, negative, or zero value adjustment. Nonetheless, BCBS deals only with the negative value adjustment which corresponds to the additional capital requirement due to the default of the counterparty.

7.2.1 Margin Requirements and Agreements

Margin requirements try to ensure the availability of adequate collaterals to offset possible losses resulting from counterparty defaults on OTC derivative deals. Likewise, they aim at reducing systemic risk, as well as avoiding *contamination effects* due to counterparty default. As the notional outstanding amount assigned to OTC derivatives is on the scale of trillions of dollars, a small percentage of systemic risk may result in a significant amount of losses. The probability of systemic risk losses may explain why regulators aim to render central clearing mandatory for most standardised derivatives in many jurisdictions.

However, margin regulatory requirements differ from capital requirements. The former retains only a complementary role in risk mitigation and loss absorbance, acting as a source of payout from the defaulted counterparty to the survivor (bank). On the other hand, capital requirements act as a source of payout from the bank's resources. By employing margins, counterparties in OTC derivative markets may be demotivated to default, which implies lower PDs and subsequently more resilient counterparties over normal and stressed times.

The definition of capital requirements relies on the probability-weighted loss-given default of a portfolio rather than on covering the entirety of the loss arising from a counterparty default. Seeing it from a portfolio management perspective, it is somewhat difficult for capital requirements to rapidly adjust to responses in changing portfolio positions and the related risk factors. In contrast, margin requirements focus on particular exposures, absorbing their potential losses.

To maintain a sufficient and effective level of margin, banks should include in it highly liquid and easily accessible collateral if needed to compensate for the default of counterparties. Having high-quality liquid collaterals allows margin to act as an efficient and reliable risk mitigant. The classification of collaterals under different liquidity levels should take into consideration a standard base of BCBS initiatives[3] that help practitioners to have a common understanding of the use of liquid collaterals across markets such as in the usage of margin agreements.

7.2.2 Mechanism of Margin Agreements

Active practitioners in OTC derivative markets are increasingly using margin agreements to reduce the net exposure and subsequent credit losses arising from counterparty risk. A margin agreement is a financial contract that requires *one or both counterparties* to post collateral in situations where an uncollateralised exposure exceeds a defined level of threshold H. The full or part of the collateral returns to the counterparty upon the final settlement of the contract, after the profits and losses have been settled.

Traditionally an initial amount of margin (IM) is applied on agreements of OTC derivatives and central counterparties (CCPs). Should delays in receiving collateral and potential costs in the close-out exist, IM reduces the associated risk and losses.

As the price of the derivative instrument fluctuates, the value of the margin account changes accordingly, requesting each of the counterparties to post or receive collateral, usually at the end of each trading day. However, before the recognition and requirement to depositing additional margin, the initial margin amount may be unable to collateralise the potential losses from the unfavourable price movements of the instrument. Hence, an additional margin deposit is placed, named variation margin (VM), and is used to bring the collateral amount back to its initial margin level. Posting IM and VM together with collaterals lowers the exposure and thus CVA losses and capital charges.

Below are the critical features of margin agreements:

- **Type and currency of collateral**: The types of collateral included in margin agreements can be cash and high-quality sovereign debt, liquid equity securities and corporate bonds, securities, for example, treasury bills, or futures[4] forming the initial margin. Unlike the initial margin, VM is a cash or highly liquid asset. The potential market volatility of the latter must be estimated to define haircuts, considering, therefore, the valuation margin.

- **Unilateral and bilateral nature of margin agreement**: Margin agreement can be either *unilateral* or *bilateral,* that is, when it refers to only one or two counterparties agreeing on posting collaterals, respectively.
- **Threshold**: There is a level of exposure below which there is no need of posting collateral. This level of collateral, named as threshold H, represents the amount of uncollateralised exposure. As soon as this amount exceeds the level of threshold H, one of the counterparties should post the appropriate collateral to cover the incremental exposure. The usage of the threshold implies that collateralisation is essential when the exposure exceeds a certain level,[5] that is, the threshold. Thresholds may also be related to the credit rating of the counterparty.
- **Minimum transfer amount (MTA)**: Collateral exchanges may be too frequent and thus may increase the degree of the operational burden resulting in excessive costs of monitoring the transactions. To avoid such burden, an MTA of collateral is specified. Such an amount defines an upper level which, when reached, triggers the transfer of additional collateral. If the amount of collateral that needs to be posted or returned is less than the MTA, no transfer of collateral occurs.
- **Net independent collateral amount (NICA)**: NICA represents the largest exposure that would not trigger the VM call; assuming no initial margin, the NICA is determined as the threshold plus any MTA, that is, $H + MTA$.
- **Effective threshold**: In practice, the effective threshold often replaces the actual threshold H. The effective threshold is the sum of thresholds and the MTA, that is, $H^{(e)} = H + MTA$, and by also subtracting, if considered, the NICA, $H^{(e)} = H + MTA - NICA$.

The following time periods are essential for margin agreements:

- **Margin call frequency (also named call period or remargin period)** is the (monitoring) period which specifies how frequently[6] the revaluation of a portfolio is being undertaken to determine the amount of collateral (if any) that needs to be posted "called" or returned.
- **Cure period (also called grace period)** defines the time interval (e.g. the number of days) after default necessary to close out the counterparty's position (get collateral and liquidate or replaced position) and rehedge the resulting market risk.
- **Margin period of risk (MPoR)** defines the time interval from the last exchange of collateral until the defaulting counterparty is closed out and the resulting market risk is rehedged; it is usually assumed[7] to be $T_M = Call\ Period + Cure\ Period$ (~2 weeks). As banks must be able to determine the availability of collateral at any given point in time, the exposure model must assume that collateral is posted or returned within the MPoR before that point in time.

There are two alternative supervisory floors set by supervisors and BCBS:

1. The supervisory floor, determined in business days, based on the "alternative one" (*a1*), SF_{a1}, is set to $SF_{a1} = 9 + N$, where N is the remargining period specified in the margin agreement[8]; and
2. As specified in the final framework (BCBS, 2011, 2017: 116, para 30), a supervisory floor based on the transactions subject to daily remargining and mark-to-market valuation, multiple margin calls, and remargining with periodicity.

Margin agreements can substantially reduce the counterparty credit exposure; however, they pose a challenge in identifying and modelling the collateralised exposure. In fact, one needs to consider time intervals and margin calls during the exposures' evolution, the default events, and estimate the value of the collateral at future times.

Moreover, with regards to (CCPs), a bank should apply the following rules:

- All members of the CCP are required to contribute to a default fund for covering losses in the event of counterparty default. All of this additional collateral needs to be funded through unsecured borrowing and hence gives rise to *margin valuation adjustment (MVA)*, which is the additional collateral needed due to a downgrade event of the counterparty;
- Initial margin is calculated using VaR models; and
- The Basel Committee proposal on bilateral margin for financial counterparties (BCBS, 2015a) similarly gives rise to a funding required to maintain the initial margin collateral buffer.

7.2.3   Exposures Evolution

The projection of the evolution of future credit exposure relies on generating future scenarios of market risk factors. There are two alternative steps in calculating future exposures:

- Generation of future scenarios of risk factors under real[9] measures on the simulation dates; and
- Adjustments of the actual measure to a risk-neutral measure to calculate the future values which in turn depends on the future performance of financial risk factors, and on the valuation rules of these factors.

Likewise, banks have to generate scenarios[10] to anticipate the future performance of the underlying market risk factors at a sequence of a fixed future simulation date $\{t_k\}_{k=1}^{M}$.

To generate the possible future risk factors one can employ:

- Path-dependent simulation (PDS) which, as illustrated in Fig. 7.1, generates a future "path" of market factors through consecutive steps in time, that is, from time $t = 0$ to the longest simulation date, $t = T$; or
- Direct jump-to-simulation (DJS) date which, as shown in Fig. 7.1, generates future markets directly by jumping from time $t = 0$ to the relevant simulation future date t.

The future performance of risk factors is unknown, and heavily depends on the selection of scenarios and the method, that is, PDS or DJS, to generate a spectrum of their possible evolution. The application of stochastic processes is a useful tool to derive some evidence on the impact of each of the methods on the future market value of the contracts. This tool enables the simulation of many market scenarios on the evolution of various underlying risk factors, that is, interest rates (IRs), foreign exchange (FX) rates, as well as stock/equity and commodity prices. The stochastic differential equations (SDEs) approximate the stochastic process of the evolution of future market prices. The geometric

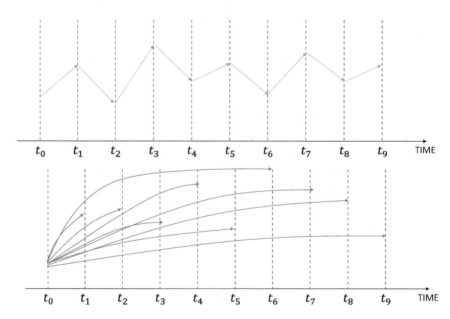

Fig. 7.1 Approaches to path-dependent simulation (PDS) and direct jump-to-simulation (DJS) date

Brownian motion shown in Eq. (7.4) is the SDE stochastic that is most widely used for simulating the evolution of the FX rates and stock indices.

$$dX(t) = \mu(t)X(t)dt + \sigma(t)X(t)dW_t \qquad (7.4)$$

where $\sigma(t)$ is time-dependent deterministic volatility and $\mu(t)$ is time-dependent *drift*.

The simulation of the evolution of risk factors enables the estimation of the distribution of credit exposures over time. Of course, the degree of complexity and sophistication to create such distributions can be high as there is a need to employ the use of several risk factors and different scenarios.

An alternative way is to employ simpler approaches that may consider one scenario or a limited number of deterministic scenarios for the evolution of market risk factors but this would render the estimation of the future path a rather subjective task which depends only on the researcher's judgement.

Figure 7.2 illustrates the exposure evolution of an IR swap contract using stochastic processes on the risk factors involved. The example simulates the

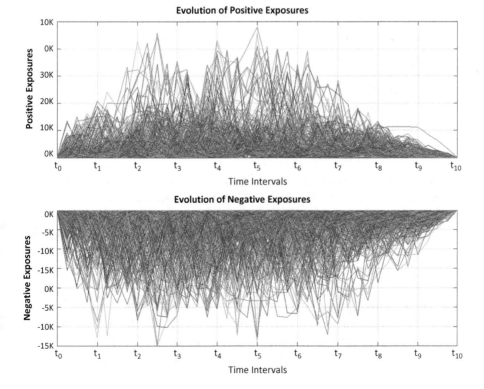

Fig. 7.2 Evolution of positive and negative exposures of interest rate swaps

short-term IR, where the bank is assumed to receive a fixed rate IR and pay floating IR. At the time of issuance, the swap's cash flows are assumed to be neutral ensuring that the estimated cash flows from the floating IR leg equal the cash flows from the fixed IR leg. Based on this condition, if IRs increase over time, the bank pays a higher floating rate and thus has a negative income on the swap position. In this case, there is no counterparty risk and the contract valuation is in the negative territory and thus the bank has nothing to lose from a potential default of the counterparty. On the other hand, if the IR decreases the bank is gaining on its position. This time, the bank faces a certain level of counterparty risk arising from the probability of a counterparty's default which would subsequently result in losing the positive cash flows from the swap position. In the latter case, the posting of collateral would cover the potential losses. The rules of posting collateral are specified in a legally enforceable margin agreement and signed by both counterparties upon the initiation of the contract.

7.2.4   The Role of Valuation

Apart from the selection of the methods for the evolution of risk factors and the scenarios involved, the level of the simulated derivative credit exposure depends on the valuation methodology involved. The simulation process uses the simulated risk factors as inputs in the valuation models. The use of valuation models enables the production of derivative prices (e.g. swap prices) and thus the simulation of the counterparty credit exposures between today and the future time. As mentioned above, there are two different ways to simulate the risk factors' evolution, that is, path-dependent scenarios (PDS) and direct-jump scenarios (DJSs).

The use of simulated, or deterministic, scenarios estimates the price of derivative instruments at discrete future points in time[11] for each scenario and market risk factor. The type of instruments and the evolution of their underlying market risk factors drive the valuation approach considered in pricing. For instance, financial instruments, whose valuation is path-dependent,[12] need to adjust their mark-to-market valuation conditional to the price evolution over time.

Therefore, the approach of conditional valuation is a scenario-based probabilistic technique to define these adjustments. Thus, the values of path-dependent instruments at a future simulation point in time depend on either the event occurring at a time before the simulation date or the entire scenario path up to the end simulation point.

As discussed earlier, the valuation process can become complicated and computationally demanding. Hence, the valuation models for the calculation of exposure should have as low a degree of complexity as possible to enable timely estimations of the distribution of instrument's prices. What matters most from the estimated distributions is the realisation of the turning points between *in-the-money* and *out-of-the-money* positions changing sides between the bank and its counterparty. The identification of such changes in flagging the position is essential to identify whether the combined likelihood of a default event and an in-the-money position results in positive CCR.

7.2.5 Counterparty Expected Exposures

The basic rule in the assessment of counterparty risk over time is to assess which of the counterparties is in the money. In cases where a bank (Bank A) is in the money this places its counterparty (Bank B) in an out-of-the-money position, and vice versa. As already mentioned, the bank with an out-of-the-money position has zero exposure to its counterparty, while if the institution is in the money, the positive exposure results in a CCR exposure. The "replacement cost" of the counterparty that defaults stand for the CCR. This cost is positive for in-the-money positions only.

In both positive and negative evolutions of credit exposures,[13] there are two potential sources of impact on P&L evolution over time. One is the "diffusion effect" which appears during the increasing path of the exposure. The increased variability over time gives a boost to the PD. The other is the "amortisation effect" which tends to decrease the exposure over time due to the reduction of the remaining cash flows exposed to default. Figure 7.2 illustrates the diffusion and amortisation effects for both positive and negative evolutions of credit exposures. In the first-time buckets $\{t_1, \ldots t_5\}$, during the diffusive phase of the exposure there is a long remaining maturity, many remaining cash flows, and thus sensitivity to market uncertainty. In the last half of the time buckets $\{t_6, \ldots t_{10}\}$, where the exposure is already in the amortisation phase, there is a short remaining maturity, and only few remaining cash flows and little sensitivity to market uncertainties. In each future simulation time point (future date) t_k and for the p number of generating scenarios, there will be a distribution of discounted positive and negative exposures up to a future time t_k $\{E_1(t_k), E_2(t_k), \ldots, E_j(t_k)\}$.

7.2.6 Scenarios for Discounted Exposure

The BCBS proposes two options for generating scenarios for discounted exposure: (a) accounting-based and (b) regulatory-based (including in the IMM-based [BCBS, 2011, 2015b] and standardised approach [SA] based [BCBS, 2017]).

The accounting-based CVA option requires banks to use the same paths as the ones used by front-office accounting CVA. This type of CVA is also considered when defining the market and transaction data, the model implementation, and the calibration process of regulatory CVA.

The adaptation of the IMM-based CVA option is subject to supervisory approval by the national competent authority. This approval allows the use of the corresponding IMM discounted exposure method to estimate exposure-at-default (EAD) used by the CVA sensitivities analysis.

In both options, banks should use the same set of scenarios in the exposure analysis for all financial instruments contained in the portfolios under study. Using the same set of scenarios, the bank ensures consistency in the simulation and pricing methodologies and facilitates the comparison across different portfolios. Models should follow a risk-neutral dynamic and be frequently calibrated, for example, daily, by employing the same market parameters used in mark-to-market valuation.

The analysis evaluates the counterparty exposure at the portfolio level, allowing for any possible netting effects. Correspondingly, an offset in the simulated positive and negative market values is applied under the set netting agreements only.

With regard to the paths of market risk factors of the underlying exposures, their drifts must be risk-neutral. Moreover, their volatilities and correlations have to be calibrated based on market data unless they are insufficient. In this case, unlike the risk-neutral drifts, historical calibration can be applied. The distribution of the resulting simulation risk factors can be non-normal, including leptokurtosis shapes.[14] Such distributions have fat tails containing, therefore, extreme events where for instance significant price moves, higher than in a normal distribution, are likely to occur.

7.2.7 Expected Exposures

To better monitor the result of the simulation of counterparty level exposures, we use a multidimensional matrix. In this matrix, r number of rows represent the different simulation time points t_k (e.g. date), c is the number of columns where each *column* refers to a different counterparty (*cp*), and *p* is the number of pages where each "page" refers to the different scenarios *j* resulting from the simulation process.

The mean of the distribution of exposures at the simulation point in time (t_k) is the EE. For each of the simulation time points, the sequence of exposures {$EE(t_1)$, $EE(t_2)$, ...$EE(t_k)$} defines a vector, presented as a curve. As t varies over future dates, the curve[15] of $EE(t_k)$ provides the EE profile, also called expected positive exposure (EPE). In other words, EPE is the weighted average exposure to the counterparty, across all paths at each point in time as defined in Eq. (7.5) and illustrated in Fig. 7.3.

$$EPE = \sum_{t_k \leq 1yr} EE(t_k)\Delta t_k \qquad (7.5)$$

where the weight of $EE(t_k)$ is defined as time intervals $\Delta t_k = t_k - t_{k-1}$.

In fact, EE represents the expected loss amount in the event of a counterparty default. Thus, it is used, when combined with other quantities, for the calculation of EPE which stands for the economic capital of diversified port-

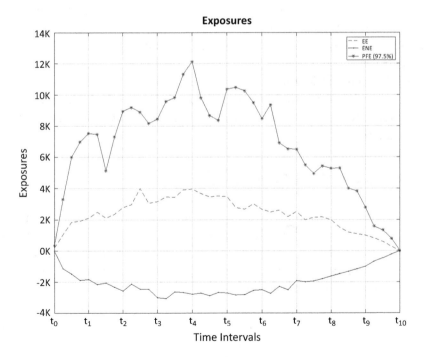

Fig. 7.3 Expected positive and negative exposures, potential future exposures

folios of counterparties but also for the capital requirements assigned to the counterparty risk. The process for providing a point estimation of the minimum capital requirement for CVA employs the average over a defined time horizon, for example, the first year or, if all contracts in the netting set (NS) expire before the fixed time horizon, over the period of the longest-maturity contract in the NS.

7.2.8 Potential Future Exposure

The potential future exposure (PFE) considers the estimation of the possible EPE that banks may have on the counterparties over the life of the derivative. The PFE is given by a high quantile (typically 99th) of the discounted (positive) value distribution over the desired time horizon and is given by Eq. (7.6) and illustrated in Fig. 7.3.

$$PFE = \left[sup\{X | \mathbb{P}(X) \le 0.99\} \right]^{+} \tag{7.6}$$

where $\mathbb{P}(X)$ denotes the cumulative probability distribution of $PV(t)$.

As indicated by its name, *PFE* estimation takes into account only non-negative values, that is, there a floor at zero. Also, regulators consider *PFE* as representing the counterparty exposure that a bank may have during the next one-year period.

For the computation of *PFE*, the process involves two elements: (a) a stochastic model (i.e. Monte Carlo simulation) for the evolution of risk factors that determine the price of the derivative, and (b) pricing model for the derivative valuation.

7.2.9 Calibration of Exposures

Banks may apply a number of scenarios by using either real-world data and probabilities or the risk-neutral probabilities. The real-world measures of drifts and volatilities use actual historical data of risk factors whereas, under the risk-neutral probability measures, drifts must be calibrated assuming the absence of arbitrage opportunities.

The Monte Carlo simulation framework applying stochastic processes such as the Ornstein-Uhlenbeck (1930) uses a risk-neutral evolution of risk factors across several asset classes. The same framework uses market data to calibrate the drift term and market-implied volatilities derived from quoted option prices.

The existence of different types of calibration could pose a dilemma for a bank as to which is the most appropriate calibration the bank should use in stochastic processes. Each method could affect market risk factors and impact the counterparty exposures and credit spreads, which eventually would have an impact on the estimated CVA.

When simulating the evolution of credit exposures, the bank needs to show that the model's projection is consistent with real-world probabilities. Hence, the model needs to rely on the past performance of risk factors. Notably, the BCBS requires that risk models be back-tested and stress-tested based on historical performance (BCBS, 2011). The use of historical observations for identifying changes in risk factors implies that the parameters of each factor distribution are based on the real-world drift. Thus, the forward-looking estimates of the real-world simulation process of market risk factors (such as IRs) could incorporate historical averages of market-implied volatilities in the PFE calibration methods. Nonetheless, in the latest revision of minimum capital requirements for CVA risk in the SA utilising exposure models, BCBS states a requirement that *the drifts of risk factors must be consistent with a risk-neutral probability measure whereas historical calibration of drifts is not allowed* (BCBS, 2017: 117, para 32).

Regulators and supervisors also require that the estimation of exposures should be the result of an approved exposure model that would also be used to compute the EAD for the CCR under the IMM. An essential requirement is that the exposure model must satisfy back-testing requirements. The approved model calibration, based on the IMM framework, usually requires the use of historical data rather than market-implied[16] parameters since the former are more easily observable by the supervisors. In other words, banks should approximate the drifts and volatilities of the diffusion processes with descriptive statistics of historical data. On the other hand, the use of accounting CVA-IFRS standards (2013)[17] and the estimation of accounting exposure must be risk-neutral, calibrated to market-implied parameters wherever possible.

Historical calibration is the most common approach for Monte Carlo models used for PFE. However, the Basel framework does not specify the exact approach for the calculation of the EE. However, the fact that most IMMs (for credit risk measurement) use historical calibration leads to the use of this method.

The stress VaR calculation must be used for a stressed model calibration, that is, a model that simulates extreme adverse market conditions. The BCBS states that for the calibration of stress VaR is based on a period of significant stress to the bank's trading book (supervised by the national regulators)

(BCBS, 2013: 18, para 1.4). Moreover, the VaR model calibration must use, at least, one year of historical data.

The application of Monte Carlo simulation typically increases the calculation burden and may raise some performance issues. Several factors may contribute to the calculation performance burden, including the numbers of scenarios, time buckets, and underlying market risk factors, as well as the revaluation frequency and process. Furthermore, the trade maturity plays a critical role, that is, the longer the duration the higher is the processing simulation time. Another critical factor is the amount and type of instruments comprising the trade portfolio; for example, exotic trades may demand more computation than plain vanilla swaps.

7.2.10   Risk-Neutral Versus Historical-Based Models

Banks may utilise historically calibrated Monte Carlo models to compute capital requirements for the CCR and CVA Basel framework. On the one hand, the use of historical calibration for the CVA Monte Carlo simulation ensures consistency with the credit risk PFE estimation, whereas CVA losses closely relate to the real-world historical credit loss. However, the use of historical data does not meet the arbitrage-free condition in the valuation of financial instruments, rendering the use of hedge instruments less efficient. Another drawback in using historical data is the access and collection of historical data (proxy data could partially resolve such issues).

Contrary to the above, market-implied risk-neutral CVA models sustain the consistency of the model with standard derivative valuation practices and make the hedging of derivative exposures more efficient. The risk-neutral models also align with the accounting standards. For the CVA capital term, BCBS (2011) suggested that banks employing advanced approaches (IMM) could use risk-neutral default probabilities. Furthermore, in the estimation of the counterparty-specific regulatory SA-CVA (BCBS, 2017), banks should generate risk-neutral exposures (see also principle 5 in Sect. 7.4.8).

The accounting-based CVA requires the use of risk-neutral drifts as well as risk-neutral calibrations of volatilities and correlations to market data. At the same time, the CVA trading desks use risk-neutral Monte Carlo models to pricing, valuation, and accounting of CVA.

All in all, the CVA is the present value of the CCR and estimates the amount needed to pay for buying protection against the variability in CCR. However, as mentioned above, the main drawbacks in computing CVA are the high demand for market data, the inconsistency with PFE, and the mismatch with the historically observed expected loss, as well as the employment of risk-neutral models that are typically very computationally expensive.

The following sections discuss the CVA estimations which use the VaR model and are driven by risk-neutral parameters. However, they apply deterministic shocks to the risk parameters, allowing the CVA measurements to be consistent with the regulatory risk measures against capital.

7.3   CVA VaR

7.3.1   Evolution of Credit Risk Factors under Real-World and Risk-Neutral Default Probabilities

The evolution of credit risk factors is a fundamental analysis in the estimation of CVA. Quantitatively speaking, the expectations on such evolution are based on either the real economic world or risk-neutral probabilities. These approximations serve different but also complementary purposes. Figure 7.4 illustrates the main elements included in the risk-neutral and real-world probability analysis discussed in the following paragraphs.

Real-world probabilities are based on the observed frequency of the various possible outcomes, and thus reflect the actual historical default observations and corresponding default distribution. In fact, real-world default events quantitatively assess the counterparty risk by estimating the probability of the counterparty to default. The PD is associated with the credit rating of the counterparty. The real-world probabilities of default are also the basis of designing the scenarios in the generating models of future credit events.

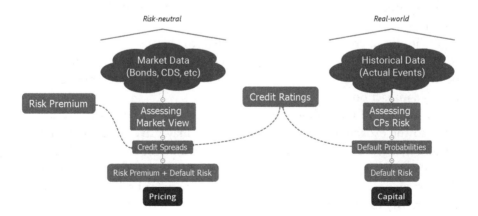

Fig. 7.4   Main elements included in real-world and risk-neutral probabilities analysis

Thus, the analysis applies the real-world probabilities on a going concern basis when granting new credit that would be potentially associated with future credit events. Profitability and risk management analysis typically consider real-world default probabilities for measuring their actual impact in regard to profits or losses in instruments' market values and liquidity shortages against default credit events.

Unlike the analysis of real-world probabilities, risk-neutral probabilities are the basis of valuation models and utilise the concept of arbitrage-free market models.[18] Driven by risk neutrality, investors are risk-averse and pay due attention to the risks that real-world estimators contain. The risk-aversion characteristic of investors implies that they prefer a deal with a reduced payoff which is counterbalanced by a level of default risk which minimises the overall[19] losses.

In addition to default risk, markets expect an additional risk premium similar to the premium embedded in IR risk, which acts as a compensating element for undertaking excessive default risk. The arbitrage-free assumption is the decisive factor for determining the premiums. The application of this assumption relies on discounting credit spreads derived from market data, for example, from bonds or credit default swaps (CDSs). Thus, the risk-neutral probabilities which correspond to the risk-neutral expectation lead to the fair value pricing after being discounted with the risk-free rates.

The observed market credit spread reflects the perception of market participants and is widely accepted as a fair spread. At the same time, credit spreads could reveal significant evidence about the credit quality of the counterparty and be linked to the actual credit rating of the counterparty.

The use of credit spreads for different time horizons/maturities defines the term structure of credit spreads. Both credit ratings and the term structure of credit spreads are subject to change, which in the end drive the future output.

The jumps in credit spread values as well as the jumps in ratings or defaults should also be included in the analysis of credit spread evolution. The analysis below relies on the generation of scenarios on credit spreads to measure their possible impact on value and liquidity.

The analysis of CCR should include not only the idiosyncratic risk factors but also the exogenous economic factors that may drive the probabilities of default. The use of structural models can limit the probabilities of default by addressing some idiosyncratic factors, for instance, by setting credit limits to the borrowing of counterparties. Likewise, it is easy for both the bank and its counterparty to set an upper bound to the counterparty risk assessed on idiosyncratic grounds.

However, many counterparties find it difficult to access and follow up the economic and market risk factors that would impact their PD. Therefore, the bank can employ reduced-form models to trigger alert mechanisms of increased PD without necessarily explaining it rationally. In the complete absence of efficient markets, however, one could use real-world probability models.

Quantitatively speaking, the probability distribution is a complete set of information banks could retrieve to identify future events. Practitioners may face difficulties to grasp intuitively the vast amount of information that such distribution contains. It is upon their discretion to use a set of measures for describing some essential characteristics such as mean (average) as the expected future point estimation and volatilities as a measure to represent the uncertainty. The most widely used methodologies which make use of measures of uncertainties are the VaR and expected shortfall (ES), with both playing a central role in CVA analysis.

In the course of the process of pricing counterparty risk and applying CVAs banks should estimate the fair[20] value adjustment of derivatives by using market-implied data based on CDS spreads or proxy[21] spreads. The use of implied market data indicates the risk neutrality in CVA estimation. The following paragraphs discuss how the use of stochastic process models simulates the evolution of risk-neutral probabilities of default on CVA.

7.3.2 Generating Default Probabilities

The intensity credit risk (reduced-form) models include inherently the exogenous factors which drive the probability and the timing of credit default events. In fact, such models do not demonstrate the economic fundamentals of the counterparty (e.g. examining the balance sheet of the given company), nor do they attempt to capture and explain[22] the arrival of default.

However, they try to model the possible patterns which could trigger defaults. Moreover, recovery rates are also exogenously specified.[23] Thus, stochastic variables identify the timing of default events and the expected recovery rates. As already mentioned, such variables have no direct or indirect links to a counterparty's idiosyncratic factors. Although they lack the intuitive understanding of an idiosyncratic default event and recovery, they have become increasingly popular, as they require minimum effort for their implementation. A significant strength of such models is their ability to embed the probability of unexpected default events.

The necessary information needed to operate the reduced-form models is less detailed and relatively more accessible compared to the respective information needed by structural models.

In such models, the implied PD over a certain time interval is modelled as a proportion of the initial length of the time interval used for the estimation of PD. The frequency of default events in the time interval $(t, t + \Delta t)$ is described by a number known as "intensity" and denoted as $\lambda(t)$. The same notion can be found as *hazard rate*; see Schönbucher (2003) and Bluhm, Overbeck, and Wagner (2010).

Banks can then assume that the PD is proportional to the degree of the intensity. The higher the intensity values, the lower is the credit quality, that is, high PD. The default event occurs at the first jump. A way to get such jump is the application of a stochastic process to approximate intensity. The key features relating to the parameters of reduced-form models are (a) the assumptions underlying a complete set of arbitrage-free credit, market-implied conditions, (b) the use of credit spread data to estimate risk-neutral probabilities; (c) the estimation of recovery rates (stochastically or deterministically); and, (d) the evolution of credit spreads which is closely related to the intensity λ and the recovery rates.[24]

Banks can intuitively describe such relation by assuming that an instantaneous increase of PD, driven by intensity λ, result in the high rise of credit spread while the expected recovery rate decreases. Based on the intensity models, the default event arrives via an underlying counting process $N(t)$, which increases progressively to the value of one as defined in Eqs. (7.7) and (7.8).

$$N(t) = \sum_{s=0}^{t} \Delta N(s) \tag{7.7}$$

$$\Delta N(s) = N(t + \Delta t) - N(t) \begin{cases} 1 & \text{if event arrives in} \left[t, t + \Delta\tau\right] \\ 0 & \text{if no event arrives in} \left[t, t + \Delta\tau\right] \end{cases} \tag{7.8}$$

The time of default is the instance of the first jump of N, that is,

$$\tau = \inf\{t\epsilon\,\mathbb{R}_{+}\,|N(t) > 0\} \tag{7.9}$$

The process then specifies the counting process $N(t)$ to get the default event, or, otherwise, defines how it jumps so that τ has the "desired" properties. The upward trend of the $N(t)$ can be decomposed into martingale and compensator processes. The value of the former at time t equals the conditional expectation of future values, while the latter captures the upward trend of N. The compensator describes the cumulative, conditional likelihood of default. It is parameterised through the intensity process λ in which the default process $N(t)$ jumps. As mentioned above, the higher the intensity λ, that is, the more the $N(t)$ jumps, the greater the PD. Then, the time of default τ is given by

$$\tau = \inf\{t \in \mathbb{R}_+ \mid \int_t^T \lambda(s)\,ds\} \tag{7.10}$$

where the variable $\lambda(s)$ describes the conditional default rate or intensity.

Thus, the key modelling quantity is $\int_t^T \lambda(s)\,ds$ where the intensity can be a constant value, a deterministic function, or based on a stochastic process.

7.3.2.1 Constant Intensity

The constant of the intensity function assumes a homogeneous Poisson process, where the intensity λ stops at its first jump. A Poisson process $N(t)$ with intensity $\lambda > 0$ is a positive non-decreasing integer-value number, that is, $N(t) \in \{0, 1, 2, 3, \ldots\}$ so that $N(t)$ continuously increases, with independent increments, starting from zero. The constant parameter λ denotes the intensity of the jump in the next instant, for example, at the default event. Such a process designates that the probability of occurrence of N jumps in the next small time interval $[t, t + \Delta t]$ is proportional to Δt, that is, the local probability of a jump of a Poisson process over a small time step is proportional to the length of this time interval.

$$\mathbf{P}\left[N(t + \Delta t) - N(t) = 1\right] = \lambda \Delta t \tag{7.11}$$

According to the above framework, the time of default event coincides with the observation of the first jump of the Poisson process, which, nonetheless, is rare and constitutes a shock event.[25] The pricing (or risk-neutral) PD is given by:

$$q(t) = e^{-\lambda(t)} \tag{7.12}$$

7.3.2.2   Time-Dependent Intensity

As the intensity parameter reflects the PD and credit spread, a constant value implies an unchanged PD and a flat term structure. Thus, to achieve a more realistic degree of PD and spread curve, the intensity of default must change over time. If the intensity λ of the Poisson process is a non-negative function of time, that is, $\lambda(t)$, we end up with an inhomogeneous Poisson process. The inhomogeneous Poisson process models defines the hazard rates which depend on time horizon T, $\lambda(T)$. The PD is given by

$$q(T) = e^{-\int_t^T \lambda(s)ds} \qquad (7.13)$$

In this approach, both PD and the term structure of credit spreads may change (term structure of spreads is not flat) and are a function of the time horizon or the maturity of the contract. Thus, the appropriate selection of the determinist function $\lambda(\bullet)$ can produce every desirable probability and term structure of hazard rates.

The market data is useful to replicate the term structure which is a tool for the calibration of a model that assumes determinist intensities.

However, would deterministic intensity models be suitable for the valuation of credit default instruments? Before answering the question, banks have to assume that the parameters of recovery, risk-free spread curve, and IR are constant and that the deterministic intensity model and the forward CDS spread are deterministic and continuous. The above set of assumptions would make the *precise* estimation of credit default instruments somewhat unrealistic.

That is because it is like assuming that banks can determine, by providing a point estimation, the future counterparty's credit quality. However, in the real world, observed credit spreads are highly irregular and thus unpredictable by a deterministic model. Thus, the pricing of credit derivatives, which pay out according to the level of the credit spread, would require a more realistic modelling of the credit spread evolution. Hence, banks should consider intensity models that allow a generation of credit spreads based on stochastic processes to retrieve a more realistic distribution of the outcomes. In this case, the valuation of credit derivatives relies on stochastic dynamic models, instead of time-inhomogeneous Poisson processes.

7.3.2.3   Stochastic Intensity

The stochastic intensities are more appropriate to capture changes in the credit quality. However, the adaptation of the model to the conditions of the real world results in an additional complexity.

Cox (1955) processes are Poisson-type stochastic models, where the time-dependent intensity $\lambda(t)$ is itself a stochastic process. As mentioned above, the probability of jump of the process $N(t)$ over a small time interval[26] Δt is given by Eq. (7.11). The intensity $\lambda(t)$ can be modelled as a stochastic process by assuming that $\lambda(t)$ is a diffusion process, that is, $d\lambda(t) = \mu(t)dt + \sigma(t)dW(t)$, with $\mu(t)$ and $\sigma(t)$ such that $\lambda(t) > 0$ is defined as a standard Brownian motion for every t and dW. Therefore, the time-dependent intensity $\lambda(t)$ exhibits volatility whereas for different products[27] correlation should also be considered. Moreover, the choice of drift and volatility processes must ensure that $\lambda(t)$ is never negative, aligned with the assumption that PD and spreads are floored to zero.

7.3.2.4   Market Filtration

By utilising a stochastic process model, the market filtration[28] $\left(\mathcal{M}_t\right)_{t\geq 0}$ defined in the Cox process should contain all relevant economic information. There are two subfiltrations:

- The $\left(\mathcal{G}_t\right)_{t\geq 0}$ filtration contains all *default-free market* information, equivalent to a default-free model where the same stochastic processes apply to all market risk factors, such as IRs, exchange rates, share prices, and so on, but not on the PD arrivals and the recovery rates.
- The $\left(\mathcal{F}_t\right)_{t\geq 0}$ filtration contains all *credit risk event* information. Thus, this filtration holds the information on whether or not a credit/counterparty risk factor(s) causes credit event, as if a credit default has occurred at time t, that is, appearing at the first jump of a Cox process.

Thus, market filtration is defined as $\left(\mathcal{M}_t\right)_{t\geq 0} = \left(\mathcal{G}_t\right)_{t\geq 0} \cap \left(\mathcal{F}_t\right)_{t\geq 0}$. The elements of the two subfiltrations can be handled in a reduced form; for instance, the pricing of a corporate bond is directly proportional to the pricing of a risk-free bond (with IR $r(s)$), including the credit risk spread $\lambda(s)$, that is, by applying a higher discounting factor $r(s) + \lambda(s)$. This higher discounting rate factor is fully consistent with the market practice of pricing credit risk.

Moreover, it is consistent with how market practitioners interpret spreads' yield curves of corporate bonds based on the expectations of their likelihood to default.

An essential element is also the modelling of the correlation between the risk factors contained in the two subfiltration types. This correlation implies that they affect each other's performance. For instance, the default probabilities may be highly correlated with market IRs under specific economic stress conditions, while both market and credit spreads may be volatile. Therefore, the pricing of such instruments should incorporate the information in subfiltrations and the risk factors' correlations and their volatilities, depending on the available information, the accuracy target, and the desired complexity.

An additional challenge in the implementation of reduced-form models is the necessity to consider the probability of the underlying market and assets subject to credit risk to face drainage of market liquidity. In almost all cases, liquidity risk arises when more than a single risk factor performs under stress conditions. Thus, the number and the integration of risk factors causing liquidity drainage would bring additional complexity to the valuation models along the calibration process.

The valuation of illiquid instruments requires risk integration analysis as well as external historical information, or strong assumptions, in the medium- to long-term performances of market and counterparty risk factors.

7.3.2.5   Multi-Stochastic Process

The valuation adjustment should consider the application of multi-stochastic processes on market and credit risk factors under expected and unexpected conditions. Banks should consider that stochastic processes drive market and credit risks in CVA as a multi-stochastic process. This process includes the stochastic evolution of market risk factors (excluding credit spreads) which impacts the valuation of exposures.

Moreover, the process of stochastic movements of the credit spreads associated with hazard rates, together with the exposure evolutions, results in the formulation of CVA distribution.

The implementation of intensity $(\lambda(t))$, which defines the hazard rate, can adopt the respective provisions and short-term IR models based on IR theory. The Cox–Ingersoll–Ross (CIR) (1985) model falls under this category of models. Banks have to define the hazard rate function of PDs and then apply the CIR model to simulate the risk-neutral credit spreads.

7.3.2.6   Defining Hazard Rate/Function

The hazard function (aka hazard rate[29]) quantifies the PD in a small interval dt for entities that have survived until time t; this implies that all defaulted, prior to t, entities are not taken into consideration. In other words, it characterises the PD of the underlying exposure that will occur within a period of time Δt.

As already discussed, there are three approaches for estimating the hazard rate:

1. A continuous form, where $h(t)\Delta t$ is approximately equal to the PD between t and $t + \Delta t$, conditional to survival time t. As mentioned earlier, the intensity is the hazard rate defined in Eq. (7.12), reflecting a set of default probability and/or flat line term structure of credit spreads.
2. Deterministic function of time, where the PD occurs before time t is $e^{-\bar{h}(t)}$. In this approach, $\bar{h}$ is the average hazard rate between time zero and time t. The hazard rate, which now depends on the time intensity $\lambda = \lambda(t)$, is a deterministic function of time while the PD is given by Eq. (7.13).
3. Stochastic changes, where the PD between time zero and time t is based on stochastic intensity models, for example, by applying the CIR model.

The stochastic simulation of credit spreads in the third approach (CIR) aligns with the CVA (VaR) implementation.

7.3.3   CIR Model on Market-Implied Credit Spreads

CIR proposed a single-factor model for the term structure of IRs. The approximation is widely used in risk-free short-term IR modelling, but banks can also adapt it to credit modelling. Based on the CIR process the dynamics of the intensity λ is expressed as in Eq. (7.14).

$$d\lambda(t) = \kappa(\theta - \lambda(t))dt + \sigma\sqrt{\lambda(t)}dW(t) \qquad (7.14)$$

where

- θ defines the mean of the spread representing the intensity's long-term value. If the intensity $\lambda(t)$ at any point is below θ the drift will be positive and will push the intensity towards its long-term value (mean level), and vice versa

- κ defines the rate of mean reversion and determines the speed of the adjustment towards the long-term value
- σ defines volatility
- $W(t)$ is the standard Brownian motion process

where κ, θ, and σ are positive values.

An essential characteristic of the CIR model is that in the intensity dynamics[30] it employs the term "square root" in the diffusion coefficient which makes the intensity always positive. This is also true for the PDs and associated credit spreads. Moreover,

- if $\lambda(0) > 0$, then $\lambda(t)$ is never negative;
- if $2\kappa\theta \geq \sigma^2$ then $\lambda(t)$ remains strictly positive for all t, which secures that the intensity can never reach zero, a property required by the CIR model. This is called the Feller condition (Feller, 1951).
- The condition $2\kappa\theta \geq \sigma^2$ also implies that if σ is large, k and/or θ are also forced to assume large values. A drastic increase of θ implies an increase in the mean reversion level of the intensity process, so that λ tends to high values.[31]
- The form of the drift in Eq. (7.14) suggests that $\lambda(t)$ is pulled towards θ at a speed controlled by κ.
- The diffusion term $\sigma\sqrt{\lambda(t)}$ decreases to zero as $\lambda(t)$ approaches the original value and this prevents $\lambda(t)$ from taking negative values.

The features of Eq. (7.14) are sufficient to model IRs as well as stochastic intensity for a jump process, for example, modelling default probabilities and credit spreads.

This SDE for λ can be interpreted in terms of its discrete-time approximation as in Eq. (7.15).

$$\lambda_{t+\Delta t} - \lambda_t \cong \kappa\left(\theta - \lambda_t\right)\Delta t + \sigma\sqrt{\lambda_t}.\epsilon_t \tag{7.15}$$

where

- Δ is the length of a short time period, and
- ϵ_t is a mean-zero independent normally distributed random variable with variance Δt.

It is worth noting that λ_t must not be negative to consider $\sqrt{\lambda_t}$ for this discrete-time approximation. Any negative output of $\lambda_{t+\Delta t}$ should be floored

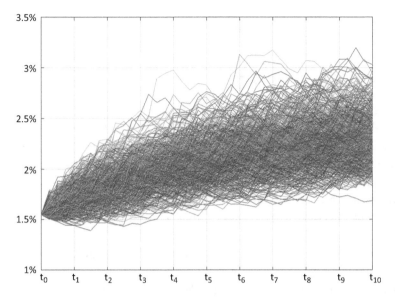

Fig. 7.5 Simulated spreads using the CIR model

at zero. Moreover, the spread correlation is a minor driver when compared to default correlations, so it can be assumed that the two Brownian motions of ϵ s are independent.

Starting with an initial term structure of a credit spread, banks may apply the CIR model to generate their evolution stochastically. Figure 7.5 shows the results of the simulation using a CIR model based on a reference CDS spread.

7.3.4   Survival and Default Probabilities

Based on stochastically simulated spread curves defined by Eqs. (7.14) and (7.15) the conditional survival probability is estimated as in Eq. (7.16).

$$S(t) = \mathbf{P}(\tau > t) = e^{\left(a_{CIR} + b_{CIR} * s(t)\right)}, \qquad t \geq 0 \tag{7.16}$$

where

$$qa_{CIR}(t) = \frac{2\theta\kappa}{\sigma_\lambda^2} \log\left(\frac{2\gamma e^{(\gamma + \kappa)t/2}}{(\gamma + \kappa)(e^{\gamma t} - 1) + 2\gamma}\right) \tag{7.17}$$

$$b_{CIR}(t) = \frac{-2(e^{\gamma t} - 1)}{(\gamma + \kappa)(e^{\gamma t} - 1) + 2\gamma} \tag{7.18}$$

$$\gamma = \sqrt{\kappa^2 + 2\sigma_\lambda^2} \tag{7.19}$$

The above survival function (Eq. (7.16)) represents that the PD at time τ is greater than the PD at time t. The same function indicates that survival time is longer than t or, in other words, the entity survives until time t. Assuming that at time $t = 0$ there is no information about the future prospects for the survival of a firm, $S(t)$ measures the likelihood that it will survive until time t. The duration between the two states, that is, from the original state s to the default state k, is called the survival time.

Having defined the survival probability over time, banks can derive the probability of changing from original (non-defaulted) to defaulted status. The PD between time s and $t \geq s$ is simply $S(s) - S(t)$. In particular, if $s = 0$, and because $S(0) = 1$, then the PD at time t, denoted as $q(t)$, is defined as in Eq. (7.20). The survival function is a monotonic non-increasing continuous function of time t, with $S(0) = 1$ and $s(\infty) = \lim_{t \to \infty} q(t) = 0$.

$$q(t) = 1 - S(t) = \mathbf{P}(\tau \leq t), \qquad t \geq 0 \tag{7.20}$$

The survival probabilities for simulated spread curves can estimate the distributions of both survival and default probabilities.[32] The cumulative distribution function, defined in Eq. (7.21), represents the probability that τ is less than or equal to a value t and denotes the probability that the event occurs before time t. As τ represents the first occurrence of the default event then $q(t)$ represents the distribution of events or default times.

$$q(t) = \mathbf{P}(\tau \leq t) = \int_0^t f(x)dx, \qquad t \geq 0 \tag{7.21}$$

The probability distribution can be specified as a cumulative distribution function, a survivor function, a probability density function, or a hazard function.

7.3.5   Hazard Rate Approximation of Spreads and Recoveries

The approximation of an average, risk-neutral hazard rate between time points of 0 to t should consider the available credit spreads and recovery rates. The relationship between market-based CDS spreads and hazard rate is given by Eq. (7.22).

$$h(t) = \frac{S_i^{CDS}}{(1-\delta_i)} \qquad (7.22)$$

where S_i^{CDS} is the CDS spread at t_i and δ_i is the assumed recovery rate at t_i.

The recovery rate implies that any low recovery rate should be balanced with a reasonable degree of survivor probabilities, and vice versa. Since δ_i is hard to define in practice, the market standard is to use data collected from rating agencies to estimate the average recovery rate by seniority and instrument type.

As the hazard rate function $h(t)$ is used to characterise the distribution of survival,[33] at time zero the probability of survival will occur before time t and is defined as in Eq. (7.23):

$$q = e^{-h(t)} = \exp\left[-\frac{S_i}{1-\delta_i}t_i\right] \qquad (7.23)$$

Thus, the marginal PD over time is defined as in Eq. (7.24):

$$q_{i(marginal)} = \exp\left(-\frac{S_{i-1} \cdot t_{i-1}}{(1-\delta)}\right) - \exp\left(-\frac{S_i \cdot t_i}{(1-\delta)}\right) \qquad (7.24)$$

The BCBS (2011) uses a similar type of hazard rate approximation on spreads and recoveries to define the marginal default probability under the CVA advanced approach.

7.3.6   Key Factors in Implementing Intensity-Based Models

In the analysis of CVA, banks have to specify the stochastic dynamics of credit spreads as well as other market risk factors, that is, the dynamics of the default-free IR r and the intensity of the default process $\lambda(s)$. A suitable specification should have the following properties:

- Both $r(s)$ and $\lambda(s)$ are stochastic;
- Stochastic default-free IRs are indispensable for fixed-income analysis, and stochastic default intensity function is required to reach stochastic credit spreads values and changes, which are necessary to approximate meaningful prices for credit spread options;
- The dynamics of $r(s)$ and $\lambda(s)$ are informative enough to allow for a realistic description of the real-world prices. Thus, in many cases a multifactor model for the credit spreads is necessary;
- It should facilitate the pricing of the building blocks based on a closed-form function to calibrate the model accordingly.[34] Such analytical tractability implies a good knowledge of the level and behavioural characteristics of the correlation between r and λ;
- There should be scope to include correlation between credit spreads and default-free IRs as well as any other market risk factors driving the exposures subject to CVA. The analysis of wrong-way risk (WWR) aligns with the scope to include correlation between credit spreads and other market default-free rates and prices as discussed in Sect. 7.3.8;
- It is desirable that the processes to ensure IRs and credit spreads remain positive[35] at all times.

7.3.7 The VaR and ES Approaches in CVA Calculation

Despite the fact that VaR is not a coherent measurement (discussed in Chap. 6), VaR models have been used by banks and have been considered for years as one of the best practices for measuring risk. The VaR plays a significant role in the estimation of the CVA regulatory requirements (CVA [VaR]) by estimating the capital charges of the BCBS (2011) advanced CVA approach (see Sect. 7.4.3) and also in the SA of CVA exposures under the new revised market risk framework for CVA risk (BCBS, 2017), discussed in Sect. 7.4.7.

The ES measure is an enhanced VaR measure as it is more coherent than the original VaR measure; see McNeil, Frey, and Embrechts (2015). Unlike VaR estimation, which considers an individual quantile (point estimation), the estimation of ES relies on the average of all loss events observed beyond the point estimation provided by the VaR. However, the exclusion of IMA in the CVA risk framework (BCBS, 2017) does not allow banks to use the ES to calibrate the capital requirements for estimating the capital charge for the CVA. Notably, the proposed FRTB-CVA framework (BCBS, 2015b) introduced the estimation of the average impact amongst extreme events which appear in the tail of loss distribution, that is, the ES for measuring how bad an extreme event might be, given that it exceeds the VaR measure. In the final Basel III framework, the new set of standards switches from estimating capital charges on the basis of ES to the estimation of CVA sensitivities and CVA (VaR) utilised in the SA of CVA.

7.3.8 Wrong- and Right-Way Risk

Before implementing the modelling, banks should observe potential interdependencies between the evolution of exposures and credit spreads, which are the two main parameters for the estimation of the CVA. Another element which requires banks' attention is the relationship between the exposure and credit quality of the counterparty.

The pattern of the interdependencies between exposures and credit spreads does not necessarily follow across all financial products; that is, they could move towards the same or opposite directions. The increase of spreads alongside the exposures indicates a higher probability of losses, which designates an unfavourable correlation called WWR. The inverse relationship between credit spreads and exposures signifies a favourable dependency, in terms of potential reduction of losses, between the two parameters used in the valuation adjustment process. This is called right-way risk (RWR).

Table 7.1 summarises the cases of WWRs and RWRs based on exposures, credit spreads, and losses. The CVA should be revalued on a mark-to-market basis. The frequent revaluation of CVA demands the consideration of WWRs and RWRs, respectively. Given that both spreads and exposures are market driven variables, banks can estimate the covariance and correlation coefficient factor ρ which indicate the degree of these variables to be positively or inversely co-dependent.

The factor ρ gets values[36] from 1 to −1 and, thus, can define the percentage of WWRs or RWRs ($a = 1 + \rho$), that is, $-1 \leq a < 0$ and $-1 \leq a < 0$ for WWR and RWR, respectively. Thus, the distribution of CVA values are now also driven by the distribution of the co-dependency factor ρ. Notably, only WWR increases the value of CVA, and the respective capital against CVA risk, in the CVA formulae.

Table 7.1 Wrong- and right-way risk, based on exposures, credit spreads, and losses

	Wrong-way risk		Right-way risk	
	Co-dependency			
	Positively		Negatively (inversely)	
Exposures	↑	↓	↑	↓
Credit spreads	↑	↓	↓	↑
Losses	↑	↓		↓

An easy way of dealing with WWR is to apply a multiplier factor "alpha" to the exposure used in CVA calculations. The effect of this is that when WWR is recognised the CVA is increased by the multiplier. The Basel II rules set alpha equal to 1.4 but also give banks the option to estimate their own alpha, subject to a floor of 1.2 (BCBS, 2016). Supervisors keep the high level of the alpha floor due to the awareness of systemic risk, and of the dangers of WWR.

As already mentioned, the Monte Carlo simulation can approximate the distribution of exposure values, spreads over time, and corresponding hazard rates. These distributions are set at discrete time points t_i within the set of Monte Carlo paths $k = 1, \ldots, N$. Banks may approach the possible joint distribution of co-dependencies by determining the positive and negative correlation of the historically or stochastically generated variables of exposure, spread, and (relative hazard rate) evolution over time. The low demand in computations counterbalances the accuracy implied by the simplicity of such an approach.

Banks can also estimate the co-dependency for each time interval and then apply the resulting vector of WWR and RWR to the corresponding exposures and spreads; however, this would result in a great computational demand. Moreover, the estimation of correlations could produce more precise results when banks identify the co-dependencies between default probabilities (or survival probabilities) and exposures using copula approaches; see Schönbucher (2003) and McNeil et al. (2015). Nevertheless, the high degree of complexity and burden that the application of such models imposes may be disproportionate in relation to the benefits from the holistic estimation of CVA risk.

The dependency of exposures on the counterparties' credit quality incorporates both WWR and RWR but also increases the complexity of the model and the calibration process. Thus, the approach of WWR and RWR is not always an easy task, and under certain conditions, it is not a necessity that the models have to address. The additional effort and a high degree of complexity in CVA models may explain why regulators, supervisors, and banks have been putting minimum efforts in proposing concrete methodologies for the implementation of WWR and RWR analyses.

7.4   CVA Capital Charge

7.4.1   Calculation of Capital Requirements of CVA Risk

Driven by different incentives, banks may employ CVA for accounting, pricing, and economic and regulatory capital estimations. Thus, it is somewhat naïve or simplified to assume that banks can apply a "one-size-fits-all" approach to the estimation of CVA.

The BCBS proposes approaches within the counterparty risk framework that define the minimum capital requirements for OTC trades against counterparty default volatility. Thus, in addition to Basel II standards, which deal with the expected losses due to actual counterparty default risk, the new frameworks address those risks resulting in CVA losses. Such losses[37] occur due to unfavourable changes in (a) credit exposures, (b) credit spreads and default probabilities, and (c) expected recoveries. These elements are not only counterparty-driven but also, to a certain extent, market-driven, defining the market value of the counterparty risk.

Within the initial framework of regulatory CVA capital charges (BCBS, 2011), the proposed BCBS framework allows banks to mitigate CVA risk, and the potential corresponding losses, by using plain vanilla hedging instruments which directly link to the counterparty risk. The advanced hedging instruments are excluded from the scope of eligible hedges, due to the higher degree of complexity and possible "fuzziness" in the analysis, and the controversy as to whether they bring benefits on mitigating the counterparty risk. Thus, the use of hedges with the use of exotic financial products would have no impact on CVA risk capital charge calculations.

In the treatment of mark-to-market counterparty risk losses (CVA capital charge) BCBS (2011) introduced two methods for the estimation of CVA risk capital charges: the standardised and the advanced approaches. Banks which apply the standardised CVA approach to calculate the risk charge employ given analytical formulae as a more straightforward measurement. Banks which apply the advanced CVA risk capital charge deal with a higher degree of complexity. Thus, this approach is the natural candidate for application by large banks,[38] given that banking supervisors have already granted approval to an IMM for the estimation of EAD or have allowed banks to use the SA-CCR. Both standardised and advanced approaches of CVA risk presume that banks must take into account only variability in credit spreads. Considering only the credit spreads variability explains why only hedges[39] against spread risks are recognised under this framework.

Both approaches seek to define the capital that banks need to reserve against exposures to counterparties, as well as to cope with the volatility of the CCR, excluding, as mentioned, the other market risk factors. Thus, this unidimensional view of CVA embeds the volatility of the counterparty's credit quality but excludes the volatility of other CVA attributes, such as the ones assigned to market-related volatilities.

An extension to the above-mentioned CVA approaches has been proposed under the minimum capital requirements for the CVA risk of market risk framework (BCBS, 2015b, 2017). This extension applies to all OTC[40] derivatives and securities financing transactions (SFTs) irrespective of whether they are part of the trading or banking book. The new CVA framework is lined up with the FRTB market risk framework (BCBS, 2013, 2016). The proposals of the consultative paper of the BCBS (2017) propose a few options to address different capabilities or preferences of banks to estimate CVA capital charges, that is, the reduced and the full version of the basic approach of CVA (BA-CVA), and the SA of CVA framework (SA-CVA). The internal model approach (IMA-CVA) introduced by the FRTB-CVA framework (BCBS, 2015b) is excluded by the new CVA framework (BCBS, 2017).

The two versions of basic approaches involve the application of simplified formulae and risk weights (RWs) that banks should take into account to estimate the capital charge. The SA estimates the capital charge based on sensitivities of CVA to credit spreads, as well as sensitivities to market risk factors which underline the formulation of the exposures. Thus, banks should estimate the corresponding delta and vega risks which are the primary measures that banks should compute under this approach.

7.4.2   The Standardised CVA Risk Capital Charge

The standardised CVA risk capital charge applies formulae proposed by the framework that approximate the dynamics of CVA (VaR) risks (BCBS, 2011: 34, para 104). The capital charge measurement assumes that the CVA follows a *normal distribution*. The confidence level of CVA (VaR) is set at 99% and the time horizon H is set to one year. The approach considers single-name credit spreads driven by the combination of a systematic (market) risk factor and an idiosyncratic risk factor.

The formula contains correlation parameters amongst single-named credit spreads, as well as the correlation between single-named credit spreads and the part of credit spreads attributed to systemic risk factors. The correlation values are set at 50% and 75%, respectively. Credit spreads have a flat term structure, that is, spreads are independent of tenor.

Also, the formulae contain weighting factors w_i on counterparties assigned to counterparty ratings.[41] Subject to supervisory approval, banks map the RWs to the corresponding external or internal rating of the counterparty. Moreover, this approach includes a weighting factor to index hedges, that is, w_{ind}, which relies on the average spread of the index in question.

The standardised CVA also considers three types of maturity factors: the effective maturity, M_i, which refers to transactions with a counterparty, and two other maturities linked to hedge instruments, M_i^{hedge}, and index hedge(s), M_{ind}. Additionally, the notional amounts of purchased hedge instruments (B_i) and index hedge(s) (B_{ind}) are part of the parameters used for the estimation of capital charge.

Finally, the EAD[42] estimation, against the counterparty i, considers netting and collateral effects in the CVA introduced by the SA formula. Equation (7.25) defines the formula proposed by the BCBS framework, and Fig. 7.6 summarises the main elements considered in CVA (VaR) of the standardised CVA risk capital charge approach.

$$K = 2.33 \cdot \sqrt{H} \cdot \sqrt{ \left(\sum_i 0.5 \cdot w_i \cdot \left(M_i \cdot EAD_i^{\text{total}} - M_i^{\text{hedge}} \cdot B_i \right) - \sum_{\text{ind}} w_{\text{ind}} \cdot M_{\text{ind}} \cdot B_{\text{ind}} \right)^2 + \sum_i 0.75 \cdot w_i^2 \cdot \left(M_i \cdot EAD_i^{\text{total}} - M_i^{\text{hedge}} \cdot B_i \right) } \qquad (7.25)$$

Box 7.1   Analysing the Sensitivity of CVA to Risk Weights and EAD Parameters

A high degree of sensitivity in the resulting CVA could arise from the application of RWs and EAD parameters. Figure 7.7 shows the impact of these two parameters in CVA capital charge, by combining the full spectrum of counterparty credit ratings, that is, from AAA to CCC, with a sample evolution of EAD from 0 to 100. In this example maturities are set constant. As shown in the same figure, the highest applicable RW (for Caa1/CCC ratings) leads to the highest capital charge. The use of regulatory RWs in the standardised method is one of the main differences compared to the advanced method which requires the application of market-implied spreads.

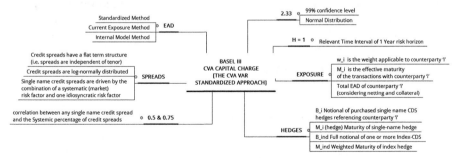

Fig. 7.6   Main elements in estimating standardised CVA capital charge based on CVA (VaR) (BCBS, 2011)

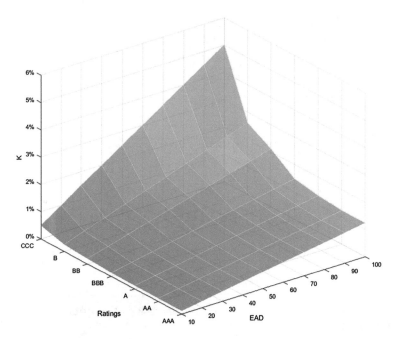

Fig. 7.7 Impact of EAD and ratings on the CVA capital charge under the standardised CVA risk capital charge approach

7.4.3   The Advanced CVA Risk Capital Charge

Equation (7.26) describes the advanced approach to CVA risk capital charge[43] proposed by BCBS (2011). The marginal default probability between t_{i-1} and t_i is the difference between the cumulative default probabilities $DP(t_{i-1}, t_i)$ multiplied by the discounted average IMM[44] EPE $\dfrac{EE_{i-1} \cdot D_{i-1} + EE_i \cdot D_i}{2}$ at the interval between revaluation time points t_{i-1} and t_i, as well as by the market-implied loss-given-default (LGD) of the counterparty (LGD_{MKT}).

$$CVA = \left(LGD_{MKT} \right) \cdot \sum_{i=1}^{T} DP\left(t_{i-1}, t_i \right) \cdot \left(\frac{EE_{i-1} \cdot D_{i-1} + EE_i \cdot D_i}{2} \right) \qquad (7.26)$$

The cumulative default probabilities $DP(t_{i-1}, t_i)$ are estimated by recalling Eq. (7.24), that is,

$$DP\left(t_{i-1}, t_i \right) = \max\left[0; \exp\left(-\frac{s_{i-1}}{LGD_{MKT}} \cdot t_{i-1} \right) - \exp\left(-\frac{s_i}{LGD_{MKT}} \cdot t_i \right) \right].$$ The term structures of market-implied default probabilities are estimated using observed credit spreads.

Thus, the factor s_i defines the credit spread of the counterparty at tenor t_i, based on market-observed credit spread of a market instrument. The term $exp\left(-\dfrac{s_i}{LGD_{MKT}}\cdot t_i\right)$ is an expression for the approximation of the risk-neutral default probability up to a given time t_i. The term $\dfrac{s_i}{LGD_{MKT}}$ defines the hazard rate driven by credit spreads, as discussed in Sect. 7.3.5. Banks have to simulate the evolution of credit spreads of all counterparties associated with instruments subject to CVA risk. The LGD of the counterparty LGD_{MKT}[45] is a market assumption on recovery rates. It is rather challenging to model and estimate recovery rates accurately. Nonetheless, we anticipate that they have a significant impact on CVA calculations. The advanced CVA uses market-implied recoveries based on information such as seniority, type of counterparty, and so on. Since market-observed credit spreads and recoveries may not always be available, banks may use proxies based on different counterparty or exposure characteristics such as rating, industry, region, currency, seniority to define proxy-based spreads and recoveries.

For estimating CVA risk capital charge, banks must apply a CVA (VaR) model based on the stochastic evolution of credit spreads (discussed in Sect. 7.3) employed in Eq. (7.24). In case the VaR model is based on credit spread sensitivities for specific tenors, BCBS (2011) introduced a formula of the regulatory credit spread sensitivity as illustrated in Eq. (7.27). Furthermore, in the case of applying parallel shifts to the credit spreads (Regulatory CS01), the formula for the regulatory credit spread sensitivity is defined as in Eq. (7.28). In both regulatory formulae of sensitivity measures a change at a degree of one basis point (bp) is applied.

$$\text{Regulatory } CS01_i = 0.0001.t_i.\exp\left(-\frac{s_i}{LGD_{MKT}}.t_i\right).\left(\frac{EE_{i-1}.D_{i-1}+EE_i.D_i}{2}\right)$$

(7.27)

Regulatory

$$CS01 = 0.0001.\sum_{T}^{i=1}\left(\begin{array}{c}\exp\left(-\dfrac{s_i}{LGD_{MKT}}.t_i\right)\\[2mm]-\exp\left(-\dfrac{s_{i-1}}{LGD_{MKT}}.t_{i-1}\right)\end{array}\right).\left(\frac{EE_{i-1}.D_{i-1}+EE_i.D_i}{2}\right)$$

(7.28)

The BCBS (2011) framework proposes that the formula of the advanced CVA (Eq. 7.26) estimates the VaR and stressed VaR at a 99% confidence level of the resulting distribution of CVA losses for each counterparty after accounting for the eligible hedges. The framework defines the advanced CVA risk capital charge as the sum of the non-stressed VaR and stressed VaR.

The fact that the present approach does not consider scenarios to approximate the evolution of exposure means that this framework does not recognise the variability of market risk factors, with the exception of the variability of credit spreads, in the estimation of the advanced CVA risk capital charge. Therefore, VaR and stressed VaR computation take into account only the variability of counterparties' credit spreads. Thus, as earlier discussed, the bank excludes hedges aimed at mitigating losses arising from market risk factors' volatility.

Also, banks assume that there are no correlations among market and counterparty risk factors, that is, they assume that there is no impact of IRs on the default probability of the counterparty. One can argue that considering such correlations may increase the complexity of the CVA model but excluding them may result in misspecification of the capital charge.

The existing (BCBS, 2015b, 2017) proposals and the respective framework of most of the jurisdictions do not recognise debit valuation adjustments (DVAs). A possible recognition of DVA would offset CVA risk. The acknowledgement of DVA would result in less economic capital charges than the ones proposed by the BCBS framework. Moreover, DVA may alter the hedging strategies as the current ones consider only the CVA risk. The proposed framework (BCBS, 2015b, 2017) restricts the application of the unilateral CVA in the advanced approach, not allowing banks to use their own internal CVA models that may be used for the estimation of accounting CVA or other risk management purposes.

Banks can employ the CIR model to simulate the evolution of counterparty credit spreads, as discussed in Sect. 7.3.3 and illustrated in Fig. 7.5. Note also that, based on these spreads and defined recoveries, the bank can even approximate the hazard rates (Eq. 7.22) using the marginal default probability (Eq. 7.24) employed in the regulatory CVA formula (Eq. 7.26). Figure 7.8 illustrates a CVA (VaR) at 99.9% confidence level resulting from a distribution of CVA values calculated based on the stochastic evolution of credit spreads.

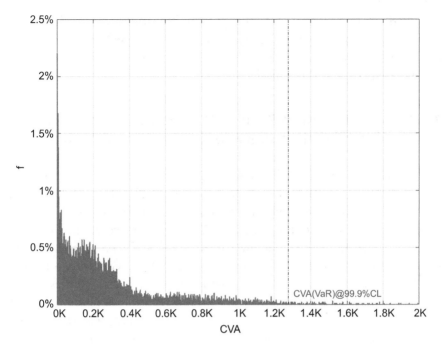

Fig. 7.8 Distribution of CVAs at a percentage of frequency (f) identifying the CVA (VaR) at the 99.9% confidence level

7.4.3.1 The Definition of Expected Recoveries, Credit Spreads, and Hedges

The latest proposals allow the mitigation of CVA risk within the advanced approach framework with the use of "eligible hedges", including CDS indices, purchased and contingent single-name CDS, and other plain vanilla hedging instruments, referred to as counterparty risks.

Banks should move these hedges from the trading book to the CVA book. Based on the new framework, regulators may also allow CVA "proxy hedges", which do not make direct reference to the counterparty but may have a significant impact on the CVA estimation. Eligible hedges do not include exotic instruments, for example, *nth-to-default* credit derivatives, synthetic collateralized debt obligations (CDOs) divided into credit tranches.

From market practitioners' point of view, the degree of the recovery rate may depend on the efficiency of hedging applied against exposures to counterparty risk. The absence of hedging reduces the expected level of recovery, whereas applying efficient hedging techniques increases the seniority of the exposure. Often, hedging and expected recoveries play a vital role to the formulation of the expected default probability, ratings, and credit spreads. However, mixing up straightforward estimations of hedging activity with behaviour assumptions on recoveries and expected defaults increases the complexity and fuzziness of the model.

7.4.4   Adjustments in Revised Market Risk Framework of Minimum Capital Requirements for CVA Risk

The new revised market risk framework on minimum capital requirements for CVA risk (BCBS, 2017) is replacing the FRTB-CVA framework (BCBS, 2015b). Under the new framework, banks do not have the option to apply the IMA-CVA approach proposed by the FRTB-CVA framework. The IMA-CVA was an adaptation of the IMA applied for the TB (Chap. 6) to capture the impact of extreme events in CVA by applying ES for a reduced set of market risk factors. The absence of the internal modelled approaches on estimating CVA risk capital aligned with the view of the Basel committee that banks should be implementing more conservative and unified approaches that could be more comparative and applicable across the banking sector.

Hence, in the new revised CVA framework banks can choose, based on hedging recognition, the *reduced* or the *full* version of basic approach (BA-CVA); or the standardised approach (SA-CVA) for calculating CVA capital charge. Remarkably, unless banks receive from their relevant supervisory authority the approval to develop and utilise SA-CVA, they must use one of the versions of the BA-CVA approach (BCBS, 2017: 109 para 2). The BCBS also proposed an alternative option to CVA capital charges for those banks exposed to non-centrally cleared derivatives up to the materiality threshold of 100 billion euros. Banks having exposure of the aggregate notional amount of the entire derivative portfolio below this threshold, as well as approval from the supervisory authority, may set the CVA capital equal to capital charge estimated for CCR.

As discussed above, the BCBS (2011) framework on CCR estimates the capital charge against future changes in CVA, caused only by the variability in counterparty credit spreads. However, losses also result from the variability of exposures[46] subject to changes in market risk factors. In the newly proposed market risk framework on CVA risk (BCBS, 2015b, 2017), banks include the exposures' variabilities assigned to all market risk factors, resulting in a vast alignment between capital charges on CVA and economic risks. Thus, capital charges take into account the fair value adjustments on derivatives due to variations in both market and credit spreads. The BCBS states that "CVA risk is defined as the risk of losses arising from changing CVA values in response to changes in counterparty credit spreads and market risk factors that drive prices of derivative transactions and SFTs" (BCBS, 2017: 109, para 2).

Under the proposed framework, the bank calculates the capital charge against the variability of CVA for all covered derivative transactions and SFTs, at fair value, in the trading book.[47] However, should derivatives be transacted via qualified CCPs the bank is eligible to omit from the estimation of BA-CVA and SA-CVA capital charge. Furthermore, NSs may be carved out from the SA-CVA calculations and thus must be calculated via the BA-CVA.

The market risk framework of CVA risk aims to approach[48] the CVA risk capital charge of the trading book, including its eligible hedges. The new framework relies on fair value sensitivities of market risk factors for all traded instruments. Based on the same concept, the framework capitalises the CVA risk for the bank's CVA book. The part of the portfolio subject to CVA includes banks' portfolios of derivative positions and the corresponding CVA-eligible hedges. Hence, banks must identify the eligible hedges to be used for hedging all the underlying factors of CVA variability.

7.4.5 Hedges in Market Risk Framework of CVA Risk

To avoid the variability in P&L due to CVA risks, the standardised approach, SA-CVA, of the new revised market risk framework of CVA risk considers as eligible the hedges of the counterparty credit spreads and of market risk factors which affect the underlying exposures. The inclusion of the volatility of exposures in CVA risk motivates banks to use hedges against market risk factors. Nonetheless, in the full version of BA-CVA banks recognise only the counterparty spread hedges, while in the reduced version of BA-CVA, implemented by less sophisticated banks, no hedging recognition is allowed.

Banks can utilise external or internal hedging instruments. The former concerns hedging with an external counterparty while the latter with the bank's trading desk. The external CVA hedges must be included in the estimation CVA but excluded in the market risk capital charge calculation. External hedges of CVA portfolio that are non-eligible under the new framework are treated as trading book instruments and thus are capitalised under the market risk rules for the trading book (BCBS, 2016).

The perfectly offsetting positions of CVA and trading desks are involved in internal CVA hedging. Should the internal CVA hedge not be eligible there is no impact in capitalisation on both desks. Nonetheless, eligible internal CVA hedges are part of the capitalisation on both desks by applying the new revised

CVA framework and the revised market risk standard (Chap. 6). Finally, eligible internal hedges applying to curvature risk, default risk, or the residual risk add-on are the only ones that perfectly offset the positions of CVA and trading desks.

7.4.6 Reduced Version of the BA-CVA (Not Recognised Hedges)

Banks can calculate the CVA capital charge proposed by the BCBS framework using the reduced version of the BA-CVA formula shown in Eq. (7.29).

$$K_{reduced} = \sqrt{\left(\rho \cdot \sum_c SCVA_c \right)^2 + \left(1 - \rho^2\right) \cdot \sum_c SCVA_c^2} \qquad (7.29)$$

The correlation parameter (ρ) between systematic and counterparty credit spread risk factors is set at 50%, and the squared correlation (ρ^2) between two counterparties' credit spread risk factors is set at 25%.

The stand-alone CVA capital estimate at the counterparty level defined by the framework is as shown in Eq. (7.30).

$$SCVA_c = \frac{RW_c}{a} \cdot \sum_{NS \in c} M_{NS} \cdot EAD_{NS} \cdot DF_{NS} \qquad (7.30)$$

- The risk weight RW_c designates the volatility of its credit spread. To derive the RW_c banks should have already assigned the counterparty to the appropriate sector, as well as have classified the underlying credit quality of the counterparty of the instrument as investment grade (IG) or high yield (HY), or not rated (NR).
- The following RWs with the corresponding counterparty sector and credit quality are set by the framework: (1) sovereigns including central banks, multilateral development banks, IG: 0.5%, HY&NR: 3.0%; (2) local government, government-backed non-financials, education and public administration, IG: 1.0%, HY&NR: 4.0%; (3) financials including government-backed financials, IG: 5.0%, HY&NR: 12.0%; (4) basic materials, energy, industrials, agriculture, manufacturing, mining and quarrying, IG: 3.0%, HY&NR: 7.0%; (5) consumer goods and services, transportation and storage, administrative and support service activities, IG: 3.0%,

HY&NR: 8.5%, (6) technology, telecommunications, IG: 2.0%, HY&NR: 5.5%; (7) health care, utilities, professional and technical activities, IG: 1.5%, HY&NR: 5.0%; and (8) other sectors, IG: 5.0%, HY&NR: 12.0%.

- The conversion factor a is used to transform effective expected positive exposure (EEPE) to EAD; this factor is set at 1.4 ($a = 1.4$);
- The effective maturity for the NS, denoted as M_{NS}, is estimated as in Basel II framework[49] (BCBS, 2006);
- The EAD of the NS, denoted as EAD_{NS}, is estimated as the bank calculates it for minimum capital requirements for CCR (BCBS, 2014);
- The supervisory discount factor denoted as DF_{NS} equals 1 for banks using the IMM to calculate EAD, and is formulated as $DF_{NS} = \dfrac{1 - e^{-0.05.M_{NS}}}{0.05.M_{NS}}$ for banks not using IMM.

For a given EAD_{NS}, M_{NS}, and DF_{NS}, Fig. 7.9 illustrates the impact of RWs set for the different sectors to $SCVA_c$ estimations.

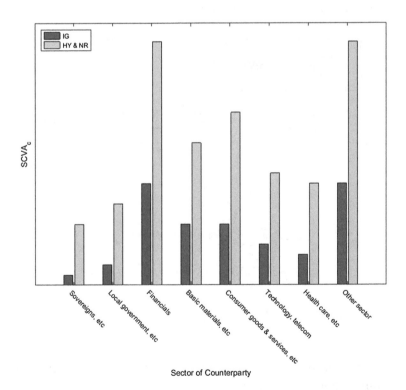

Fig. 7.9 *Impact of RWA set for the different sectors to* $SCVA_c$ *estimations*

7.4.7   Full Version of the BA-CVA (Recognised Hedges)

In addition to perfect single-named CDS and contingent CDS hedges, index CDS with direct reference to counterparty the full version of BA-CVA allows imperfect single-named hedges, that is, hedges with an indirect legal link or common region/sector with the counterparties.

In the final Basel framework, the full version of the BA-CVA approach for estimating CVA capital charges, denoted as K_{full}, relies on the given formula (BCBS, 2017: 112 para 18) shown in Eq. (7.31).

$$K_{full} = \beta \cdot K_{reduced} + (1 - \beta) \cdot K_{hedged} \tag{7.31}$$

The capital charge K_{full} includes:

- The reduced version of the BA-CVA capital charge $K_{reduced}$ (Eq. 7.29);
- The hedging floor parameter β determined at $\beta = 0.25$; and
- The capital requirements that recognises eligible hedges K_{hedged} calculated by a given formula shown in Eq. (7.32).

$$K_{hedged} = \sqrt{ \underbrace{\left(\rho \cdot \sum_c SCVA_c - SNH_c - IH \right)^2}_{Systematic} + \underbrace{(1 - \rho^2) \cdot \sum_c (SCVA_c - SNH_c)^2}_{Idiosyncratic} + \underbrace{\sum_c HMA_c}_{Indirect\ hedges} } \tag{7.32}$$

where

$$SNH_c = \sum_{h \in c} r_{hc} \cdot RW_h \cdot M_h^{SN} \cdot B_h^{SN} \cdot DF_h^{SN} \tag{7.33}$$

$$IH = \sum_i RW_i \cdot M_i^{ind} \cdot B_i^{ind} \cdot DF_i^{ind} \tag{7.34}$$

$$HMA_c = \sum_{h \in c} (1 - r_{hc}^2) \cdot (RW_h \cdot M_h^{SN} \cdot B_h^{SN} \cdot DF_h^{SN})^2 \tag{7.35}$$

The calculation of capital charge (K_{hedged}) of the exposures where eligible hedges are recognised should consider the following:

- The correlation (ρ) between counterparty credit spread and the systematic factor, set at ρ = 50%,
- The stand-alone CVA capital ($SCVA_c$) (Eq. (7.30)) described in Sect. 7.4.5, containing:

  - The counterparties' characteristics, for example, the sector where the counterparty belongs;
  - The EAD;
  - The effective maturities;
  - The supervisory discount factor denoted as DF_{NS};

- The recognition parameter (SNH_c) of using single-name hedges of credit spread risk defined by the framework as shown in Eq. (7.33) including:

  - The supervisory correlation (r_{hc}) between counterparty c credit spreads and the spread of single-name hedge h of the counterparty c set[50] from 50% to 100%;
  - The supervisory risk weight RW_h of single-name hedge h. The RW_h indicates the volatility of the credit spread of the reference name of the hedging instrument and is set in the exact manner as the RW_c explained in Sect. 7.4.5.
  - The remaining maturity $\left(M_h^{SN} \right)$ of single-name hedge h;
  - The notional $\left(B_h^{SN} \right)$ of single-name hedge h;
  - The supervisory discount factor formulated as $DF_h^{SN} = \dfrac{1 - e^{-0.05 \cdot M_h^{SN}}}{0.05 \cdot M_h^{SN}}$;

- The index hedges parameter IH defined by the framework as shown in Eq. (7.35) containing the following parameters:

  - The supervisory risk weight RW_i of the index hedge i equals to 70% of the RW_c defined in Sect. 7.4.5 following the classification rules of the sector and the credit quality of the index;
  - The remaining maturity $\left(M_i^{ind} \right)$ of index hedge i;
  - The notional $\left(B_i^{ind} \right)$ of the index hedge i;
  - The supervisory discount factor formulated as $DF_i^{ind} = \dfrac{1 - e^{-0.05 \cdot M_i^{ind}}}{0.05 \cdot M_i^{ind}}$.

- The quantity HMA_c reflects the indirect hedges that are not fully aligned with counterparties' credit spreads. The definition of the HMA_c function, shown in Eq. (7.35), is driven by the same parameters defined in SNH_c;
- The systematic and idiosyncratic risk components of single-named hedges.

The first two aggregation terms of the *systematic* and *idiosyncratic* components of the square root in Eq. (7.32) shows that banks should subtract the stand-alone CVA capital ($SCVA_c$) from the single-name hedge parameter (SNH_c). The systemic component is again reduced by the index hedges parameter IH. The resulting output of the systematic components is finally weighted by the systematic factor ρ. The respective sum of the second component (idiosyncratic) is accordingly weighted by the idiosyncratic risk factor $(1 - \rho^2)$.

In the third aggregation term, which refers to the indirect hedges, banks have to sum the quantity HMA_c for all counterparties and indirect single-named hedges. In all three components, the calculation applies to all counterparty exposures and then it is summed up. The square power applied to the sums ensures that capital charges are positive even in cases where the subtractions result in a negative number.

Therefore, banks have to optimise their positions (exposures and hedges) to optimise the systematic and idiosyncratic risk components as well as the indirect hedges and eventually minimise the capital charge. The optimisation of banks' positions does not only include changing the reference entities which underline the instruments but it also includes altering the maturity and the notional amounts of the exposures and hedges which could lead to different RWs.

Box 7.2   Example for Optimal Capital Charge Under BA-CVA

As an example, consider a case where there are two positions against respective counterparties: the first position refers to a two-year US $8 million bond of Vodafone, hedged by a Swisscom bond, and the second position is a three-year US $2 million depth security from Apple, hedged by IBM bonds. In both hedges the bank may apply a maximum level of 75% of the positions' exposures. Both positions and hedges are assigned to technology and telecommunications sectors with RWs set at 2%. There are also indirect index hedges that apply to both positions assigned to a sector with underlying credit quality of the counterparty falling to 3% of RW. The bank may use the indirect index hedges covering up to 25% of the positions' exposures. To simplify the example there is no maturity mismatch between positions and reference hedges.

The stand-alone CVA capital ($SCVA_c$) (Eq. (7.30)) for both positions are

$$SCVA_{c(Vodafone)} = \frac{2\%}{1.4} \times 2 \times 8 \times 0.97 = 0.22 \quad \text{and} \quad SCVA_{c(Apple)} = \frac{2\%}{1.4} \times 3 \times 2 \times 0.97 = 0.08.$$ Given

the $SCVA_c$, the capital $K_{reduced}$ of the reduced version of the BA-CVA is estimated using Eq. (7.29).

(continued)

Box 7.2   (continued)

Given the exposures, maturities, RWs of the positions and individual hedging position the bank may optimise the notionals $\left(B_h^{SN}\right)$ of single-name hedge and $\left(B_i^{ind}\right)$ of the index hedge to get the minimum capital charge.

Banks now estimate the quantity HMA_c of the systematic and idiosyncratic components utilising the $SCVA_c$, SNH_c, IH, keeping the maturities constant and applying hedge amounts starting from 0% to 75% for B_h^{SN} and to 25% for B_i^{ind} of the two positions' exposures. The resulting amounts of capital requirements that recognise eligible hedges K_{hedged} (Eq. (7.32)) together with $K_{reduced}$ lead to the evolution of K_{full}.

Figure 7.10 illustrates the evolution of K_{full} with respect to the sum amount of hedge notionals. Table 7.2 shows the optimal values of $SCVA_c$, SNH_c, IH, B_h^{SN}, and B_i^{ind} for reaching the minimum capital charge $K_{full} = 0.2081$ (Eq. (7.31)). In this respect the optimal notionals of each hedging position (Swisscom, IBM, and indirect index hedging) leads to the optimal aggregated hedge amount of 5.5, which is only 55% of the total positions' exposures that are being hedged.

Of course, banks could apply an alternative approximation by optimising the level of maturities. In fact, this is an optimisation problem where we try to achieve the values for K_{hedged} parameters which result in the minimum capital K_{full}.

7.4.8   Standardised Approach CVA Framework

Under the SA-CVA, banks consider CVA sensitivities and hedges of both market and CCR factors. Thus, banks have to estimate CVA sensitivities arising from small changes in market risk factors, including interest and inflation rates, equity, commodity, FX, and reference credit spreads, as well as sensitivities assigned to small changes in market-implied counterparty credit spreads. The standard risk factors and classes are common between SA-CVA and SA under the FRTB framework. The SA-CVA framework follows the same sensitivities-based methods used under the market risk SA for the trading book (FRTB) (Chap. 6). The sensitivity measures can be significantly useful in cases where volatilities of market risk factors cause large movements in net exposures, hedging instruments' valuation, and CVA assessment.

Table 7.2 Optimal values of $SCVA_c$, SNH_c, IH, B_h^{SN}, and B_i^{ind} in order to minimise capital charge K_{full}

	SNH_c	IH	HMA_c	B_h^{SN}	B_i^{ind}
Swisscom	0.0628	0.0628	0.0118	3.3000	1.1000
IBM	0.0230	0.0230	0.0016	0.8250	0.2750

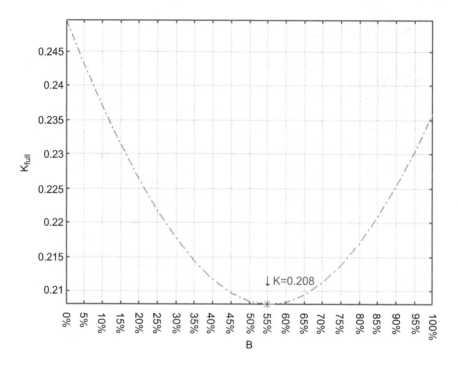

Fig. 7.10 Capital charge K_{full} with respect to the evolution of the aggregated amount of single-name and index hedges

Banks should use delta and vega risk calculations to measure the sensitivities of value adjustments to market risk factors. Again, the sensitivities to counterparty credit spread are measured only by delta risk calculation.

Nevertheless, this approach does not include the estimation of vega risk in CVA as the impulse-response relationship of counterparty credit spreads to CVA sensitivities is approximately linear. The counterparty default risk is out of consideration under this approach as the CCR capital charge already accounts for it. Moreover, to reduce computational intensiveness, gamma risk is also excluded. This exclusion, together with the reduction in granularity of risk factors, may result in insufficient capturing of both risk and capital measurements.

Table 7.3 summarises the main differences between SA-CVA, covered in this chapter, and SA for TB disused in Sect. 6.2 under the SA to market risk section. From this comparison, one can observe that the SA-CVA is less demanding for a set of market risk factors, as well as in the inclusion of other risk factors, which may result in insufficient capturing of risks. This may explain why risk aggregation under the SA-CVA is more conservative than under the SA of the FRTB framework. Hence, the SA-CVA framework does not recognise any diversification effects between delta and vega risks nor any potential perfect correlation between CVA risks and their corresponding hedges. For each risk factor, the proposed framework does not allow any correlation between the CVA exposures and hedges, if the exposures are not perfectly hedged.

The fact that correlations of imperfect hedges are not eligible impacts the diversification and results in higher capital requirements[51]; moreover, banks must always keep additional capital for the part of CVA risk which is not fully hedged.

7.4.9 The Estimation of Counterparty-Specific Regulatory SA-CVA

The main principles that define and estimate the unilateral regulatory SA-CVA are:

Principle 1:   Banks must assume themselves as default risk-free. Hence, exposure to counterparty default is the only source of risk that may result in CVA losses.

Table 7.3 Comparison of the elements used in SA to CVA risk and SA to market risk in the FRTB framework

	SA-CVA (FRTB) (Standardised approach to CVA risk)	SA (FRTB) (Standardised approach to market risk)	
	Risk types/classes IRs, FX, equity, commodity, reference credit spread	General interest rate risk (GIRR), FX, equity, commodity, CSR non-securitisations, CSR securitisations (CTP), CSR securitisations (non-CTP)	Sensitivity method
Market risk factors	Delta and vega	Delta, vega, curvature risk	
Counterparty (reference) credit spread	Delta and vega		
Counterparty credit spread	Delta		
Default risk	Not considered	Default risk charge (gross jump-to-default risk)	
Other risks	None	Residual risk add-on	

Principle 2:   The parameter elements of the CVA calculations are the term structure of market-implied PDs, the market-implied expected loss-given default (ELGD), and the simulated paths of discounted future exposure.

Principle 3:   The estimation of the term structure of market-implied PDs, aka the risk-neutral PDs, uses credit spreads obtained by liquid traded instruments. In the case of illiquid counterparties, banks should map and appropriately use the observed credit spreads of their liquid peers.

The algorithm used for such indirect extraction of credit spreads must use variables such as counterparty's credit quality (e.g. rating), sector, and region or country. Also, banks can collectively map illiquid counterparties to a single liquid reference name, for example, mapping of municipalities to the state that they belong to. A bank may also rely on analysis based on more fundamental characteristics of credit risk to proxy the spread of illiquid counterparties. Such characteristics must still be—to a reasonable and convincing degree—linked to market-driven, rather than historical data (BCBS, 2017: 115 para 30).

Banks estimate the market-implied ELGD by following the same rules as in estimating risk-neutral PDs from credit spreads.

Principle 4:   Banks should use the observed counterparty credit spreads as market risk factors that are driving the exposures, and defining the market-implied default probabilities.

Principle 5:   Banks should duly generate and calculate the risk-neutral exposures to market-implied risk factor parameters. In this fashion, the drifts of the generated risk factors must be consistent with a risk-neutral probability measure. Exposures distribution could be non-normal or containing fat tails. Historical calibration may be permitted for the volatilities and correlations of market risk factors while historical drift calibration is disallowed.

Principle 6:   Banks should simulate an appropriate number of paths of the underlying risk factors to the discounted exposures, as well as of the counterparty credit spreads stochastically. The set of future time points must be aligned to the maturity of the longest transaction.

Principle 7:   Banks should take into account the dependence between exposure and the counterparty's credit quality.

Principle 8:   Banks should apply a supervisory floor of 9 + N business days
                 on the MPoR (see Sect. 7.2.2).
Principle 9:   Recognition of netting is in the same fashion as in the account-
                 ing CVA and allowance of modelling netting uncertainty.
Principle 10:   Allowance of banks in hedging CVA sensitivities.

The estimation of CVA should take into consideration these principles
before using the formula defined in Eq. (7.1). Notably, banks should only
calculate the unilateral CVA which means that they should ignore the own
estimation of default probabilities.

The CVA makes use of the market-implied parameters, based on fair value
under risk-neutral environment. Risk neutrality is widely used by market
participants in the pricing of accounting CVA. Moreover, the pricing under
risk neutrality allows banks to hedge (mitigate) efficiently the CVA sensitivities of traded instruments which are exposed market-driven risk factors.

7.4.9.1   Hedges

Banks may hedge CVA sensitivities against market risk factors, by trading
derivative contracts such as IR and FX swaps and FX forwards, to reduce the
volatility of CVA capital charges, attributable to potential variations of derivative values.

Thus, banks hedge both changes and variabilities in the underlying exposures, which impact the CVA, by taking opposite positions on the corresponding market risk factors that affect these exposures. They also hedge changes in
counterparty credit spreads of long positions, which impact the CVA, by taking short positions in the relevant spreads.

Banks can use single-named financial instruments to hedge counterparty
credit spread risk. Moreover, the new proposal on SA-CVA allows the recognition of market risk hedges for mitigating CVA sensitivities to market risk
factors affecting the exposures. To that end, eligible hedges are not only the
ones that hedge the counterparty credit spread but also those that hedge the
other risk components that affect the CVA. Naturally, the ability to include
counterparty and exposure hedges reduces the CVA risk and thus the CVA
capital charge. Nonetheless, only instruments included in the IMA for market risk under the revised market risk standard (BCBS, 2016) can be eligible
CVA hedges.

7.4.10   Multiplier Factor on SA-CVA

The complexity of calculating CVA exposures and sensitivities could aggravate model-error risk, which may partly explain why supervisors require the scaling up of the capital charges, using a multiplier m_{CVA}.[52] Moreover, this multiplier addresses the potential existence of WWR (Sect. 7.3.8). Banks that do not take into account the WWR into their CVA models but have a significant level of dependence on exposure and the counterparty's credit quality must apply a higher degree of multiplier m_{CVA}.

7.4.11   Sensitivity Analysis of CVA Capital Charges

Banks should apply a sensitivity analysis based on delta and vega risk measurements to the estimation of CVA capital charges for CVA portfolios. Thus, for each risk factor k of the five risk types, banks should calculate the aggregate sensitivities of CVA (s_k^{CVA}) as well as of all eligible hedges of CVA portfolios (s_k^{Hdg}). The sensitivity analysis employs the ratio of the change of these quantities as a result of small changes (i.e. deterministic shocks by one bp) of the underlying financial risk factors, including shifts in the values of risk factors and their volatilities.

Banks should estimate delta sensitivities of the CVA exposures (and of eligible CVA hedges) as a response to a small deterministic shift on the counterparty market-implied credit spread risk factor $k_{(spreads)}$ as well as on other market risk factors ($k_{(MRF)}$) which drive the underlying CVA exposures (E_k). The general formulae of CVA sensitivities for the delta to underlying risk factors are defined in Eqs. (7.36) and (7.37).

$$\Delta s_{k_{(CPspreads)}}^{CVA} = \frac{\partial CVA}{\partial k_{(CPspreads)}} \qquad (7.36)$$

$$\Delta s_{E_k}^{CVA} = \frac{\partial CVA}{\partial E_{k_{(MRF)}}} \qquad (7.37)$$

The credit spread sensitivity comprises the default probability and recovery rate. The exposure sensitivity contains all variables that have an impact on exposure.

With regard to co-dependency between credit spread and exposure, aka WWR, sensitivity is defined as $\partial^2 CVA / \partial k_{(CPspreads)} \partial E_{k_{(MRF)}}$. However, this sensitivity term is not part of the BCBS CVA sensitivity framework.

Furthermore, banks should calculate vega risk sensitivities of the CVA as a result of a volatility shift applied to market risk factors, which will impact the underlying CVA exposures as well as the pricing of options through the exposure valuation models. The general formula of CVA sensitivities for the vega risk is defined in Eq. (7.38).

$$vs_{E_k}^{CVA} = \frac{\partial CVA}{\partial E_{\sigma k}} \qquad (7.38)$$

The CVA is always sensitive to changes in volatilities of market risk factors, even in the absence of options from the portfolio. Nevertheless, as banks need to apply simulation of exposures' evolution for all trades even the existence of plain vanilla derivative contracts in a small notional may require exhaustive calculation processing power and time.

7.4.12 Delta and Vega Risks Charge for CVA Book

The CVA capital charge under the SA-CVA approach stands for the sum of capital charges for delta and vega risks. Delta (Δs) and vega (vs) CVA sensitivities are defined as Δs_k^{CVA} and vs_k^{CVA}, while for CVA hedges as Δs_k^{Hdg} and vs_k^{Hdg}, respectively. These are the core measurement elements of the estimation of capital charges which are analytically shown in the set of formulae provided in Eq. (7.39).

$$\Delta s_k^{CVA} = \frac{\partial CVA}{\partial k}, \ \Delta s_k^{Hdg} = \frac{\partial V^{CVA\_Hdg}}{\partial k}, \ vs_k^{CVA} = \frac{\partial CVA}{\partial k}, \ vs_k^{Hdg} = \frac{\partial V^{CVA\_Hdg}}{\partial k}$$

$$(7.39)$$

where ∂CVA_i is the change in the aggregate CVA (or the value of CVA hedges) by applying a shift value in the risk factor k of volatility of one bp, that is, 0.01%.

The proposed set of rules provides RWs for the weighting of these sensitivities. Then, the weighted sensitivities for each particular risk factor k defined as $WS_k^{CVA} = RW_k \Delta s_k^{CVA}$ and $WS_k^{Hdg} = RW_k \Delta s_k^{Hdg}$ are aggregated to produce the net weighted sensitivity as illustrated in Eq. (7.40).

$$WS_k = WS_k^{CVA} + WS_k^{Hdg}, \ WS_k = RW_k \cdot s_k^{CVA} + RW_k \cdot s_k^{Hdg} \qquad (7.40)$$

Within each bucket b, banks should aggregate the net weighted sensitivities for each of the different risk factors, that is, k, l, considering the correlation set by the framework (ρ_{kl}). Based on the above elements, the bucket-specific capital charge is provided in Eq. (7.41).

$$K_b = \sqrt{\left[\sum_{k \in b} WS_k^2 + \sum_{k \in b}\sum_{l \in b\ l \neq l}\rho_{kl} \cdot W_k \cdot W_l\right] + R \cdot \sum_{k \in b}\left[\left(WS_k^{Hdg}\right)^2\right]} \qquad (7.41)$$

The banks which apply the proposed framework should note that as defined in the framework (BCBS, 2017: 119 para 51) a specific hedging disallowance R factor, set at [0.01], prevents the possibility of perfect hedging of CVA risk.

The capital charge across all buckets is defined, as shown in Eq. (7.42), by aggregating the bucket-level capital charges, considering the correlation factors for each risk γ_{bc} among the buckets.

$$K = m_{CVA}\sqrt{\sum_b k_b^2 + \sum_b\sum_{c \neq b}\gamma_{bc}K_bK_c} \qquad (7.42)$$

7.4.13   Setting Parameters for Delta and Vega Risks Charge

The main elements that influence the estimation of capital charge are the definitions of buckets and risk factors, the correlations between cross-bucket as well as amongst risk factors, the measurements of sensitivities, and the determination of RWs.

7.4.13.1   Interest and Inflation Rates

Regarding the changes in the values of risk factors, potential alterations in inflation rates and market IRs could significantly affect the CVA of the existing positions.

Buckets: The buckets of the IR delta and vega risks are distinguished according to the currency of denomination, that is, USD, EUR, GBP, JPY, and [all] other currencies.

Cross-bucket correlation: The cross-bucket correlation γ_{bc} amongst buckets for *all currency pairs* is set at 50%.

Delta and vega risk shifts: Delta and vega risks measure the IR sensitivities, under a given currency (bucket), assuming shocks on the risk-free yield curve,[53] IRs, and inflation rates. Thus, banks should apply a deterministic shift to yield curve, inflation rate, IR of a given currency by applying a shock of one bp and a shock of 1% on all IRs and/or inflation rate implied volatilities.

RWs and risk factors correlations: The delta sensitivity analysis assumes that, for specific currency buckets, the level of RWs and correlations between pairs of risk factors ρ_{kl} depends on the maturities of the yield curves. Specifically, the RWs span between 1.06% and 1.59%[54] and the correlations, ρ_{kl} between different maturity buckets are set between 40% and 91%.[55] For the other currencies, RWs for both risk-free yield curve and inflation rates are set at $RW_k = 2.25\%$ and the correlations, ρ_{kl} between risk-free yield curve and inflation rate are set at $\rho_{kl} = 40\%$.

Under vega sensitivity, RWs for both IR and inflation volatilities are set at $RW_k = RW_\sigma \times \sqrt{6} \approx 1.35\%$, with $RW_\sigma = 55\%$, while the correlation, ρ_{kl} between IR volatilities and inflation volatilities is set at 40%.

7.4.13.2 Foreign Exchange

The CVA portfolio, inter alia, is exposed to FX. Thus, banks should accordingly estimate the sensitivities in relation to FX delta and vega risks.

Buckets: The buckets that define the calculation of FX delta and vega risks consist of buckets of individual currencies, excluding, though, the bank's domestic currency as it is not subject to any FX fluctuations.

Cross-bucket correlation: The cross-bucket correlation (γ_{bc}) for all currency pairs is set at 0.6.

Delta and vega risk shifts: Deterministic shocks of 1% are applied to the FX rate as well as in the market-implied volatilities of the FX rate to measure the corresponding sensitivities of both FX spot rates and FX volatilities. Sensitivity is estimated as in Eq. (7.39) where the shift is expressed in percentage value.

Risk weights: The RWs for all FX rates is set at $RW_k = 21\%$ and for FX volatilities is defined as $RW_k = RW_\sigma \times \sqrt{4} = 110\%$, with $RW_\sigma = 55\%$.

7.4.13.3 Counterparty Credit Spread

The delta risk measures the sensitivity of counterparty credit spreads.

Buckets and sectors: Seven buckets are defined by the new framework for the estimation of delta risk for counterparty credit spreads. The first bucket is associated to two groups of sectors; each of the remaining buckets (i.e. 2 to 7) links to a set of sectors[56] where the counterparties are assigned.

Cross-bucket correlation: The cross-bucket correlation (γ_{bc}) for counterparty credit spread delta risk ranges between 0% and 25%.[57]

Delta risk shifts: In the new framework banks shift deterministically the counterparty credit spreads by one bp for a particular bucket and for different tenors.[58] Vega risk for counterparty credit spread is not calculated.

RWs and correlations: The new framework assigns the same RWs (RW_k) as the risk weight RW_c designates the volatility of credit spread in BA-CVA (Sect. 7.4.5). The RWs[59] for all tenors depend on the bucket and credit quality categories. The framework also defines the degree of correlation factor[60] ρ_{kl} that relies on: tenors' identity; as well as the relation and credit quality of the entities.

7.4.13.4   Reference Credit Spread

The delta and vega risks measure the sensitivity of the counterparty reference credit spread.

Buckets, credit qualities, and sectors: The final Basel standards define 15 buckets separated into three groups for the estimation of delta risk for reference credit spreads. The first group includes the buckets from 1 to 7, the second from 8 to 14, and the third consists of only the 15th bucket. The first group corresponds to "IG" credit quality, the second group to HY&NR credit quality, whereas the third group to "other sectors", where credit quality is "not applicable". Each bucket links to a set of sectors[61] where the counterparties are assigned.

Cross-bucket correlation: The cross-bucket correlation (γ_{bc}) within the same credit quality category (i.e. either "IG" or HY&NR), for reference credit spread, ranges[62] between 5% and 75%. However, the level of these correlations drops by 50% when cross-buckets belong to separate credit categories. Finally, a cross-bucket correlation of 0% applies across the bucket of sectors having a "*not applicable*" credit quality, with another bucket.

Delta risk shifts: A simultaneous absolute shift of one bp applies to reference credit spread of all tenors for all reference names in a particular bucket. The impact of the shock on aggregated CVA exposures and hedges for different combinations of counterparties and tenor points are eventually classified according to the degree of the shock.

Vega risk shift: The BCBS expects banks to estimate the vega risk of a reference credit spread and a given bucket by applying a simultaneous relative shift of 1% on volatilities for all tenors and reference names in the bucket.

Risk weights: The new framework assigns RWs (RW_k) to counterparty bucket and credit quality categories. Likewise, the first seven buckets, which belong to the "IG" credit quality category, have lower RWs than the 8th to 15th buckets, which have lower credit quality attached.

The RWs assigned to reference credit spread volatilities are set at $RW_k = RW_\sigma \times \sqrt{25} = 275\%$, with $RW_\sigma = 55\%$.

Box 7.3   Example for Estimating Capital on Derivative Portfolio

An example case for estimating capital based on the SA-CVA sensitivity method is described below. Banks which have headquarters in the Euro zone hold an OTC portfolio that contains an interest rate swap (IRS) with four counterparties which are all financial institutions. Two of them are located in the Euro zone (henceforth labelled as "EU-B-I" and "EU-B-II"), and the other two are located in the US (henceforth labelled as "US-B-I" and "US-B-II"). This portfolio has two different classes of maturities, that is, up to one year and from one to two years, as well as two currencies of denomination, domestic EUR and USD, which are the following: (a) one-year maturity EUR/EUR-IRS, (b) two-year maturity EUR/EUR-IRS, (c) one-year maturity EUR/USD-IRS, (d) two-year maturity EUR/USD-IRS. All contracts have the same notional values, resulting in each one of them comprising 25% of the value of the portfolio. In the portfolio above, the recovery rate δ for all counterparties is set at 25%, resulting therefore in a value of market-implied LGD of 0.75 (75%).

Steps of the application of the SA-CVA approach.

In the calculation of *SA-CVA* the bank must obtain (1) the term structure of market-implied PD; (2) the market consensus ELGD; and (3) the simulated paths of discounted future exposure.

As illustrated in Fig. 7.11, the reference market implies that counterparty spreads are extracted from reference to counterparties' single-named CDSs. Based on these spreads, the corresponding survival and default probabilities are estimated. The resulting term structure of market-implied PD is used as an input to regulatory CVA calculation.

Based on the sixth principle discussed in Sect. 7.4.8 all market risk factors material for the transactions with a counterparty must be stochastically simulated. Thus, *n* number of scenarios are applicable to the evolution of the market risk factors including credit spreads and IRs. The resulting exposure changes over time, causing the positions of the bank and its counterparty to switch between "in the money" and "out of the money" accordingly. As already discussed, banks should consider only the discounted net positive exposures for CVA analysis, that is, cases where the bank is in the money, and the counterparty is out of the money. Figure 7.12 illustrates the generation of market risk factor paths underlying the exposure model of the four IRS positions over time.

By identifying the correlation between the exposures and credit spreads, banks may examine WWR in the estimation of CVA, as discussed in Sect. 7.3.8. Figure 7.13 illustrates the correlation between exposures and spreads observed for each time interval reflecting the WWR. However, the analysis of this example does not include the resulting values of WWR as the new framework does not consider it in the estimation of CVA to calculate the capital charge, whereas the impact of WWR is included in the capital charge by incorporating the multiplier m_{CVA}.

The CVA sensitivities $\partial CVA/\partial k_{(CPspreads)}$ and $\partial CVA / \partial E_{k_{(iit)}}$ are applied with respect to credit spreads and exposure. Figure 7.14 illustrates the resulting values of the CVA sensitivities. In this portfolio, we do not apply any CVA hedges to the underlying risk factors. Thus, their sensitivities are set to zero. By applying the SA-CVA approach, the bank has to follow the rules defined under the IRs and counterparty credit spread risk factors.

Interest rates

The bank in question may apply the following steps for the estimation of CVA capital charges:

(continued)

Box 7.3 (continued)

1. The IRS portfolio retains two currencies of denomination, that is, EUR and USD, which indicate two buckets: bucket 1 (b_1) refers to the EUR-denominated IRS (EU-B-I and EU-B-II) and bucket 2 (b_2) refers to the USD-denominated IRS (US-B-I and US-B-II);
2. There are also two different maturities in the IRS portfolio, that is, 1 year and 2 years with corresponding RWs of $RW_k = 1.59\%$ and $RW_k = 1.33\%$, respectively;
3. The CVA sensitivities against IR changes (s_k^{CVA}) are estimated as illustrated in Fig. 7.14;
4. The weighted sensitivities are estimated based on the product of RWs and sensitivities, that is, $WS_k^{CVA} = RW_k \cdot s_k^{CVA}$. As there are no hedges, $WS_k^{Hdg} = 0$;
5. The net weighted sensitivity for each trade is estimated as defined in Eq. (7.40), that is, $WS_k = WS_k^{CVA} + WS_k^{Hdg} = WS_k^{CVA}$;
6. The correlation factor ρ_{kl} between the pairs of risk factors (i.e. 1 year and 2 years) where the EU and US trades fall is $\rho_{kl} = 91\%$;
7. The capital charges K_{b1} assigned to bucket b_1, which fall under EUR currency, is estimated by Eq. (7.41);

   where

   (a) The hedging disallowance parameter (R) is set at 0.01;
   (b) For the two risk factors:

   - The squared weighted sensitivities (WS_k^2) for the two trades is summed to produce the term $\sum_{k \in b} WS_k^2$;
   - The product of all paired net weighted sensitivities, of the two trades, is weighted by the correlation factor, that is, $\rho_{kl} \times WS_k \times WS_l$, where multiplication is applied to WS_k referring to trade EU-B-I, WS_l referring to trade EU-B-II. Having two risk factors, the above weighted product is applied to two trade pairs, that is, $2 \times (\rho_{kl} \times WS_k \times WS_l)$, to get the corresponding summation $\sum_{k \in b} \sum_{l \neq k} \rho_{kl} . W_k . W_l$;
   - The square of the weighted hedge sensitivity $\left(WS_k^{Hdg}\right)^2$ and $\left(WS_l^{Hdg}\right)^2$ is added for both of the risk factors considered;

8. The capital charge (K_{b2}) for bucket b_2 is estimated by following the exact steps described above for b_1;
9. The IR capital charges (K_{IR}) is aggregated across buckets estimated based on Eq. (7.42);
   where

   (a) The multiplier m_{CVA} is set at 1.25;
   (b) The cross-bucket correlation for currencies EUR and EUS is set at $\gamma_{bc} = 0.5$;
   (c) The calculation of the square of the capital charge K_b for buckets b_1 and b_2 is being performed; and
   (d) The product between capital charges of the two buckets b_1 and b_2 is weighted by the cross-bucket correlation γ_{bc} above.

(continued)

Box 7.3   (continued)

Counterparty credit spread

Equation (7.41) highlights the steps for the calculation of capital charges for the counterparty credit spread which are shown below:

1. The credit quality for all entities is defined to "IG" and thus the buckets for delta risk are set to two. All trades belong to the same sector (*Financials*) and are associated with bucket b_2;
2. The RW of b_2 is set at $RW_k = 5\%$;
3. Figure 7.14 illustrates the CVA sensitivities against counterparty credit spreads (s_k^{CVA}) which are used in the computations;
4. The product of the above sensitivities and RWs define the weighted sensitivities for all trades, that is, $WS_k^{CVA} = RW_k \cdot s_k^{CVA}$. As there are no hedges, $WS_k^{Hdg} = 0$;
5. For all four trades, the net weighted sensitivity is given by Eq. (7.40), that is, $WS_k = WS_k^{CVA} + WS_k^{Hdg} = WS_k^{CVA}$;
6. As all counterparty entities of the four trades are unrelated but have the same credit quality, the correlation factor ρ_{kl} is set at $\rho_{kl} = 45\%$;
7. The capital charge K_b for the single bucket b is estimated based on Eq. (7.41);

where

(a) The hedging disallowance (R) parameter is set at 0.01;
(b) For all four risk factors

- The sum of the squared weighted sensitivities ($WS_k{}^2$) for all trades produces is given by $\sum_{k \in b} WS_k^2$;
- The product of all paired net weighted sensitivities, between all trades, is weighted by the correlation factor, that is, $\rho_{kl} \times WS_k \times WS_l$. The weighting above is applied for all trade pairs to retrieve the corresponding aggregation $\sum_{k \in b} \sum_{l \in b, l \neq k} \rho_{kl} \cdot W_k \cdot W_l$;
- For all trades, the square of the hedge weighted sensitivity $\left(WS_k^{Hdg} \right)^2$;
- The resulting capital charge for bucket b, referring to all trades, is estimated based on Eq. (7.41);

10. The capital charges K_{Spread} is given by Eq. (7.42);

where

(a) The multiplier m_{CVA} is set at 1.5;
(b) As there is only one bucket, there is no cross-bucket correlation; thus, the second part of Eq. (7.42) is zero.

The above two capital charges are aggregated resulting in the overall capital charge $K = K_{IR} + K_{Spread}$.

In regard to the above case, Table 7.4 shows the numerical results on different parameters used for estimating the overall capital charge K.

Table 7.4 Estimating different parameters used for calculating capital charge

Risk type/class	EU-B-I	EU-B-II	US-B-I	US-B-II
	IRs			
Bucket	b_1 (USD)		b_2 (EUR)	
RWs	$RW_k = 1.59\%$	$RW_l = 1.33\%$	$RW_m = 1.59\%$	$RW_p = 1.33\%$
Sensitivities	$s_k^{CVA} = 8.1$	$s_l^{CVA} = 10.2$	$s_m^{CVA} = 12.7$	$s_p^{CVA} = 13.3$
Weighted sensitivities	$WS_k^{CVA} = 0.13$	$WS_l^{CVA} = 0.14$	$WS_m^{CVA} = 0.19$	$WS_p^{CVA} = 0.2$
Correlation ρ_{kl}	$\rho_{kl} = 91\%$		$\rho_{mp} = 91\%$	
Product of weighted sensitivities	$WS_k \cdot WS_k = 0.017$ $WS_k \cdot WS_l = 0.016$ $WS_l \cdot WS_l = 0.018$		$WS_m \cdot WS_m = 0.041$ $WS_m \cdot WS_p = 0.036$ $WS_p \cdot WS_p = 0.031$	
Capital charge at bucket level	$K_{b1} = 0.258$		$K_{b2} = 0.379$	
Buckets' correlation γ_{bc}	$\gamma_{b1b2} = 0.5$			
Multiplier m_{CVA}	$m_{CVA} = 1.25$			
Capital charge	$K_{IR} = 0.69$			

Risk type/class	Counterparty credit spread			
Bucket	b_2 (bucket number 2)			
RWs	$RW_k = 5\%$	$RW_l = 5\%$	$RW_m = 5\%$	$RW_p = 5\%$
Sensitivities	$s_k^{CVA} = 17.6$	$s_l^{CVA} = 20.3$	$s_m^{CVA} = 25.9$	$s_p^{CVA} = 27.2$
Weighted sensitivities	$WS_k^{CVA} = 0.88$	$WS_k^{CVA} = 1.02$	$WS_m^{CVA} = 1.30$	$WS_p^{CVA} = 1.36$
Correlation ρ_{kl}	$\rho_{kl} = 45\%$			
Product of weighted sensitivities				
	WS_k^{CVA}	WS_l^{CVA}	WS_m^{CVA}	WS_p^{CVA}
WS_k^{CVA}	0.774	0.402	0.513	0.539
WS_l^{CVA}	0402	1.03	0.591	0.621
WS_m^{CVA}	0.513	0.591	1.677	0.793
WS_p^{CVA}	0.539	0.621	0.793	1.85
Capital charge at bucket level	$K_b = 3.5$			
Multiplier m_{CVA}	$m_{CVA} = 1.25$			
	$K_{spread} = 4.37$			
Capital charge	$K = K_{IR} + K_{spread} = 5.07$			

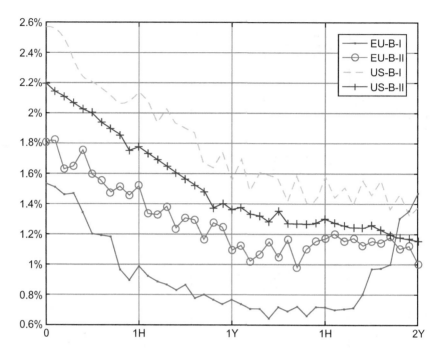

Fig. 7.11 Market-implied spread curves of IRS: EU-B-I, EU-B-II, US-B-I, US-B-II

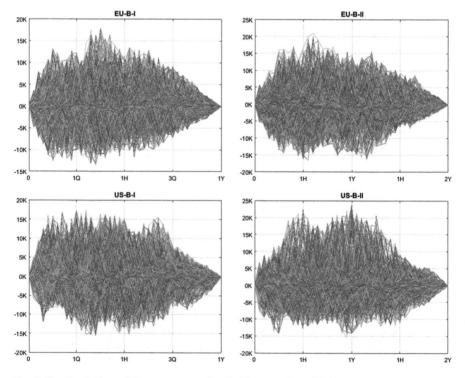

Fig. 7.12 Evolution of the exposures for the four trades of IRS

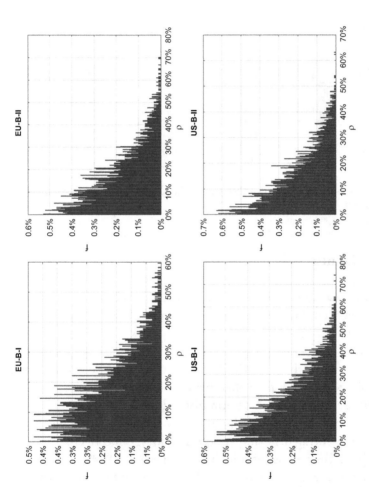

Fig. 7.13 Distributions for the correlations ρ between exposures and spreads, defined as wrong-way risk, applied in CVA calculations for the four trades of IRS. The degree of positive correlations ρ is estimated up to 60% expected at frequency f of the n scenarios

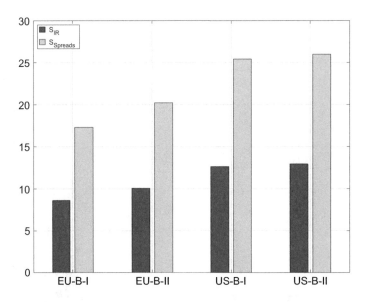

Fig. 7.14 CVA sensitivities to counterparty credit spreads and exposures with underlying interest rate (IR) risk factor

7.4.13.5 Equity

Buckets, size, and region: There are 11 buckets for the equity delta and vega risks, grouped according to reference size[63] and regions.[64] Also, buckets refer to sector[65] classifications.

Cross-bucket correlation: The cross-bucket correlation (γ_{bc}) for all cross-bucket pairs b and c that fall within bucket numbers 1 to 10 is set at 15%. However, all cross-bucket pairs that include bucket 11 are set at 0%.

Delta and vega risk shift: A deterministic shift of 1% on both equity spot prices and market-implied volatilities for all reference names in the bucket apply when measuring delta and vega sensitivities, respectively.

Risk weights: The new set of rules links the level of RWs[66] to the number of reference name buckets. Moreover, the RWs assigned to equity volatilities are set at $RW_k = RW_\sigma \times \sqrt{2}$ for large capitalisation buckets, and $RW_k = RW_\sigma \times \sqrt{6}$ for small capitalisation buckets, with $RW_\sigma = 55\%$.

7.4.13.6 Commodity

Buckets: There are 11 buckets defined for the estimation of commodity delta and vega risks wherein 11 different types (buckets) of commodity groups[67] are assigned to:

Cross-bucket correlation: The correlation (γ_{bc}) of all cross-bucket pairs b and c falling within buckets 1 to 10 is set at 20%, while the correlation of all cross-bucket pairs which include bucket 11 is set at 0%.

Delta and vega risk shift: The shift in commodity spot prices and market-implied volatilities, intended to measure delta and vega risk, is deterministically set at 1%.

Risk weights: Like other market risk factors, the RWs are assigned to 11 different buckets of commodities,[68] while the RW assigned to commodity volatilities is set at $RW_k = RW_\sigma \times \sqrt{12} \approx 191\%$, with $RW_\sigma = 55\%$.

7.4.14 Conclusion

To estimate the CVA capital charges, it is essential for banks to know, at all times, the market value of the OTC derivative exposures. Likewise, they should be in a position to estimate the value of their instruments whenever a default event occurs. However, due to the potential uncertainties in the underlying market conditions, these exposures cannot be estimated deterministically. Therefore, banks are forced to estimate the evolution of the exposure as a result of a number of scenarios which define the variability of the underlying risk factors.

The valuation of default events should consider all rules applicable to collateralised exposures, via margin requirements and agreements, to approximate the net exposures. The expected positive or negative PFEs are the types of exposures expected in the CVA analysis.

The calibration of exposure evolution may use a risk-neutral or historically based data and models. Risk-neutral probabilities are much more aligned to instruments' valuation and accounting valuation, while real-world probabilities are more appropriate for the estimation of PFEs. The evolution of exposures and credit spreads are the main elements for the estimation of CVA (VaR) and CVA (ES), which are both driven by the variability of underlying market and counterparty risk factors. The market risk factors drive the evolution of exposures, whereas counterparty spreads define the survival and default probabilities.

In the current chapter, we show how banks may employ stochastic intensity, reduced-form models, to generate risk-neutral credit spreads and the associated probability and time of credit default events.

In principle, BCBS proposes the *reduced* or the *full* version of the basic approach (BA-CVA) or the standardised approach (SA-CVA) for calculating CVA capital charge.

In both *reduced* and the *full* version of BA-CVA approaches, the RWs assigned to the exposures are based on the classification of the counterparty sector and credit quality. In the *reduced* BA-CVA the bank has to compute the stand-alone CVA capital. The capital charge resulting from the *reduced* BA-CVA is also included in the capital charge of the *full* BA-CVA. The latter also comprises systematic and idiosyncratic components and the quantity HMA_c reflecting the indirect hedges that are not fully aligned with counterparties' credit spreads.

The SA uses the sensitivities-based methods aligned with the FRTB framework of the trading book. However, SA-CVA reduces the granularity of risk factors and the complexity of the related methods used in sensitivity analysis. The estimation of the SA-CVA capital charge relies on a given set of formulae and estimated sensitivities provided by the new framework. Under the new CVA banks estimate the sensitivity to each risk factor of the aggregate CVA and of the market value of all eligible hedging instruments in the CVA portfolio.

It is noteworthy that the latest proposals do not suggest any formula for the estimation of the CVA but, instead, provide guidance to banks to employ the most appropriate CVA function.

Notes

1. From banks' point of view.
2. The analysis of debt valuation adjustments, rising due to an institution's default risk, is currently beyond the Basel regulatory market risk frameworks.
3. BCBS's liquidity coverage ratio (LCR) and net stable funding ratio (NSFR).
4. Using futures to form the initial margin implies a "good faith" collateral assuming that the investor will satisfy the obligation of the contract.
5. A threshold of zero implies that any exposure is collateralised whilst a threshold of infinity is used to specify that one of the counterparties will not post collateral under any circumstances.
6. Intraday margining is common for vanilla products such as repos but other instruments such as swaps require a daily margin call frequency for the relevant valuations to be carried out.
7. In practice, collaterals are not delivered immediately; moreover, the portfolio is not settled and replaced immediately when the collateral is not posted. It may take several days for the bank to realise that the counterparty is defaulting; moreover, there is a grace period after the bank issues a notice of default. During this grace period the counterparty may still post a collateral; however, it may take a while to close out and replace complex trades.
8. Note that for margin agreements with daily or intra-daily exchange of margin the minimum MPoR is ten business days.

9. As opposed to the risk-neutral measures.
10. Each market scenario is a realisation of a set of price factors that affect the values of the trades in the portfolio, for example, FX rates, interest rates, equity prices, commodity prices, and credit spreads.
11. The use of discrete time intervals reduces the demand in computation resources.
12. Such as American/Bermudan and asset-settled derivatives.
13. For a single or a portfolio of transactions linked to a single counterparty.
14. The central peak is narrower, but the tails are significantly longer and fatter.
15. Also defined as a "credit-equivalent" or "loan-equivalent" exposure curve.
16. Implying, therefore, an absence of risk neutrality in volatilities and drifts for the diffusion processes of the risk factors.
17. International Financial Reporting Standards, Fair Value Measurement, entered into force on 1 January 2013. In estimating the accounting CVA exposure, institutions should be using risk-neutral drifts, calibrating both correlations and volatilities based on market data whenever information on market data is available and also defining the ten-business-day floor for the margin period of risk; see also IVSC (2013).
18. Risk-neutral probabilities assume the absence of arbitrage opportunities.
19. Assuming that not all assets will default at the same time in a well-structured portfolio.
20. Market participants have not always accepted and adopted the regulatory methodologies for estimating the fair value of derivative exposures as the most appropriate for the estimation of economic capital arising from the same exposures.
21. Based on the current supervisory standards, when a CDS is unavailable, banks "shall use a proxy spread that is appropriate taking into consideration the rating, industry and region of the counterparty" (BCBS, 2011).
22. Even though this process is not necessary and neither always the best practice to identify the default probability.
23. Whereas the value of the firm's assets and liabilities at default determines the recovery rates in structural models.
24. Recovery rates usually take the form of a percentage of the expected value of the security at the time of default. Key elements of the recovery rate are (a) the amount of the recovery; and (b) the time interval between default and the recovery being realised. Generally, recovery rates are related to the seniority of the debt, which implies that in case the seniority of debt changes the recovery of the debt may change.
25. In addition, these models use the risk-neutral transition matrix, for example, rating agencies' transition probabilities to determine the probability of default.
26. Discrete-time approximation of the Poisson process.
27. That is, the protection buyer, the protection seller, and the reference credit.

28. Filtration is a function with the purpose of filtering and controlling information propagation. In mathematical terms a filtration is a non-decreasing collection of σ algebras $\{\mathcal{M}_t \subseteq \mathfrak{I} : t \geq 0\}$ such that $\mathcal{M}_s \subseteq \mathcal{M}_t$, for $\forall s, t \geq 0$ with $s \leq t$. Where $\mathcal{M}_t$ defines the information available at time t, assuming that this information is always kept and has been available as long as $s \leq t$.

29. That is, the number of events per interval of time.

30. Proposed by Vasicek (1977); see reference list.

31. Alternatively, increasing k results in a large speed of mean reversion so the system will have less stochasticity for a given value of σ. Due to the positivity condition, an increasing θ will force an increase in k, whose effect will counterbalance the initial increase in σ.

32. Also called lifetime distributions.

33. Also known as "credit curve" due to its similarity to a yield curve.

34. Detailed description of calibration process and methodologies is beyond the scope of this book. For further reading the reader may refer to the books in the reference list of this chapter.

35. Although credit spreads must always be positive, interest rates can be negative under market stress conditions.

36. The correlation coefficient equals one or minus one. The former implies a perfect positive co-dependency (or co-movement) while the latter a negative co-dependency, that is, the variables move in the same or opposite directions, respectively. A correlation of less than one defines the degree of positive or negative strength in correlation. Correlations equal to zero implies no co-dependencies.

37. Based on UK Financial Service Authority (2010), CVA losses, during the financial crisis, increased in the UK five times the amounts of actual default losses.

38. In fact, banks permitted to employ and use both the VaR and the IMM modes have the obligation to implement the advanced CVA charge method.

39. Eligible hedges are single-name credit instruments that reference directly to counterparty and, under certain conditions, to CDS index hedges.

40. Not cleared through central counterparties.

41. Based on the external rating of the counterparty on the rating scale AAA, AA, A, BBB, BB, B, and CCC, the weights are 0.7%, 0.7%, 0.8%, 1%, 2%, 3%, 10%, respectively.

42. EAD is calculated following IMM or SA-CCR replacing the standardised and current exposure methods.

43. As since 2010, CVA (VaR) under BCBS (2011) has already been approached by the market, and extended description of this approach is beyond the scope of this book. This book focuses more on final Basel approaches referring to minimum capital requirements for the CVA risk framework (BCBS, 2017).

44. Based on the regulation, exposure profiles are used in the internal model method approval; moreover, if the IMM does not cover all transactions subject to the CVA risk charge and non-IMM transactions consist of a limited number of smaller portfolios, an institution can also be allowed to use the advanced approach for these portfolios.

45. It should be noted that LGD_{MKT}, used as input in the calculation of the CVA capital charge, is different from the LGD that is determined under the IRBA and CCR default risk charge. LGD_{MKT} is market assessment rather than an internal estimate. It is based on the provision of BCBS (2011) which mentions that "where market instrument of single counterparties should be driving the market-implied LGD or where a counterparty instrument is not available, [the estimation of the LGD should be] based on the proxy spread that is appropriate based on the rating, industry and region of the counterparty".

46. The last financial crisis indicated that the majority of losses do not arise from counterparty defaults but rather from market variabilities of derivative portfolios.

47. The Basel II/Basel III market risk framework estimates the capital charge against only the actual variability in the derivatives' market.

48. Note, however, that the CVA capital charge for both frameworks is calculated on a stand-alone basis, that is, interactions among the CVA book and trading book are not allowed.

49. M_{NS} for the banks with supervisory approval to use IMM, see BCBS, 2006: 262–263 para 38, 39, excluding, however, the five-year cap in para 38. For those banks with no supervisory approval to use IMM, see BCBS, 2006: 75–76 para 320–323, excluding, however, the five-year cap in para 320.

50. The supervisory prescribed correlations r_{hc} set as in the table below:

Single-name hedge h of counterparty c	Value of r_{hc}
References counterparty c directly	100%
Has legal relation with counterparty c	80%
Shares sector and region with counterparty c	50%

51. Applying to the entire CVA book including eligible hedges.

52. The default value of m_{CVA} set by the BCBS at 1.25; however, the supervisory authority may determine a higher degree based on the evaluation of the bank's CVA model risk as well as the dependence on the counterparty's credit quality and the bank's exposure to the counterparty known as WWR (BCBS, 2017: 118 para 40).

53. Distinguished amongst maturities of 1 year, 2 years, 5 years, 10 years, and 30 years.

54. For the risk factors 1 year, 2 years, 5 years, 10 years, and 30 years, and inflation, the RWs are set to 1.59%, 1.33%, 1.06%, 1.06%, 1.06%, and 1.59%, respectively.

55. The proposed set of rules has set the correlations between the pairs of risk factors as in the table below:

Risk factor	1 year	2 years	5 years	10 years	30 years	Inflation
1 year	100%	91%	72%	55%	31%	40%
2 years		100%	87%	72%	45%	40%
5 years			100%	91%	68%	40%
10 years				100%	83%	40%
30 years					100%	40%
Inflation						100%

The first bucket associated to sectors (1 a) sovereigns including central banks, multilateral development banks; (1 b) local government, government-backed non-financials, education, and public administration; (2) financials including government-backed financials; (3) basic materials, energy, industrials, agriculture, manufacturing, mining and quarrying; (4) consumer goods and services, transportation and storage, administrative and support service activities; (5) technology, telecommunications; (6) health care, utilities, professional and technical activities; (7) all other sectors.

56. The cross-bucket correlations of delta risk for counterparty credit spread are set in the table below:

Bucket	1	2	3	4	5	6
1	100%	10%	20%	25%	20%	15%
2		100%	5%	15%	20%	5%
3			100%	20%	25%	5%
4				100%	25%	5%
5					100%	5%
6						100%

57. The cross-bucket correlations across bucket 7 and another bucket are set to $\gamma_{bc} = 0\%$.

58. Tenors are set at 0.5, 1, 3, 5, and 10 years.

59. The buckets 1 a), 1 b), 2, 3, 4, 5, 6, and 7 for investment grade (IG) receive the RWs of 0.5%, 1.0%, 5.0%, 3.0%, 3.0%, 2.0%, 1.5% and 5.0%, respectively; and, for high-yield/non-rated (HY/NR) the same buckets receive the RWs of 3.0%, 4.0%, 12.0%, 7.0%, 8.5%, 5.5%, 5.0%, and 12.0%, respectively.

60. Correlations between different tenors for the same entity are set to 90%; for unrelated entities of the same credit quality (IG and IG or HY/NR and HY/NR) correlations between the same tenors are set to 50% and between different tenors are set to 45%; for unrelated entities of different credit quality (IG and HY/NR) correlations between the same tenors are set to 40% and between different tenors are set to 36%; for entities that are legally related

correlations between the same tenors are set to 90% and between different tenors are set to 81%.

61. The first two bucket groups contain six groups of sectors which are (1) sovereigns including central banks, multilateral development banks; (2) local government, government-backed non-financials, education, public administration; (3) financials including government-backed financials; (4) basic materials, energy, industrials, agriculture, manufacturing, mining and quarrying; (5) consumer goods and services, transportation and storage, administrative and support service activities; (6) technology, telecommunications; (7) health care, utilities, professional and technical activities. The third bucket group contains all other sectors.

62. The cross-bucket correlations of delta risk are set in the table below:

Bucket	1/8	2/9	3/10	4/11	5/12	6/13	7/14
1/8	100%	75%	10%	20%	25%	20%	15%
2/9		100%	5%	15%	20%	15%	10%
3/10			100%	5%	15%	20%	5%
4/11				100%	20%	25%	5%
5/12					100%	25%	5%
6/13						100%	5%
7/14							100%

63. Large size for the 1st eight buckets, small size for the 9th and 10th buckets, and not applicable size for the 11th bucket number.

64. Regions are classified as (a) emerging market economies associated to bucket numbers 1, 2, 3, 4, 9; and (b) advanced economies associated to bucket numbers 5, 6, 7, 8, and 10. Bucket number 11 is not associated to any region.

65. Buckets 1 and 5: consumer goods and services, transportation and storage, administrative and support service activities, health care, utilities; buckets 2 and 6: telecommunications, industrials; buckets 3 and 7: basic materials, energy, agriculture, manufacturing, mining and quarrying; buckets 4 and 8: financials including government-backed financials, real estate activities, technology; bucket 9: all sectors are described under bucket numbers 1 to 4; bucket 10: all sectors described under bucket numbers 5 to 8; bucket 11: other sectors.

66. The RWs for bucket numbers 1, 2, 3, 4, 5, 6, 7, 8, 9, 10, and 11 are set to 55%, 60%, 45%, 55%, 30%, 35%, 40%, 50%, 70%, 50%, and 70%, respectively.

67. The commodity group are assigned to 11 different buckets as follows: bucket 1: energy—solid combustibles; bucket 2: energy—liquid combustibles; bucket 3: energy—electricity and carbon trading; bucket 4: freight; bucket 5: metals—non-precious; bucket 6: gaseous combustibles; bucket 7: precious metals (including gold); bucket 8: grains and oilseed; bucket 9:

livestock and dairy; bucket 10: softs and other agriculturals; bucket 11: other commodity group.

68. Based on the reference name's bucket, the RWs assigned to buckets 1, 2, 3, 4, 5, 6, 7, 8, 9, 10, and 11 receive RWs of 30%, 35%, 60%, 80%, 40%, 45%, 20%, 35%, 25%, 35%, and 50%, respectively.

References

Basel Committee on Banking Supervision (BCBS). (2006, June). International convergence of capital measurement and capital standards: A revised framework comprehensive version. Retrieved December 2006, from http://www.bis.org/publ/bcbs128.htm

Basel Committee on Banking Supervision (BCBS). (2011, June). Basel III: A global regulatory framework for more resilient banks and banking systems – Revised version. Retrieved September 2011, from https://www.bis.org/publ/bcbs189.pdf

Basel Committee on Banking Supervision (BCBS). (2013, October). Fundamental review of the trading book: A revised market risk framework. Retrieved October 2013, from https://www.bis.org/publ/bcbs265.pdf

Basel Committee on Banking Supervision (BCBS). (2014, April). The standardised approach for measuring counterparty credit risk exposures. Retrieved May 2014, from https://www.bis.org/publ/bcbs279.pdf

Basel Committee on Banking Supervision (BCBS). (2015a, March). Margin requirements for non-centrally cleared derivatives. Retrieved March 2015, from http://www.bis.org/bcbs/publ/d317.pdf

Basel Committee on Banking Supervision (BCBS). (2015b, July). Review of the Credit Valuation Adjustment (CVA) risk framework – Consultative document. Retrieved July 2015, from http://www.bis.org/bcbs/publ/d325.pdf

Basel Committee on Banking Supervision (BCBS). (2016, January). Minimum capital requirements for market risk. Retrieved January 2016, from https://www.bis.org/bcbs/publ/d352.pdf

Basel Committee on Banking Supervision (BCBS). (2017, December). Basel III: Finalising post-crisis reforms. Retrieved December 2017, from https://www.bis.org/bcbs/publ/d424.pdf

Bluhm, C., Overbeck, L., & Wagner, C. (2010, June). *Introduction to credit risk modelling*, 2nd ed. Boca Raton: Chapman and Hall/CRC.

Cox, D. R. (1955). Some statistical methods connected with series of events. *Journal of the Royal Statistical Society, 17*(2), 129–164.

Cox, Ingersoll and Ross. (1985, March). A theory of the term structure of interest rates. *Econometrica, 53*(2), 385–407.

Feller, W. (1951). Two singular diffusion problems. *Annals of Mathematics, 54*, 173–182.

Financial Services Authority (FSA). (2010, August). The prudential regime for trading activities – A fundamental review. Retrieved November 2017, from http://www.fsa.gov.uk/pubs/discussion/dp10_04.pdf

IASB (2012). IFRS 13: *Fair value measurement.* International Accounting Standards Board.

IVSC International Valuation Standards Council (2013). Credit and debit valuation adjustments. Retrieved November 2017, from https://www.ivsc.org/files/file/download/id/100

McNeil, A. J., Frey, R., & Embrechts, P. (2015). *Quantitative risk management: Concepts, techniques and tools – Rev. ed.* Princeton Series in Finance. Princeton: Princeton University Press.

Schönbucher, P. (2003). *Credit derivatives pricing models: Models, pricing and implementation.* Wiley Finance Series. Chichester; Hoboken, NJ: Wiley.

Uhlenbeck, G. E., & Ornstein, L. S. (1930). On the theory of Brownian motion. *Physics Review, 36,* 823–841.

Vasicek. (1977). An equilibrium characterization of the term structure. *Journal of Financial Economics, 5,* 177–188.

8

Revisions to Operational Risk

Chapter 8 describes the current operational risk framework, the final specifications of the proposed standardised measurement approach (SMA) for its estimation under the final Basel III (BCBS, 2017), and their comparison with the initial proposals for the SMA (BCBS, 2016).

Within the description of SMA methodology, Chap. 8 compares the core SMA proposals with the alternative specifications proposed by the authors. Also, the chapter presents the interaction between the business indicator component (BIC) and the internal loss multiplier (ILM) and infers the sensitivity of how banks' operational risk requirements are affected by the new framework.

8.1 The Current Framework for Operational Risk Regulatory Capital

There have been many attempts to define the notion of operational risk. The BCBS defines operational risk as "the risk of loss arising from inadequate or failed internal processes, people and systems or from external events" (BCBS, 2011: 3). Nonetheless, the above definition is not exhaustive as to describing the nature of operational risk as it includes legal risk and does not include business and reputation risks. That is why the BCBS definition attracted a lot of criticism from researchers and academics, and motivated them to provide alternative definitions. Nonetheless, the alternative definitions cover the entire spectrum from negative references (by defining what operational risk does not consist of) to self-defined (by defining it as the risk of operational losses), or incomplete references (by focusing only on a part of operational losses).

© The Author(s) 2018
I. Akkizidis, L. Kalyvas, *Final Basel III Modelling*,
https://doi.org/10.1007/978-3-319-70425-8_8

Amongst all the attempts to define operational risk, a rather comprehensive one is the one describing it as "the risk of business disruption, control failures, errors, misdeeds, or external events, and is measured by direct and indirect economic loss associated with business interruption and legal risk costs, and also by 'immeasurable' such as reputation risk cost" (see Moosa, 2007).

The introduction of operational risk regulatory capital by Basel II intended to confront with the enormous losses arising from the misconduct of business relating to the activities of international banks, which in some cases were of high magnitude and high frequency. This combined characteristic of operational losses could cause bank insolvency.

Even prior to the publication of the Basel II framework, international banks had taken the initiative to establish advanced operational risk measurement, and management systems based on granular databases, to enable the calculation of economic capital with a view to absorb potential losses arising from operational risk. To this end, Basel II intended to bridge the obvious gap between the methodology for the estimation of economic capital and the absence of any framework for the estimation of regulatory capital for operational risk. Basel established a new era for the assessment of operational risk which bridges this gap. Having said that, the Basel II operational risk framework cannot be perceived as free of structural flaws or inconsistencies between the advertised and the de facto functionality of the regulatory framework relating to operational risk.

The Basel II framework allows the use of three alternative measures for the calculation of the regulatory capital requirements against the operational risk. In ascending order of complexity, these approaches are the following: the basic indicator approach (BIA), the traditional standardised approach (TSA), the alternative standardised approach (ASA), and the advanced measurement approach (AMA). Given the absence of evidence on the applicability of the ASA amongst international banks, the book does not examine the implicit impact of switching from this method to the SMA.

The publication of operational risk framework kicked off a debate amongst regulators, market participants, and academics as to whether the new, at that time, framework was sufficient to address the intended related risks borne by the banks. The main focal point of the debate was the simplicity of the standardised approaches, hereafter BIA, TSA, and ASA, which contradicts the structure of international banks which by nature are complex and diverse amongst them. In other words, the regulatory framework provides a simple and universal solution which had been proved to be the result of the complex operations of international banks. Instead, the standardised approaches are implicitly more appropriate for banks with simpler structure.

Despite the expressed view of the BCBS that internationally active banks are expected to use more sophisticated approaches for complex operations, which by nature encompass higher operational risk, there is no mechanism to force these banks to create or use these models to calculate operational risk requirements under Pillar I. Instead, internationally active banks are allowed to use the standardised approaches for the calculation of Pillar I capital requirements. If national supervisors judge that the capital arising from Pillar I is not sufficient to cover potential operational risk losses, they could increase it through additional Pillar II capital requirements. All in all, it is doubtful whether the Basel II framework for operational risk promotes the level playing field under Pillar I capital requirements.

Another part of the criticism focuses on the fact that the Basel II operational risk framework uses the gross income. This implies that operational malfunctions could only harm the part of the revenues without considering any adverse impact on the part of the costs, that is, an increase in the costs due to operational malfunctions could also have been taken into consideration.

8.1.1   Basic Indicator Approach

Usually, banks opt to apply the BIA in cases where they cannot meet the eligibility criteria of other operational risk approaches or they find that it better suits their functionality. The BIA is the simplest of all approaches and is implicitly designed to cover the lack or inability to split operations into business lines and disproportionate cost of small banks to develop sophisticated operational risk models.

$$K_{BIA} = 15\% \times \frac{\sum_{i=1}^{n} GI_i}{n} \qquad (8.1)$$

where

K_{BIA} is the minimum capital requirement under BIA;

GI_i is the gross income of the year i preceding the year of the calculation of operational risk capital requirements;

i could be 1, 2, or 3, depending on the number of years with observations of positive gross income over the last three years.

For BIA the gross income is defined as the net interest income plus the non-interest income which is gross of (1) provisions for any unpaid income and (2) operating expenses and does not include "realised profits/losses from the sale of securities in the BB and extraordinary or irregular items as well as income derived from insurance" (BCBS, 2006: 145, para 650).

The operational risk capital requirement for a bank which applies the BIA is simply the three-year average of the positive annual gross income multiplied by a factor of 15%. In cases where the annual gross income has not been always positive over the last three years, then, only the positive values are used for the estimation of capital requirements. To avoid distortions due to the lack of sufficient data, for example, in the extreme case where the gross annual has been negative throughout the last three years, the national supervisor could impose additional capital requirements under Pillar II to ensure that the bank capital base is always adequate to cope with operational risk events.

A good proxy for the estimation of Pillar II capital requirements by the national supervisors, for banks which completely lack positive gross income observations over the last three years, would be the average of the most recent three years with positive gross income (even if they are older than three years) after adjusting these observations for the business growth rate and inflation rate.

8.1.2 (Traditional) Standardised Approach (TSA)

Alike BIA, the TSA also relies on the calculation of capital requirements on the metric of gross income. However, unlike BIA, the gross income which arises from different business lines bears different risk weights (betas) which correspond to the riskiness of each business line. Within each business line, the gross income represents the magnitude of business operations within the business line and thus is deemed to be best approximation of operational risk exposure within each business lines. The capital charge for each business line is given by multiplying the gross income by a factor (denoted beta) assigned to the specific business line. The total capital charge is calculated as the three-year average of the simple sum of the regulatory capital charges across each of the business lines in each year. The negative capital charges (resulting from negative gross income) in any business line, in any given year, may offset positive capital charges in other business lines (Table 8.1).

The net interest income for retail banking is calculated as the "interest earned on loans and advances to retail customers" less "the weighted average cost of funding of the loans (from whatever source)". Similarly, the net interest income of commercial banking is calculated as the interest earned on loans and advances to corporate, interbank, and sovereign customers less the weighted average cost of funding these loans (from whatever source).

Table 8.1 Mapping and risk weights of different business lines

Level 1—(Risk weight)	Level 2	Activity groups	Supplementary guidance for the calculation of TSA capital requirements
Corporate finance (18%)	Corporate finance Municipal/government finance Merchant banking Advisory services	Mergers and acquisitions; underwriting; privatisations; securitisation; research; debt (government, high yield); equity; syndications; initial public offerings; secondary private placements	Gross income consists of net fees/commissions earned from "corporate finance"
Trading and sales (18%)	Sales Market making Proprietary positions Treasury	Fixed income; equity; foreign exchanges; commodities; credit; funding; own positions securities; lending and repos; brokerage; debt; prime brokerage	Gross income consists of (1) P&L on instruments held for trading purposes net of (2) funding cost, plus (3) fees from wholesale broking
Retail banking (12%)	Retail banking Private banking	Private lending and deposits; banking services; trust and estates; investment advice (for "private banking" only)	Gross income consists of (1) net interest income on loans and advances to retail customers and SMEs treated as retail, plus (2) fees related to traditional retail activities, (3) net income from swaps and derivatives held to hedge the retail BB, and (4) income on purchased retail receivables
	Card services	Merchant/commercial/corporate cards; private labels and retails	
Commercial banking (15%)	Commercial banking	Project finance; real estate; export finance; trade finance; factoring; leasing; lending; guarantees; bills of exchange	Gross income consists of (1) net interest income on loans and advances to corporates, SMEs treated as corporates, interbank and sovereign customers; (2) income on purchased corporate receivables; plus (3) fees related to traditional commercial banking activities; (4) net income on securities held in the banking book (e.g. from coupons/dividends); and (5) P&L on swaps and derivatives held to hedge the commercial BB

(continued)

Table 8.1 (continued)

Level 1—(Risk weight)	Level 2	Activity groups	Supplementary guidance for the calculation of TSA capital requirements
Payment and settlement (18%)	External clients	Payments[a] and collections; funds transfer; clearing and settlement	Gross income consists of fees to cover provision of payment/settlement facilities for wholesale counterparties
Agency services (15%)	Custody	Escrow; depository receipts; securities lending (customers); corporate actions	Gross income consists of net fees/commissions earned from "agency services"
	Corporate agency / Corporate trust	Issuer and paying agents	
Asset management (12%)	Discretionary fund management	Pooled; segregated; retail; institutional; closed; open; private equity (only for "discretionary fund management")	Gross income consists of fees/commissions for the management of assets on behalf of others
	Non-discretionary fund management		
Retail brokerage (12%)	Retail brokerage	Execution and full service	Gross income consists of net fees/commissions earned from "retail brokerage"

Source: BCBS (2006)

[a]"Payment and settlement" losses related to a bank's own activities would be incorporated in the loss experience of the affected business line

8.1.3   (Alternative) Standardised Approach (ASA)

At national discretion, a supervisor may allow a bank to use the ASA provided it is in the position to ensure that the ASA provides an improved basis of avoiding double counting of risks. A bank that uses the ASA cannot revert to the TSA without the prior permission of its supervisor. Although the Basel II did not envisage the use of ASA by large diversified banks, there is no evidence that small banks use this approach either.

Under the ASA, the operational risk capital charge/methodology is the same with the standardised approach except for two business lines—retail banking and commercial banking. For these business lines, the loans and advances—multiplied by a fixed factor m—replace the gross income as the exposure amount used for the calculation of capital charges. The betas for retail and commercial banking are those given by the standardised approach.

The ASA operational risk capital charge for retail banking (with the same basic formula for commercial banking) can be expressed as:

$$K_{ASA*} = \beta_{SA} \times m_{ASA} \times LA_{ASA*} \qquad (8.2)$$

where

K_{ASA*} is the capital charge for the retail and commercial banking business lines;

β_{SA} is the beta for the retail and commercial banking business line, that is, 12% and 15%, respectively; and

LA_{ASA*} is total outstanding retail loans and advances (non-risk-weighted and gross of provisions), averaged over the past three years; m is 0.035.

For the purposes of the ASA, total loans and advances in the retail banking business line consist of the total drawn amounts in the following credit portfolios: retail, SMEs treated as retail, and purchased retail receivables. For commercial banking, total loans and advances consist of the drawn amounts in the following credit portfolios: corporate, sovereign, bank, specialised lending, SMEs treated as corporates, and purchased corporate receivables. The above definition includes the accounting value of securities held in the banking book. Banks which apply the ASA may aggregate retail and commercial banking using a beta of 15%, which would increase the capital charge arising from the ASA, but decrease the complexity of separating the two business lines. Similarly, those banks that are unable to disaggregate their gross income into the other six business lines can aggregate the total gross income for these six business lines using a beta of 18%. Similar to the TSA, the total capital charge for the ASA is calculated as the aggregation of regulatory capital charges across the eight business lines.

8.1.4   Advanced Measurement Approach (AMA)

Unlike the standardised approaches, the advanced measurement approach (AMA) intended to become the most appealing method with respect to the (lower) level of operational risk capital requirements that it would produce. At the inception of Basel II, national supervisors deemed this method as producing the most risk-sensitive results, while banks favour it amid the lowest capital requirements it produces. However, the development of AMA was not an easy task nor was it suitable for all banks. Since this method requires a significant investment of time and resources for its development, it is prohibiting for small banks. The associated cost is often above the relevant benefit from the reduced capital requirement that the AMA would produce in relation to the standardised approaches.

To apply the AMA, banks have to prove that the estimation of the operational risk capital requirements is well-integrated into the day-to-day risk management process, while the top management should regularly receive updates about the measurement of operational risks produced by the AMA. The national supervisory authorities and external auditors should also monitor the performance of AMA. All in all, ongoing monitoring of AMA's performance is necessary to ensure that the reduced operational risk capital requirements reflect the riskiness of banks' operations.

The BCBS does not provide detailed technical/methodological guidelines for the application of AMA. Instead, banks are expected to develop their own approach, provided that their model takes into account both expected and unexpected losses. Banks could exclude unexpected losses from the capital requirements if they were in the position to prove that there is enough budget to cover for such losses. The BCBS (2001), in an effort to encourage banks to produce their own AMA models, affirmed that AMA capital requirements would be lower than the capital required under the standardised approaches.

Every AMA model should rely on internal and external data, carry out scenario analysis, and be subject to internal controls. These are the minimum quantitative requirements for a bank to qualify as eligible for the estimation of regulatory capital under the AMA. Beyond these general requirements, AMA banks should adopt several definitions as to the estimation of operational risk. These are the following:

- *Definition of operational risk:* The Basel II definition of operational risk (which remained unchanged under Basel III) describes it as "the risk of loss resulting from inadequate or failed internal processes, people and systems, or from external events". The definition that the bank adopts should as minima include the Basel II definition and, if deemed appropriate, other elements which could enhance this definition;

- *Definition of operational risk loss:* The operational risk loss is considered as the financial impact which arises or is linked to an operational event that is recorded in the bank's financial statements and could be classified as (a) internal fraud; (b) external fraud; (c) employment practices and workplace safety; (d) clients, products, and business practices; (e) damage to physical assets; (f) business disruption and system failures; and (g) execution, delivery, and process management.

- *Definition of operational risk exposure:* The part of the risk-weighted asset (RWA) that stems from the loss event that appears once in 10,000 operational risk events. In other words, it is the RWA equivalent that covers operational risk events with a 99.99% confidence level. The estimated loss at 99.99% should be multiplied by 12.5 to obtain the part of RWA equivalent which corresponds to operational risk.

- *Business environment and internal control factor assessments:* These are the tools used to provide objective assessment of the level and trends of operational risk within a bank. Irrespective of the type of AMA models used by a bank, they should provide the tools for the identification of all key operational risks, for example, key performance indicators, audit scores, and so on.

Every AMA model should estimate and apply objective correlations amongst operations, operational risk, and operational risk events. Nonetheless, this book will not concentrate on the qualitative aspects of AMA models and/ or the pre-requisites that the national supervisor sets for the approval of AMA. Instead, it provides a simple method of comparison between the AMA and the final SMA for operational risk.

For the purpose of comparison with the SMA approach, the book presents a simple non-parametric AMA model which is based on a variation of the "block maxima" model. The "block maxima" model is applicable on high-frequency data which are supposed to be independently and identically distributed according to an unknown distribution.

The entire data set is separated into m identical, consecutive, and non-overlapping periods (blocks) with n length (the number of observations within each block). The block should be sufficiently populated to correspond to the occurrence of operational risk events. The set of extremes is populated by the maxima values M_j which are collected from each block j, ending up to a set of m values (block maxima).

The model in its original form selects the maximum (extreme) values (M_j) selected from each block (j) to create a sample of total m block maxima, that is, a sample consisting of the maximum values from all subsamples. As mentioned, this assumes the existence of many subsamples (m) and observations within each subsample (n).

In the absence of actual data for operational risk events, the forthcoming analysis suggests the generation of random data sets of operational events comprising of 10,000 data points for each day over a period of one year, that is, 365,000 data points. The process of generating 10,000 alternative operational risk events (scenarios) for each day creates 10,000 alternative total annual losses for each day of the year. In turn, the maximum value (or the 99.9th percentile) is selected for each year to create a data set of ten block maxima for the entire period of ten years. The analysis assumes that the block maxima follow the generalised extreme value (GEV) distribution. The cumulative distribution function of GEV, aka generalised Pareto distribution (GPD), takes the following form (see Embrechts, 2000):

$$H_\xi(y) = \begin{cases} \exp\left(-\left[1 - \xi \times y\right]^{-\frac{1}{\xi}}\right), & \text{where } \xi \neq 0 \\ \exp\left(-\exp(-y)\right), & \text{where } \xi = 0 \end{cases} \tag{8.3}$$

The variable y in the above distribution function represents the normalised M_j's by using the Central Limit Theory (Fisher & Tippett, 1928):

$$y_j = \frac{M_j - \mu}{\sigma} \tag{8.4}$$

The variable y should fulfil the condition $1 + \xi y > 0$ (or $\xi > -1/\xi$). The μ and σ represent the position (mean) and scale (standard deviation) parameters of the distribution of the M_j of the normal distribution, while ξ is the parameter that governs the shape of the distribution, aka the "shape parameter", including the shape and length of the tail of the distribution. When $n \to \infty$, y follows the distribution H which according to the parameterisation used, that is, according to the values that ξ and y take, is transformed to one of the Gumbel, Fréchet, or Weibull distributions (Eq. (8.3)). If $\xi = 0$ the generalised cumulative extreme value distribution function belongs to Type I (Gumbel) distribution, if $\xi < 0$ it belongs to Type II (Fréchet) distribution while if $\xi > 0$ it belongs to Type III (Weibull) distribution.

Gumbel distribution (Type I distribution)

$$\Lambda(y) = \exp\bigl(-\exp(-y)\bigr) \; for \; \xi = 0, \; y \in R \tag{8.5}$$

Fréchet distribution (Type II distribution)

$$\Phi_\zeta(y) = \begin{cases} 0 \; for \; y \le 0 \\ \exp\bigl(-y^{-\zeta}\bigr) \; for \; y > 0, \; \zeta > 0 \end{cases} \tag{8.6}$$

Weibull distribution (Type III distribution)

$$\Psi_\zeta(y) = \begin{cases} \exp\bigl(-\bigl(-y^{-\zeta}\bigr)\bigr) for \; y \le 0, \; \zeta < 0 \\ 1 \; for \; y > 0, \end{cases} \tag{8.7}$$

The ξ parameter is equal to zero for Gumbel distribution, ζ^{-1} for Fréchet distribution and—ζ^{-1} for Weibull distribution function. Gumbel distributions can be considered as the distribution which bridges Fréchet and Weibull distributions when $\xi \to 0$, that is, both distributions are gradually transformed to Gumbel distribution as ξ approaches zero.

If the shape and location parameters are both zero ($\xi = \mu = 0$), the GPD is equivalent to the exponential distribution. The generation of random values which would resemble operational losses distribution function (GPD) is a two-step process. First, the module produces random values (z_u) which are uniformly distributed in the range of (0,1]. Then, the cumulative GPD function is inverted to obtain the set of equations which will be used for the generation of random values that are distributed according to the GPD[1] (z_{gpd}). This set of equations is the following:

$$z_{gpd} = \begin{cases} \mu + \dfrac{\sigma\bigl(z_u^{-\xi} - 1\bigr)}{\xi} \; for \; \xi \ne 0 \\ \mu - \sigma \ln(z_u) \; for \; \xi = 0 \end{cases} \tag{8.8}$$

The BCBS (2016) provides that only losses above the equivalent of EUR 10,000 are used for the calculation of capital requirements under AMA. Thus, after the generation of random values distributed according to GPD, the calculation of AMA capital requirements will exclude the losses which are lower than the above threshold.

8.2 The Standardised Measurement Approach (SMA)

The SMA intends to substitute the currently applied methods for the estimation of operational risk capital requirements. According to the finalised framework, all three approaches will be discontinued and consequently be substituted by SMA after a transitional period. Banks which currently apply the AMA will face more increased capital requirements compared to other approaches. From an administrative point of view, AMA banks will also confront major structural changes in the estimation of losses: whereas capital requirements produced by the AMA use forward-looking estimators of losses, that is, they try to model the future behaviour of operational losses, the SMA is purely based on past observations relating to the size of observed losses and business activities subject to operational risk. Likewise, the latter avoids any subjective modelling in the estimation of losses.

The new approach is based on the estimation of the BIC, that is, the component which represents the volume of business which is subject to operational risk, and the ILM which represents an approximation of past years' losses in relation to BIC.

Concretely, the proposed methodology for the calculation of capital requirements under SMA is determined by the multiplication of the business indicator (BI) component and the ILM component as shown below:

$$SMA = BIC \times ILM \tag{8.9}$$

Figure 8.1 shows the two different legs for the estimation of SMA capital requirements, that is, the estimation for BIC and ILM, respectively. The BIC estimation differentiates according to the clustering of BI; the BIC for BI lower than the equivalent of EUR 1 billion is multiplied by a BI of 12%, for BI in excess of EUR 1 billion and up to EUR 30 billion the BI is multiplied by 15% while any amount in excess of EUR 30 billion is multiplied by 18%. Going backwards in the calculation process, the BI measure comprises the "interest, operating lease, and dividend component" (ILDC), "service component" (SC), and "financial component" (FC), which are calculated according to the set of equations below.

The other leg of SMA estimation involves the estimation of ILM. The ILM estimation takes into consideration the realised losses above a certain threshold, that is, it does not take into account the low-impact losses which are unlikely to cause any harm in the functioning of the bank under consideration. The definition of "low impact" is set at EUR 10,000 according to the

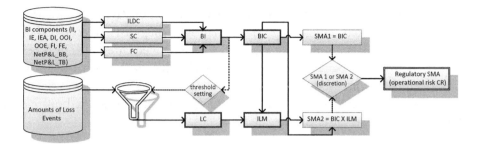

Fig. 8.1   Process for the calculation of the Standardised Measurement Approach (SMA)

current framework. Nonetheless, the SMA allows the differentiation of this threshold between small and large banks, that is, banks with low and high BIs. The redesign of the structure of operational loss threshold implies that higher thresholds would reduce the number of individual operational events and thus the total annual loss to be used as input in the estimation of LC and ILM. In turn, the increase of the threshold would result in a reduction of SMA capital requirements.

8.2.1   Business Indicator Component

The BIC is a function of the estimation of the BI which in turn is composed by the following elements:

The "ILDC" which comprises the absolute value of average income minus the average expenses retrieved by the conduct of business produced by the above types of income/expenses over a period of time. The interest component is adjusted by the ratio of the net interest margin (NIM) cap (set at 2.25%) to the actual NIM;

The "SC" arises from adding the maximum value between fee income and fee expense to the maximum value between other operating income and other operating expense; and

The "FC" arises from adding the average absolute value of net P&L of the trading book to the average absolute value of net P&L of the banking book.

Expressed in mathematical terms, the BI for a given year is defined as the sum of the three-year average of its components:

$$BI = ILDC_{average} + SC_{average} + FC_{average} \qquad (8.10)$$

The BCBS (2016) proposed the discrete estimation of BIC depending on different BI buckets, suggesting that banks with high BIs receive higher weights for the BI amounts which exceed a pre-specified threshold. In other words, the BICs for banks with high BIs would be higher than what the proportionate weighting would indicate. Specifically, the first consultative document (BCBS, 2016) provides that the BIC calculation is structured on five buckets where banks' BIs are allocated:

$$
BIC = \begin{cases}
0.11 \times BI, \text{ for bucket 1} \\
EUR\,110\,mn + 0.15 \times (BI - EUR\,1\,bn), \text{ for bucket 2} \\
EUR\,410\,mn + 0.19 \times (BI - EUR\,3\,bn), \text{ for bucket 3} \\
EUR\,1.74\,bn + 0.23 \times (BI - EUR\,10\,bn), \text{ for bucket 4} \\
EUR\,6.34\,bn + 0.29 \times (BI - EUR\,30\,bn), \text{ for bucket 5}
\end{cases} \quad (8.11)
$$

where
Bucket 1: from EUR 0 to EUR 1 billion.
Bucket 2: from EUR 1 to EUR 3 billion.
Bucket 3: from EUR 3 to EUR 10 billion.
Bucket 4: from EUR 10 to EUR 30 billion.
Bucket 5: higher than EUR 30 billion.

The excessive granularity (five buckets) of the BI buckets in the initial proposals implies that the banks with BIs between EUR 1 billion and EUR 10 billion could frequently jump from one bucket to another, rendering their supervision a difficult task. Having said this, a less granular allocation of BIs into buckets would be more efficient and promote a level playing field for banks which have BIs of medium level and have similar BIs. Following this rationale, the BCBS (2017) agreed on rearranging the buckets (Eq. (8.12)). This rearrangement includes the unification of the buckets between EUR 1 billion and EUR 30 billion BI and a new weighting for the all buckets. The revised framework for the estimation of the BI, according to the new bucketing, takes the following form:

$$
BI = \begin{cases}
0.12 \times BI, \text{ for bucket 1}(new) \\
EUR\,120\,billion + 0.15 \times (BI - EUR\,1\,billion), \text{ for bucket 2}(new) \\
EUR\,4470\,billion + 0.18 \times (BI - EUR\,29\,billion), \text{ for bucket 3}(new)
\end{cases} \quad (8.12)
$$

where
  Bucket 1 (new): from EUR 0 to EUR 1 billion.
  Bucket 2 (new): from EUR 1 to EUR 30 billion.
  Bucket 3 (new): higher than EUR 30 billion.
  The properties of the rebucketing are examined later in the current chapter.

8.2.1.1 The Calculation of BI According to the Consultative Document

The high-level description of the SMA framework, as set out in the first consultative document (BCBS, 2016), involves the estimation of ILDC, SC, and FC according to the methodology below.

$$ILDC_{average} = \min\left\{ Abs\left(II_{average} - IE_{average}\right); 0.035 \times IEA_{average}\right\}$$
$$+ Abs\left(LI_{average} - LE_{average}\right) + DI_{average} \tag{8.13}$$

$$SC_{average} = \max\left(OOI_{average}; OOE_{average}\right) + \max$$
$$\left\{ \begin{matrix} Abs\left(FI_{average} - FE_{average}\right); \min \\ \left[\begin{matrix} \max\left(FI_{average}; FE_{average}\right); 0.5 \times uBI \\ +0.1 \times \left(\max\left(FI_{average}; FE_{average}\right) - 0.5 \times uBI\right)\end{matrix}\right] \end{matrix}\right\} \tag{8.14}$$

$$uBI = ILDC_{average} + \max\left(OOI_{average}; OOE_{average}\right)$$
$$+ \max\left(FI_{average}; FE_{average}\right) + FC_{average} \tag{8.15}$$

$$FC_{average} = \left[Abs\left(Net\ P\ \&\ L\ TB\right)\right]_{average} + \left[Abs\left(Net\ P\ \&\ L\ BB\right)\right]_{average} \tag{8.16}$$

where the "average" denotes the equally weighted average of the last three annual observations.

The final standards differ from the original BCBS proposals. The structure of Eqs. (8.14) and (8.15) implied that the estimation of SC depends also on the level of ILDC and FC via the estimation of the unadjusted business indicator factor (uBI). Also, the part of the SC formula which refers to the comparison between the net financial income and the maximum between the financial income and financial expenses will always produce the former as output and thus render the latter redundant. Nonetheless, the inclusion of only the maximum value between income and expenses is consistent with the treatment of other operational income and expenses in the same formula (SC).

Thus, one could reduce the complication of the SC formula by removing the uBI, that is, the BI which does not include the adjustment for high fees, and the expressions relating to net financial institutions (FI) income. The simplified SC formula would take the form shown in Eq. (8.18).

8.2.1.2 The Calculation of BI According to the Final SMA Framework

Following the rationale described above, the BCBS revised the calculation of the SC. However, the BCBS also revised the ILDC formula to allow the inclusion of the average absolute net interest income instead of the absolute net interest income based on the average income and expenses values. It changes the multiplication factor of the interest-earning assets which implies that the ILDC is now reduced in relation to the level implied in the SMA CD (BCBS, 2016).

$$ILDC_{average} = \min\left\{\left[Abs\left(II - IE\right)\right]_{average}; 0.0225 \times IEA_{average}\right\} + DI_{average} \quad (8.17)$$

$$SC_{average} = \max\left(OOI_{average}; OOE_{average}\right) + \max\left(FI_{average}; FE_{average}\right) \quad (8.18)$$

The $FC_{average}$ is again given by Eq. (8.16). The definitions of the BI components are provided in Table 8.2.

8.2.2 The Internal Loss Multiplier and Loss Component

As shown in Eq. (8.9), the second component for the determination of SMA capital charge is the ILM which according to the initial proposal (BCBS, 2016) is an exponential function of the LC-to-BIC ratio. In turn, the loss component is nothing else, but the realisation of losses above certain thresholds multiplied by factors. The initial proposal suggested the application of different multiplication factors on average annual losses assumed by different materiality thresholds. Specifically, it suggests the multiplication of average annual losses above the lowest loss materiality threshold by a factor of seven, the average annual losses above the medium loss materiality threshold by a factor of seven, whereas the average annual losses above the highest loss materiality threshold by a factor of five. The set of equations below presents this scheme (hereafter "7-7-5" multiplication scheme).

Table 8.2 Business indicator definitions

BIC	P&L or balance sheet items	Description	Typical subitems
Interest, operating lease, and dividend	Interest income	Interest income from all financial assets and other interest income (interest income from financial and operating leases should be **included**)	• Interest income from loans and advances, assets available for sale, assets held to maturity, and trading assets • Interest income from hedge accounting derivatives • Other interest income
	Interest expenses	Interest expenses from all financial liabilities and other interest expenses (interest income from financial and operating leases should be included)	• Interest expenses from deposits • Interest expenses from debt securities issued • Interest expenses from hedge accounting derivatives • Other interest expenses
	Interest-earning assets (balance sheet item, not P&L)	Total gross outstanding loans, advances, and interest bearing securities (including government bonds) measured at the end of each financial year	
	Financial and operating lease income (LI)	• Interest income from financial leases • Interest income from operating leases • Profits from leased assets	
	Financial and operating lease expenses (LEs)	• Interest expenses from financial leases • Interest expenses from operating leases • Losses from leased assets • Depreciation and impairment of operating leased assets	
	Dividend income	Dividend income from investments in stocks and funds not consolidated in the bank's financial statements, including dividend income from non-consolidated subsidiaries, associates, and joint ventures.	

(continued)

Table 8.2 continued

BIC	P&L or balance sheet items	Description	Typical subitems
Services	Fee and commission income	Income received from providing advice and services. Includes income received by the bank as an outsourcer of financial services.	Fee and commission income from: • Securities (issuance, origination, reception, transmission, execution of orders on behalf of customers) • Clearing and settlement • Asset management • Custody • Fiduciary transactions • Payment services • Structured finance • Servicing of securitisations • Loan commitments and guarantees given • Foreign transactions
	Fee and commission expenses	Expenses paid for receiving advice and services. Includes outsourcing fees paid by the bank for the supply of financial services, but not outsourcing fees paid for the supply of non-financial services (e.g. logistical, IT, human resources)	Fee and commission expenses from: • Clearing and settlement • Custody • Servicing of securitisations • Loan commitments and guarantees received • Foreign transactions
	Other operating income	Income from ordinary banking operations not included in other BI items but of similar nature (income from operating leases should be excluded)	• Rental income from investment properties • Gains from non-current assets and disposal groups classified as held for sale not qualifying as discontinued operations (IFRS 5.37)

Other operating expenses	Expenses and losses from ordinary banking operations not included in other BI items but of similar nature and from operational loss events (expenses from operating leases should be excluded)	• Losses from non-current assets and disposal groups classified as held for sale not qualifying as discontinued operations (IFRS 5.37) • Losses incurred as a consequence of operational loss events (e.g. fines, penalties, settlements, replacement cost of damaged assets), which have not been provisioned/reserved for in previous years • Expenses related to establishing provisions/reserves for operational loss events
Financial[2]	Net profit (loss) on the trading book	• Net profit/loss on trading assets and trading liabilities (derivatives, debt securities, equity securities, loans and advances, short positions, other assets and liabilities) • Net profit/loss from hedge accounting • Net profit/loss from exchange differences
	Net profit (loss) on the banking book	• Net profit/loss on financial assets and liabilities measured at fair value through P&L • Realised gains/losses on financial assets and liabilities not measured at fair value through P&L (loans and advances, assets available for sale, assets held to maturity, financial liabilities measured at amortised cost) • Net profit/loss from hedge accounting • Net profit/loss from exchange differences

Source: BCBS (2016)

$$ILM = \ln\left(\exp(1) - 1 + \left(\frac{LC}{BIC}\right)^a\right) \tag{8.19}$$

$$LC = 7 \times l_{10-year\ average}^{>EUR\ 10,000} + 7 \times l_{10-year\ average}^{>EUR\ 10mn} + 5 \times l_{10-year\ average}^{>EUR\ 100mn} \tag{8.20}$$

where $\alpha = 1$, and $l_{average}^{>EUR\ 10,000}$, $l_{average}^{>EUR\ 10\ mn}$, and $l_{average}^{>EUR\ 100\ mn}$ are the average total annual losses over the last ten years which take into account the losses above EUR 10,000, EUR 10 million, and EUR 100 million, respectively.

The calibration of the "7-7-5" scheme targets to achieve an average LC-to-BIC of one which subsequently means that the ILM would also be one. Although ILM could significantly deviate from unity when assessing an individual bank, the initial calibration intended to produce an average ILM for the international banking system which is close to one.

To simplify the estimation of LC in Eq. (8.20) the final BCBS agreement suggests the estimation of SMA capital based on a unique multiplication factor which would replace the existing "7-7-5" scheme. The new factor applies to the average annual losses above a materiality threshold for the operational losses.

The operational loss materiality threshold of the final SMA framework is set at EUR 20,000 for banks belonging in bucket 1, and at EUR 100,000 for banks in buckets 2 and 3. Analytically, the formula for the calculation of ILM for a bank falling under a given BI bucket i is presented below:

$$ILM = \ln\left(\exp(1) - 1 + \left(\frac{LC_i}{BIC}\right)^a\right) \tag{8.21}$$

$$LC_i = \lambda \times \begin{cases} l_{10-year\ average}^{>EUR\ 20,000}, & for\ i = 1 \\ l_{10-year\ average}^{>EUR\ 100,000}, & for\ i = 2,3 \end{cases} \tag{8.22}$$

where $\alpha = 0.8$; and $\lambda = 15$ which is deemed equivalent to the "7-7-5" scheme of Eq. (8.22):

The estimation of the ten-year averages involves the following process: first, the aggregation of all losses above the threshold for a specific year formulate the total annual loss amount; second, the ten-year average takes into account the simple average of the total annual losses for the last ten years. In years where there are no data of good quality for ten years, as judged by the supervisor, a bank could exceptionally use only five years of observations.

8.2.3   Implications of the Application of SMA Alternative Specifications

To sum up, the amendments of the SMA revises the SC and the reclassifies the BI buckets. However, the outcome of the consultation on the initial SMA proposals (BCBS, 2016) triggered further amendments which are reflected in the final framework. The following are the elements which change under the new framework:

- The LI and LEs are included in the definition of interest income (II) and interest expenses (IE);
- The cap for high NIM, as a percentage of interest earning assets (IEA), is introduced in the formula for the calculation of ILDC;
- The reduction of the weights assigned to the BI which downwards the estimation of BIC and ILM, except for banks with BI < EUR 1 billion whose SMA is affected upwards.

The proposed adjustment in the SC formula simplifies the calculation of BI without producing materially different results in most of the instances. Essentially, the unadjusted BI in the previous framework (Eq. (8.15)) was removed. The non-ILDC and non-FC components of what used to be the uBI comprise the SC (Eq. (8.18)).

As implied in the current provisions of SMA (BCBS, 2016), there is a linear relationship between BI and BIC within each of the BI buckets. This linear relationship represents the marginal increase of BIC resulting from an increase of 1 EUR of BI.

The sensitivity analysis of SMA capital requirements as a result of the changes in the BI is discussed in Sect. 8.2.4.

8.2.4   Sensitivity of SMA Capital Requirements to Changes in the Components

This section analyses the interaction between the stand-alone changes in BI or LC and the SMA capital requirements. The sensitivity analysis below intends to provide banks and supervisors with evidence on what would be the adjustments to their business model in view to reduce the SMA capital. On the other hand, the sensitivity analysis could provide national regulators with a better understanding on how the SMA capital will be affected if they choose to apply national discretions when transposing the final Basel III into the national regulatory framework, for example, ILM equal to one.

A potential change in the level of BI does not only affect SMA capital requirement directly through the formulation of the BIC, but it also affects indirectly through changes in the LC-to-BIC ratio which is the main determinant of the formulation of ILM. A potential increase in the LC-to-BIC ratio would push upwards the ILM factor and vice versa. Thus, from a theoretical perspective, a reduction of BIC does not necessarily cause an increase in SMA capital requirements. Although the BIC constituent would become lower, it is a subject of empirical investigation whether, and in which instances, this reduction will also diminish the SMA capital requirements. The empirical analysis below examines whether a negative shift in the BIC is counterbalanced by a second-order positive impact stemming from a higher LC-to-BIC ratio. The values in parentheses of x-axis labels of Fig. 8.2 indicate the LC-to-BIC ratio after the relevant change in the BIC.

The increase of the loss materiality threshold under the final Basel III reduces the LC and subsequently the SMA capital requirements. Although it is not deemed substantial, the impact of changing the materiality threshold cannot be precisely estimated, given the different distribution of bank-specific operational losses. Also, a potential change of α factor from the initially

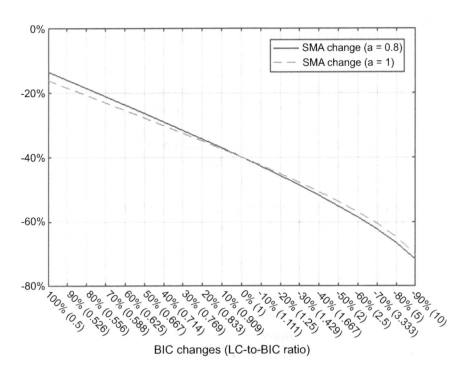

Fig. 8.2 The sensitivity of SMA to changes in BIC level

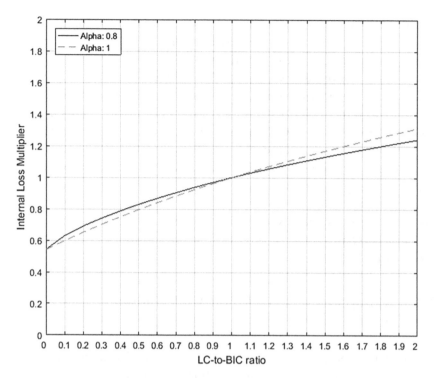

Fig. 8.3 The evolution of ILM for various LC-to-BIC ratios and alphas of 0.5, 1.0, and 1.5

proposed of $\alpha = 1$ (BCBS, 2016) to the final of $\alpha = 0.8$ would further reduce the ILM.

The following section shows the causal relationship between LC-to-BIC ratios and ILM for given values of alphas. The framework initially proposed by the BCBS implied an alpha of one, while the final revision applies an alpha of 0.8. As shown in Fig. 8.3, a bank with negligible LC-to-BIC ratio (i.e. LC-to-BIC ~ 0, or operational risk losses ~ 0) would apply an ILM of less than 0.6 to the BIC amount under both regimes (initial and final). Keeping everything else constant, this means that the SMA capital would appear reduced by approximately 40% compared to the level of SMA that would solely rely on the BIC or the SMA that is based on an LC-to-BIC ratio equal to 1. The SMA capital requirement would also be the same under both regimes if the LC-to-BIC ratio equals one.

Keeping everything else constant, the change in the alpha value from one to 0.8 increases the SMA capital requirements of banks which exhibit LC-to-BIC ratio lower than one and decreases the SMA of those with ratios above unity.

Looking at the right end of Fig. 8.3 (LC-to-BIC ratio > 1), a bank which suffers from high operational losses would be subject to less capital requirements compared to the initial proposals where an alpha of one was implied (BCBS, 2016, 2017). This change stems solely from the change in the value of alpha. Also, a bank with an LC-to-BIC ratio of 2 would have to set aside 30% additional capital compared to what the BIC would indicate.

All in all, the application of lower alphas would increase the SMA capital for banks with low LC-to-BIC ratios (<1) and decrease the SMA capital for banks with high LC-to-BIC ratios (>1). In other words, the new specification treats banks with low operational losses less favourably and banks with high operational losses more favourably compared to the initial proposals. The impact of changes in alphas is less apparent for LC-to-BIC values around 1 while there is no impact for LC-to-BIC which equals 0 or 1. On the other hand, the upsurge of alphas to levels higher than 1 would decrease the SMA capital, relative to the initial proposals, for banks with an LC-to-BIC ratio lower than one (Figs. 8.4a, b).

8.2.5   Comparison of SMA and AMA Capital Requirements

As implied in the presentation of the currently applied methods, the BIA, TSA, and ASA rely on the size of operations, which is subject to operational losses, to calculate the operational risk capital requirements. On the other hand, the AMA is based on the size of actual losses to estimate future losses. The estimated losses will then be the input and main determinant of the calculation for operational risk capital requirements.

Contrary to this, the SMA (BCBS, 2016, 2017) appears as a hybrid approach inspired by elements existing in both the current standardised methods and AMA methods. The new method derives the business size of operations from the standardised approaches whereas the AMA inspired the inclusion of the level of losses in the calculation of SMA capital requirements. Nonetheless, banks are now requested to use the actual losses without being allowed to develop any bespoke modelling for the estimation of future losses. In other words, the SMA is backward-looking rather than forward-looking as the AMA used to be. The backward-looking characteristic of the SMA aligns also with the attributes of the input parameters in credit risk, rendering the use and scope of data consistent throughout the new framework.

The comparison between the level of capital requirements produced by the AMA and the SMA approach is vital to understand the impact caused by the different specifications. To make the capital requirements comparable between the AMA and the SMA, the analysis assumes that the AMA does not apply

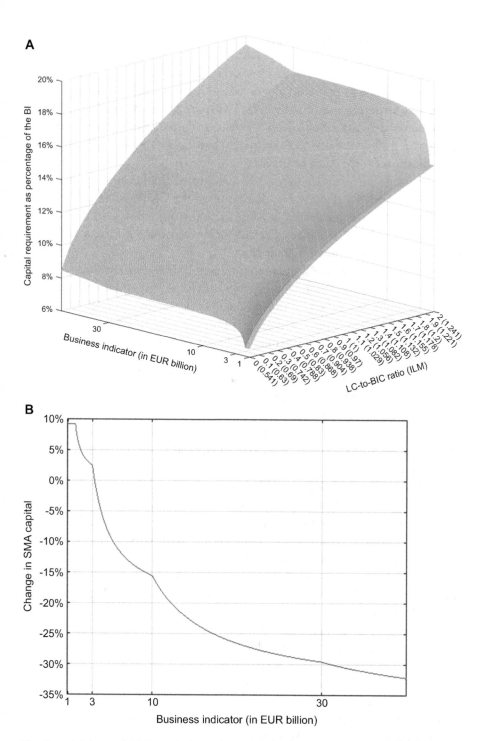

Fig. 8.4 (a) (upper) SMA capital requirements for various levels of BI and LC-to-BIC (ILM); (b) (upper) SMA capital requirements for various levels of BI and LC-to-BIC (ILM); (lower) the difference between the initial proposals and final revisions of SMA

any parameterisation or modelling of past losses data series, but instead assumes that the past operational risk losses are unbiased predictors of future losses. This assumption is broadly in line with the SMA proposal. The analysis also assumes that the AMA meets all the qualitative criteria and conditions which would allow the national competent authorities to grant permission for its application for regulatory purposes.

The existence of a reliable data set of operational risk losses is a prerequisite and one of the two factors for determining the SMA, as it is the main determinant for the calculation of AMA capital requirements. In the absence of actual operational risk losses, the analysis involves the estimation of AMA and SMA based on simulated daily data.

Regarding the AMA, the simulation produces 10,000 alternative daily values, for each of the days in a year, ranging from 0 to EUR 150 million. The routine makes use of the natural logarithmic probability density function (PDF) for the derivation of random values, assuming a thin tail after the threshold of EUR 100 million. The specific approximation follows the approach adopted by the SMA framework which implicitly penalises losses above the threshold of EUR 100 million. The routine subsequently produces 10,000 simulated total annual losses by simply aggregating the randomly produced daily values after excluding those which are lower than EUR 10,000 which is the loss materiality threshold for the application of the AMA. In turn, the level of capital requirements under AMA is the 99.9th percentiles of the simulated total annual losses over a period of ten years.

Given that the SMA uses actual losses as inputs (and not the estimation of the 99.9th percentile), the routine produces only one data set (instead of 10,000) for each of the ten years used for averaging the total annual losses. To isolate the impact of various levels of operational loss events on capital requirements, the analysis assumes that the BI remains.

For the estimation of capital requirements under AMA the block maxima approach is used. The block maxima method selects the 99.9th percentile of the 10,000 iterations of the total annual losses experienced every year to build a sample of ten block maxima (one value for each year) to be used for the estimation of the average across the ten-year period. The same process is repeated for the estimation of capital requirements under two scenarios: (a) individual loss events follow a natural logarithmic density function and are distributed between EUR 0 and EUR 15 million and (b) individual loss events follow a natural logarithmic density function and are distributed between EUR 0 and EUR 150 million.

The analysis considers the case of a bank with a medium-to-high size of BI (EUR 20 million). The natural logarithmic density function for operational losses distributed between 0 and EUR 150 million produces an LC-to-BIC ratio higher than 17, that is, a ratio relatively high in relation to the size of business conducted by the specific bank. Instead, when the analysis assumes the distribution of losses between EUR 0 and EUR 15 million, the LC-to-BIC ratio is approximately 1.1.

The ten-year average operational loss is the input for the estimation of LC and subsequently influences the level of LC-to-BIC ratio which, in turn, produces the ILM. The analysis compares the capital requirements under the initial and final specifications of the SMA framework, assuming unique loss materiality threshold of EUR 20,000.

The analytic comparison of AMA and SMA properties and capital requirements are provided in Table 8.3. As inferred from Table 8.3, should the calculation of SMA capital requirements neglect the influence of past losses, it would be equal to the BIC. In such cases the calculation of SMA capital requirements would be conceptually equivalent to the current standardised approaches which are free of any influence from historical or estimated future losses.

It is worth mentioning that, by omitting the multiplication factor that corresponds to past losses in the SMA formula, is not equivalent to implying that the past losses are zero. The former implies a structural change of a feature of the SMA framework which would harmonise the treatment of all banks irrespective of the losses they experienced in the past. According to the latter, the ILM component is still included in the calculation of SMA; an input of zero losses would produce a low ILM which will reduce the SMA capital requirement by approximately 40%.

As shown in Table 8.3, the capital requirement arising from all SMA specifications (initial, revised, and revised assuming an alpha of 1) exceeds the AMA by more than 200% when the scenario of high-magnitude losses is examined. The magnitude of the increase appears consistent for all rounds of the simulation. Having in mind that the operational loss generation of scenario 2 implies an LC of approximately 17 times the BIC, the chosen scenario is considered adequately conservative and the impact should be considered as being close to the maximum that a bank could face.

When comparing the final SMA framework with the "7-7-5" specification proposed in the initial consultation document, the former appears lower for the scenario of high-magnitude losses and slightly higher for low-magnitude losses.

From the analysis above, it cannot be safely concluded that the implementation of SMA will increase capital requirements compared to the AMA given that the magnitude of the increase depends on the current estimation of AMA capital requirements. Banks whose current estimate of AMA is low compared to their volume of business (BI) would be impacted more than those which

Table 8.3 Comparison of AMA and SMA capital requirements for different operational loss distribution functions

BIC parameters	Alternative SMA (alpha = 0.8)	Alternative SMA (alpha = 1)	SMA/7-7-5
ILDC	3.0	3.0	3.0
Abs(II-IE)_AVG	2.0	2.0	2.0
IEA_AVG	500.0	500.0	500.0
DI_AVG	1.0	1.0	1.0
FC	8.0	8.0	8.0
NetPandLBB_AVG	5.0	5.0	5.0
NetPandLTB_AVG	3.0	3.0	3.0
SC	9.0	9.0	9.0
OOI_AVG	2.0	2.0	2.0
OOE_AVG	3.0	3.0	3.0
FI_AVG	5.0	5.0	5.0
FE_AVG	6.0	6.0	6.0
uBI	N/A	N/A	20.0
BI	20.0	20.0	20.0
BIC	2.960	2.960	4.040
ILM parameters—Scenario 1: Distribution of losses between 0 and 150 EUR billion			
BIC	2.960	2.960	4.040
LC	51.394	51.394	43.084
ILM	2.445	2.949	2.516
LC-to-BIC	17.363	17.363	10.664
AMA capital requirements	10.591	10.591	10.591
SMA capital requirements	7.237	8.728	10.166
OpRisk RWA equivalent	90.460	109.102	127.073
Changes relative to the AMA	−31.67%	−17.59%	−4.01%
Changes relative to the initial SMA proposals	−28.81%	−14.14%	N/A
ILM parameters—Scenario 2: Distribution of losses between 0 and 15 EUR billion			
BIC	2.960	2.960	4.040
LC	4.950	4.950	2.451
ILM	1.172	1.221	0.844
LC-to-BIC	1.672	1.672	0.607
AMA capital requirements	1.072	1.072	1.072
SMA capital requirements	3.468	3.614	3.408
OpRisk RWA equivalent	43.349	45.177	42.606
Changes relative to the AMA	223.46%	237.10%	217.92%
Changes relative to the initial SMA proposals	1.74%	6.03%	N/A

Note: Scenario 1: high-magnitude operational losses; Scenario 2: low-magnitude operational losses

currently estimate higher AMA capital. The increase arising from the application of SMA capital requirements would widely vary amongst banks. According to the estimations in Table 8.3, the impact would range from slightly negative to massively positive for banks which currently have average actual losses-to-BIC ratio above 100% (high-magnitude losses) (Box 8.1).

Box 8.1 Example on the Calculation of SMA

The practical example below shows the sequence for the calculation of SMA capital requirements according to the consultative document (BCBS, 2016) (values in EUR billion).

SMA capital requirements/ operational risk RWAs (1)	Inputs for the estimation of SMA capital and RWA equivalent (2)	Inputs for the estimation of BIC and ILM (3)	Inputs for the estimation of BI (4)	Inputs for the estimation of ILDC, FC, and SC (5)
SMA capital = 1.240 (RWA equivalent = 15.500)	BIC (=0.938)	BI (=5.778)	ILDC (=1.050)	Abs(II_AVG—IE_AVG) (=1.000)
				IEA_AVG (=50.000)
				Abs(LI_AVG—LE_AVG) (assumed to be included in the abs(II_AVG—IE_AVG))
				DI_AVG (=0.050)
			FC (=3.600)	NetPandLBB_AVG (=1.500)
				NetPandLTB_AVG (=2.100)
			SC (=1.130)	OOI_AVG (=0.150)
				OOE_AVG (=0.285)
				FI_AVG (=0.843)
				FE_AVG (=0.500)
	ILM (=1.322)	LC (=1.907) BIC (=0.938)		Losses > EUR 20k (=0.101)

8.3   Conclusions

The current chapter articulated the methodology for the calculation of operational risk capital requirements under current Basel III (BIA, TSA, ASA, and AMA) and final Basel III (SMA) according to the latest BCBS proposals. It also presented the impact of migrating from the AMA (current Basel III) to the SMA (final Basel III), presenting alternative scenarios on the composition of banks' business component and observed operational losses.

It also presented the impact on the SMA capital requirement by assuming alternative specifications of the "alpha" factor and the impact of regrouping the BI buckets together with lowering the weights assigned to the second BI bucket. Finally, the analysis examined the sensitivity of the impact of potential changes in the BIC on the SMA capital, as result of managerial decisions to reduce the size of the banking business and thus the BI.

Notes

1. Matlab Statistics Toolbox uses the command *gprnd* to generate generalised Pareto random numbers.
2. The following P&L items do not contribute to any of the items of the BI: (a) income and expenses from insurance or reinsurance businesses; (b) premiums paid and reimbursements/payments received from insurance or reinsurance policies purchased; (c) administrative expenses, including staff expenses, outsourcing fees paid for the supply of non-financial services (e.g. logistical, IT, human resources), and other administrative expenses (e.g. IT, utilities, telephone, travel, office supplies, postage); (d) recovery of administrative expenses including recovery of payments on behalf of customers (e.g. taxes debited to customers); (e) expenses of premises and fixed assets (except when these expenses result from operational loss events); (f) depreciation/amortisation of tangible and intangible assets (except depreciation related to operating lease assets, which should be included in financial and operating lease expenses); (g) provisions/reversal of provisions (e.g. on pensions, commitments, and guarantees given) except for provisions related to operational loss events; (h) expenses due to share capital repayable on demand; (i) impairment/reversal of impairment (e.g. on financial assets, non-financial assets, investments in subsidiaries, joint ventures, and associates); (j) changes in goodwill recognised in profit or loss; and (k) corporate income tax (tax based on profits including current tax and deferred tax).

References

Basel Committee on Banking Supervision (BCBS). (2001, January). Operational risk – Consultative document. Retrieved from https://www.bis.org/publ/bcbsca07.pdf

Basel Committee on Banking Supervision (BCBS). (2006, June). Basel II: International convergence of capital measurement and capital standards: A revised framework – Comprehensive version. Retrieved from http://www.bis.org/publ/bcbs128.pdf

Basel Committee on Banking Supervision (BCBS). (2011, June). Principles for the sound management of operational risk. Retrieved from http://www.bis.org/publ/bcbs195.pdf

Basel Committee on Banking Supervision (BCBS). (2016, March). Standardised measurement approach for operational risk – Consultative document. Retrieved from http://www.bis.org/bcbs/publ/d355.pdf

Basel Committee on Banking Supervision (BCBS). (2017, December). Basel III: Finalising post-crisis reforms – Standards. Retrieved December 7, 2017, from https://www.bis.org/bcbs/publ/d424.pdf

Embrechts, P. (Ed.). (2000). *Extremes and integrated risk management*. London: RiskBooks.

Fisher, R. A., & Tippett, L. H. C. (1928). Limiting forms of the frequency distribution of the largest and smallest member of the sample. *Proceedings of the Cambridge Philosophical Society, 24*, 180–190.

Moosa, I. A. (2007). *Operational risk management*. London: Palgrave Macmillan.

9

Output Floor, Leverage Ratio, and Other Regulatory Requirements

Chapters 4, 5, 6, 7, and 8 described the impact of the final Basel III on the risk weights (RWs) and capital requirements that correspond to individual risk categories, that is, credit risk, market risk, CVA, and operational risk. In addition to the capital requirements set aside by banks for individual risks, the new framework introduces a general add-on applicable to the overall risk-weighted assets (RWAs) to cope with cases where the estimates of internal models after the application of input floors are still at low levels compared to the equivalent RWAs estimated by the standardised approach (SA).

The newly proposed banking supervision standards have triggered ambiguity amongst banks and supervisors (Economist, 2017) as is always the case before the finalisation of the Basel framework (see also Economist, 2007 for the debate on Basel II/III). Supervisors from certain jurisdictions echoed that the internal models produce RWs which are unjustifiably lower than the SA-equivalent RWs and thus lead to less capital which could place financial stability at stake.

Also, the current chapter discusses the final Basel III amendments on leverage ratio (LR) framework (BCBS, 2016, 2017a) without, however, providing evidence on the direction of a potential impact. Finally, this chapter refers to the residual impact of other Basel regulatory reforms (total loss-absorbing capacity [TLAC]) and how banks could approximate the assessment of the holistic impact of all reforms on RWA, capital requirements, and the cost of funding.

© The Author(s) 2018
I. Akkizidis, L. Kalyvas, *Final Basel III Modelling*,
https://doi.org/10.1007/978-3-319-70425-8_9

9.1 Output Floors: Past and Present

The major innovation, and point of controversy between regulators and banks in the final framework, is the implementation of an output floor on the internal models' RWA (output). The rationale behind the implementation of the output floor is to not allow banks to produce unjustifiably low values of RWA vis-à-vis their SA-equivalent RWAs. Basel II set a similar floor between Basel II internal models' RWAs and Basel I SA RWAs. This floor, aka the "Basel I" floor, is still in place under the existing framework.

The initial intention of the Basel I floor was to smooth out the changes in capital requirements stemming from the transition from Basel I SA for credit risk to the newly implemented at that time Basel II IRBA framework (BCBS, 2006). Its implementation implicitly limits the effect of any model-error risk arising from the development and application of the IRBA models, amid the novelty that the IRBA models introduced at that time. The Basel I floor can also be interpreted as a backstop for biases generated by the lack of representative data for the calibration of IRBA models. Albeit proposed by the BCBS, there is no detailed evidence on whether and which of the BCBS members apply it and whether its application is consistent amongst them.

The outbreak of the financial crisis revealed the inadequacy of some of the internal models to predict the magnitude of credit losses for some asset classes. The IRBA (for credit risk), the IMA (for market risk), and the AMA (for operational risk) failed, to some extent, to set aside a sufficient level of capital to absorb losses produced by the respective risks resulting from turbulences in the international financial system and intervention of the governments to support banks which struggled because of the crisis.

The failure of internal models created a lack of confidence in the national supervisory authorities as to whether the risks of the banking sector are adequately addressed. A similar scepticism prevailed amongst investors, which resulted in increased volatility in the secondary markets for banking equity.

The final Basel III framework attempts to ease the unintended effects of having too low IRBA RWAs by introducing an output floor on internal models' estimations as a percentage of the final Basel III SA-equivalent RWAs. This structural difference in the estimation of the output floor add-on, vis-à-vis the Basel I floor, requires banks to adjust the way they see and calculate capital requirements. To calculate the capital requirements under the new framework, banks have to integrate their market risk and credit risk functions and motivate the two operational units to cooperate with a view towards achieving the most optimal portfolio.

The BCBS deems that the new framework promotes the consistent application of Pillar I requirements and a level playing field and, thus, healthy competition amongst banks. By calibrating the output floor at 72.5% of the SA-equivalent RWA, it does not disregard the idiosyncratic risks of individual banks. The new output floor framework aims at balancing between retaining the risk sensitivity in the assessment of credit and market risk and bridging the (wide in some cases) gap between the internal models and SAs.

The BCBS decision on the abolition of AMA eliminated a factor which was a "black box" for the estimation of operational risk for both national supervisory authorities and investors alike, leaving the IRBA and IMA the only applicable internal models and thus the ones subject to the output floor.

9.1.1 Basel I Output Floor

The background for the establishment of an output floor has its origins back in 2004, when the major part of Basel II was finalised. A provision in the Basel II framework (BCBS, 2006) suggested that the newly implemented, at that time, IRBA for credit risk and the AMA for operational risk will be subject to an output floor vis-à-vis the respective Basel I requirements (BCBS, 1999). The additional RWA and capital requirements stemming from the implementation of Basel I floor is calculated as the difference between (1) the floor, defined as a proportion of Basel I SA capital requirements, and (2) the amount calculated according to what is set out in the Basel II documentation (BCBS, 2006). If the floor amount is higher than the amount estimated by the Basel II internal models, banks are required to add an RWA amount.

The minimum capital equivalent of the Basel I RWA floor derives from the application of an adjustment factor on the sum of the following elements: (1) 8% of the RWAs, (2) plus Tier 1 and Tier 2 deductions, and (3) less the amount of general provisions that may be recognised in Tier 2 (Fig. 9.1; BCBS, 2006: 13, para 47). The adjustment factor for banks using the foundation IRB approach for 2006 was 95%. The adjustment factor for banks using the foundation and/or advanced IRB approaches and/or the AMA for 2007 was 90%, while in 2008 it became 80%. Table 9.1 illustrates the application of the adjustment factors. Additional transitional arrangements including the parallel calculation were set out in Basel II documentation (BCBS, 2006: 62–63, paras 263–269).

The general formula for the estimation of Basel I floor is set below:

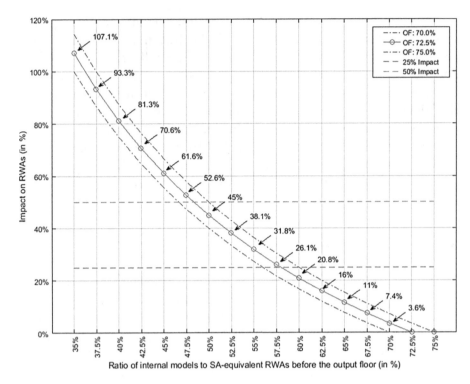

Fig. 9.1 Illustration of the output floor impact on RWs relating to various levels of the ratio of internal models to the SA equivalent (IRBA-to-SA ratios of 75% and above are not subject to output floor impact should the output floor be set at 75%)

Table 9.1 Transitional arrangements of Basel I floor

Internal models	End 2006	End 2007	End 2008
FIRBA (credit risk)	95%	90%	80%
AIRBA (credit risk) and AMA (OpRisk)	–	90%	80%

$$B1\text{floor} - RWA\,\text{add} - \text{on} = 12.5 \times \max$$

$$\begin{pmatrix} 0, \left\{\left[8\% \times B1SA + \left(T1DED + T2DED\right) - GPR\right] \times 80\%\right\} - \\ \left\{8\% \times B2IRBA + \left(T1DED + T2DED\right) - \left(TPRIRBA - EL\right)\right\} \end{pmatrix} \quad (9.1)$$

where

$B1$floor–RWA add-on: RWA corresponding to "Basel I floor" add-on.

$B1SA$: RWA according to the Basel I SA equivalent.

$T1DED$: Tier 1 deductions.

$T2DED$: Tier 2 deductions.

*B*2IRBA: Internal models' RWA according to the Basel II IRBA.

GPR: General provisions under the SA.

TPRIRBA: Total provisions under the IRBA.

EL: Expected losses under the IRBA.

The Basel I floor capital requirements is the positive difference between the Basel I SA-equivalent capital requirements and the Basel II internal models' capital requirements. It constitutes a separate component of RWA for credit risk, which should be added to the amounts produced by SA and IRBA for credit risk. As seen in the mathematical expression above, the Basel I floor add-on derives from the comparison of two different versions of Basel standards, that is, Basel I and Basel II.

9.1.2   The Final Basel III Output Floor

In 2009 and 2013, the BCBS postponed the application of the Basel I floor to set a minimum amount for the Basel III framework subject to 80% of Basel I RWA. The postponement enforced the comparison between Basel III and Basel I. Since this comparison is outdated and out of the initial scope of setting a floor, the BCBS proposed the substitution of the old with a new output floor framework which would compare the total RWA, inclusive of internal models, and the total SA equivalent after the application of the respective SAs. To replace the Basel I floor, the BCBS considered many alternative calibrations which ranged from 70% to 80%.[1] The analysis examines the 70%–75% range which, according to the understanding of the authors, the BCBS has been considering up until before the finalisation of the reforms. The analysis below presents the methodology, and illustrative examples, on the estimation of the output floor impact.

To estimate the incremental output floor impact, banks need to have conducted the mapping between SA and IRBA asset classes (see Chap. 5) before calculating the SA-equivalent RWA. The mapping provides researchers, analysts, or bank professionals with a tool for the estimation of internal models' RWA (i.e. RWA arising from market risk [IMA] and credit risk [IRB] internal models) and the SA equivalent of the same exposures using the correct risk-weighting framework.

The direction of the interaction between the level of impact arising from individual risk-based categories (i.e. market risk, credit risk, operational risk) and the level of output floor impact is not straightforward. It is highly dependent on whether the internal model or the SA is driving the changes for the relevant risk category (credit or market risk) and what is the direction of these changes, that is, increase or decrease of RWA stemming from individual approaches. An overall reduction in RWA, entirely attributed to the IRBA, implies a subsequent increase in the output floor impact, while an increase in the IRBA RWA leads to the reduction of the output floor impact. On the contrary, an overall reduction in RWA, entirely attributed to the SA, implies a decrease in the output floor impact, and vice versa. It is not certain whether the impact of the changes in individual risk categories will be higher or lower than the impact of the output floor. The same principles apply to the IMA and SA for market risk.

Figure 9.1 designates the impact on RWA stemming from the application of three alternative output floor scenarios, that is, 70%, 72.5%, and 75%. The impact solely depends on the ratio of revised internal models' RWA to the SA-equivalent RWA estimated for the same assets after implementing the revisions to the credit and market risks of internal models. The illustration shows that the application of an output floor which is equal to or below the ratio of internal models to SA equivalent (IM-to-SAeq) does not imply any RWA add-on attributed to the output floor.

The application of a 72.5% output floor implies an impact of less than 25% of the RWA if the estimated IM-to-SAeq ratio is higher than 58% (not shown as a discrete number in Fig. 9.1), while the impact will be higher than 50% of the RWA should the estimated IM-to-SAeq ratio be below 48.4% (not shown as a discrete number in Fig. 9.1). Similarly, the application of a 75% output floor would raise the RWA by less than 25% for banks with envisaged IM-to-SAeq ratio higher than 60%, whereas banks with IM-to-SAeq ratio lower than 50% will face an increase of more than 50%.

The impact described above is useful to observe the mechanics of the output floor. While the output floor is binding for non-prudent (non-conservative) internal models, it is becoming less and less binding as the internal models become more conservative, that is, the IRBA RWAs are closer to their SA equivalent. On the other hand, any reduction of the SA equivalent, through the reduction of the RWs in the final provisions, would reduce the impact of the output floor.

9.1.3   Relative Contribution of Input and Output Floors in the Increase of Risk Weights

As mentioned, the implementation of input and output floors is a potential source of additional RWA and thus capital requirements in the credit risk category. However, they are counterbalancing: the higher the input floor the lower the impact of the output floor, and vice versa. Some argue that the introduction of output floors is obsolete as input floors already cope with the model-error risk embedded in the estimations of IRBA models. Nonetheless, we showed that the impact of the final revisions does not imply any significant impact stemming from the input floors (at least not from PD floors), implying that the output floor will be higher.

The analysis below shows the relative contribution of each type of floor by examining the modelling properties arising from their implementation of credit risk revisions only. Going back to Fig. 5.7 in Chap. 5, the analysis below selects the part of the example that refers to the fully unsecured corporate exposures (vertical arrow) to examine the impact of different levels of output floor on RWs for corporate exposures, with different estimated PD levels, assessed under the FIRBA. As also observed in Fig. 5.7 in Chap. 5, the application of the revised PD floors, assuming that bank's own estimate of LGD is 5 percentage points lower (20%) than the LGD floor for the AIRBA, implies an impact of 62.76%, given that the bank's own PD estimate is equal to or lower than 0.03%. The impact of unsecured corporate exposures whose bank's own PD estimate is equal to or higher than 0.05% would be 17.92%. The RW impact of corporate exposures with 0.03% < PD < 0.05% would be between 17.92% and 62.76%.

Figure 9.2 shows that the high impact of the input floor on low-PD exposures implies that the output floor impact would be low as the input floor is responsible for a big part of the total impact (input and output). Thus, the impact on corporate exposures' RWs, assuming a current PD ≤ 0.03%, is 7.2% for 70% output floor, 9.7% for 72.5% output floor, and 12.2% for 75% output floor. The respective values of the impact on corporate exposures with PDs higher than 0.05% are 52.1%, 54.6%, and 57.1% (Fig. 9.2). From the illustration in Fig. 9.2, it is inferred that the differentiation stemming from the impact of different output floors becomes less apparent, in percentage terms, for exposures not affected by the input floor.

The following analysis investigates in depth the behaviour of RRE exposures due to the revisions to IRBA specifications, that is, the alteration of the input floors and the implementation of the output floor. The analysis will examine the response of different RRE LTV buckets, assuming a counterparty risk weight of 100%. To estimate the increase attributed to input floors, the analysis uses the set of proposed floors on PD and LGD (BCBS, 2015), while for the output floor it estimates the impact assuming an output floor of 72.5%. As shown in Fig. 9.3, the contribution of output floors is higher than that of input floors on all points on the surface defined by the current PD = 0.03%. The scenario of bank's own estimate of PD = 0.03% implies that the PD floor (set at 0.05%) will have an impact on RWs while a current PD

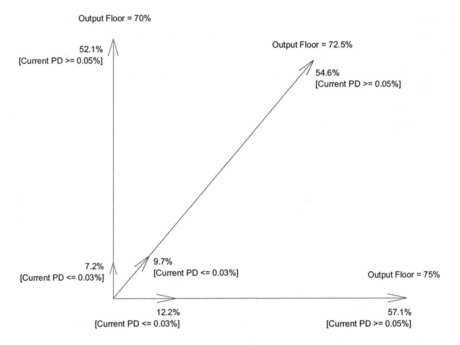

Fig. 9.2 The joint impact of input and output floors on A-rated corporates exposures assessed under the AIRBA

= 0.10% does not imply any impact. This attribute places the surface that corresponds to the bank's estimated PD of 0.03%, being lower than the surface defined by higher PD estimations.

Examining the attributes of the "bank's internal estimate of PD = 0.03%", the contribution of output floors increases for lower internally estimated LGDs and for higher LTVs. The contribution of the output floor impact to the total impact peaks at internally estimated LGD = 10% and LTV > 100%, while its lowest level is observed at LGD = 40%² and LTV < 40% (72.26%).

The contribution of the output floor drops for internally estimated LGDs lower than the set LGD floor for this type of exposure (10%). At the same time, the reduction in the input floor impact increases the contribution of the output floor in the formulation of the total effect. Hence, the output floor participation in the total impact of the floors diminishes together with the level of LGD and LTV, reaching its lowest level at LGD = 1% and LTV < 40% (87.89%). Thus, the output floor impact remains the predominant factor which drives the overall impact of the floors where credit risk is concerned.

The examination of the surface labelled as "bank's internal estimate of PD = 0.10%" indicates that the RRE exposures for all LTV buckets, which relate

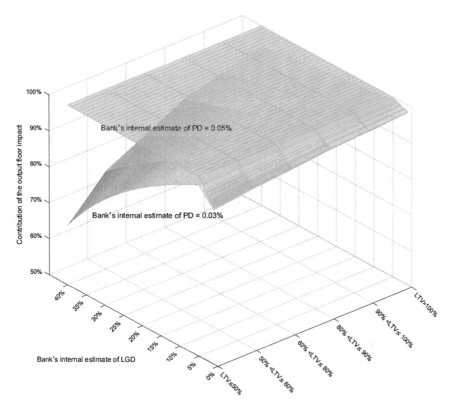

Fig. 9.3 Contribution of 72.5% output floor to the total impact on RW attributed to (input and output) floors per LTV bucket (SA RRE RW: BCBS, 2015) and various LGD levels, LTVs in %

to an internal estimate of LGD higher than 10%, would be affected only by the output floor as the input floors are not binding. The input floor affects[3] only the RRE exposures with a lower LGD, which implies that the participation of the output floor impact increases, reaching its peak at 81.52% (LTV < 40%, bank's internal estimate: LGD = 1%).

9.1.4 Alternative Proposals for the Calibration of the Output Floor

Some believe (Euromoney, 2015) that the implementation of the output floor could be a first step to address potential misspecifications of internal models and could provide markets with the confidence that banks indeed hold sufficient capital buffers to cope with their risks. Others argue that the output floor will cause misrepresentation of the real risks (Villeroy de Galhau, 2017) or reduce the risk-sensitive attribute of internal models, which was the initial intention of Basel II. According to the latter view, it would be more appropriate to harmonise the application of internal models and intensify the supervision of them than to add an arbitrary capital add-on. Nonetheless, if it were calibrated robustly at an appropriate level, the application of the output floor might provide a balance between the two views.

The BCBS has proposed a level of output floor on the basis of the RWA. However, this approach does not take into account the surplus or deficit of credit provisions. The authors believe that the level of credit provisions should be a decisive factor for the final formulation of the output floor impact and thus should be included in the relevant computation. The empirical part of the analysis below provides the reader with evidence about the impact of calibrating the output floor slightly differently than the BCBS proposal (BCBS, 2016, 2017a, b).

Currently, the output floor is simply a percentage of the SA-equivalent RWAs. The BCBS implies that the RWA add-on, stemming from the comparison of the IRBA with its SA-equivalent amount, is converted into the capital requirement by simply multiplying it with the minimum capital requirement ratios, without accounting for the credit provisions.

$$RWA^*_{of} = RWA^*_{SAeq.} \times ofr^* \qquad (9.2)$$

$$RWA^{**} = \max\left(RWA^*,\ RWA^*_{of}\right) \qquad (9.3)$$

$$\Delta RWA^*_{of} = \max\left(0,\ RWA^{**} - RWA^*\right) \qquad (9.4)$$

$$\Delta T1^*_{of} = \left(T1r^* + CCBr^* + G - SIIr^*\right) \times \Delta RWA^*_{of} \qquad (9.5)$$

where
RWA^*_{of} is the estimated output floor level (in RWA);
$RWA^*_{SAeq.}$ is the estimated fully implemented SA-equivalent RWA, which includes only SA estimations;
RWA^* is the estimated fully implemented RWA, which includes internal models' estimations;
ofr^* is the output floor ratio as of the full implementation date (72.5%);
RWA^{**} is the final reference RWA to be used for the calculation of the minimum required capital (MRC);
ΔRWA^*_{of} is the RWA add-on stemming from the application of the output floor;

$\Delta T1^*_{of}$ is the estimated impact of the implementation of the output floor on T1 MRC;

$T1r^*$ is the T1 MRC ratio as of the full implementation date;

$CCBr^*$ is the capital conservation buffer ratio as of the full implementation date (2.5%); and

$G - SIIr^*$ is the G-SIB surcharge ratio as of the full implementation date (0–3.5%).

The above-mentioned approach targets the misspecifications in assessing the riskiness of asset portfolios using IRBA models. On the other hand, a bank may (or may not) cope with the riskiness of its asset portfolio by holding (or not) credit provisions in excess of the expected losses. On the other hand, the Basel III framework provides a different treatment of the deficit of credit provisions: any shortfall of provisions to expected losses should be deducted from Common Equity Tier 1 (BCBS, 2011: 22, para 73), and thus from T1 capital, under the IRBA. Analogically, the shortfall of provisions should be added to the MRC since it would constitute an additional capital requirement that the bank should comply with.

By combining the treatment of provisions in the calculation of the T1 MRC with the methodology for the calculation of the output floor impact, the book suggests an alternative approximation for the estimation of the output floor add-on which could be considered by the BCBS in future revisions of the framework. This proposal is expressed by the following set of equations:

$$T1^*_{of} = \max \left(\begin{array}{l} T1^*, \left\{ RWA^*_{SAeq.} \times \left(T1r^* + CCBr^* + G - SIIr^* \right) \times ofr^* \right\} \\ -\min \left\{ \left[P - EL^* \right], 0 \right\} \end{array} \right) \qquad (9.6)$$

$$T1^{**} = \max \left(T1^*, T1^*_{of} \right) \qquad (9.7)$$

$$\Delta T1^*_{of} = \max \left(0, T1^{**} - T1^* \right) \qquad (9.8)$$

where

$T1^*_{of}$ is the estimated output floor level (in T1 MRC);

$T1^*$ is the estimated fully implemented T1 MRC, which includes the deficit of provisions;

P is the actual amount held for credit provisions against impaired assets;

EL^* is the estimated level of expected losses as of the full implementation date; and

$T1^{**}$ is the final T1 MRC after taking into account the deficit of provisions.

The above methodology appropriately penalises the banks with a deficit of provisions by increasing the minimum T1 capital stemming from the output floor. However, it does not reward banks with a surplus of provisions. To take into account the potential surplus of provisions, the methodology could be further adjusted as follows (Eqs. (9.9)–(9.11)).

$$T1^{**}_{of} = \max \left(\begin{array}{l} T1^*, \left\{ RWA^*_{SAeq.} \times \left(T1r^* + CCBr^* + G - SIIr^* \right) \times ofr^* \right\} \\ - \left[P - EL^* \right] \end{array} \right) \quad (9.9)$$

$$T1^{+**} = \max \left(T1^*, \ T1^{**}_{of} \right) \quad (9.10)$$

$$\Delta T1^{**}_{of} = \max \left(0, T1^{+**} - T1^{**} \right) \quad (9.11)$$

where

$\Delta T1^{**}_{of}$, the estimated output floor level accounting for the surplus or deficit of provisions, is expressed in T1 capital;

$T1^{+**}$ is the final T1 MRC after accounting for the surplus and deficit of provisions; and

$\Delta T1^{**}_{of}$ is the estimated impact on T1 MRC due to the implementation of the output floor according to the alternative approach.

9.2 Revisions to the Leverage Ratio Framework

The SA for measuring the counterparty credit risk (SA-CCR) revises the existing scope of application and calibration of the "standardised method" (SM) for counterparty risk. Also, the proposed revisions to the SA for credit risk will have a significant impact on the definition and level of EAD, mainly through the changes in the credit conversion factor (CCF), which will affect the level of on-balance sheet equivalent of off-balance sheet exposures. Currently, the existing framework for the calculation of LR does not align with the proposals relating to the SA-CCR and SA for credit risks. To this end, two sets of revisions set the tone for the recalibration of LR framework.

9.2.1 The Current Framework for the Estimation of Leverage Ratio

Currently, the measurement of derivatives exposures is being conducted using the current exposure method (CEM) and the SM, the two prescribed measures for measuring counterparty credit exposure values for derivatives under the risk-based capital requirements. Focusing on the CEM, some support the use of CEM in the Basel III LR exposure measure as it includes a margin of conservatism to address the exposure to the underlying assets and it is comparatively easy to understand and implement.

Others support that there are several deficiencies of the CEM framework, the most important being that "the CEM did not differentiate between margined and unmargined transactions; that the supervisory PFE add-on factors did not sufficiently capture the level of volatilities as observed over recent stress periods; and that the recognition of netting was too simplistic and not reflective of economically meaningful relationships between derivative positions" (BCBS, 2016: 2). The above-mentioned caveats renders the current CEM a method which does not assess appropriately the risks of the real market portfolio.

Also, the current LR framework permits certain assets, already accounted for in the risk-based Tier 1 capital, to be ignored by the total exposure measure which is used as the basis for the calculation of LR. Nonetheless, this treatment is not universally applied to the provisions which have already been included in the Tier 1 capital. Specific provisions can offset exposure values of non-derivative positions whilst general provisions do not reduce the exposure measure. Further, neither specific nor general provisions are recognised in reducing exposure values of off-balance sheet items.

9.2.2   The Revised Framework for the Estimation of Leverage Ratio

The embedded caveats in the application of the CEM necessitated the development of the SM for measuring the counterparty credit risk (SA-CCR) under the risk-based framework. The SA-CCR will substitute the current methods for the risk-based capital requirements, while the BCBS proposed the alignment of the LR framework by applying the SA-CCR to the treatment of OTC derivatives, exchange-traded derivatives, and long settlement transactions.

In general, the SA-CCR is considered as a more risk-sensitive and improved approach, compared to the CEM or the current SM, for measuring counterparty risk. The SA-CCR accounts for the trades that are collateralised and distinguishes between finalised (cleared) transactions, and not irrevocably finalised transactions (uncleared).

Despite the obvious advantages of the SA-CCR in the application of the risk-based framework, the calculation of the LR exposure cannot blindly rely on the entire SA-CCR framework as, by definition, the LR exposure ignores all kinds of credit risk mitigation except for the cash variation margin (CVM). Given the differences in the scope of application between the SA-CCR framework and LR exposure measure, the BCBS proposed the application of a modified version of SA-CCR to only allow the recognition of CVM as eligible collateral.

More specifically, the BCBS (2016) issued its proposals for revisions to the LR framework standards in January 2014. The revisions mainly aim to sufficiently reflect the actual exposures and the allocation of risks associated with these exposures.

The revisions to the LR framework are linked to the following:

9.2.2.1   Additional Quantitative Requirements for G-SIBs

The BCBS proposed the application of an add-on for setting out a discrete minimum LR for G-SIBs. This add-on equals half of G-SIBs surcharge which is applicable to the risk-based capital requirements, that is, CET1, T1, and total capital (TC) ratios. Although several jurisdictions may have already implemented the add-on LR requirement under Pillar II capital requirements, the current Pillar I MRC is 3% across all banks. The aim of the add-on requirement is to create a universal Pillar I standard for G-SIBs which would mitigate the risk of systemic contagion by enhancing the resilience of systemically important banks. The BCBS set this add-on at half of the G-SIB surcharge which is applied to risk-based capital requirements.

9.2.2.2   Measurement of Derivative Exposures

To measure derivative exposures, the BCBS proposed the use of a modified version of the SA for measuring the counterparty credit risk (SA-CCR) exposures, instead of the CEM which is currently used (see BCBS, 2016).

9.2.2.3   Treatment of Provisions

The BCBS provides clarification on the treatment of provisions and prudential valuation adjustments for less liquid positions, so as to avoid double counting. More specifically, the current framework allows the assets which have already been accounted for Tier 1 capital to not be accounted in the exposure measure.

Responding to the caveats of the current framework, the BCBS revisions now permit both general and specific provisions to reduce the total exposure measure. This change is consistent with the current framework, which permits assets already accounted in the Tier 1 capital to be ignored in the exposure measure. Similarly, exposures from off-balance sheet items, after applying the relevant CCF, are also now to be reduced by provisions, both general and specific. The recognition of specific and general provisions for the calculation of the exposure measure under the proposed framework reduces the level of required minimum Tier 1.

9.2.2.4   Credit Conversion Factors for Off-Balance Sheet Items

The new framework addresses the need for aligning the CCFs for off-balance sheet items, for the purposes of LR calculations, with those suggested by the revised SA for the purposes of credit risk calculations.

9.3   Macroeconomic Impact

The outbreak of the financial crisis in 2007–2008 provides evidence on the cost—direct and indirect, transitory as well as permanent—of public "bailouts" for the recovery or resolution of systemically important banks. As a lesson learnt, the FSB, after being mandated by the G20, developed global standards to manage or prevent future crises by disseminating the "Principles on loss-absorbing and recapitalisation capacity of G-SIBs in resolution", whereas the capital needed to contribute to the resolution of troubled banks is an additional requirement known as the TLAC capital (FSB, 2015a).

According to these standards, the designated resolution authorities will have specific powers to deal with banks which failed or are likely to fail, including the power to bail in financial institutions' shareholders and creditors by writing down equity or converting debt into equity. The principal objective of these global standards is the orderly winding down of troubled institutions, without undermining the stability of the financial system or the real economy, while at the same time protecting the public finances and—to a certain extent—unsophisticated creditors (FSB, 2014, 2015b).

9.3.1   Total Loss Absorbing Capacity (TLAC) Capital and Its Jurisdictional Implementation

Albeit the BCBS designed the TLAC capital for implementation only by G-SIBs, the European Union (EU) extended its application to cover all banks in its jurisdiction. The EU has implemented these global supervisory standards via a dedicated legislative framework[4] to make them binding for all EU banks. Consistent with the "FSB Key Attributes" (2014), this framework requires the resolution authorities to avail of a bail-in tool to ensure that shareholders and creditors participate in the resolution of a failing bank. To credibly and effectively implement resolution strategies, the framework further specifies the criteria of setting up a minimum requirement for own funds and minimum required capital and eligible liabilities (MREL), that is, a minimum amount of own funds and liabilities eligible for bail-in to facilitate sufficient loss absorbing capital (LAC), recapitalisation capacity (RCC), and market confidence.

The general sentiment of the banking sector as reflected in the press (e.g. (The) Economist, 2017) is that the recent regulatory initiatives of the BCBS render the conduct of banking business a burdensome and costly task. They echo to supervisors that the revisions are burdensome due to the significant operational effort and regulatory costs that the newly adopted capital requirements imply. On the other hand, national supervisors agree on the need to enhance the resilience of the international banking sector, even though they represent different views as to how the appropriate level of capital could be calibrated.

Regulators and banks reckon the necessity of a holistic approach for the estimation of the impact of regulatory reforms by accounting for all elements which could potentially affect the future level of banks' capital and profitability. The assessment of the joint impact is imperative for regulators to appropriately and holistically calibrate the new framework and for banks to prepare medium-term business plans.

In principle, the EU regulatory framework requires banks to avail of own funds and "bail-in-able" liabilities twice the requirement for the authorisation to operate as a bank (once for the loss absorption capacity and once for the RCC) plus an additional requirement for the combined capital buffers (to ensure sufficient market confidence).

While it is the explicit objective of the EU co-legislators to design the resolution framework in the EU consistently with the global standards, a few specificities of the EU framework are notable. Firstly, while the global FSB standards apply to banks identified as systemically important, the relevant EU directive is generally applicable for all groups and/or entities of the EU banking sector. Secondly, unlike the FSB TLAC standard, the EU framework envisages MREL to represent a firm-specific amount, set by resolution authorities in accordance with the relevant legal provisions. This provision differentiates amongst the bank's business model, funding model, risk profile, size, and systemic importance. Thirdly, the EU framework stipulates the MREL to apply at the solo (individual institutions) and consolidated (group) level.

The entirety of the book has focused on the assessment of the impact arising from the implementation of the final Basel III rules. However, the evaluation of the total impact of major banking regulation on banks' capital should also account for the additional capital requirements of TLAC/MREL. To this end, TLAC/MREL requirements could absorb part or even the entirety of the impact coming from the final Basel III if the former is lower. This could happen since banks would anyway have to raise capital for TLAC/MREL capital, which could potentially suffice to comply with the minimum capital requirements.

In principle, the impact from the joint implementation of the final Basel III and TLAC/MREL requirements is given by following equation:

$$J\Delta C = \max\left(\Delta BIV, \Delta TLAC\right) \qquad (9.12)$$

where

$J\Delta C$ is the change in T1 MRC stemming from the combined implementation of Basel III and TLAC/MREL standards;

ΔBIV is the change in T1 MRC that arises from the full implementation of the final Basel III requirements;

$\Delta TLAC$ is the change in T1 MRC that arises from the full implementation of TLAC/MREL requirements.

9.3.2   Impact on the Cost of Capital

The current section presents a stylised model on how the capital impact could conceptually translate into funding costs, profitability, deleveraging, or derisking (macroeconomic costs of regulation) on the one hand and reduced probability and severity of crises (macroeconomic benefits) on the other hand. For that purpose, the analysis below explains the mechanism in a simplified fashion.

The first-order effect of going concern regulation (Basel framework) and gone concern (resolution) standards (TLAC) is the increased amount of capital required. This capital acts as a cushion to reduce the probability of bank failures and strengthen the individual bank's resilience and capacity to absorb losses should a failure happen. Everything else being equal (e.g. ignoring the stylised fact that better capitalised banks have been found able to borrow at lower rates), capital is a relatively costly instrument of funding, reflecting the inherent risk of losing value and/or missing dividends. Such an increase in funding costs adversely affects bank profitability (and potentially the ability to retain earnings). Assuming that (1) banks target a certain profitability ratio, (2) banks do not avail of or do not want to offset increased funding costs by cuts in other cost categories, such funding cost increases could be countered by adjustments to the banks' assets. These asset side adjustments could take the form of either deleveraging (reducing non-profitable lending and/or investments) or assuming more risk (investing in riskier and more profitable assets, changing the composition of assets). For simplicity, in the below analysis we assume the adjustment to take the form of balance sheet shrinkage, for example, banks reducing unprofitable lending and investments. Reduced levels of bank lending would—in the assumed absence of alternative providers of funding—lead to reduced real economic activity and growth.

On the other hand, previous studies have shown that higher bank-capital requirements and loss absorption capacity significantly reduce the probability of systemic bank crises and sector-wide bailouts. In addition, higher loss absorption capacity of banks also reduces the impact of bank failures on the real economy and public finances, requiring private investors to bear losses. In sum, these benefits of bank-capital regulation and standards on loss-absorbing capacity need to be compared with the expected costs.

The higher capital can lead either to an increased cost of borrowing for the banks' counterparties or to increased cost of funding for the bank itself. The latter could hamper banks' role as intermediaries between lenders and borrowers by reducing the provision of funding to the real economy as a whole (deleveraging) or to the risky sectors only (derisking), yet the sectors with the highest expected return. This would subsequently reduce the profitability of the real economy and economic growth and therefore the average disposable income of taxpayers. The indirect cost incurred by the taxpayers should be compared with the direct cost of the bailout in times of crises to figure out how the additional cost of regulatory compliance, indirectly borne by the real economy, compares with the direct cost of bailout, directly borne by the economy. To evaluate the impact of diffusing the banks' incremental cost of regulatory compliance in either direction, one should start with the quantification of the funding cost.

Banks fund their asset exposures by raising borrowings or equity. Assuming banks would retain the same exposure to the economy (no deleveraging), the additional capital arising from the Basel and TLAC/MREL provisions results in a (forced) increase in the equity used for the funding of the real economy. This enables banks to forego the utilisation of borrowings by the same amount. This could potentially increase the cost of equity but at the same time decrease the funding cost from the utilisation of the borrowings (liabilities). The cost of funding can be assessed by the following formula (APRA, 2012; Damodaran, 2016; Kalyvas & Akkizidis, 2006):

$$\Delta IR = J\Delta C \times (\text{Cost of equity} - \text{Cost of borrowing}) \times BIV\_ARW \quad (9.13)$$

where

ΔIR represents the difference in interest rates due to the joint implementation of the final Basel III and TLAC;

$J\Delta C$ is the percentage change of T1 MRC stemming from the combined implementation of the final Basel III and TLAC/MREL standards; and

BIV_ARW is the average risk weight stemming from the joint Basel III and TLAC/MREL full implementation.

Based on data provided by Damodaran (2017), the average cost of equity of international banks is approximately 7.34% while the after-tax cost of debt is 2.10%. This combination would result in a transformation of Eq. (9.13) into the following form:

$$\Delta IR = J\Delta C \times 5.24\% \times BIV\_ARW \quad (9.14)$$

Assuming the final Basel III and TLAC/MREL T1 MRC are the same across the globe and that all international banks hold exactly the minimum capital needed to comply with the minimum risk-based and LR capital requirements, Eq. (9.14) becomes:

$$\Delta IR = J\Delta C \times 5.24\% \times 0.375 = J\Delta C \times 1.97\% \quad (9.15)$$

The approximation of the funding cost impact after substituting for the cost of equity and debt (Eq. (9.15)) indicates that for every 10 percentage points of the impact of the new Basel framework and TLAC/MREL implementation, the impact on banks' funding cost would be approximately 20 basis points. However, one should bear in mind that this is just a rough approximation of the average cost for a typical international bank which participated in the survey conducted by Damodaran (2017). When considering individual cases, the BIV_ARW changes according to the riskiness of the exposures and banks. Similarly, the cost-of-funding-to-cost-of-borrowing spread varies amongst banks according to their credit ratings, causing the additional funding cost to change accordingly. However, this, by itself, is an area of further investigation which is out of the scope of the current book. The publications of international and European organisations, involved with the impact assessment of the Basel reforms (BCBS, 2017b; EBA, 2017), is a good source to further analyse the cost of funding for the banking system.

9.4   Conclusions

To cope with cases where internal models produce unjustifiably lower RWAs, and MRC, than the respective SA RWA, the final Basel III introduced an update to the existing framework (Basel I floor) by suggesting the application of an output floor of 72.5%. The analysis of this chapter focused on the attributes of setting an output floor between 70% and 75% and provided evidence on the share of input and output floors on the TC increase in the credit risk RW, since it is by far the risk category with the largest contribution to the total RWA. Also, the analysis provided evidence on the joint impact of input and output floors on various credit risk asset classes, assuming various levels of internally estimated PDs and LGD.

It also described the theoretical aspects of the LR implementation. Also, the analysis suggested a methodology for the holistic impact assessment of the reforms. Finally, the use of publicly available data showed that for every 10 percentage points of capital increase the corporate cost of funding will be affected by approximately 20 basis points.

Notes

1. At least, this was the range that was reflected in the economic press and literature.
2. Albeit this is rather a theoretical level of LGD for RREs, as this type of exposure usually relates to much lower LTVs.
3. The input floor is ineffective if the internal estimates are higher than the floor.
4. European Union, Bank Recovery and Resolution Directive (BRRD); European Union, Delegated Regulation on methodology for setting MREL; subject to amendments proposed by the EC (Nov 2016), with a view to strengthen consistency with TLAC and proportionality of application.

References

Australian Prudential Regulation Authority (APRA). (2012). Regulation Impact Statement (RIS): Implementing Basel III capital reforms in Australia (OBPR ID: 2012/13813).

Basel Committee on Banking Supervision (BCBS). (1999, June). A new capital adequacy framework. Retrieved from http://www.bis.org/publ/bcbs50.pdf

Basel Committee on Banking Supervision (BCBS). (2006, June). Basel II: International convergence of capital measurement and capital standards: A revised framework – Comprehensive version. Retrieved from http://www.bis.org/publ/bcbs128.pdf

Basel Committee on Banking Supervision (BCBS). (2011, June). Basel III: A global regulatory framework for more resilient banks and banking systems – Revised version.

Basel Committee on Banking Supervision (BCBS). (2015, December). Revisions to the standardised approach for credit risk – Second consultative document.

Basel Committee on Banking Supervision (BCBS). (2016, April). Revisions to the Basel III leverage ratio framework – Consultative document.

Basel Committee on Banking Supervision (BCBS). (2017a, December). Basel III: Finalising post-crisis reforms – Standards. Retrieved December 7, 2017, from https://www.bis.org/bcbs/publ/d424.pdf

Basel Committee on Banking Supervision (BCBS). (2017b, December). Basel III monitoring report – Results of the cumulative quantitative impact study. Retrieved December 7, 2017, from https://www.bis.org/bcbs/publ/d426.pdf

Basel Committee on Banking Supervision. (2016, March). Reducing variation in credit risk-weighted assets – Constraints on the use of internal model approaches – Consultative document.

Damodaran, A. (2016). January 2016 data update 4: The costs of capital. Retrieved October 24, 2017, from http://people.stern.nyu.edu/adamodar/pdfiles/country/CostofCapitalShort.pdf

Euromoney. (2015, March 5). Bank regulation: 'Basel IV' sparks banker fury.

European Banking Authority (EBA). (2016, August). Report on the Leverage Ratio requirements under Article 511 of the CRR. Retrieved from https://www.eba.europa.eu/documents/10180/1360107/EBA-Op-2016-13+(Leverage+ratio+report).pdf

European Banking Authority (EBA). (2017, December). Ad hoc cumulative impact assessment of the Basel reform package. Retrieved from https://www.eba.europa.eu/documents/10180/1720738/Ad+Hoc+Cumulative+Impact+Assessment+of+the+Basel+reform+package.pdf/76c00d7d-3ae3-445e-9e8a-8c397e02e465

Financial Stability Board (FSB). (2014, October). Key attributes of effective resolution regimes for financial institutions.

Financial Stability Board (FSB). (2015a, November). Historical losses and recapitalisation needs – Findings report.

Financial Stability Board (FSB). (2015b, November). Principles on loss-absorbing and recapitalisation capacity of G-SIBs in resolution – Total loss-absorbing capacity (TLAC) term sheet.

Kalyvas, L., & Akkizidis, I. (2006). *Integrating market, credit and operational risk.* London: Riskbooks.

Stern New York University Database maintained by Damodaran A, Cost of Capital by Sector. (2017). Retrieved October 24, 2017, from http://people.stern.nyu.edu/adamodar/New_Home_Page/datafile/wacc.htm

The Economist. (2007, February 22). A twist or two of Basel: Europe and America cannot agree on new global banking rules.

The Economist. (2017, January 5). Polishing the floor: Supervisors put off finalising reforms to bank-capital rules – Disagreement over revisions to Basel 3 cause delay.

Villeroy de Galhau, François. (2017, May 29). *Governor of the Bank of France and Chairman of the Autorité de contrôle prudentiel et de resolution (ACPR)*. Press conference that followed the presentation of the 2016 Annual Report of the ACPR, Paris.

Index[1]

---

[1] Note: Page numbers followed by 'n' refer to notes.

© The Author(s) 2018
I. Akkizidis, L. Kalyvas, *Final Basel III Modelling*,
https://doi.org/10.1007/978-3-319-70425-8